Cavendish
Publishing
Limited

INTELLECTUAL PROPERTY LAW

TITLES IN THE SERIES

Cavendish
Publishing
Limited

INTELLECTUAL PROPERTY LAW

**Michael Edenborough, MA (Cantab), D Phil (Oxon),
Barrister**

First published in Great Britain 1995 by Cavendish Publishing Limited, The Glass House, Wharton Street, London WC1X 9PX

Telephone: 0171-278 8000 Facsimile: 0171-278 8080

British Library Cataloguing in Publication Data

Edenborough, Michael
Intellectual Property Law – (Lecture Notes Series)
I Title II Series
344.20648

ISBN 1-874241-47-3

Cover photograph by Jerome Yeats
Photograph of the author by Peter Kinnear
Printed and bound in Great Britain

Foreword

Only a short time ago, the mention of an interest in intellectual property at any gathering of academic lawyers, would elicit blank looks and a rapid change of topic. I can even recall a speaker at the annual conference of the Society of Public Teachers of Law giving it as an example of a subject totally unsuitable for teaching in law schools. In 1981 when the first edition of Professor Cornish's excellent textbook appeared, the subject was, in fact, hardly taught either at undergraduate, or at postgraduate, level. Today, the situation is quite different. Intellectual property courses are available in very many law schools, either as part of a general commercial law programme, or as options in their own right.

Again, there was virtually no academic research carried on in the area in this country as recently as 10 years ago (in Germany, where intellectual property's central importance to many fields of industry was recognised, the situation was quite different). This too has changed dramatically: research is going on in many universities, and my own Institute has expanded its activities considerably.

The increasing importance of intellectual property as a subject which students not only can, but, perhaps, *ought*, to study, is reflected in the rapidly expanding choice of textbooks available to them. This range of textbooks reflects a market where, because of its size, differing needs can be met. The present work is a worthy addition to the *oeuvre*, and is aimed at the student who needs a comprehensive and authoritative treatise covering the whole area.

The great advantage of a relatively new field, is that the textbook writer has, as it were, a *tabula rasa*, rather than having to try to update for the needs of the present day a text first written by a long dead author, for almost equally long dead students. The author of this book has taken full advantage of the possibilities which the challenge of producing an entirely new text presents. He is eminently well qualified to write it, straddling as he does both the disciplines of law and chemistry. In fact, he is the only barrister, to my knowledge, who has produced textbooks in both fields. I am delighted to recommend this work.

John N Adams, Barrister,
Professor of Intellectual Property, University of Sheffield,
Director of the Common Law Institute of Intellectual Property

Preface

The aim of this book is to provide a thorough introduction to the intellectual property law of the UK. It is suitable for undergraduate students taking the subject as a separate topic, and for the specialist student who needs a comprehensive introductory textbook for a postgraduate course. In particular, this book is suitable for any modular course on IP, because each topic is dealt with in a discreet manner. I hope that this book will also be of value to solicitors, as a readable introduction to the subject before he or she reaches for one of the major practitioners' works.

This book covers all the major areas that need to be considered in order to have a balanced and informed knowledge of this large area of law. The current legislation has been strongly influenced by the UK's membership of the European Union, and the requirement for harmonisation across the Member States. This has resulted in a complex body of statutes, both of domestic and European origin, that is coupled with some residual common law, all of which is continually being updated to keep up with the advances in technology.

By examining a little of the history of the domestic statutes and their relationship with the common law, the present day complexities are more easily understood. Similarly, the effect upon the domestic law of the Regulations and Directives, which emanate from the Council of the Ministers and the European Commission, and the decisions of the Court of Justice of the European Communities may be analysed in terms of the goals which the European Union is attempting to reach.

This book was written at a time of great change in the national laws that concern intellectual property rights within the UK. Principal among these changes was the passing of the Trade Marks Act 1994. This Act came into force on 31 October 1994. As yet there have been no reported cases decided under this Act. Furthermore, cases that were started under the Trade Marks Act 1938 are still in the process of going through the courts. Hence, both Acts have been examined. On the European stage, the case of *IHT Internationale Heiztechnik GmbH v Ideal Standard GmbH* (1995) and Directive 89/104 and Regulation 40/94 will have a profound effect on trade mark law. In the copyright area, there is the effect of Directive 93/98, on the harmonisation of term of copyright protection, that needs to be considered. Further, the cases of *Anacon Corporation Ltd v Environmental Research Technology Ltd* (1994), *Ibcos Computers Ltd v Barclays Mercantile Highland Finance Ltd* (1994), and *John Richardson Computers Ltd v Flanders* (1993) have developed the law on copyright substantially. In registered design law, the House of Lords has now considered what is meant by an 'article' in *R v Registered Design Appeal Tribunal, ex parte Ford Motor Co Ltd* (1994). In patent law, the cases of *Biogen Inc v Medera plc* (1995), and *Assidoman Multipack Ltd v The Mead Corporation* (1995) are important.

Even though only one name may appear on the front cover, this book, like all others, is the culmination of the hard work of many different people. I would like to thank Elizabeth Hambley and Susan Hall in particular, as well as Jane Moore, Ellen Gredley, Ashley Roughton and Natalie Langridge for all the time and effort that they have expended in reading the draft text and for the many valuable comments and criticisms they have offered. Without their hard work, this book would have been the poorer. In addition, I would like to thank all the members of the Chambers of Christopher Morcom QC who between them have enriched my understanding of the subject and so contributed to this book. Furthermore, I would like to acknowledge the unstinting help and attention that has been afforded me by the staff at Cavendish Publishing Limited, in particular Jo Reddy, Kate Nicol and Hannah Ward who between them ensured the smooth production of this book.

However hard one attempts to produce a book without errors such an achievement is rarely attained. If any mistakes are found, be they typographical, factual or legal, then please write to me, care of the publishers, and I will endeavour to remedy them in a future edition. I would also welcome comments of a more general nature, for example suggestions on parts of the text that need elaborating or suggestions for others topics that ought to be included.

For simplicity I have used the masculine throughout the text to refer to a natural person of either sex. By so doing, I do not wish it to be inferred that there is any limitation upon the gender of the protagonist.

I have attempted to state the law on intellectual property in the UK as it stands at 1 January 1995.

Michael Edenborough
One Essex Court, Temple, London
Saint George's Day, 1995

Table of Contents

Table of Cases

Table of Statutes

Chapter 1

Intellectual Property Rights

Society values the creative fruits of the human mind, believing that they enrich the fabric of life for all of its members. Thus, a system of laws has been developed that confers rights on the creators of these fruits. These rights are collectively known as intellectual property rights, which is commonly abbreviated to 'IPRs'.

The single all encompassing term of intellectual property rights belies their diversity, and also the different approaches that the legislature has adopted in protecting them. However, underlying all of these rights, there is the fundamental point that by conferring some rights on the creators, the freedom of the remainder of society is curtailed in some manner. This conflict between a free and unregulated market, and a market on which restrictions have been placed is one that has taxed the legislature throughout the centuries. Furthermore, this conflict remains in a constant state of flux as the legislature enacts statutes to cope with the ever-changing technological and economic conditions within society.

Intellectual property law includes many diverse topics. Protection is conferred on the authors of creative works such as books, music or artistic works. This generally takes the form of copyright protection that prohibits other individuals from copying the original work. In addition to the copyright that subsists in original creative works, copyright protection has been extended to cover derivative works such as films, sound recordings and broadcasts. The protection conferred by copyright does not stop another person from producing the same work independently of the original, ie the protection is not monopolistic in nature.

Related to copyright *simpliciter*, are the moral rights that are associated with being an author of a creative work. These, as their name suggests, are concerned with the protection of the integrity of the author rather than protecting his commercial interests. There are also rights that accrue to the performers of live shows. Such shows often do not involve the intermediary of any copyright work on which to base the rights that would normally prevent exploitation by way of unofficial recordings. Broadly, all these rights protect the creative arts.

1.1 Introduction

1.2 Examples of IPRs

There are works which, although technically falling within the definition of a work protectable by copyright, are in practice technical drawings that will be used in the production of engineering components. These industrial designs are treated separately from true artistic works, and the protection that is conferred is substantially restricted. The protection is provided by a modified form of copyright and a special right called design right. All of the rights mentioned so far arise automatically when the work is created, ie there are no formalities that must be completed before protection becomes available.

Ideas that result in truly technical advances, such as inventions or better designs for everyday objects, are protected by patents and registered designs respectively. These rights are different in nature from those conferred on copyright works, in that the work must be novel, and in the case of inventions, the work must also be 'not obvious', ie it must be inventive. In order for an inventive work to be protected, it must be registered, which involves an examination to test whether or not the work meets the statutory requirements. Correspondingly, the registration system confers protection of a different nature from that which arises automatically for copyright works. So, in the case of a patent or registered design, a true monopoly is granted in return for the full disclosure of the subject matter to the public. Thus, regardless of whether a different person subsequently invents the same thing totally independently, that person is unable to take advantage of his invention, because all rights will have already been given to the first inventor.

The last main category of intellectual property rights concerns the rights of traders to protect themselves from other traders who might otherwise attempt to take unfair advantage. A body of legislation has evolved to prevent the misappropriation of the marks that one trader may use in order to distinguish his goods from those of another trader. This protection is provided by a system of registration for trade marks, and by the common law tort of passing-off for those marks which have not been officially registered. The protection provided by trade marks, like patents and registered designs, only accrues to the owner of the right once an application has been successfully submitted and the necessary formalities have been completed.

In addition to registered and unregistered trade marks, the businessman has the protection of an equitable duty of confidentiality that provides protection from people disclosing confidential information to others who should not be privy to such information. Furthermore, there are various statutory provisions that ensure the owners of the principal forms of intellectual property rights cannot use those rights to intimidate other traders by issuing groundless threats of legal proceedings. Finally, there is the common law tort of malicious falsehood which prevents one trader from falsely denigrating another trader's business or produce. This is similar to an action for defamation, but rather than regulating the interactions between natural persons, malicious falsehood is concerned with the interactions between companies and other trading organisations. This close link is reflected by an alternative name for malicious falsehood, namely trade libel.

The requirement for registration is a prerequisite in the UK before monopolistic rights are granted under English law. The grant of such monopolistic rights gives the owner of these rights a monopoly to exploit these rights to the exclusion of anyone else, regardless of whether or not any other person has independently come up with the same idea. In contrast, rights that are not registrable and which arise automatically when the work comes into existence, such as copyright, tend only to confer protection against copying, ie the subsequent independent creation of an identical work would be an absolute defence to an allegation of infringement of copyright.

Historically, patents, registered designs and trade marks were referred to as *industrial* property rights, because they were associated with industry and commerce. This label also covered unregistered trade marks and the duty of confidentiality, because these too were primarily associated with commercial dealings. With the addition of copyright, the related rights in performances and moral rights the modern definition of *intellectual* property rights is completed.

1.3 Related rights

There are, however, a number of statutes that deal with matters related to the core intellectual property rights. For example, the Trade Description Act 1968 is concerned with the false application of marks upon goods that belie their true origin and nature. This is closely related to the function that a trade mark is intended to fulfil.

Another example of these related rights is provided by competition law. On the Continent it is common for there to be some statutory prohibition against unfair competition that attempts to prevent the exploitation of a market by a powerful company. In this country there are the Restricted Trade Practices Act 1976 and the Competition Act 1980 which between them regulate whether or not a restrictive agreement between trading associations may be enforced. There is, however, no fully developed regime within the UK concerned with regulating unfair competition between traders, although the UK, being a member of the European Union does have to abide by the competition regulations that operate within the Community.

1.4 Influences on domestic intellectual property law

The majority of the protection for intellectual property rights in the UK is provided by statute, as opposed to the common law or equity. As a member of the European Union, the UK's legislation has been influenced by Community law, and any consideration of domestic intellectual property law must take this into account. In addition to this European dimension, the UK is a signatory to a number of international treaties that regulate the exploitation of intellectual property rights, and these too have an effect within the UK. Principal amongst these international treaties is the Paris Convention for the Protection of Industrial Property 1883.

In addition to these purely legislative matters, other influences, originating from the commercial world, affect the rights that accrue to the owners of intellectual property rights. For example, the Uruguay Round of the General Agreement on Tariffs and Trade ('GATT') was commenced in 1986, and in the latter half of 1993 agreement was finally reached. Although intellectual property rights *per se* were not a subject of the negotiations, it was recognised during the negotiation that the differences in the substantive laws of the signatory states could lead to the distortion of a free-trading market. Thus, the Trade Related Intellectual Property Rights ('TRIPs') Agreement, which was annexed to the GATT Uruguay Round, deals with substantive rights and obligations as well as procedural issues such as enforcement.

1.5 European Union legislation

The European Union, in the guise of the Council of Ministers, the European Commission and the European Parliament, promulgates a vast amount of legislation which affects each and every Member State.

The principal sources of European law are the founding Treaties of the European Union and the amendments that have been made to them. These Treaties, of which the most important is the Treaty of Rome 1957, comprise many different Articles, of which many have a direct effect within the Member States. For example, the competition rules of the Treaty of Rome 1957, which are contained in Articles 85 and 86, have horizontal direct effect. This means that economic undertakings may invoke these Articles against each other in the national courts. In the UK, a breach of an Article is

Article is actionable as a breach of statutory duty (*Garden Cottage Foods Ltd v Milk Marketing Board* (1984)).

Apart from the founding Treaties, the two most important types of legal pronouncements that the Council and the Commission make are Regulations and Directives.

A Regulation, which is said to be 'made', has general application, ie it affects all Member States. This means it is binding in its entirety and directly applicable to all Member States. Generally, a Regulation is used to introduce new rights and obligations throughout the whole Community. A Regulation does not need any additional implementation by the Government of a Member State to be effective within that Member State. As a consequence, an individual may rely on the contents of a Regulation. Thus, if that Regulation makes provision for a new right, then the individual can rely on that new right to found a cause of action against another individual.

A Directive, which is said to be 'issued', is binding as to the result to be achieved upon each Member State to which it is addressed, but it leaves to the national authorities the choice of form and method for implementation (Treaty of Rome 1957, Article 189). Under the terms of a Directive the Member State has an obligation to pass national implementing legislation to give effect to the Directive within its national legal system (*Commission of the European Communities v Italian Republic* (1980)). In the main, Directives are used to harmonise national laws, for example Directive 93/98 is designed to equalise all of the differing periods of copyright protection that are found within the various Member States. There is no requirement on the Member State to implement legislation that reproduces *verbatim* the provisions of the Directive. However, the Member State must adopt the most appropriate forms and methods to ensure that the Directive is fully effective (*Commission of the European Communities v Italian Republic* (1983)).

Once a Directive has been implemented by national legislation, a private party must rely on the national legislation rather than on the Directive. However, if the implementary legislation fails to give full effect to the Directive, then a private individual may continue to rely on the provisions of the Directive (*Commission of the European Communities v Kingdom of Belgium* (1980)).

If a Directive has not been implemented, the position is more complicated. A Directive will have direct effect if, and only if, it satisfies the following three-fold test:

(1) the relevant obligation(s) must be clear, precise and unconditional;

(2) the nature of the Director must be capable of creating rights for individuals; and

(3) the implementation date for the Directive must have expired.

A Directive is 'unconditional' when there is no need for further action by the Community institution or the Member States in order to define its content. If all of these conditions are met then an individual may rely on any rights introduced, but only against the Member State itself: it does not introduce a cause of action against another private party, ie there is no horizontal, only vertical effect (*Marshall v Southampton and South West Hampshire Area Health Authority (Teaching)* (1986)). Where an individual has suffered loss as a result of a Member State's failure to implement a Directive, that individual may be entitled to recover damages from the Member State (*Francovich and Bonifaci v Italian Republic* (1991)).

In applying national law, a national Court must interpret it, as far as possible, in the light of the wording and purpose of any relevant Directive, whether the national law originated before or after the adoption of the Directive, and this, in effect, gives rise to a horizontal effect, the so-called 'indirect effect' (*Marleasing SA v La Comercial Internacional De Alimentación SA* (1992)).

Traditionally, the English courts have been ill-disposed towards the grant of any monopolistic rights that might fetter competition within the business community. On the continent the principle of unfettered competition is of paramount importance. This is evidenced by the prominent position afforded to the Articles in the Treaty of Rome 1957 that are concerned with the establishment of the principle of the free movement of goods between Member States of the European Economic Community. Yet, in practice, the European Union has tended to grant greater rights to the owners of intellectual property rights than has occurred in the domestic laws of the UK. For example, in the UK under the Patents Act 1949, the term of protection for a patent was 16 years, but under the Patents Act 1977, which conforms to the European Patent Convention 1973, the term has been extended to 20 years.

Not only do continental countries grant monopolies of greater duration, but they also confer protection in areas that the UK used not to protect. For example, continental countries have long provided for the existence of moral rights for authors. Only recently, under the Copyright, Designs and Patents Act 1988, has an author been entitled to such protection within the UK.

Thus, there is an inconsistency between the principle of free trade, which is lauded by many continental countries, and their practice of granting a multitude of intellectual property rights of long duration.

Within the European Union there is strong pressure for greater integration between Member States. For example, the existing domestic laws of the Member States are seen as barriers to free trade between them. Hence the new Trade Mark Act 1994 enacts provisions that are designed to harmonise the manner in which trade marks are treated within the UK with their treatment throughout the Community.

In addition to the harmonisation of individual legislative frameworks, the European Union intends to instigate common procedural systems to regulate the application for, and the granting of, intellectual property rights. Thus, the European Patent Convention 1973 provides a mechanism whereby with one application a number of domestic patents may be granted.

Furthermore, it is proposed that unitary rights should operate throughout the European Union. Under the Community Patent Convention 1973 and the Trade Mark Regulation 40/94, there are provisions for the introduction of a unitary Community-wide patent and trade mark. These pan-European rights will displace the operation of the domestic rights, and will be adjudicated upon by European, rather than domestic courts.

Apart from the pressures from within the European Union, there are also external pressures that are exerted from other large trading blocks, such as the US, Japan, and the Pacific Basin. Eventually, these will lead to the harmonisation of property rights world-wide and the corresponding adoption of world-wide unitary rights. This, however, is still a long way in the future, and, for the present, most IPRs within the UK are governed directly by domestic and not international legislation. It is with these domestic rights that this book is predominantly concerned.

1.6 Possible future developments

Intellectual Property Rights

Intellectual Property Rights ('IPRs') protect the fruits of the creative mind.

Introduction

Conflict exists between free trade and the restrictions imposed by the exercise of IPRs.

Copyright protects creative works like literary, musical and artistic works.

Examples of IPRs

Derivative works include films, sound recordings and broadcasts.

Copyright provides protection against copying, but not against independent creation.

Moral rights of the author protect his artistic integrity.

Performance rights protect performers of live shows.

Industrial designs are protected by a modified form of copyright and design right.

All these rights arise automatically when the creative work comes into existence.

Innovative works are protected by patents and registered designs.

These latter two rights are monopolistic in the nature of the protection conferred and correspondingly must satisfy the registration requirements.

Trading rights include:

- trade marks for registered trade marks;

- the tort of passing-off for unregistered trade marks;

- the equitable duty of confidentiality for confidential information.

There is statutory protection against groundless threats of legal proceedings for the infringement of IPRs.

Common law right against malicious falsehood prohibits the denigration of a trader or his products by another trader.

Related rights	Trade Descriptions Act 1968 deals with false trade descriptions.
	Competition laws, eg Restricted Trade Practices Act 1976 and Competition Act 1980.
	The Treaty of Rome 1957 regulates the free movement of goods within the Community, and Articles 85 and 86 prohibit abuses of the market by trading organisations.
Influences on domestic intellectual property law	Most IPRs are conferred by UK statutes, some by the common law or equity.
	Legislation from the European Union is in the form of Treaties, Regulations and Directives.
	International Conventions.
	TRIPs resulting from GATT will affect IPRs.
European Union legislation	Founding Treaties and their amendments, eg Treaty of Rome 1957.
	Garden Cottage v MMB (1984): breach of an Article actionable as a breach of statutory duty.
	Regulations have direct effect, used to introduce new rights and obligations.
	Directives usually must be implemented by each Member State before becoming effective. They are used to harmonise the differing laws and procedures of the Member States.
	A Directive, if clear and precise, may have direct effect even if not implemented.
	Marshall v Southampton AHA (1986): directives generally have no horizontal effect.
	Marleasing (1992): national law must be applied to give effect to Directive.
Likely developments	Greater integration within EU, ie harmonisation of rights.
	European Patent Convention and the Madrid Protocol harmonise procedure.
	Introduction of unitary Community-wide trade marks and patents.

Chapter 2

Copyright: Historical Introduction

Copyright was originally concerned with preventing the unlawful physical copying of printed material, but over the centuries it has evolved considerably in order to keep pace with technological developments. Copyright may now be used to protect a wide range of divergent concepts from the reproduction of cartoon characters on T-shirts to the broadcasting of audio/visual material from satellites.

Not only has the subject matter encompassed by copyright protection been expanded, but, concomitantly, the acts that are held to constitute infringement have been extended. At first, copyright only proscribed the physical reproduction of a literary work, but it now covers such activities as the performance of dramatic or musical works, and the electronic reproduction of the source code of a computer program within a microprocessor.

The history of copyright in this country is long and contains many different threads. The protection conferred started as a mere licence that was granted to printers as an exercise of the Royal prerogative. Initially, copyright was a property right which existed only at common law and lasted in perpetuity. Statutory copyright was first introduced for published works by the Copyright Act 1709, but unpublished words still only received copyright protection by virtue of the common law. There then followed two centuries in which the types of work protected, and the protection conferred, was increased by piecemeal legislation. The Copyright Act 1911 attempted to unify all these divergent branches into a single coherent system and, furthermore, it abolished common law copyright. Henceforth, copyright only existed by virtue of statute. The Copyright Act 1956 was passed in a attempt to keep pace with international and technological developments. This is the Act which is still in force in Hong Kong, and so is still of great importance today. The Copyright, Designs and Patents Act 1988 was passed in response to further international and technological developments and is the basis for the current legislation in the UK.

It should be remembered that copyright is a legal *chose in action* that relates to the intangible property right to reproduce, for example, the text of a book. It is not concerned with the tangible property right that relates to the legal ownership of, eg, the physical book, ie the *chose in possession*. I may buy a book and own it, but I may not reproduce the text without a licence from the copyright owner.

2.2	**Early developments of copyright**	In 1709 the first true Copyright Act was passed. It is also commonly referred to as the Statute of Anne. This gave the author of a new book the sole right of printing it for a term of 14 years, at the end of which the book could be freely printed, unless the author was still living in which case a second term of 14 years was granted. Authors of books that were already published retained the right of sole publication for 21 years from 10 April 1710. All books that were published had to be registered at the Stationers' Company. This was the first time that the property right of copyright was conferred by statute.

Initially, it was thought by legal commentators that this Act merely enhanced the pre-existing common law rights of copyright during the first few years of publication, and that the common law right of copyright was not extinguished by publication, and so would continue in perpetuity (*Millar v Taylor* (1769)). However, in a later decision by the House of Lords it was held that this Act had the effect of destroying the common law copyright in published works (*Donaldson v Beckett* (1774)), but that the common law copyright in unpublished works remained, and this lasted in perpetuity. This everlasting right at common law was finally abolished by the Copyright Act 1911 s 31, and from then on the only type of copyright that could exist was as a result of statute.

2.2.1	Non-literary copyright works	The origin of copyright lay in the control by the Crown of the spread of ideas contained in literary works. This control was exercised by restricting the printing of books. Other types of works, which are now commonly associated with copyright protection, did not actually receive copyright protection until much later. The spur to conferring protection was the development of technology, which allowed an ever-increasing number of articles to be reproduced easily. This has continued to act as an impetus to the evolution of copyright law to increase both the class of works protected and also the acts that are to be considered an infringement of the copyright rights vested in those works. In parallel with this technological impetus was the growing commercial value of the original works themselves, and also the rapid growth in value of products that were derived from the original works.
2.3	**Developments during the 19th century**	During the 19th century, Parliament continued to modify the precise period of protection conferred by copyright, and also the ambit of works that could be protected by copyright. By

the Copyright Act 1814 s 4, the period for which the author had the sole right to print was extended to 28 years from the first day of publication, and if the author was still alive at the end of that period, then the sole right continued for the remainder of his natural life. The Literary Copyright Act 1842 extended the duration of protection again. This time to the life of the author plus seven years, or 42 years from publication whichever was the longer; or, if the work was published posthumously, then 42 years from the date of publication. In addition to extending the period of protection, registration at Stationers' Hall was no longer compulsory. However, it was still a precondition before an action could be commenced for infringement.

The decision in *Donaldson v Beckett* (1774) (which, it will be recalled, held that the Copyright Act 1709 extinguished the perpetual common law right of copyright once a work was published, and replaced it with a right that was limited in duration) had a fundamental influence in determining the development of copyright protection in the succeeding centuries, because it highlighted the conflict between the common law right and the statutory right.

In *Jefferys v Boosey* (1854), a related issue arose. At that time, statute did not confer copyright protection to a foreign author. However, did any right accrue as a result of the residual action of the common law? Pollock CB commented that copyright was:

'... altogether an artificial right, not naturally and necessarily arising out of the social rules that ought to prevail among mankind, but ... a creature of the municipal laws of each country, to be enjoyed for such time and under such regulations as the laws of each state may direct.'

Accordingly, the House of Lords held that the statute defined the scope of the rights of the author in respect of any copyright property. It can be readily appreciated that this case follows the underlying reasoning contained in *Donaldson v Beckett* (1774), namely the displacement of the common law right by one based on statute.

The performance of a dramatic work was not a restricted act until the Dramatic Copyright Act 1833 was passed. This Act, which is also know as the Bulwer Lytton's Act, conferred the exclusive right of public performance for a period of 28 years, with a further reversionary period to the author for the residue of his life. There was, however, a common law right to prevent the performance of a work that had not been published (*Morris v Kelly* (1820); and *Jefferys v Boosey* (1854)).

2.3.1   Dramatic and musical works

The Literary Copyright Act 1842 provided similar protection for the performance of musical works. This Act also extended the period of protection to 42 years from the date of publication, or the life of the author plus seven years, whichever was the longer, and so brought the protection conferred upon these types of works into line with that granted to literary works.

2.3.2	Royal Commission of 1875	

Copyright protection had developed piecemeal over several centuries slowly replacing the common law right of copyright. In parallel with this development, the range of works protected was greatly expanded from just original literary material. As a result of this expansion there were many different statutes in this area that had been drafted without any consideration to forming a uniform system.

A Royal Commission was formed in 1875 to consider these problems, and in its report of 1878, summarised the situation with respect to copyright in the UK by stating that:

> 'The law is wholly destitute in any sort of arrangement, incomplete, often obscure, and, even when it is intelligible upon long study, it is in many parts so ill-expressed that no one who does not give such study to it can expect to understand it. The common law principles which lie at the root of the law, have never been settled.'

It is notable that even though the report of the Royal Commission was wide-ranging, there was no mention of any moral rights to which an author of a work might be entitled. This clearly contrasts with the situation on the continent, where such rights were recognised.

2.3.3	Berne Convention 1886

In addition to the domestic complexities of the law on copyright, the subject had increasingly become one of international importance. The issue of reciprocal rights for foreign authors was a matter of great concern, particularly on the continent. Hitherto, copyright did not subsist in a work unless it was published first in the UK. The UK, which exported large amounts of valuable copyright material, wished to secure reciprocal protection from other countries. This was achieved initially by a series of independent bilateral treaties. These treaties conferred copyright in the UK on works that had been first published abroad. In 1886 the Berne Convention was formulated. This was the first multi-national agreement that enabled copyright protection to be secured in all the Member States so long as either the author had a personal connection with a Member State or the work was first published in a Member State. The UK became a signatory to this Convention, and as a consequence, the International

Copyright Act 1886 was passed in order to fulfil the international obligations to foreign authors which thereby arose upon the UK ratifying the Berne Convention on 5 September 1887.

In 1908 the Berne Convention was substantially revised at Berlin, and, in response to this, a Committee was appointed to report to Parliament on any changes that would be necessary in order to give domestic effect to the revised Convention. This Committee recommended that a consolidating and amending Act be passed (Report of the Committee on Copyright 1909). The result was the Copyright Act 1911, which repealed, with only a few small exceptions, all the previous legislation on copyright that hitherto had been in force within the UK.

2.4   Developments in the 20th century

The Copyright Act 1911 came into force on 1 July 1912. Common law copyright, which existed in perpetuity for unpublished works, was abolished (CA 1911 s 31). Henceforth, the only protection that existed was that conferred by statute. The CA 1911 explicitly granted copyright in both published and unpublished works, as protection now arose out of the act of *creation* and not the act of *publication*.

2.4.1   Copyright Act 1911

There were other significant changes that were introduced by the CA 1911 as a consequence of the Berlin revision of the Berne Convention. The period of protection was increased for most works to the life of the author plus 50 years. The CA 1911 also widened the acts that were to be considered an infringement. For example, the producers of sound recordings gained an exclusive right to prevent others reproducing their recordings (CA 1911 s 19(1)), or playing their recordings in public (*Gramophone Co Ltd v Stephen Cawardine and Co* (1934)). Furthermore, literary, dramatic and musical works could now be infringed by the making of a film or other mechanical performance (CA 1911 s 1(2)(d)).

The Berne Convention was further revised at Rome in 1928 and at Brussels in 1948, each of which strengthened the position of an author in the Convention countries. However, throughout this period, the US was not a signatory to the Berne Convention, or any of the subsequent revisions. This left the US isolated from any international agreement for the reciprocal granting of copyright. There had been temporary agreements during the two World Wars, but these had been allowed to lapse.

2.4.2   Further international developments

In an attempt to bring the US into an international agreement on copyright, UNESCO organised a new convention. This agreement aimed to guarantee reciprocal treatment, but on terms less stringent than those required by the Berne Convention. For example, the minimum term of protection was for the life of the author plus 25 years, or, alternatively, if the country already measured the term of copyright protection from the date of publication, then that period had to be at least 25 years. This new agreement was called the Universal Copyright Convention (the 'UCC') and was signed at Geneva in 1952. Notably, it contained no provisions concerning the moral rights of the authors, for this had been one of the obstacles to the US satisfying the Berne Convention. The US agreed to sign this Convention, and, indeed, was one of the original signatories.

The Berne Convention, as reflects its European origins, requires no formalities to be fulfilled before protection accrues (Article 5(2)). The US, in contrast, required that all works be registered before copyright protection vested. In order to accommodate this requirement, the UCC stated that if a work bore the symbol ©, together with the name of the copyright owner and the year of first publication, then it would be deemed that all registration requirements had been satisfied (Article III(1)). This is the origin of the use of the symbol © on works published in the UK, for it allowed the work to receive reciprocal protection in, for example, the US. An important difference between the Berne Convention and the UCC concerns works that have fallen into the public domain because the term of copyright protection has expired. Under the UCC, once copyright has been lost, it cannot acquire protection retrospectively should its country of origin subsequently ratify the UCC. However, under the Berne Convention, this retrospective protection does occur.

The UK was a founding signatory to the UCC, and as a consequence, another Parliamentary Committee was appointed to consider whether or not any changes were needed in the domestic legislation in order to comply with its revised international obligations. Furthermore, the Committee also was to consider the effect of new technology upon copyright works. The Committee, known as the Gregory Committee after its chairman, reported to Parliament (Report of the Committee on the Law of Copyright 1952) and as a result the Copyright Act 1956 was passed.

2.4.3   Copyright Act 1956

This Act came into force on 1 June 1957. It repealed the few remaining Acts on copyright that had not been repealed by the Copyright Act 1911. Furthermore, it also repealed all of the CA 1911, save for ss 15, 34 and 37. The CA 1956 added three new types of works on which copyright could subsist, namely cinematograph films, broadcasts and the typographical format of published editions. The arrangement of this Act was such that original works, such as literary, dramatic, musical and artistic works, appeared in Part I, while derivative works, such as sound recordings, cinematograph films, broadcasts, cable programmes and typographical format of published editions, were covered in Part II. The term 'derivative work' comprises works that (in the legislator's view) have been derived from some underlying primary copyright material. Examples would include the film of a book, and the sound recording of a concert. The right conferred in the latter type of work is called a neighbouring right on the continent. The continental term again implies that such derived works are one removed from the central creative work. However, in the modern day, when, for example, films are lauded as creations of aesthetic merit in their own right, without any reference to an underlying work (if there is one), this distinction is becoming increasingly outdated.

One of the principal changes to the CA 1956 was brought about by the Design Copyright Act 1968 which was intended to deal with the position of copyright in design drawings for mass-produced items. The issue of copyright in design drawings for industrial objects is interrelated to the protection conferred on such items by the Registered Designs Act 1949. The issue of the protection for industrial designs is discussed in Chapters 11 and 12.

The CA 1956, even though repealed in its entirety in the UK by the CDPA 1988 Schedule 8, is still in force in Hong Kong, and so it remains of great importance.

The development of smaller and more sensitive recording equipment has allowed the unauthorised recording of musical performances and films to be easily achieved. These illicit recordings can then be sold to the general public at a large profit to the person who had made the recording. This practice of making, and then selling, illicit recording is called 'bootlegging' and is a source of great financial loss to the performing artists. Some protection was provided by the Dramatic and Musical Performers' Protection Act 1925, which introduced some limited criminal sanctions. The protection was strengthened by the Dramatic and Musical Performers' Protection Act 1958, the Performers' Protection Act 1963 and the Performers' Protection Act 1972. However, in the opinion of the recording industry, none of these measures provided sufficient protection, and this lacuna in the protection of their rights was one of the major commercial pressures that lead to a review of the law of copyright as a whole that was eventually to lead to the repeal of the CA 1956.

2.4.4   Illicit recording of performances

2.4.5	Whitford Report 1977	In order to consider all of these issues, and other related problems that had arisen due to the new methods by which material could be reproduced (for example, the development of computers and the advances in audio/visual reproduction and transmission) another Committee was appointed in 1973. This Committee also considered the international developments that resulted from the revision of the Berne Convention at Stockholm in 1967 and Paris in 1971, and the revision of the Universal Copyright Convention at Paris in 1971. This Committee submitted its report in 1977, which is known as the Whitford Report after the High Court judge who presided over its preparation (Report of the Committee to consider the Law on Copyright and Designs 1977). There were two important government papers on this issue before a Bill was presented to Parliament (Reform of the Law relating to Copyright, Designs, and Performers' Protection 1981; and Intellectual Property and Innovation 1986).
2.4.6	Copyright, Designs and Patents Act 1988	The result of the Whitford Report was the Copyright, Designs and Patents Act 1988, which is the current framework for copyright law in this country. The 1988 CDPA repealed the whole of the CA 1956, the Copyright (Computer Software) Act 1985 and the Performers' Protection Acts of 1958, 1963 and 1972. The new copyright provisions came into force on 1 August 1989.

The 1988 Act introduced some new rights, such as a rental right in respect of sound recordings, films, and computer programs (CDPA 1988 s 18(3)); it also introduced a comprehensive system of moral rights for authors (CDPA 1988 ss 77-89). The vexed issue of industrial designs, which had troubled the Courts and Parliament, resulted in the creation of a new property right called design right (CDPA 1988 ss 213-264). This new right is discussed in Chapter 12.

However, even though this is the principal Act concerning copyright, it is not the sole source that needs to be consulted to obtain a full account of copyright law in the UK, for it in turn has been extensively amended by the Broadcasting Act 1990. Furthermore, a large amount of subordinate legislation has been passed under the powers conferred by the 1988 Act.

2.4.7	Recent developments	Intellectual property law issues, which affect the UK, continue to arise, both within the EU, and on the international stage. For example, the US ratified the Berne Convention (as revised at Paris in 1971) with effect from 1 March 1989, while the UK formally ratified this amended version with effect from 2 January 1990. All Member States of the European Union have undertaken to become parties to this Paris revision of the

Berne Convention by 1 January 1995. This will provide increased protection for copyright and neighbouring rights (Council Resolution of 14 May 1992, Article 1).

Within Europe, the Commission has made a large number of proposals. For example, there is a proposal for a Council Regulation laying down measures to prohibit the release for free circulation, export or transit of counterfeit and pirated goods, which is now subject to further consultation with the European Parliament (Regulation 2842/86 and COM (93) 329). There is also a proposed Council Directive on the legal protection of databases.

Copyright: Historical Introduction

Copyright originated to prevent the unlawful copying of books and other written material.

    Both the type of works protected and the acts restricted by copyright have gradually increased over the centuries.

    Currently, UK copyright is governed by the Copyright, Designs and Patents Act 1988.

Introduction

The Statute of Anne 1709 was the first true Copyright Act in the UK, and it conferred upon the author the sole right to print a book for a term of 14 years, renewable for a further 14 years.

    It was first thought that the Act merely enhanced common law rights (*Miller v Taylor* (1769)).

    However, *Donaldson v Beckett* (1774) established that the 1709 Act destroyed the common law copyright in published works, but the common law copyright in unpublished works remained and lasted forever.

The Statute of Anne 1709

The development of new technology enabled cheaper and easier reproduction of various articles. Other types of work, therefore, required protection and between 1734 and 1862, for example, artistic and sculptural works, and the performance of dramatic and musical works were brought within the scope of copyright protection.

    Reciprocal rights for foreign authors were secured by a multi-national treaty known as the Berne Convention 1886. The latest revised version of this Convention was formulated at Paris in 1971, and the UK is a signatory to this version.

Early developments in other types of copyright

The Copyright Act 1911 abolished perpetual common law copyright in unpublished works. Copyright now exists solely as a statutory right protecting both published and unpublished works. The 1911 Act also extended protection to include sound recordings.

Developments in the 20th century

The Universal Copyright Convention (UCC) was concluded in 1952. The US became a signatory, because its terms were less stringent than those of the Berne Convention. The use of the copyright symbol © followed by the name of the copyright owner and year of publication, originates from the provisions of the UCC.

Further international developments

The Copyright Act 1956 brought cinematograph films, broadcasts and the typographical arrangements of published editions into the realms of copyright protection.

The Copyright, Designs and Patents Act 1988 (CDPA) was introduced as a result of the Whitford Report 1977.

It has introduced the following:

- A rental right (s 18(3));
- Moral rights (ss 77-89);
- A design right (ss 213-264).

The CDPA 1988 has been amended by the Broadcasting Act 1990.

Recent developments

The US has ratified the Berne Convention as from 1 March 1989.

All EU Member States are to ratify the Berne Convention by 1 January 1995.

There is a move towards greater international agreement, and in the EU this has developed into the harmonisation of the substantive laws that exist within each Member State.

Chapter 3

Copyright: Types of Works Capable of Protection

In Chapters 3 to 8 inclusive, which all concern copyright, all references to 'Act' or sections thereof are to the Copyright, Designs and Patents Act 1988 unless otherwise stated. This Act came into force from 1 August 1989 and is the principal Act dealing with copyright in the UK.

The types of works in which copyright may potentially subsist are described in s 1(1):

'1(1) (a) original literary, dramatic, musical or artistic works,

(b) sound recordings, films, broadcasts, cable programmes, and

(c) the typographical arrangement of published editions.'

If a work falls into one of the categories outlined in s 1(1), it must in addition fulfil a number of the qualifying conditions contained in ss 153-162 (s 1(3)). This chapter deals in detail with the various types of work that are potentially capable of copyright protection. The other prerequisite conditions are dealt with in the subsequent chapters.

However, it should be noted at the outset that copyright does not protect a mere idea, but only the expression of that idea. In the field of computer programs this has been explicitly recognised in Council Directive 91/250/EEC on the legal protection of computer programs which states that:

'Protection in accordance with this directive shall apply to the expression in any form of a computer program. Ideas and principles which underlie any element of a computer program, including those which underlie its interfaces, are not protected by copyright under this directive.' (Article 1(2)).

3.1   Introduction

A literary work is defined by s 3(1) to mean 'any work, other than a dramatic or musical work, which is written, spoken or sung and accordingly includes (a) a table or compilation, and (b) a computer program'. Section 3(1)(c) was added by the Copyright (Computer Programs) Regulations 1992 reg 3, to include the phrase 'preparatory design material for a computer program'. This amendment was effective from 1 January 1993 (C(CP)R 1992 reg 1(1)).

3.2   Literary works

3.2.1	No requirement for literary merit	There is no requirement that a literary work should have any literary merit. In *Exxon Corporation v Exxon Insurance Consultants International Ltd* (1982), the court approved the definition in *Hollinrake v Truswell* (1884) that a literary work is one which '... is intended to afford either information and instruction or pleasure in the form of literary enjoyment'. As a consequence of this definition, a work may be devoid of literary enjoyment, but rather merely supply the reader with information (such as, say, a menu) and yet still qualify as a 'literary' work under this Act.

Therefore, the use of the word 'literary' in the definition means no more than 'pertaining to printed matter', rather than importing a reference to the aesthetic merit of the work (*University of London Press Ltd v University Tutorial Press Ltd* (1916)).

3.2.2	Examples of literary works	As we have seen, literary works are not limited to works that have literary merit, but also include works in a written format that convey information. This has been interpreted widely by the courts. Thus, all of the following have been held to be literary works: private letters (*Donoghue v Allied Newspapers Ltd* (1938)); mathematical examination papers (*University of London Press Ltd v University Tutorial Press Ltd* (1916)); telegraph codes (*Anderson (DP) & Co Ltd v The Lieber Code Co* (1917)); a system of shorthand (*Pitman v Hine* (1884)); football fixture list (*Football League Ltd v Littlewoods Pools Ltd* (1959)); tables of five-letter combinations for a newspaper competition (*Express Newspapers plc v Liverpool Daily Post & Echo plc* (1985)); and various compilations such as an arrangement of broadcasting programmes (*Independent Television Publications Ltd v Time Out Ltd* (1984)); an alphabetical list of railway stations contained in *Bradshaw's Railway Guide* (*Blacklock (H) & Co Ltd v Arthur Pearson (C) Ltd* (1915)); a list of election results (*Press Association Ltd v Northern and Midland Reporting Agency* (1905-1910)); and a race card for a greyhound meeting comprising, *inter alia*, the dogs in each of the races, the time, the length and type of race and the prize money (*Bookmakers' Afternoon Greyhound Services Ltd v Wilf Gilbert (Staffordshire) Ltd* (1994)). Electronic circuit diagrams have also been held to be a literary work, because they contain information that can be read by someone, as opposed to being appreciated solely with the eye (*Anacon Corporation Ltd v Environmental Research Technology Ltd* (1994)).
3.2.3	Works denied literary protection	Even though a very large number of works have been held to be capable of protection as a literary work, the genus is not completely open ended. Thus, not all works that consist of printed words will be granted protection as a literary work, eg

the name of a political party such as the 'Social Democratic Party' (*Kean v McGiven* (1982)). Some works have been held to be too trivial to qualify eg four commonplace sentences that formed an advertising slogan (*Kirk Ltd v J & R Fleming* (1928-35)). Similarly, the title to a song 'The man who broke the bank at Monte Carlo' was held to be too brief to attract copyright (*Francis Day & Hunter v Twentieth Century Fox Corporation Ltd* (1940)) as was the title 'The Lawyer's Diary 1986' (*Rose v Information Services Ltd* (1987)). The various tables of useful information at the front of a pocket diary have also been denied copyright (*GA Cramp & Sons Ltd v Frank Smythson Ltd* (1944)), as has a race card which merely gave the name of the competitors in the order in which they were drawn from a hat (*Greyhound Racing Association Ltd v Shallis* (1923-28)). Thus, it is not sufficient for the work to comprise merely of words. In addition, there must have been the expenditure of sufficient labour, judgment or skill to justify the protection conferred by statute. Clearly, there was little labour, judgment or skill exercised in drawing the names of the competing dogs from a hat and writing down the result of the draw, and so the final race card did not merit copyright protection.

A dramatic work may include 'a work of dance or mime', while a musical work means 'a work of music, exclusive of any words or actions intended to be sung, spoken or performed with the music' (s 3(1)). The definition of literary work thus excludes any overlap with either a dramatic or musical work. Thus, a song consists of two separate copyrights: the literary copyright in the words, and the musical copyright in the musical components (*Redwood Music Ltd v B Feldman & Co Ltd* (1979)), and these are mutually exclusive.	**3.3 Dramatic and musical works**

The term 'dramatic work' implies that it is capable of performance (*Green v Broadcasting Corporation of New Zealand* (1989)). Furthermore, a dramatic work ought to involve action. As a consequence, if there is only a recital by the actor, without any movement, then such a performance would not constitute a dramatic work, but merely amount to a performance of a literary work. In such a case, any background scenic effects would only be protectable as artistic works in their own right. However, once movement is introduced, then the scenic effects become part of the dramatic work as a whole, and so subject to protection as a dramatic work (*Tate v Fullbrook* (1908)).

It is necessary for a literary, dramatic or musical work to be recorded in writing or in some other manner, before copyright may subsist (s 3(2)). Thus, there can be no copyright in a mere unrecorded idea. As a consequence, copyright cannot subsist	**3.4 The requirement for a permanent form of a literary, dramatic or musical work**

in any ad lib improvisations of a play that have not been recorded in some manner (*Tate v Thomas* (1921)). The justification for this is that it is expedient for there to be certainty in the subject matter receiving the protection.

3.5   Artistic works

An artistic work is defined as meaning:

'4(1) (a) a graphic work, photograph, sculpture or collage, irrespective or artistic quality;

(b) a work of architecture being a building or a model for a building; or,

(c) a work of artistic craftsmanship.'

3.5.1   Graphic works

A graphic work is further defined as meaning:

'4(2) (a) any painting, drawing, diagram, map, chart or plan; and

(b) any engraving, etching, lithograph, woodcut or similar work.'

It has been held that the facial make up on Adam Ant was not a painting, because it lacked permanence (*Merchandising Corporation of America Inc v Harpbond Ltd* (1983)). Similarly, artistic copyright did not subsist in the transient patterns produced by a mixture of sand and glycerine (*Komesaroff v Mickle* (1988)). Thus, even though there is no explicit requirement within the CDPA 1988 for an artistic work to be recorded before copyright may subsist, as there is for literary, dramatic or musical works, the courts have implicitly imposed such a requirement anyway.

Artistic copyright has been held to exist in the drawings of very simple items such as rivets (*British Northrop Ltd v Texteam Blackburn Ltd* (1974)) and the point patterns for knitwear (*Lerose Ltd v Hawick Jersey International Ltd* (1974)).

3.5.2   Photographs or sculptures

A photograph is defined within the Act to mean a recording of light or other radiation on any medium on which an image is produced or from which an image may by any means be produced so long as it is not part of a film (s 4(2)). This definition is wide enough to include a hologram. The phrase 'light or other radiation' must refer to electromagnetic radiation and not the type of radiation associated with radioactive decay, namely alpha and beta particles, even though gamma rays would be included. This definition of a photograph would not include an image that was stored on a CD ROM, because the picture in such a case is encoded using magnetic information, and is not a recording of light or any other form of electromagnetic radiation.

A carved wooden model, which was required in the manufacturing development of frisbees, has been held to be a sculpture, yet the final article was held not to be a sculpture (*Wham-O Manufacturing Co v Lincoln Industries Ltd* (1985)). The temporary models made from plasticine, which were used in the production of prototypes and were not intended to have any permanent existence, were held not to be sculptures (*J & S Davis (Holdings) Ltd v Wright Health Group Ltd* (1988)). This demonstrates again that the courts have imposed a requirement of permanence before copyright may be granted for a work.

A separate copyright can exist in an actual building, as well as a model of that building (s 4(1)(b) and *Meikle v Maufe* (1941)). The internal features of the design are also capable of protection (*Vincent v Universal Housing Co Ltd* (1928-1935)), as is a landscaped garden (*Meikle v Maufe* (1941)). The omission of the words 'irrespective of artistic quality' from the defining subsection implies that the work must have some artistic character, and so, for example, a purely functional breeze block building could be denied protection.

3.5.3   Architectural works

There have been few cases under this heading, and so the exact scope is ill-defined. In *Margot Burke Ltd v Spicers Dress Designs* (1936), Clauson J was reticent to hold that a lady's dress was a work of artistic craftsmanship, for his Lordship doubted whether the designer was cultivating:

3.5.4   Works of artistic craftsmanship

> ' ... one of the fine arts in which the object is mainly to gratify the aesthetic emotions by perfection of execution whether in creation or representation.'

Given the high profile that modern day fashion designers enjoy, it would seem that if this point were before the court today, a different opinion might prevail. Furthermore, it is now common place to secure protection for a dress pattern by reference to the underlying cutting pattern that has been used to produce the individual pieces from which the completed dress is fashioned (*Radley Gowns Ltd v Costas Spyrou (t/a 'Touch of Class' and 'Fiesta Girl')* (1975)).

In *George Hensher Ltd v Restawile Upholstery (Lancs) Ltd* (1976) the plaintiff claimed that the prototype to a piece of mass-produced furniture was a work of artistic craftsmanship. The House of Lords rejected the claim that the prototype furniture was a work of artistic craftsmanship, and further thought that the defence had needlessly conceded that the prototypes were even works of craftsmanship.

In a subsequent case Walton J opined that, by a majority, the House of Lords in *George Hensher Ltd v Restawile Upholstery*

(*Lancs*) *Ltd* (1976) had held that the intention of the author was paramount in deciding whether or not the work was artistic. His Lordship applied this criterion when holding that a prototype for a raincape for a mother and child, even though a work of craftsmanship, was a basic commodity and that its creator did not intend it to be considered as a work of artistic merit. Instead, the designer intended the cape merely to shield a child from inclement weather (*Merlet v Mothercare plc* (1984)).

3.6	**Sound recordings and films**	Sound recordings are defined in s 5(1). This confers a separate copyright in the recording of a work, that may also be the subject of a separate literary, dramatic or musical copyright. It also provides for copyright to subsist in a recording of a work that may not have an underlying copyright, such as an *ex tempore* conversation, a bird song, or a recording of a work in which copyright no longer subsists. There is no limitation on the method by which the recording is made, or the medium upon which it is stored.

A film is defined in s 5(1) as a 'recording on any medium from which a moving image may by any means be produced'. This definition is wide enough to include a digitised picture stored on a computer disc or a pack of 'flick-cards'.

3.7	**Broadcasts**	A broadcast is defined in s 6(1) as meaning 'a transmission by wireless telegraphy of visual images, sounds or other information which is capable of being lawfully received by a member of the public or is transmitted for presentation to members of the public'. Accordingly, the distinction that existed between television and sound broadcasts under CA 1956 s 14(10) has now been removed. Under CA 1956 only the British Broadcasting Corporation and the Independent Broadcasting Authority were entitled to copyright protection in the broadcasts. This restriction now no longer holds true.

Terrestrial and satellite broadcasts are treated in the same manner. Thus, for the purpose of Part I of the CDPA 1988 the place from which a broadcast is made is, in the case of a satellite transmission, the place from which the signals carrying the broadcast are transmitted to the satellite rather than the satellite itself in its geostationary orbit (s 6(4)), and references to the reception of a broadcast include reception of a broadcast relayed by means of a telecommunications system (s 6(5)).

3.8	**Cable programmes**	Section 7(1) defines a cable programme as 'any item included in a cable programme service', which in turn is defined as 'a service which consists wholly or mainly in sending visual

images, sounds or other information by means of a telecommunications system, otherwise than by wireless telegraphy, for reception at two or more places (whether for simultaneous reception or at different times in response to requests by different users) or for presentation to members of the public'. Thus, cable programmes and broadcasts are mutually exclusive.

(It is to be noted in passing that when used in conjunction with the word 'cable', the word 'programme' is spelt in the French manner, which was adopted by the English during the 19th century. However, when used in conjunction with the word 'computer', the word 'program' reverts to the former English spelling, which was preserved by the speakers of American English. This difference in spelling is used in the CDPA 1988, thus 'computer program' in s 3(1)(b), and 'cable programme' in s 7(1).)

3.9 Typographical arrangements of published editions

Typographical arrangements of published editions receive copyright protection under s 1(1)(c). Section 8(1) defines a 'published edition' as referring to the whole or part of a literary, dramatic or musical work. There is no requirement that the work itself should be still be in copyright, or indeed that it was ever the subject of copyright protection (*Machinery Market Ltd v Sheen Publishing Ltd* (1983)). Therefore, copyright can be claimed for a particular imprint of a book, even though the book is no longer protected by literary copyright. This is how particular reprints of, say, a Shakespearian play may be accorded protection, so long as the new edition does not reproduce the typographical arrangement of a previous edition (s 8(2)).

Copyright: Types of Works Capable of Protection

Types of works in which copyright may potentially subsist are described in s 1(1):

Introduction

'1(1) (a) original literary, dramatic, musical or artistic works;

(b) sound recordings, films, broadcasts or cable programmes; and

(c) the typographical arrangement of published editions.

Other qualifying conditions, which must be fulfilled, are contained in ss 153–162.

A literary work is any work, other than a dramatic or musical work, that is written, spoken or sung (s 3(1)). This includes a table, a compilation and a computer program.

Literary works

There is no requirement for the work to have any literary merit (*Exxon Corporation v Exxon Insurance Consultants International Ltd* (1982)). Examples of literary works include: private letters (*Donoghue v Allied Newspapers Ltd* (1938)) and examination papers (*University of London Press Ltd v University Tutorial Press Ltd* (1916)). Works denied literary protection include: the name of the Social Democratic Party (*Kean v McGiven* (1982)) and an advertising slogan (*Kirk Ltd v J & R Fleming* (1928–35)).

No requirement for literary merit

Dramatic and musical works include a work of dance or mime (s 3(1)). A song has typically two copyrights, one in the music and one in the words (*Redwood Music Ltd v B Feldman & Co Ltd* (1979)). For a dramatic work, there is a requirement that it be capable of performance (*Green v Broadcasting Corporation of New Zealand* (1989)).

Dramatic and musical works

Literary, dramatic and musical works must be recorded in writing or otherwise (s 3(2)). Writing is defined to include any code or notation (s 178). The recording need not be authorised (s 3(3)).

The requirement for a permanent form

Definition in s 4(1):

Artistic works

(a) a graphic work, photograph, sculpture or collage, irrespective of artistic quality;

(b) a work of architecture being a building or a model for a building; or

(c) a work of artistic craftsmanship.

Graphic works

Definition in s 4(2):

(a) any painting, drawing, diagram, map, chart or plan; and

(b) any engraving, etching, lithograph, woodcut or similar work.

Photographs or sculptures

A photograph is a recording of light or other radiation (s 4(2)).

A prototype model for frisbees was held to be a sculpture (*Wham-O Manufacturing Co v Lincoln Industries Ltd* (1985)). However, temporary plasticine models that were going to be used to produce a mould were held not to be sculptures (*Davis (Holdings) Ltd v Wright Health Group Ltd* (1988)).

Architectural works

The exterior of a house, the accompanying landscaped garden and the interior design have all been held to be architectural works (*Meikle v Maufe* (1941) and *Vincent v Universal Housing Co Ltd* (1928-35)).

Works of artistic craftsmanship

The prototypes of prefabricated furniture are not works of artistic craftsmanship (*George Hensher Ltd v Restawile Upholstery (Lancs) Ltd* (1976)). The artistic intention of the designer is important. Thus a mother and baby rain-cape, even though a work of craftsmanship, had not been intended by its designer to be artistic and therefore did not fall into this category (*Merlet v Mothercare plc* (1984)).

Sound recordings and films

A sound recording has a separate copyright from the underlying work (s 5(1)). The sound track of a film now has separate copyright from that of the film.

Films are defined as a moving image recorded on any medium by any means (s 5(1)).

Broadcasts

Broadcasts are defined as any transmission by wireless telegraphy of visual images, sounds or other information (s 6(1)).

Cable programmes

Cable Programmes are defined as any programme included in a cable programme service (s 7(1)).

Typographical arrangements of published editions relate to the whole or part of a published edition of a literary, dramatic or musical work (s 8(1)). In this way, the typographical arrangement of a new edition of a book may receive protection, independently of whether or not the underlying work is in copyright.

Chapter 4

Copyright: Subsistence

Having described the types of works in which copyright may potentially subsist in s 1(1), subsection 1(3) goes on to state that copyright will not subsist unless the requirements in ss 153–162 of the Act are met. In general, qualification is satisfied for both published and unpublished works if the author fulfils certain conditions (s 153(1)(a)). In the case of published works, qualification may also be satisfied if the country in which the work was first published meets certain requirements (s 153(1)(b)). In the case of a broadcast or cable programme, the country from which the broadcast was made or the cable programme was sent is the relevant criterion for satisfying the qualification requirements (s 153(1)(c)).

4.1   Introduction

Works in which Crown or Parliamentary copyright vests are regulated by separate provisions contained in ss 163–167. Similarly, the copyright that vests in certain international organisations, such as the United Nations, is regulated by separate provisions contained in s 168.

Once the qualification conditions for copyright subsistence have been met, then it will not cease by reason of any subsequent event (s 153(3)). Therefore, for example, if a work qualified for copyright by virtue of the author being a qualifying person when the work was first made, then that work would not cease to qualify for copyright protection if the author ceased to satisfy the pre-requisite conditions. So once a work has qualified, it retains copyright even if the reason for its qualification in the first place is no longer valid.

Most commonly, a work qualifies by virtue of the fact that the author satisfies the qualifying conditions. These requirements will now be considered in detail.

4.2   Qualification by reference to the author

Any type of work in which copyright may potentially subsist, will qualify for copyright protection if the author was at the *material time* a qualifying person (s 154(1)); that is, a British citizen or subject, an individual domiciled or resident in the UK, or any other country to which the relevant provisions of the CDPA 1988 extend, or a body incorporated under the law of the UK or any other country to which the Act extends. Works of joint authorship qualify so long as at least one of the authors is a qualifying person (s 154(3)), in which case the qualifying author determines the first ownership of copyright

4.2.1   Personal status

and its duration under ss 11 and 12 respectively. Duration and ownership are discussed in Chapters 5 and 6 respectively.

4.2.2 Material time	The 'material time' for an unpublished work, such as a literary, dramatic, musical or artistic work, is when the work was made or, if the making of the work extended over a period, a substantial part of that period (s 154(4)(a)). It must be remembered that for the purpose of the Act a literary, dramatic or musical work is not made until such time as it is recorded (s 3(2)), which may be later that when it was first created or performed. By restricting the relevant period to that in which the work is 'made', ie recorded, no account will be taken of the time when an idea is merely developed as a thought. Instead, only the time during which concrete manipulation of the work was produced will count towards the period of creation for the purpose of this section. For a published work, the 'material time' is when the work was first published, or if published posthumously, then at the time just before the author died (s 154(4)(b)).

For other works, such as sound recordings, films, or broadcasts, the material time is when the work in question was made (s 154(5)(a) and (b)); for a cable programme, when it was included in the cable programme service (s 154(5)(c)); and for the case of a typographical arrangement, when the edition was published (s 154(5)(d)).

4.3 Qualification by reference to place of first publication	Instead of qualifying by reference to the author's status, a work may qualify by reference to the place of its first publication. Thus, a literary, dramatic, musical or artistic work, a sound recording or a film, or the typographical arrangement of a published edition may qualify for copyright protection if it is first published in the UK or any other country to which the relevant provisions of the Act have been extended (s 155(1)). Furthermore, so long as the publication occurred within a qualifying country simultaneously or within 30 days of the publication within a non-qualifying country, then the work will still qualify for publication (s 155(3)).

4.3.1 Meaning of publication	Section 175(1) defines publication of a work as the issuing of copies to the public, or in the case of literary, dramatic, musical or artistic works making the same available by means of an electronic retrieval system, so long as (in each case) it satisfies the reasonable requirements of the public and is not just 'merely colourable' (s 175(5)). Accordingly, a conversation between the users on a public access bulletin board on the Internet would amount to publication. In contrast, a similar conversation held on a secure line would not amount to

publication, because it does not satisfy the 'reasonable requirements of the public'.

A literary, dramatic or musical work is not published merely because it has been performed in public (s 175(4)(a)(i)). Thus, the oral delivery of a lecture read from written notes is not publication; but by virtue of s 19(2)(a) such an action constitutes a performance of the lecture.

An artistic work is not published by virtue of it having been exhibited (s 175(4)(b)(i)). Nor is a work of artistic craftsmanship or a sculpture deemed to have been published by reason of either photographs or copies of a graphic work representing it having been issued to the public. The only way in which a three dimensional artistic work, or a work of artistic craftsmanship, may be published is by the issue of three dimensional copies of such work. In contrast, a two dimensional artistic work may be published by the issue to the public of a graphic representation or a photograph of the work, or even of a three dimension reproduction of a drawing (*Merchant Adventurers Ltd v M Grew & Co Ltd* (1972)).

A photograph may be published merely by the act of developing and printing the film on which the photograph was initially recorded (*R v Taylor (Alan)* (1994)).

A sound recording or a film is not published by the work being played or shown in public, nor is it if the work is included in a broadcast or a cable programme service (s 175(4)(c)). Thus, such a work is only published when copies are 'issued to the public' (s 175(1)(a)). The meaning of this term will now be examined.

Not only must copies of the work be made, but those copies must then be 'issued to the public'. There is no requirement that the copies be issued for the purpose of sale (*British Northrop Ltd v Texteam Blackburn Ltd* (1974)), but if they have been issued for that purpose and subsequently sold, that would be sufficient for publication (*White v Geroch* (1819)). However, the mere offer or exposure for sale does not constitute publication (*Infabrics Ltd v Jaytex Shirt Co Ltd* (1982)).

4.3.2   Issued to the public

The requirement of issuing to the public is not satisfied if the work is only issued to a limited class, for example, the Academy Award winners to whom the Oscar statuette is presented (*OSCAR Trade Mark* (1980)).

However, publication does not depend upon a minimum certain number of the works being available. It is all a question of fact, so, for example, the offering for sale of only six books, but with the intention of satisfying any further demand should that demand present itself, has been held to constitute publication (*Francis Day & Hunter v Feldman & Co* (1914)).

4.3.3	Subsistence of copyright in existing works	Every work in which copyright subsisted (by virtue of the CA 1956) immediately prior to 1 August 1989 is deemed to satisfy the requirements of Part I of the CDPA 1988 as to the qualification for copyright protection. This is the case even if such a work would not receive protection under the CDPA 1988 (CDPA 1988 Schedule 1 para 35). This is an example of the continuity of vested rights. Unless there is a good reason for removing a right that a person has enjoyed under previous legislation, then that accumulated right will continue under the new regime, even if a person new to the scene could not claim a similar right under the new legislation.

When dealing with the opposite scenario, the CDPA 1988 does not confer copyright protection on those works in which copyright did not subsist under the CA 1956 Act immediately prior to 1 August 1989 but which would now be protected (CDPA 1988 Schedule 1 para 5(1)). Accordingly, there is no windfall for a person who had a work that did not qualify under the CA 1956, but would qualify under the CDPA 1988. The new rights will only be conferred on works that are produced after the commencement of the CDPA 1988.

There are a couple of exceptions to the general principle that an existing work in which copyright did not subsist would not be granted copyright protection by virtue of the CDPA 1988. The first exception concerns the situation in which a work was unpublished and did not qualify for copyright under the CA 1956, but was subsequently published for the first time after 1 August 1989 in a manner that would have secured copyright protection if it had been a new work. In this case, copyright will subsist in the work (CDPA 1988 Schedule 1 para 5(2)(a)).

The second exception is contained in para 5(2)(b) of Schedule 1. This concerns the situation in which an existing work did not enjoy copyright prior to 1 August 1989, but may now enjoy such protection if an Order in Council is made pursuant to s 159. In this way copyright protection may be conferred on pre-existing foreign works as and when the country becomes a signatory to the Berne Convention or otherwise gives adequate protection to the owners of copyright (Copyright (Application to Other Countries) Order 1993 as amended by Copyright (Application to Other Countries) (Amendment) Order 1994).

4.4	**Originality in literary, dramatic, musical and artistic works**	The principle case on originality prior to the Copyright Act 1911 was *Walter v Lane* (1900) in which the defendant was found to have infringed the plaintiff's copyright of a *verbatim* report which the latter had made of a public speech given by

Lord Rosebery. This case was decided under the Literary Copyright Act 1842. Lord Halsbury LC considered that the lack of the word 'original' in the statute was the basis for finding in the plaintiff's favour because, in His Lordship's view, a work that merely recorded *verbatim* someone else's speech was devoid of originality. In contrast, Davey LJ considered that it was more important that the defendant should not benefit from the appropriation of the skill and labour that the plaintiff had exercised in recording the speech *verbatim*. Accordingly, His Lordship was not concerned with the issue of originality *per se*.

It was suggested by Cross J that the insertion of the requirement for originality in the CA 1911, which was repeated in the CA 1956, rendered *Walter v Lane* (1900) no longer good law (*Lady Helen Robertson v Harry Lewis (t/a Virginia Music)* (1976)). However, this suggestion was explicitly rejected by Browne-Wilkinson VC in *Express Newspapers plc v News (UK) Ltd* (1990). Thus, the remarks made by Davey LJ concerning the skill and labour involved in the creation of a work that merits copyright protection are still relevant today. The fact that it has taken 90 years for this issue to be explicitly resolved highlights the care that is needed when using old cases decided under different legislation to support a present day proposition.

The concept of originality in copyright law has acquired a technical meaning, which is different from either the meaning in common parlance or the meaning in other areas of intellectual property law. Originality in copyright law is not concerned with the embodiment of an idea that is new to the world in the sense that it is novel, inventive, or unprecedented in any way.

4.4.1	The nature of originality

The concept of originality in copyright law was expounded by Peterson J in *University of London Press Ltd v University Tutorial Press Ltd* (1916) in which His Lordship said:

> 'The word original does not in this connection mean that the work must be the expression of original or inventive thought. Copyright Acts are not concerned with the originality of ideas, but with the expression of thought, and, in the case of literary work, with the expression of thought in print or writing. The originality which is required relates to the expression of thought. The Act does not require that the expression must be in an original or novel form, but that the work must not be copied from another work – that it should originate from the author'.

This further elaboration of the term 'original' indicating that the work should originate from the author means in practice that the work must be original to the particular author who is seeking copyright protection, rather than requiring that a work is either an original idea or an original expression of that idea *per se*. A logical consequence of this is that two works that are identical may each be original in copyright law. For example, two sets of logarithmic tables, which if both have been calculated correctly should be identical, may each be entitled to copyright protection This will be true so long as both authors independently produced them (ie one table was not copied from the other) because then each set of tables would have originated from a different author and so be original to that particular author. This would result in each having copyright protection (*Bailey v Taylor* (1829)).

| 4.4.2 | The expenditure of effort |

There is no requirement that labour be expended in the creation of a work before it may qualify for copyright. Thus, very simple designs have been held to be original, such as a few decorative lines on a price label (*Charles Walker & Co Ltd v British Picker Co Ltd* (1961)); as have three concentric circles when drawn to precise dimensions as a plan for a technical device (*Solar Thomson Engineering Co Ltd v Barton* (1977)). For the creation of these simple works, little physical labour was expended: rather, skill and judgment were exercised in their creation.

Similarly, for artistic works the mere expenditure of labour may not suffice to make a work original, and so a tracing has been held not to be original (*J & S Davis (Holding) Ltd v Wright Heath Group Ltd* (1988)). If the contrary had been held, then the copyright in a work could be extended indefinitely merely by the act of redrawing the original work. This holds true even when the new drawing may require great skill and labour in its production (*Interlego AG v Tyco Industries Inc* (1988)).

| 4.4.3 | Use of pre-existing material |

It is commonly said that there are only a handful of plots that any play can be based upon, and that all of these have been exemplified by the Classic writers. If this is so, then any play produced today must be based upon a pre-existing work to a greater or lesser extent. In the world of the novel, this seems to occur repeatedly. For example, David Lodge queried whether Pauline Harris had based her book *The Iron Master* on his book *Nice Work*. In the ensuing libel action, the defendants admitted that Mrs Harris had not copied Lodge's work. In contrast, it appears that both authors had been influenced by Elizabeth Gaskell's work *North and South* (*Harris v Jack* (1995)).

If the work is not entirely novel to the author, then the question is whether or not sufficient embellishment has been made in order to produce a new work that is capable of being original. When determining this, the new work must be considered as a whole, rather than just considering those parts that originated from the author and ignoring the material that was incorporated from a pre-existing source (*Ladbroke (Football) Ltd v William Hill (Football) Ltd* (1964)).

Translations of traditional literary works, such as books, have always been considered to require sufficient skill and labour to confer originality (*Byrne v Statist Co* (1914)). However, this is not the case for computer programs, in which a mere translation has been held not to be a new work in which a separate copyright could subsist (*John Richardson Computers Ltd v Flanders* (1993)).

4.4.4   Examples of derived literary, dramatic and musical works

In *Ibcos Computers Ltd v Barclays Mercantile Highland Finance Ltd* (1994), Jacob J held that a fresh copyright could arise each time a modification to a computer program had occurred, and furthermore that the subsistence and extent of copyright was not affected by the fact that the original work embodied practical elements that could only be achieved in one or a limited number of ways.

An abridgement may qualify as an original work so long as it is not merely the result of copying out short sections of the main work, whilst omitting other parts (*Macmilllan & Co Ltd v K & J Cooper* (1924)). This principle was approved by the House of Lords in *G A Cramp & Sons Ltd v Frank Smythson Ltd* (1944), which concerned the contents of a pocket diary. In this case the literary work consisted of tables of useful information at the front of the diary. It was held that such a compilation was not original, because the information which was contained within those tables was freely available, and insufficient skill and judgment had gone into the compilation of that information when forming the tables.

However, even though the standard of originality is seemingly rather low, it is not zero, and so it is still a requirement that *sufficient* skill and judgment be exercised by the author in forming the compilation before copyright will arise. For example, it was held that originality was not present in a list which merely extracted the times of local trains from a master railway timetable (*Leslie v J Young & Sons* (1894)).

An adaptation of a play has been held to result in an original work (*Hatton v Kean* (1859)). Similarly, a new arrangement of a work of music will result in a new original work (*Redwook Music Ltd v Chappell & Co Ltd* (1982)); as will a pianoforte score of an opera (*Boosey v Fairlie* (1877)); or selecting and arranging older tunes (*Metzler & Co (1920) Ltd v J Curwen & Sons Ltd* (1928-35)).

<table>
<tr><td>4.4.5</td><td>Examples of derived artistic works</td></tr>
</table>

4.4.5	Examples of derived artistic works

A change in the medium from that in which the work initially occurred will usually be sufficient for originality to be conferred on the new work. Examples include a photograph of an engraving (*Graves' Case* (1869)); and the engraving on a coin from a drawing of the picture (*Martin v Polyplas Manufacturers Ltd* (1969)).

Artistic copyright usually subsists in technical drawings. It is common practice that such drawings will be revised many times in the lifetime of the product. If there has been sufficient expenditure of skill and labour, then originality will be found in each the revision (*LB (Plastics) Ltd v Swish Products Ltd* (1979)), so long as the new drawing has sufficient material addition or embellishment for the new work to be visually significantly different from the previous drawing (*Interlego AG v Tyco Industries Inc* (1988)) The emphasis here is on visual significance. Thus, a change that is quantitatively small, yet carries with it a large qualitative change usually, will confer originality on the new work (*Martin v Polyplas Manufacturers Ltd* (1969)). A change in the scale of a technical drawing will not confer originality on the new drawing, because that would not normally be visually significant (*Drayton Controls (Engineering) Ltd v Honeywell Control Systems Ltd* (1992)). However, just because a finished drawing is produced from a number of preliminary sketches, the final drawing does not lack originality simply for the reason that the final version only has minor variations from one or more of the earlier drafts (*LA Gear Inc v Hi-Tech Sports plc* (1992)).

The principle of abridgement which has been developed for literary works may be extended to artistic works: thus, in a case which involved the creation of simplified navigational charts, it was held that sufficient work and skill had gone into the creation of a simplified form of the coast and geographical details and in the compilation of selected information, such as depth soundings and buoys, for the new work to be original (*MacMillan Publishing Ltd v Thomas Reed Publications Ltd* (1993)). In this case, the resultant charts created an entirely different visual appearance, because of the different styles adopted. Thus, when a derived artistic work merely takes selected parts from an original work, without any change in style, that would not amount to an abridgement in which a new copyright would arise.

As we saw in paras 4.2 and 4.3, copyright in a sound recording or a film may subsist by virtue of the author being a qualifying person (s 154(1)), or the first publication occurring in a qualifying country (s 155(1)). However, s 175(4)(c) provides that in the case of a sound recording or a film, the playing or showing of the work in public, or the broadcasting of the work or its inclusion in a cable programme service does not constitute publication for the purpose of qualification for copyright. In contrast, such a work is only published if it is sold or otherwise issued to the public, as was elaborated in para 4.3.2.

Unlike the situation for a literary, dramatic, musical or artistic work, there is no requirement for originality in order for copyright to subsist in a sound recording or a film. However, no copyright will subsist in a sound recording or a film which is, or to the extent that it is, a copy taken from a previous sound recording or film (s 5(2)).

4.5	**Sound recordings and films**

Copyright may subsist in a broadcast or cable programme by virtue of the author (s 154(1)). Section 156 states that copyright may also subsist in a broadcast or cable programme if it has been transmitted from, or sent from, a place in the UK or any other country to which the relevant provisions of the Act extend, or have been so applied by virtue of an Order in Council made pursuant to s 159. If a broadcast is transmitted from a satellite, then the country from which the signal is initially transmitted to the satellite is taken as the country of origin of the transmitted signal (s 6(4)).

4.6	**Broadcasts and cable programmes**

There is no limitation that the transmission of the broadcast or the sending of the cable programme be the first such transmission or sending in order for copyright to subsist. Copyright does subsist in a *repeat* broadcast or cable programme, but the subsequent copyrights expire at the same time as the original copyright (s 14(2)).

No copyright subsists in a broadcast made before 1 June 1957 (CDPA 1988 Schedule 1 para 9(a)). Similarly, no copyright subsists in a cable programme included in a cable programme service before 1 January 1985 (CDPA 1988 Schedule 1 paragraph 9(b)). It would appear that by the combined operation of the proviso to Schedule 1 paragraph 9(a) and Schedule 1 para 5(2)(b) that copyright can only be conferred on a pre-1 June 1957 broadcast, by virtue of an Order in Council extending the provisions of the CDPA 1988 to other countries under s 159.

4.7	**Typographical arrangement of a published edition**	As we have already seen in para 4.2 and 4.3, copyright in a typographical arrangement of a published edition may subsist by virtue of the author being a qualifying person (s 154(1)), or the first publication occurring a qualifying country (s 155(1)). The material time when the author must be a qualifying person is when the edition is first published (s 154(5)(d)).

By s 8(2) copyright does not subsist in the typographical arrangement of a published edition if, or to the extent that, it reproduces the typographical arrangement of a previous edition; this is similar in effect to the proviso of the CA 1956 s 15(1). Thus, so long as the work is original to the author of the work, which in this case means the publisher, copyright will arise. Consequently, copyright protection cannot be extended by merely reproducing a fascimile copy of a previous edition.

4.8	**Crown copyright**	Section 153(2) provides that the general requirements for the subsistence of copyright do not apply in relation to Crown copyright or Parliamentary copyright, or to the copyright which belongs to certain international organisations. Thus the requirements contained in ss 153-162 do not apply. Instead, there are special provisions for qualification for the subsistence of copyright which are contained in ss 163-169.

Where a work is created by an officer or servant of the Crown in the course of his duties, then by s 163(1) that work qualifies for copyright protection regardless of the requirements of s 153(1), ie regardless of the nationality of the author or the place of first publication. The copyright does not vest with the author of the work but, instead, it vests with the Crown (s 11(3)). There is no need for originality.

4.9	**Parliamentary copyright**	Where a work is made by, or under, the direction or control of the House of Commons or the House of Lords the work qualifies for copyright protection, regardless of whether or not the requirements of s 153(1) are met (s 165(1)(a)). The copyright is to be known as Parliamentary copyright regardless of whether it has been assigned to another person (s 165(2)).

Any work made by an officer or employee of either House in the course of his or her duties will attract Parliamentary copyright (s 165(4)(a)); as will any sound recording, film, live broadcast or live cable programme of the proceedings of the House (s 165(4)(b)), save that this shall not be the case only by reason that the work was commissioned by, or on behalf of, the House. Thus, a literary, dramatic, artistic or musical work need not be original for copyright to arise under the Parliamentary provisions.

The way in which copyright subsists in works of certain designated international organisations, such as the United Nations, differs from the arrangements for the subsistence of either Crown or Parliamentary copyright (s 168(1)). First, it is limited to original literary, dramatic, musical or artistic works, as opposed to any work; and secondly, the protection conferred by s 168 only applies if the work does not otherwise qualify for copyright protection under ss 154 or 155. Furthermore, there seems to be no restriction that the work be produced in the usual course of the duties of the officer or employee, just that the work should have been produced by the officer or employee or published by the organisation in question (s 168(1)(a)).

4.10   Copyright belonging to certain international organisations

If any one of the joint authors satisfies the requirements for copyright to subsist in a work, then the work will qualify (s 154(3)). However, only those authors who satisfy the requirements shall be considered for the purposes of determining the first ownership of the copyright and the duration of copyright (s 154(3)). These two issues are the subject of the two following chapters.

4.11   Subsistence of copyright in works of joint authorship

Summary of Chapter 4

Copyright: Subsistence

A published and unpublished work may qualify for copyright by reference to the author (s 153(1)(a)). Qualification may also be achieved by reference to the country of first publication (s 153(1)(b)). Crown and Parliamentary copyright are regulated separately by ss 163-167. Similarly, the copyright that vests in certain international organisations is regulated by s 168. Once a work has qualified, then qualification does not cease by reason of any subsequent event (s 153(3)).

Introduction

The author must be a British citizen or subject, or domiciled or resident in the UK (s 154(1)). For an unpublished primary work, the author must qualify when the work is made (s 154(4)(a)); while for a published work, the author must qualify when the work is first published (s 154(4)(b)). If a work is published posthumously, then the author must qualify at the time just before he died (s 154(4)(b)). The relevant time for sound recordings, films and broadcasts, is when they are made (s 154(5)(a) and (b)), and for a cable programme, when it is included in a cable programme service (s 154(5)(c)). The material time for a typographical arrangement is when the edition is published (s 154(5)(d)).

Qualification by reference to the author

A work will qualify for copyright if it is first published in the UK, or in a country to which the Act extends (s 155(1)).

Publication of a work means issuing copies to the public (s 175(1)). This must satisfy the reasonable requirements of the public, and may not be just colourable, ie a sham that does not satisfy the reasonable demands of the public (s 175(5)). The public performance of a literary, dramatic or musical work is not publication (s 175(4)(a)(i)). Similarly, an artistic work is not published by virtue of it having been exhibited (s 175(4)(b)(i)). A three-dimensional artistic work is only published by issuing a three-dimensional copy. However, a two-dimensional work may be published by issuing three-dimensional copies (*Merchant Adventurers v Grew* (1972)).

A photograph is published by the act of developing it (*R v Taylor (Alan)* (1994)).

To constitute publication, a work must be 'issued to the public'. If a work is sold and distributed free that is sufficient (*British Northrop Ltd v Texteam Blackburn Ltd* (1974) and (*White v*

Qualification by reference to place of first publication

Geroch (1819) respectively. However, a mere offer or exposure for sale, or distribution to a small restricted class of receivers are both insufficient (*Infabrics Ltd v Jaytex Shirt Co Ltd* (1980) and *OSCAR Trade Mark* (1980) respectively).

Subsistence of copyright in existing works

If copyright subsisted in a work created before 1 August 1989, then it subsists in the work thereafter (Schedule 1 para 35). Generally, copyright will not be conferred if it did not already subsist (Schedule 1 para 5(1)). However, if an unpublished work, in which copyright did not already subsist, was published in a manner that if it were a new work it would have qualified, then it will so qualify (Schedule 1 para 5(2)(a)). Furthermore, retrospective protection may be conferred by an Order in Council (Schedule 1 para 5(2)(b)).

Originality in literary, dramatic, musical and artistic works

Originality is a requirement for the subsistence of copyright (s 1(1)(a)). A work must be original in that it must 'originate from the author' and not be copied from another source (*University of London Press v University Tutorial Press* (1916)). Thus, identical logarithmic tables, each of which is original to their separate authors, may each have a separate copyright (*Bailey v Taylor* (1830)). Accordingly, independent creation is an absolute defence to copyright infringement.

Copyright may subsist in very simple designs, eg three concentric circles (*Solar Thomson v Barton* (1977)). However, the expenditure of effort is not irrelevant (*LB (Plastics) Ltd v Swish Products Ltd* (1979)). A mere tracing is not original, because insufficient skill has been expended in its making even if great labour expended (*J & S Davis (Holding) Ltd v Wright Heath Group Ltd* (1988) and *Interlego AG v Tyco Industries Inc* (1988) respectively).

Use of pre-existing material

A new copyright work may comprise copyrighted and uncopyrighted material. The new work must then be considered as a whole (*Ladbroke (Football) Ltd v William Hill (Football) Ltd* (1964)).

Examples of derived literary, dramatic and musical works

Translations of traditional literary works are original but not computer translations (*Wyatt v Barnard* (1814) and *John Richardson Computers Ltd v Flanders* (1993) respectively). The following have been held to be original: abridgements (*Macmilllan & Co Ltd v K & J Cooper* (1924)); and compilations (s 3(1)(a)). However, a selection of local train times from a master timetable was held not to be original (*Leslie v Young* (1894)).

A change of medium confers originality (*Graves' Case* (1869)). The new work must be visually distinctive (*Interlego AG v Tyco Industries Inc* (1988)).

What is important is the qualitative visual impression that the amendments make, rather than their quantitative significance (*Martin v Polyplas Manufacturers Ltd* (1969)). The final drawing may be original despite the fact that it is similar to earlier drafts (*LA Gear Inc v Hi-Tech Sports plc* (1992)). A simplified drawing derived from a more comprehensive drawing may be original (*MacMillan Publishing v Thomas Reed Publications* (1993)).

Examples of derived artistic works

These works may qualify by virtue of having been made by a qualifying person (s 154(1)) or the first publication occurring in a qualifying country (s 155(1)). There is no copyright in a copy that is taken from a previous sound recording or film (s 5(2)).

Sound recordings and films

Similarly, these works may qualify by virtue of a qualifying person (s 154(1)) or having been transmitted or sent from a qualifying country (s 156).

Copyright in a repeat broadcast or cable programme will expire with the original (s 14(2)). There is no copyright in a broadcast made before 1 June 1957 (Schedule 1 para 9(a)) nor is there copyright in a cable programme included in a cable programme service before 1 January 1985 (Schedule 1 para 9(b)).

Broadcasts and cable programmes

Again, copyright may subsist by reason of having been made by a qualifying person (s 154(1)) or having been first published in a qualifying country (s 155(1)).

No copyright subsists if the work reproduces the typographical arrangement of a previous edition (s 8(2)).

Typographical arrangement of a published edition

Crown copyright subsists if the work was produced by an officer or servant of the Crown in the course of his duties (s 163(1)). There is no need for originality.

Crown copyright

Similarly, Parliamentary copyright subsists if the work was made in the course of duties of an officer or employee of either House (s 165(4)(a)). Again, there is no need for originality.

Parliamentary copyright

Copyright belonging to the certain international organisations

Copyright may subsist in the works of certain designated international organisations, such as the United Nations (s 168(1)). It is limited to original works that are not otherwise protected. The work must have been produced by an officer or employee of the organisation or published by the organisation (s 168(1)(a)).

Subsistence of copyright in works of joint authorship

If any one of the joint authors satisfies the requirements, then the work qualifies (s 154(3)). The duration and joint ownership of copyright are determined only by the qualifying authors.

Chapter 5

Copyright: Duration

Statute confers copyright protection upon a work once certain pre-conditions have been met. However, copyright protection does not last forever, the protection conferred is limited in time, which is called the term of protection. Over the years, this term of protection has been gradually extended. Originally, under the Copyright Act 1709, the term of protection was only 14 years. Broadly, the term of protection for primary copyright works (namely: literary, dramatic, musical and artistic works) is now the life of the author and a further 50 years from the end of the year of death; while for derived works (namely sound recordings, films, broadcasts and cable programmes) the term is usually 50 years from the end of the year in which the work was made.

The formulation encompassed in the phrase 'life of the author plus 50 years from the end of the year of death' was introduced to remove uncertainty about exactly when copyright protection would expire. Previous to the formulation, copyright lasted for the life of the author plus 50 years. Thus, the *exact* date of death was required in order to calculate the day upon which copyright protection expired. Now, only the *year* of death is needed, which is much easier to ascertain.

The vast bulk of old copyright works are literary, dramatic, musical or artistic works. Some particular types of works in these categories have received different attention under different legislation. Accordingly, for these works in particular, there is a need to examine some of the previous legislation and transitional provisions in greater detail. However, to commence with, the position of new works will be considered.

The normal period of protection granted to literary, dramatic, musical or artistic works that have been created after 1 August 1989, is 50 years from the end of the calendar year in which the author died, regardless of whether or not, at the date of the author's death, the work has been published (s 12(1)).

Under the CDPA 1988, new photographs now enjoy the full term of protection accorded to artistic works, which is longer than that granted previously.

Computer-generated works, ie those that have no human author (s 178), have a fixed period of 50 years from the end of the year in which the work was made (s 12(3)).

5.1 Introduction

5.2 Literary, dramatic, musical and artistic works

5.2.1 Works created after 1 August 1989

5.2.2	Pre-existing literary dramatic, musical and artistic works	There is a general principle of English law that there is continuity of the law of the land as it applies to subsisting rights. Thus, if a person had a right under the old law, then that right will continue unless it is expressly abrogated.

In order to give this effect, Schedule 1 para 3 of the CDPA 1988 states that the new copyright provisions shall apply in relation to works already in existence at the commencement of the Act, ie 1 August 1989, as they apply in relation to works that come into existence after commencement, subject only to express provisions to the contrary. However, because certain works are treated less favourably under the CDPA 1988 than they were under the CA 1956, there is a need for transitional provisions. These provisions, which mainly relate to unpublished works, are found in Schedule 1 paras 12 and 13.

Unpublished literary, dramatic, or musical works of an author who died before 1 August 1989 are granted 50 years protection which will expire on 31 December 2039 (Schedule 1 para 12(4)(a)), so long as the work has not been performed in public, offered for sale, broadcasted, or included in a cable programme. If any of the acts included in the provisos has occurred, then the 50 year period of protection will already have commenced under s 2(3) of the CA 1956, and, accordingly, the term of copyright protection will then be limited to the unexpired residue under the CA 1956 (Schedule 1 para 12(2)(a)).

The perpetual copyright which was enjoyed by the Universities of Oxford and Cambridge and the colleges of Eton, Westminster and Winchester, has been abrogated. This is now replaced by a copyright which will expire on 31 December 2039 (Schedule 1 para 13).

A new right by which the Trustees of the Hospital for Sick Children, Great Ormond Street, London, may claim a royalty in respect of the public performance, commercial publication, broadcasting or inclusion in a cable programme service of the play *Peter Pan* by Sir James Barrie, or any adaptation of that work, has been created by s 301. This right is akin to copyright, but is not identical. The right exists in perpetuity so long as the conditions set out in Schedule 6 are fulfilled.

5.2.3	Pre-existing engravings and photographs	The provisions that relate to pre-existing photographs and engravings, ie ones in existence before 1 August 1989, have the overall effect of removing many examples of perpetual copyright in unpublished works that remained under the CA 1956. In their place, a fixed term of protection, which has already started to run, has been substituted.

Photographs and engravings were not treated in the same way as other artistic works under the CA 1956. Under the CDPA 1988, photographs and engravings are now treated in exactly the same manner as other artistic works (ss 4(1) and 4(2)). The commercial importance of photographs taken before 1 August 1989 make these transitional provisions important.

Photographs *published* before 1 August 1989 will continue to receive protection for the period of time they were granted under the CA 1956 (Schedule 1 para 12(2)(c)), namely 50 years from the end of the year in which they were first published (proviso (b) to s 3(4) of the CA 1956). Photographs taken before 1 June 1957, whether *published or not*, receive 50 years protection from the date when the photograph was made (s 21 of the CA 1911), and this term of protection was continued by the Schedule 7 para 2 of the CA 1956, and by Schedule 1 para 12(2)(c) of the CDPA 1988.

Unpublished photographs taken on or after 1 June 1957, but before 1 August 1989, are granted 50 years protection from 1 January 1990 (Schedule 1 para 12(4)(c)).

Under the CDPA 1988, works of unknown authorship are granted a period of protection of 50 years which runs from the end of the year in which the work is first made available to the public (s 12(2)). Thus, as well as publication *per se*, a literary, dramatic or musical work will be deemed to have been made available if it is performed in public, broadcast, or included in a cable programmes service (s 12(2)(a)). For an artistic work it will include exhibiting the work in public (s 12(2)(b)). However, no account is to be taken of unauthorised acts (proviso to s 12(2)).

5.2.4   Unknown authorship

If a work of unknown authorship remains *unpublished*, then the copyright right subsists in perpetuity. This is the last example of perpetual copyright in current existence under UK law.

For sound recordings or films made after 1 August 1989, the duration of copyright is 50 years from the end of the calendar year in which the work was made (s 13(1)(a)), or, if it is released before that date, then 50 years from the end of the calendar year in which it was released (s 13(1)(b)). A sound recording or film is released when it is first published, broadcast or included in a cable programme service (s 13(2)(a)), or, in the case of a film or film sound track, when the film is first shown in public (s 13(2)(b)), save that no unauthorised acts shall count.

5.3   **Sound recordings and films**

For pre-existing published sound recordings or films, ie those made before 1 August 1989, the term of copyright protection continues as specified under the CA 1956 (Schedule 1 para 12(2)(d) and (e)), ie 50 years from the end of the calendar year in which the work was published (CA 1956 ss 12(3) and 13(3)), or in the particular case of sound recordings, whether published or not, and made before 1 June 1957, 50 years from the end of the calendar year in which it was made (Schedule 7 para 11 of the CA 1956).

Unpublished works are granted 50 years protection from 1 January 1990, unless published during that period, in which case a further 50 years protection is granted (Schedule 1 para 12(5)).

5.4	**Broadcast and cable programmes**	A broadcast or a cable programme included in a cable programme service whether made or included before or after 1 August 1989, is granted 50 years protection from the end of the year in which the broadcast was made or the cable programme included in the service (s 14(1) and Schedule 1, para 12(6)). The copyright that subsists in a repeat broadcast or cable programme expires at the same time as the copyright in the original broadcast or cable programme (s 14(2)).
5.5	**Typographical arrangement of a published edition**	The copyright in the typographical arrangement of a published edition lasts for 25 years from the end of the calendar year in which the work was published, regardless of whether the work was published before or after 1 August 1989 (s 15 and Schedule 1 para 12(6)). This is longer than the minimum 15 years protection which is required by the Vienna Agreement for the Protection of Typefaces 1973, which is the principal international treaty dealing with this topic.
5.6	**Crown and Parliamentary copyright**	Under the 1956 Act, for those works where the copyright vested with the Crown, the term of protection lasted in perpetuity for *unpublished* literary, dramatic and musical works, and *unpublished* engravings and photographs. This has now been abrogated and has been replaced, for all literary, dramatic, musical and artistic works, with a term of protection of 125 years from the end of the calendar year in which the work was made (s 163(3)(a)). If the work is published commercially before the expiry of 75 years from the end of the calendar year in which it was made, then copyright protection will continue until the end of 50 years from the end of the calendar year in which it was so published (s 163(3)(b)). All other types of work, are granted the normal term of protection as if the copyright was not vested in the Crown (s 163(5)). The transitional provisions for pre-existing works are contained in Schedule 1 para 41.

Crown copyright subsists in Acts of Parliament for 50 years from the end of the calendar year in which the Act received Royal Assent (s 164(2)).

Parliamentary copyright in literary, dramatic, musical or artistic works continues to subsist for 50 years from the end of the calendar year in which the work was made (s 165(3)). The duration of copyright in other types of work is the same as if the copyright was not Parliamentary copyright (s 165(6)). The transitional provisions for pre-existing works are contained in Schedule 1 para 43.

The 1911 Act provided that copyright in a work of joint authorship should endure for the life of the author who died first, plus 50 years from the date of death, or for the duration of the life of the author who died last, whichever period was the longer (s 16(1)).	**5.7** **The duration of copyright in works of joint authorship**

The 1956 Act revised this to become the life of the author who died last, plus 50 years from the end of the calendar year in which he died (s 2(3) and Schedule 3 para 2). If copyright had expired under the 1911 Act before the 1956 Act came into force, then the new extended period did not apply (Schedule 7 para 10 of the CA 1956).

The extended period introduced by the 1956 Act has been preserved under the 1988 Act for literary, dramatic, musical or artistic works (s 12(4)(a)(i)).

If the identity of some of the authors of a joint work is unknown, then the period of protection is related to the death of the last of the authors whose identity is known (s 12(4)(a)(ii)).

In Germany the duration of copyright protection is the life of the author plus a further *70* years from the end of the year of death. In Spain, the duration of copyright protection is life of the author plus a further *80* years from the end of the year of death of the author. In France the period is the same as in the UK. However, in France the years of the Great War and the Second World War are excluded from the calculation. Furthermore, for 'serious music', the period is similar to that in Spain.	**5.8** **Council Directive 93/98/EEC**

The European Union has attempted to remove such discrepancies in order to minimise the distortions in competition that could otherwise arise. Accordingly, Council Directive 93/98/EEC, which concerns the harmonisation of the term of protection of copyright and certain related rights, was passed. Each Member State shall make the necessary provisions for the implementation of this Directive and suitable transition provisions by 1 July 1995 (Article 13(1)).

In the preamble to this Directive, it states that the reason for choosing the period of life plus 50 years as the minimum term of protection in the Berne Convention was to provide protection for the author and the first two generations of his descendants. Accordingly, as the average lifespan within the Community has now increased, this period is no longer deemed sufficient to cover two generations, and so the Directive proposed that the period of copyright protection should be lengthened to life plus 70 years.

Photographs, which are the product of the author's own intellectual creation, are protected as artistic works and so are entitled to this extra period of protection (Article 6). Member States may provide for the protection of other types of photographs as each Member State sees fit.

The principal director of a cinematographic or audiovisual work shall be considered as its author or one of its authors (Article 2(1)). The copyright protection shall expire 70 years after the last of the following to die: the principal director, the author of the screen play, the author of the dialogue or the composer of the music specifically created for use in the cinematographic or audiovisual work (Article 2(2)). This increases the number of people who have to be considered when calculating the date when a work of joint authorship, such as a film, finally stops being protected by copyright.

So long as a work is protected in at least one Member State on 1 July 1995, then the new terms of protection shall apply to that work (Article 10(2)). However, the provisions of Article 2(2) need not apply to cinematographic or audiovisual works created before 1 July 1994 (Article 10(4)). For cinematographic or audiovisual works the provisions of Article 2(1) must be implemented by 1 July 1997 (Article 10(5)).

To date, the UK Government has not implemented this Directive. It is not immediately obvious what happens to works for which copyright protection expires before the introduction of this Directive. For example, the stories of Kipling or the compositions of Rachmaninov. The Directive is silent on whether it is retrospective in action, like the Berne Convention, or whether it is not, like the UCC. The likely solution for works that still receive protection somewhere in the EU, is that a work will come into copyright protection again in the UK. For works that do not receive the benefit of such EU protection, they may not regain it in the UK. This would affect US works in particular. If Parliament fails to clarify this point when it enacts the necessary implementing legislation, then the matter will have to be resolved by the courts.

Copyright: Duration

These works are protected for 50 years from the end of the calendar year in which the author died (s 12(1)). New photographs now enjoy the full term of protection accorded to artistic works.

Literary, dramatic, musical and artistic works

Computer-generated works are only accorded 50 years from the end of the year in which they were made (s 12(3)).

Works created after 1 August 1989

The principle of continuity of law ensures that works created under the old Acts are integrated into the CDPA 1988 regime with the minimum of dislocation (Schedule 1 para 3). There are a few express provisions that affect settled rights (Schedule 1 paras 12 and 13). For example, unpublished works of dead authors now receive only 50 years from 1 January 1990 (Schedule 1 para 12(4)(a)); similarly, the perpetual copyright enjoyed by some colleges will expire on the 31 December 2039 (Schedule 1 para 13). In contrast, the play of 'Peter Pan' has a perpetual entitlement to royalties for commercial exploitation (s 310).

Pre-existing literary, dramatic, musical and artistic works

Photographs *published before* 1 August 1989 receive 50 years from publication (Schedule 1 para 12(2)(c)); while *unpublished* photographs taken before 1 August 1989 receive 50 years from 1 January 1990 (Schedule 1 para 12(4)(c)). Photographs taken before 1 June 1957 receive 50 years protection from when made (Schedule 1 para 12(2)(c)).

Pre-existing engravings and photographs

An anonymous work receives 50 years from when it is made available to the public (s 12(2)).

Old unpublished works receive 50 years from 1 January 1990 (Schedule 1 para 12(3)(b)).

Works of unknown authorship

Sound recordings made after 1 August 1989 receive 50 years from when made (s 13(1)(a)). Sound recordings released before 1 August 1989 receive 50 years from release (s 13(1)(b)).

Old published works receive 50 years from publication (Schedule 1 para 12(2)(d) and (e)). Sound recordings made before 1 June 1957 receive 50 years from creation (CA 1956 Schedule 7 para 11). Unpublished works receive 50 years from 1 January 1990 (Schedule 1 para 12(5)).

Sound recordings and films

Broadcast and cable programmes	If made or included before or after 1 August 1989, then receive 50 years from when made or included (s 14(1) and Schedule 1 para 12(6)).
	The copyright in repeat broadcast or cable programme expires with the original (s 14(2)).
Typographical arrangement of a published edition	This type of work receives 25 years from the year in which the work was first published (s 15 and Schedule 1 para 12(6)).
Crown and parliamentary copyright	Crown unpublished primary works receive 125 years from when made (s 163(3)(a)). If published commercially, then receive 50 years from publication, but the maximum is still 125 years' protection (s 163(3)(b)).
	Crown copyright in Acts of Parliament lasts for 50 years from receiving Royal Assent (s 164(2)).
	Other types of Crown works receive the normal period of protection as if the copyright was not vested in the Crown (s 163(5)).
	Parliamentary copyright in primary works lasts for 50 years (s 165(3)).
The duration of copyright in works of joint authorship	For primary works, the protection lasts for the life of the author who died last plus 50 years (s 12(1)).
Council Directive 93/98/EEC	This Directive increases the period of protection to life of the author plus 70 years after his death (Article 1(1)). The implementation of this Directive, and the introduction of suitable transitional provisions should be completed by 1 July 1995 (Article 13(1)).

Chapter 6

Copyright: Authorship and First Ownership

So far, we have considered the types of works in which copyright may subsist, and the various pre-conditions that must be fulfilled before a work may qualify for copyright. There remains, however, an important outstanding issue, namely who owns the right that has now come into existence? In copyright law there is an important distinction to be drawn between the person who creates the work, the 'author', and the person who is the 'first owner' of the copyright that subsists in that work. Often, the author is the first owner as well, but this is not invariably the situation. However, the issue of first ownership may always be determined by ascertaining who is the author of a work and then making any necessary adjustments for special circumstances that appertain to that person.

Section 11(1) of the CDPA 1988 has preserved the position that existed under the two previous Acts (CA 1911 s 5(1) and CA 1956 s 4(1)), namely, that generally the author of a copyright work is also deemed to be the first owner of that work. The term 'author' is defined in s 9(1), for the first time in a copyright Act as the person who created the work.

6.1 Introduction

Usually, it is clear who is to be considered the author of a work. The author of a work is the person who is responsible for physically creating it (s 9(1)); for example, the writer of a book or the drawer of a picture. In the normal course of events, the creator will also be the first owner of the copyright. However, a person who merely suggests the subject matter of a picture or the plot of a book would not be considered as the author (*Kenrick & Co v Lawrence & Co* (1890) and *Tate v Thomas* (1921) respectively).

In *Cummins v Bond* (1927), a spirit medium produced a work that she believed had been dictated to her by a spirit. The court did not feel that it could embark upon protecting the rights of people who no longer had a physical presence within the jurisdiction. Accordingly, the spirit medium, who had physically produced the work, was held to be the author of the dictated work. This should be contrasted with a mere amanuensis, who is not to be held as the author of a work dictated by a live person (*British Oxygen Co Ltd v Liquid Air Ltd* (1925)); however, a ghost writer who put the reminiscences of his principal into a written form is to be considered the author

6.2 Literary, dramatic, musical and artistic works

(*Donoghue v Allied Newspapers Ltd* (1938)). Therefore, the fact that a book is attributed to a certain person does not necessarily determine the issue of authorship for the purpose of copyright.

The 'author' of a building is the architect who drew the plans that the builder follows in order to construct the final building (*Meikle v Maufe* (1941)).

There are a limited number of exceptions to the general principle that the author of a work is also the first owner of the copyright in the work. These exceptions include those works that have no human originator, ie they are computer-generated, commissioned works, works produced by employees, works that attract Crown or Parliamentary copyright, and those works where the copyright is vested in certain designated international organisations.

| 6.2.1 | Computer-generated works |

With the increased use of technology, special provisions were made in the CDPA 1988 to deal with works that involved the use of computers in some part of their creation. Section 9(3) provides that where a literary, dramatic, musical or artistic work is generated by a computer, then the 'author shall be taken to be the person by whom the arrangements necessary for the creation of the work are undertaken'. It is not entirely clear to whom the Act is referring: the programmer, the program operator or even the company that owns the computer and the computer program. Computer-generated works are to be distinguished from those in which there has been a human author. A computer may be used by a human being to produce a work, just as if the computer were a modern-day pen, eg a word-processor, without the work becoming a computer-generated one (*Express Newspapers plc v Liverpool Daily Post & Echo plc* (1985)). However, if the computer is used to generate a random passage of text, then this would be a computer-generated work, and thus the author would be the computer operator who wrote the program that allowed the computer to generate the text.

| 6.2.2 | Commissioned works |

Commissioning involves ordering that work be done, and thereby coming under an obligation to pay for the work; however, there is no need actually to purchase the work (*Plix Products Ltd v Frank M Winstone (Merchants) Ltd* (1986)). In the informal circumstances that often accompany the ordering of a photograph, a bare request may be sufficient to constitute a commission. In contrast, the existence of the intention to pay for any photographs that may be taken, even though they had not been requested, is insufficient to establish a commission (*Apple Corp Ltd v Cooper* (1993)).

There are no special provisions under the CDPA 1988 that affect the first ownership of works which have been commissioned, and thus the author of such a work is therefore the first owner. This situation may be altered by the terms of any contract that may exist between the author of the work and the commissioner, ie an author may assign the copyright of works that are already in existence, and even the copyright of works that have yet to come into existence (s 91).

There were, however, several provisions under the CA 1956 that related to the ownership of commissioned works. For example, by s 4(3) of the CA 1956, where a person had commissioned an artistic work, and paid or agreed to pay for it in money or money's worth, and the work was made in pursuance of that commission, the commissioner was entitled to the first ownership of that work. It would appear that the commissioner was entitled to the copyright regardless of whether or not the work was completed (*Art Direction Ltd v SUP Needham (NZ) Ltd* (1977)).

For a literary, dramatic, musical or artistic work made after 1 August 1989 by an employee in the course of his employment, his employer is the first owner of any copyright in the work subject to any agreement to the contrary (CDPA 1988 s 11(2)). This transfer of the copyright from the employee to the employer reflects the public policy that because the employer takes the risks in financing the business, then the benefits should also accrue to him. Employment refers to a contract of service or apprenticeship (s 178). An apprentice 'is a person bound to another for the purpose of learning his trade or calling, the contract being of that nature that the master teaches and the other serves the master with the intention of learning' (*The Parish of St Pancras v The Parish of Clapham* (1860)).

6.2.3   Work of employees

The primary issue concerning people who work for others is whether they are employees of the latter, or whether they are in fact independent contractors. The first type are employed under a contract of service, ie a contract *of* employment, while the latter are engaged under a contract for services and so are self-employed, ie a contract *for* oneself (the self-employed person).

There have been many cases upon this issue, the force of which is that the more control that the employer exercises over the employee the more likely that a contract of service will be implied (*Ready Mixed Concrete (South East) Ltd v Minister of Pensions and National Insurance* (1968)). Under a contract of service the employee is an integral part of the machinery of the company, while a person employed under a contract for services is an accessory, albeit one who may be very important, to the company (*Stephenson Jordan & Harrison Ltd v MacDonald & Evans* (1952)). A further refinement to the test, which is used particularly when the worker is skilled, is to consider whether or not the employee is doing business on his own account (*Market Investigations Ltd v Minister of Social Security* (1969)). The answer to this further question may be found by examining where the financial risk lies, and whether and how far the worker has an opportunity of profiting from sound management in the performance of his task (*Lane v Shire Roofing Co (Oxford) Ltd* (1995)). The distinction between a contract of service and a contract for services is a question of law that is to be decided by the judge upon the available facts (*O'Kelly v Trusthouse Forte plc* (1984)).

As title to a copyright work is a prerequisite to pursuing an action for infringement it is always prudent if there is any doubt as to whether or not the work in question was made under a contract of service or a contract for services, for a prospective plaintiff to take an assignment from any possible creator of the work, or to join them in the action before commencing litigation.

| 6.2.4 | Course of employment |

Not only must the work be produced by an employee who was under a contract of service, it must also be made in the course of such employment before the copyright is deemed to vest with the employer (*Noah v Shuba* (1991)). Thus, where a translation was made by an employee of a newspaper in his own time, the copyright belonged to the employee and not the employer (*Byrne v Statist Co* (1914)). There is, however, the issue that an employee owes a duty of fidelity to his employer, and if he produces a work that is capable of being used in competition with his employer, then such a work may be deemed to be held on constructive trust for the employer (*Missing Link Software v Magee* (1989)).

| 6.2.5 | Work produced by directors |

A director of a company does not usually have a contract of service with the company, or even if there is one, then it may not be part of that contract to produce works in which copyright may subsist. Instead, the director is usually employed to manage the company (*Gardex Ltd v Sorata Ltd* (1986)). However, a director has a fiduciary duty to the company, and thus any work produced by the director would be held on trust for the company. In this situation, the legal and equitable title to the copyright is split, with the director owning the legal title and the company the equitable title. This means that a director would have to assign the legal title to the company if called upon so to do (*Antocks Lairn Ltd v I Bloohn Ltd* (1971)).

Section 9(2)(a) provides that the person who undertook the necessary arrangements for the making of the sound recording is to be taken as the author, and so consequentially will be the first owner of the copyright in that sound recording.

The situation under the CA 1956 was different. In this case the maker of the sound recording, who was defined by s 12(8) as the person who owned the record embodying the recording, was the author (s 12(4)).

New provisions have been made in the CDPA 1988 for sound recordings that accompany a film. Under the CA 1956 a sound track to a film was considered to be part of that film (CA 1956 s 13(9)), while under the CDPA 1988 such a sound track possesses an independent copyright to that present in the film (CDPA 1988 s 5(1)). Under the transitional provisions of the CDPA 1988, the copyright in a sound track of a film made before 1 August 1989 is now to be treated separately from the copyright in the film (Schedule 1 para 8(1)). However, the author and first owner of the copyright in the film is to be considered as the author and first owner of the copyright in the sound track (Schedule 1 para 8(2)(b)).

6.3   Sound recordings

Under the CDPA 1988 the same provisions apply to the author of a film as they do to the author of a sound recording, namely that the person who undertakes the necessary arrangements for the making of the film is to be taken as the author and so the first owner of the copyright (s 9(2)(a)). In particular, the entity that was responsible for the financial arrangements would be considered to have undertaken the necessary arrangements (*In re FG (Films) Ltd* (1953)). This approach may be applicable for computer-generated work, but it has not yet been decided by the courts.

Council Directive 93/98/EEC affects the position of the authorship of films. It states that the principal director of a cinematographic or audiovisual work shall be considered as its author or one of its authors (Article 2(1)). For cinematographic or audiovisual works the provisions of Article 2(1) must be implemented by 1 July 1997 (Article 10(5)).

6.4   Films

By s 9(2)(b) the person making the broadcast is to be considered the author. The term 'making' is further defined in s 6(3) as the person who transmits the programme, so long as he has responsibility for its contents, or any person who has provided the programme who makes with the person transmitting it the arrangements necessary for its transmission. If a broadcast is made by more than one person, then the work shall be treated as a work of joint authorship (s 10(2)).

6.5   Broadcasts

6.6	**Cable programmes**	Under the CDPA 1988, the author of a cable programme is the person who provides the cable programme service in which the programme is included (s 9(2)(c)). Under the CA 1956 (as amended by the Cable and Broadcasting Act 1984) identical provisions applied (s 14A(3)).
6.7	**Typographical arrangements**	By s 9(2)(d), the publisher is taken to be the author of the typographical arrangement of a published edition. The publisher is defined in s 175(1) as the person who is responsible for making copies available to the public. Thus, the typesetter is not the author. Section 15(2) of the CA 1956 was to similar effect.
6.8	**Crown copyright**	Under CDPA 1988 s 163(1) the Crown is the first copyright owner of any work that has been made by an officer or servant of the Crown in the course of his duties. There is no requirement that the author be a qualifying person, rather the work is deemed to qualify by virtue of being produced by the Crown. Furthermore, not only servants of the Crown are included, but also officers of the Crown.
		A work produced by the Crown is referred to as 'Crown copyright' notwithstanding that it may be, or may have been, assigned to another person (s 163(2)). Crown copyright does not subsist to the extent that Parliamentary copyright subsists in the work, ie they are mutually exclusive, with Parliamentary copyright taking precedence (s 163(6)).
		In addition to these works where copyright vests in the Crown, Her Majesty is entitled to the copyright in every Act of Parliament or Measure of the General Synod of the Church of England (s 164(1)). No other copyright, or right in the nature of copyright, subsists in an Act or Measure (s 164(4)).
6.9	**Parliamentary copyright**	Where a work is made by, or under, the direction or control of the House of Commons or the House of Lords the work qualifies for Parliamentary copyright (s 165(1)(a)). Furthermore, the House by whom, or under whose direction or control, the work was made is the first owner of any copyright in the work, and if the work is made by or under the direction or control of both Houses, the two Houses are joint first owners of copyright (s 165(1)(b)). Copyright in every bill vests in Parliament (s 166(1)).
6.10	**Copyright vested in certain international organisations**	Where an original literary, dramatic, musical or artistic work is made by an officer or employee of, or is published by, an international organisation to which s 168 applies, and does not qualify for copyright protection by reference to the normal conditions, ie by virtue of the author or place of first

publication, then copyright nevertheless subsists in the work by virtue of s 168 and the organisation is the first owner of that copyright (s 168(1)). The international organisations to which s 168 applies are those as to which Her Majesty has by Order in Council declared that it is expedient that it should apply (s 168(2)). The Copyright (International Organisation) Order 1989 includes such organisations as the United Nations, the Specialised Agencies of the United Nations and the Organisation of American States.

Under s 10(1) of the CDPA 1988 a work of joint authorship means a work produced by the collaboration of two or more authors in which the contribution of each author is not distinct from that of the other author or authors.

However, broadcasts are treated separately under the 1988 Act. In this case a broadcast is to be treated as a work of joint authorship where more than one person is to be taken as making the broadcast (s 10(2)). In this context, 'making' has the meaning ascribed to it in s 6(3).

A person who merely suggests the idea, which is then developed by another into a recorded work, is not a joint author with the latter (*Wiseman v George Weidenfeld & Nicholson Ltd* (1985)), nor is a person who makes minor amendments to the original work (*Samuelson v Producers Distributing Co Ltd* (1931)). However, if it has been agreed beforehand that the editor is to be treated as a joint author (*Prior v Landsdowne Press Pty Ltd* (1977)), or if both have worked together on the project with a common objective (*Nejma Heptulla v Orient Longman Ltd* (1989)), then the work will be considered to be one of joint authorship. It is presumed that if there is more than one person named as the author of a literary, dramatic, musical or artistic work, then each person so named is a joint author until the contrary is proven (s 104(2) and (3)).

In the case of a work of joint authorship in which the copyright may vest in the Crown, where one or more, but not all, of the authors are persons falling within s 163(1), then the Crown copyright provisions apply only to those authors and the copyright subsisting by virtue of their contribution to the work (s 163(4)). The exact scope of this provision is unclear, because a work of joint authorship, by definition, is one in which the individual contributions cannot be separated.

Joint authorship leads to the property in the copyright of the final work being in joint ownership. This may take two mutually exclusive forms, either tenants in common, or joint tenants. The difference is important, because when one party to a tenancy in common dies, then his portion of the copyright

6.11   Joint authorship and ownership

6.11.1   Joint ownership

will devolve upon his heirs as part of his estate; however, when one party to a joint tenancy dies, his portion is divided equally among the remaining joint tenants.

Usually, joint authors hold the copyright title as tenants in common (*Lauri v Renad* (1892)). However, the facts of the case may suggest that the authors hold the title as joint tenants, for example as in the case of the marriage photographs of a husband and wife (*Mail Newspapers plc v Express Newspapers plc* (1987)).

A licence to use a work that is co-owned must be the licence of all the co-owners (s 173(2)). Moreover, a licence cannot be granted by one co-owner that is purported to be exclusive, in the sense that it excludes the other co-owners (*Mail Newspapers plc v Express Newspapers plc* (1987)).

6.11.2	Non-qualifying author of a work of joint authorship

Copyright in an *unpublished* work may only subsist by virtue of the authors qualifying by virtue of s 154. A work of joint authorship may be created by authors, some of whom qualify, while others of whom do not. The exact position of an author of such a work who does not qualify under the Act is unclear. Such an author has no legal title, but may have some equitable right to the copyright, if only for an account of profits. It is to be doubted whether such an author would have an equitable title to the work, as he could not call for an assignment of the legal title from the qualifying author. Accordingly, it is unlikely that the author who did not qualify could initiate proceedings for infringement. Furthermore, the qualifying author could grant a valid licence without the consent of the other, non-qualifying, author.

Once the work is published such that s 155 was satisfied, ie qualification by virtue of first place of publication, then all the authors would be considered the legal co-owners.

6.12 Equitable ownership

So far we have only considered the legal title to a copyright work, ie the title to the copyright that arises by virtue of statute. It is also possible for an equitable title to exist in a work, ie one that arises by the operation of the principles of equity. Furthermore, this equitable title may vest in a different person from that in whom the legal title vests, ie the equitable and legal titles may be split.

Where a work is produced by one person at the behest of another, then the exact relationship that exists between the parties will determine who owns the legal title and who owns the equitable title to the work. We have already examined two situations in which this occurs, namely works produced in the course of employment and those produced under commission. There are other occasions, however, in which equity intervenes. Since an equitable interest will arise when the courts call upon equity to ameliorate the harshness that would otherwise be caused by the strict application of the legal principles, there are many diverse instances in which such an interest may occur. For example, the legal and equitable titles may be split in a situation where an outside draftsman produces a copyright work for a company. In such a case it has been held that the equitable title to the copyright in the drawings vested in the company (*Merchant Adventurers Ltd v M Grew & Co Ltd* (1973)). In this case the draughtsman has the legal title to the drawings, because he actually created them and so satisfies the statutory requirement as the creator of the work. Yet, equity intervenes to confer the equitable title on the company which paid for the work and requested that it be done.

Two other examples where the legal and equitable titles may be split are when (a) there is an agreement to assign the copyright in a work, rather than an actual assignment, and (b) there has been a failure to comply with the requirements that the assignment be in writing and signed by, or on behalf of, the assignor (s 90(3)). There is no need for writing to create an equitable interest (*Roban Jig & Tool Co Ltd v Taylor* (1979)), however, a written instrument is still needed to assign it (Law of Property Act 1925 ss 53 and 136). An oral promise to assign the legal title to copyright in a work that exists, or one which has yet to come into existence, will be sufficient to create an equitable title for the promisee (*Western Front Ltd v Vestron Inc* (1987)).

If an independent contractor is commissioned to make modifications to a copyright work that is owned by the commissioner, as may be the case for instance in the modification of a computer program, then the contractor holds the bare legal title, and the commissioner will have the equitable title. This amounts to the contractor holding the legal title on trust for the commissioner, and so the commissioner may call for an assignment of the legal title from the contractor (*John Richardson Computers Ltd v Flanders* (1993)).

Instead of an equitable interest arising, the author of the work may have granted only a licence to someone else to use the copyright work in a limited manner (*Ironside v HM Attorney-General* (1988)). If the licence is oral, then the exact terms may be open to debate. It is permissible to imply terms into a copyright licence by reason of business efficacy or trade custom (*Warner v Gestetner Ltd* (1988)).

Copyright: Authorship and First Ownership

Generally the author of a work is also is the first owner of the copyright work (s 11(1)). The author is the person who created the work (s 9(1)).

Introduction

The author of a play is the person who actually wrote it, rather than the person who merely suggests the plot (*Tate v Thomas* (1921)). Thus, a spirit medium who produces a work at the behest of a 'spirit' is the author of the work (*Cummins v Bond* (1927)). However, a mere amanuensis is not to be taken as the author of the letters that were dictated (*British Oxygen Co Ltd v Liquid Air Ltd* (1925)). In contrast, though, a ghost writer is the author, and not the celebrity who shared his experiences with the ghost writer ghost writer, is the author (*Donoghue v Allied Newspapers Ltd* (1938)).

Literary, dramatic, musical and artistic works

The person who makes the necessary arrangements for the computer to produce the work is the author of the work (s 9(3)). However, merely using a computer as a tool, ie as an electronic pen, does not make the work computer-generated (*Express Newspapers v Liverpool Daily Post* (1985)).

Computer-generated works

The act of commissioning is characterised by an obligation to pay for the work (*Plix Products Ltd v Frank M Winstone (Merchants)* (1986)). The commissioning arrangement may be very informal (*Apple Corp Ltd v Cooper* (1993)). There are no special provisions under the CDPA 1988 that affect the first ownership of commissioned works, hence the author is the first owner. In contrast, under the CA 1956 s 4(3) the first owner of a commissioned work was the commissioner.

Commissioned artistic works

Work produced by employees in the course of their employment belongs to the employer (s 11(2)). In order to determine whether or not there is a contract of employment, the degree of control needs to be investigated (*Ready Mixed Concrete v Minister of Pensions* (1968)).

The distinction between being in employment and self-employed is a question of law (*O'Kelly v Trusthouse Forte plc* (1984)).

Work of employees

Course of employment	Not only must the work be produced by an employee, but it must also be made in the normal course of employment (*Noah v Shuba* (1991)). Thus, the copyright in a translation made in a person's own time did not belong to the employer (*Byrne v Statist Co* (1914)). However, an employee owes a duty of fidelity to his employer and thus cannot compete with his employer while in his employment (*Missing Link Software v Magee* (1989)).
Work produced by directors	A director is usually not employed to produce copyright works and so he, not the company, will own the first legal title to the copyright work (*Gardex Ltd v Sorata Ltd* (1986)). However, a director will usually hold this legal title on trust for the company and so, if requested, have to transfer it to the company (*Antocks Lairn Ltd v Bloohn Ltd* (1971)).
Sound recordings	In regard to any soundtrack to a film, the person who undertook the necessary arrangements in order to make the recording is to be taken as the author of the recording, and so first owner of the copyright (s 9(2)(a)), independent of the copyright in that film (Schedule 1 para 8(1)).
Films	The person who undertook the necessary arrangements in order to make the film is to be taken as the author of the film, and is first owner of the copyright (s 9(2)(a)), eg the entity that was responsible for the financial arrangements could be considered as the author (*In re F G (Films) Ltd* (1953)). Council Directive 93/98/EEC provides that the director of a film must be a co-author. There is no copyright in films made before 1 June 1957 (CDPA 1988 Schedule 1 para 7(1)).
Broadcasts	The person making the broadcast is the author and so first owner of the copyright (s 9(2)(b)). The 'maker' is the person who transmits the broadcast, or makes the arrangements for the transmission (s 6(3)).
Cable programmes	The person who provides the service is the author and so first owner of the copyright (s 9(2)(c)).
Typographical arrangements	The publisher is the author and so he is the first owner of the copyright in the typographical arrangement of a published work (s 9(2)(d)). The publisher is the person responsible for making copies available to the public (s 175(1)).

The copyright in a work produced by an officer or servant of the Crown in the course of his duties vests with the Crown (s 163(1)). Furthermore, so does the copyright in all Acts of Parliament (s 164(1)). Crown copyright is displaced by parliamentary copyright (s 163(6)).

Crown copyright

The copyright in a work made under the direction or control of Parliament vests with Parliament (s 165(1)).

Parliamentary copyright

A work of joint authorship is one in which the separate collaborations are indistinguishable (s 10(1)). Note that broadcasts are treated separately (s 10(2)).

Joint authorship

A work of joint authorship may be owned as a tenancy in common or a joint tenancy. The usual situation is that the joint authors are tenants in common (*Lauri v Renad* (1892)). An example of a work where there is a joint tenancy would be marriage photographs (*Mail Newspapers plc v Express Newspapers plc* (1987)).

Joint ownership

Once the work is published so as to satisfy s 155, ie qualification by virtue of first place of publication, then all authors become legal co-owners.

If, however, the work is unpublished, then the non-qualifying author has no legal or equitable title.

Non-qualifying author of a work of joint authorship

The legal and equitable title in a copyright work may vest in different people. There is no need for writing in order to create an equitable interest (*Roban Jig & Tool Co Ltd v Taylor* (1979)).

The exact relationship between the creator of the work, ie the author, and the person at whose behest the work was made will determine who owns the legal and equitable titles in a work. For example, if the copyright owner requests that a contractor makes changes to the work, then the contractor holds the legal title to those changes on trust for the original copyright owner (*John Richardson Computers Ltd v Flanders* (1993)).

Note that in some situations the person at whose behest the work is produced may first receive only a licence from the author (*Ironside v HM Attorney-General* (1988)).

Equitable ownership

Chapter 7

Copyright: Infringement

When considering a copyright dispute, the question that is often uppermost in one's mind is whether there has been an infringement, ie has the potential defendant unlawfully appropriated some right or property belonging to the potential plaintiff. However, before that question is answered, it is necessary to ascertain whether or not the prospective plaintiff has any rights in the nature of copyright. As we have seen in the previous chapters, the subsistence of copyright requires that: (1) the works be of a certain type; (2) the creator of the work is a qualified person; (3) the ownership of (at least) the equitable title be in the possession of the prospective plaintiff; and (4) copyright still subsists and has not expired.

All of these requirements may be grouped together into one enquiry, namely: has the prospective plaintiff good title to sue? Or, more colloquially, 'First we've got to get all our ducks in a row.' Once these essential pre-conditions have been satisfied, then the question of infringement may be addressed.

The copying of a banal idea does not lead to copyright infringement (*Kenrick & Co v Lawrence & Co* (1890)). The classical justification for this is that the patents system, and not the copyright system, is the correct forum for the protection of ideas. However, in contrast to this classical statement that copyright does not protect an idea, there is a line of cases from which the opposite stance may be argued. For example, in *Sutton Vane v Famous Players Film Co Ltd* (1923-28) the plot from a novel was held to be infringed by a silent film. Obviously, little or no dialogue could have been taken, rather what was misappropriated was the plot, ie the idea of the novel. This case may be distinguished from *Kenwick & Co v Lawrence & Co* (1890) in that the latter case, the 'idea' that was copied was banal. In contrast, the 'idea' that was copied in *Sutton Vane v Famous Players Film Co Ltd* (1923-28) was the detailed plot of the novel. This distinction between the copying of a banal idea, and a detailed idea, and the corresponding consequence of whether or not copyright infringement has occurred, was highlighted by Jacob J in *Ibcos Computers Ltd v Barclays Mercantile Highland Finance Ltd* (1994), where His Lordship stated '... UK copyright cannot prevent the copying of a mere general idea, but can protect the copying of a detailed idea'. In this case, Jacob J held that not only was there

7.1   Introduction

7.2   Essence of copyright protection

literal copying, but also that there was copying of the computer program structure and other design features. Accordingly, the view that copyright does not protect the idea of a work must be considered as a simplification of the true position.

<table>
<tr><td>7.2.1</td><td>Protection of a
particular expression</td><td>The essence of copyright protection is to prevent the copying of an original work to produce another work. Copyright will protect the particular physical expression of an idea, for example, the actual words of a poem. Furthermore, as illustrated in the previous section, copyright may also protect the detailed idea as expressed in the physical expression of that idea. However, copyright does not protect ideas per se, and so, for example, if a culinary dish is made according to the recipe contained in a cookery book, there is no infringement of that recipe (J & S Davis (Holdings) Ltd v Wright Health Group Ltd (1988)). However, another interpretation of this finding of non-infringement is that the finished article, ie the cake or whatever, is not a work that can be protected by copyright, and so is not included within the ambit of copyright protection. In order to protect a mere idea, resource needs to be taken in other forms of protection, for example by imposing an equitable duty of confidentiality or the granting of Letters Patent.</td></tr>
</table>

Another scenario involves the production of a work that is based upon an original source, and then this derived work forms the basis for the production of a further, subsequent work, ie there is a chain from the original work via the derived work to the subsequent work. In this case, the fact that the derived work was based upon the original work would not provide a defence to an allegation of copying levelled at the producer of the subsequent work. The author of the subsequent work could not say that his work was actually derived from the original work, because, in fact, it was based upon the derived work. Thus, in this case, there is no defence of independent creation available to the author of the subsequent work (*Elanco Products Ltd v Mandrops (Agrochemicals Specialists) Ltd* (1979)).

<table>
<tr><td>7.2.2</td><td>Causal link</td><td>In order to found a cause of action, there must be a causal link between the original work and the alleged infringement (Billhöfer Maschinenfabrik GmbH v TH Dixon & Co Ltd (1990)). The allegedly copied work must have been derived originally from a work in which copyright subsisted. It is irrelevant that there may be links in the chain in which copyright did not exist, or could not exist. For example, if a catalogue of spare parts is put together by physically dismantling a machine and then listing the parts, the resultant list ought to be very similar to the manufacturer's genuine spare-parts catalogue.</td></tr>
</table>

However, there is, in fact, no infringement of the genuine catalogue, because the physical collection of spare parts, which was the source of the derived list, is not a work in which copyright may subsist, nor was the list derived from the genuine catalogue (*Purefoy Engineering Co Ltd v Sykes, Boxall & Co Ltd* (1955)). The situation might be different if there were photographs within the genuine catalogue and parts' diagrams in the derived work, because, in this case, the physical parts would be a reproduction of the photographs, and the diagrams would be a representation of those parts. Accordingly, there would be a chain that originates in a work in which copyright may subsist, ie the photographs, and this leads to the derived work, namely the parts' diagrams in the list. It is not necessary for each link in the chain of causation to infringe the original copyright (s 16(3)), nor is it necessary for copyright to subsist in each link of the chain.

It is very rare that there is clear evidence of direct copying, for example, the defendant admits to having seen the plaintiff's work and using it as a basis for his own work. Usually, the court is asked to infer that copying has occurred, because the close similarity between the works in question would be unlikely to have arisen by independent creation (*Antocks Lairn Ltd v I Bloohn Ltd* (1971)). This inference may be deduced from all the circumstances of the case. For example, in a literary work, the presence of the same mistakes would be indicative of copying (*Ibcos Computers Ltd v Barclays Mercantile Highland Finance Ltd* (1994)), or the planting of 'seed entries' in directories, ie entries in a customer list that actually refer to trusted employees and not genuine customers, so that if the list is used for an unauthorised mail-shot, the employees of the owner of the list will receive the unauthorised material and so be alerted to the misuse of the list (*VNU Business Publications BV v Ziff Davis (UK) Ltd* (1992)). The arrangement of topics in a similar order may be suggestive of copying (*Coral Index Ltd v Regent Index Ltd* (1970)), unless there is some industry standard or other custom that requires a particular sequence to be followed (*Kwik Lok Corporation v WBW Engineers Ltd* (1975)).

7.3   Evidence of copying

A prospective plaintiff may allege that his copyright work has been copied indirectly, rather than directly. Indirect copying is just as much an infringement as is direct copying (s 16(3)(b)).

There is still an absolute requirement for a causal link between the original work and the allegedly derived work. 'Indirect' copying is generally used to indicate that there has been a change in medium at some stage in the causal link, eg a drawing to a three-dimensional work and back to a drawing.

7.3.1   Indirect copying

In contrast, 'direct' copying usually indicates the use of only one medium, eg a picture that is photographed and then that photograph is used to produce another picture. There is, however, no hard and fast distinction, more a matter of degree.

It does not matter how long the chain of causation is, so long as it exists then the derived work will still be an infringement of the original diagrams. For example, a set of photographs of a three-dimensional reproduction of a set of diagrams has been held to infringe the original diagrams (*Dorling v Honnor Marine Ltd* (1965)).

The causal chain will still exist even if one of the links is a detailed verbal description of the original work. In *Plix Products Ltd v Frank M Winstone (Merchants) Ltd* (1986), which concerned the plastic trays that hold kiwi fruit, an independent designer had been given such detailed instructions of the form, shape and pattern of the original packaging that the description took the place of a physical copy of the original work and became an intermediate stage in the copying process. Infringement would not have been found if the description merely conveyed the overall idea of the original product.

7.3.2 Subconscious copying	In *Francis Day & Hunter Ltd v Bron* (1963), the defendant stated that he had not copied the first bars of the chorus to a piece of music entitled 'In a Little Spanish Town', when he wrote the song entitled 'Why?'. However, he admitted that it was possible he had heard it on the radio many years previously and had retained some memory of it. The court held that infringement could occur by subconscious copying, but found on the facts present in this instance that there was insufficient evidence to prove the causal link necessary to establish infringement. Obviously, this issue is of importance where an author is accused of copying a previous work of his own, of which he no longer has any rights to reproduce. This may occur if the original author has assigned the copyright to a work, but subsequently wishes to develop a theme started in the first work. For artistic works there are special provisions, whereby so long as the artist does not repeat or imitate the main design of the earlier work, no infringement will arise (s 64).

7.4   Substantiality of material copied

It is rare for cases to reach court in which there has been extensive copying of the original work with few alterations, because such cases normally settle at an early stage.

However, there is no need for the entire copyright work to be copied in order for infringement to take place, nor is there any need for the portion that is copied to be identical to the original. If either of these conditions was a requirement, then the protection afforded by copyright would be so narrow as to be virtually impotent. It is far more common in infringement proceedings for only a part of the original work to have been appropriated. In such a situation, the parts that have been taken must amount to a substantial proportion of the original work in order for copyright infringement to be made out (s 16(3)(a)). In order to determine whether or not a substantial proportion has been taken, attention is focused on the quality of the parts copied rather than the mere quantity that has been appropriated (*Ladbroke (Football) Ltd v William Hill (Football) Ltd* (1964)). Thus, substantiality is determined qualitatively, and not quantitatively, and so it is not possible to say that if more than a certain percentage of the original work is plagiarised then infringement has occurred. Thus, the value of what was appropriated needs to be assessed.

However, in contrast to this approach, Petersen J in *University of London Press Ltd v University Tutorial Press Ltd* (1916) said that 'what is worth copying is *prima facie* worth protecting'.

If the part that has been copied was not original to the plaintiff, but he in turn had copied it from another earlier source, then if only the unoriginal part of the earlier work is copied by the defendant, it is unlikely that the court will hold that it was a substantial part of the copyright work belonging to the plaintiff (*Warwick Film Productions Ltd v Eisinger* (1969)).

The CDPA 1988 makes a distinction between primary acts of infringement and secondary acts. Primary infringement of copyright is covered in ss 16-21, while secondary infringement is covered in ss 22-26.	**7.5 Primary and secondary infringement**

The owner of the copyright in a work has the exclusive right to do the following acts in the UK (s 16(1)), ie these acts are restricted to the copyright owner or his licensee:	**7.6 Primary acts of infringement**

- to copy the work;

- to issue copies of the work to the public;

- to perform, show or play the work in public;

- to broadcast the work or include it in a cable programme; and

- to make an adaptation of the work, or do any of the above acts in relation to an adaptation.

Copyright in a work is thus infringed by any person who without the licence of the copyright owner does, or authorises another to do, any of the acts outlined above (s 16(2)).

7.7 Infringement by copying

Of the many different ways in which a work may be infringed, the copying of a copyright work constitutes the commonest. The copying of a work is an act restricted by the copyright in every description of the work (s 17(1)). In relation to literary, dramatic, musical or artistic works, copying means reproducing the work in any material form, which includes storing the work in any medium by electronic means (s 17(2)). Furthermore, in relation to any description of a work, the making of copies that are transient is prohibited (s 17(6)). Thus, this explicitly covers the temporary storage by a computer of a program in its random access memory. We will now examine in more detail how different categories of copyright works may be 'reproduced'.

7.7.1 Literary works

Reproduction of a work may be by any method, eg by hand (*Chappell & Co Ltd v Columbia Gramophone Co* (1914)) or machine, eg a photocopier (*Moorhouse v University of New South Wales* (1976)).

It has previously been assumed that a literary work could not be infringed by its reproduction in an entirely different format such as a three dimensional representation. For example, a series of instructions that comprised a knitting pattern was not infringed merely by making a sweater in accordance with those written instructions (*Brigid Foley Ltd v Ellott* (1982)). In *Anacon Corporation Ltd v Environmental Research Technology Ltd* (1994), it was held that a circuit diagram for an electronic circuit was a literary work. From this circuit diagram, the plaintiff had constructed the physical circuit board. The defendants had used that circuit board to construct a 'net list' which shows all the electronic components and indicated to which other components each component was linked. From this net list, the defendants produced their own circuit board which looked entirely different from the plaintiff's. Jacob J held that the defendants' net list infringed the literary copyright in the plaintiff's circuit diagram, because it reproduced the information that was contained therein, namely the connectivity of each and every component. It was left open whether or not the defendants' circuit board infringed the plaintiff's literary copyright in the circuit diagram. The plain words of s 17(2) state that it would be an infringement to reproduce a literary work in 'any material form'. Accordingly, the circuit board would be an infringement of the circuit diagram. Hence, the decision in the case of *Brigid Foley Ltd v Ellott* (1982) must be doubted.

Apart from copying a computer program line by line, it may also be an infringement to copy the overall structure of the program if that is a part of the expression of the program (*Whelan Associates Inc v Jaslow Dental Laboratory Inc* (1987)). However, Jacob J in *Ibcos Computers Ltd v Barclays Mercantile Highland Finance Ltd* (1994) thought that the US line of authorities was unhelpful in UK copyright law. However, Jacob J did hold that copying the distribution of functions between the individual sub-programs in the overall program was an infringement.

In most cases of copyright infringement, the derived work has been altered in some manner so as to distinguish it from the original. Often this has been done to disguise the fact that the work was derived from some other source. For example, in a book entitled *The Spear of Destiny*, it was proposed that there was a link between the spear used to pierce Christ's side at the crucifixion and a spear that was later, reputedly, the source of inspiration for the rise of Nazi Germany. It was alleged that this non-fictional work, *The Spear of Destiny* was used as the basis for a fictional story entitled *The Spear*. It was held that not only had the historical facts been copied, but so had the particular incidents, the language and the overall interpretation of events. As a consequence, it was held that the novel infringed the earlier work (*Ravenscroft v Herbert* (1980)).

The written words of a dramatic work may be copied, in which case the principles that apply to literary copyright will apply. However, in addition, part of the value of a dramatic work lies in the non-verbal content, ie the characterisation of the players, the incidents of the play, and even the scenery and lighting components, ie the dramatic elements *per se*. If, instead of particular incidents being copied, only the overall bare plot of the play is copied, then no infringement will have occurred (*Sutton Vane v Famous Players Film Co Ltd* (1928-35)). There will also be no infringement if those scenes that are common to the two works are of a stock nature, and so lacked originality in the first work (*Dagnall v British and Dominions Film Corporation Co Ltd* (1928-35)).

It is also an infringement to turn a dramatic work into a non-dramatic work and *vice versa* (s 21(3)(a)(ii)).

7.7.2   Dramatic works

The same general considerations apply to musical infringement as they do to literary infringement. If only a small part has been used, then, if the piece is long enough to identify the work, that would amount to an infringement. In *Hawkes & Son (London) Ltd v Paramount Film Service Ltd* (1934), the opening 20 seconds of the march 'Colonel Bogey', which

7.7.3   Musical works

lasted four minutes in total, was used in a newsreel. This use was held to be an infringement since the opening bars were the most memorable part of the tune.

When considering whether a substantial part of a work has been copied, not only must consideration be given to the physical musical notation used in recording the work, but also attention must be paid to the similarity of the two works upon the ear (*Austin v Columbia Graphophone Co Ltd* (1917-23)). Accordingly, there is no need for there to be a single note in common, but so long as the two pieces sound sufficiently similar infringement will be established. It is also an infringement of a musical work to make an arrangement or transcription of the work (s 21(3)(b)).

7.7.4   Artistic works

Artistic works are frequently copied, and, with literary works, form the vast bulk of copyright infringement cases. The same principles apply equally to artistic works as they do to other types of works in which copyright subsists; thus, for example, if an original work provided the general idea and inspiration for the derived work, then that is not enough to impose liability *per se* (*Bauman v Fussell* (1978)). If, however, the derived work is so close to the original that it unfailingly imparts the same impression as the original work, then infringement is more likely to be upheld (*King Features Syndicate v O and M Kleeman Ltd* (1941)). If the drawings are very simple then the degree of similarity must be very close in order for infringement to be substantiated (*Politechnika Ipari Szovetkezet v Dallas Print Transfers Ltd* (1982), which concerned an alleged infringing copy of the Rubic Cube).

In the rag trade there is a common belief that so long as seven changes are made to a design that is being copied, then the new work will not infringe the copyright of the first work. In every season there is a style, for example mini, midi, maxi for hem lengths. The different designers tend to base the majority of their collections on this template. What distinguishes the various collections are the different *details* present in the designs. However, even these details are, by and large, not original *per se*. What marks out each designer is the selection, or *compilation* of details in the final article. Under this analysis, a designer who changed seven points of detail would consider reasonably that a new design had been created.

Infringement is largely a matter of impression (*Spectravest Inc v Aperknit Ltd* (1988)), even though it is usual for expert evidence to be adduced on each side in order to highlight similarities and identify features that lack originality (*Monsoon Ltd v India Imports of Rhode Island Ltd* (1993)). In helping to decide what has been appropriated from the original, attention should be paid to what is visually significant, rather than what may be of greatest importance in any other way, eg from an engineering point of view (*Rose Plastics GmbH v William Beckett & Co Ltd (Plastics) Ltd* (1989)). Thus, a feature of road cones that allowed them to be stacked when not in use was important functionally, but it was not a visually significant part of the design, and thus, even though this feature had been copied, it was not sufficient by itself to impose liability (*Johnstone Safety Ltd v Peter Cook (International) plc* (1990)). The visual significance is to be judged by the target audience. So, in the case of a T-shirt design, a member of the public may judge its visual significance, while an engineer would be the appropriate judge of an engineering diagram (*Billhöfer Maschinenfabrik GmbH v TH Dixon & Co Ltd* (1990)). In each case, the trial judge adopts the mantle of the appropriate target audience, after considering the expert evidence.

If a person has merely observed the resultant output from a computer program, and has then written his own version to imitate that original program, as, for example, in the imitation of the computer game Pac-Man by Munchkin, infringement of the literary work should not be held to have occurred, but infringement of visual output (which is an artistic work) may have (*Atari Incorporated v Philips Electronics and Associated Industries Ltd* (1988)).

For an artistic work, copying is further elaborated to include the making of a copy in three dimensions of a two dimensional work and the making of a copy in two dimensions of a three dimensional work (s 17(3)). Thus, a *tableaux vivant* may infringe a picture (*Bradbury, Agnew & Co v Day* (1915-16)), or a dress may infringe a cutting pattern (*J Bernstein Ltd v Sidney Murray Ltd* (1981)).

There are no special provisions under the CDPA 1988 that relate to copying of a sound recording, thus the previously described provisions in ss 16(1)(a), 16(3)(a), 16(3)(b) and 17(1) apply.	**7.7.5 Other copyright works**

Apart from the restrictions outlined above that concerned the making of a copy of a film, copying is further defined for films under the CDPA 1988 s 17(4) as the making of a photograph of the whole or any substantial part of any image forming part of the film.

The provisions in ss 16(1)(a), 16(3)(a), 16(3)(b) and 17(1) apply in respect to infringement for both broadcasts and cable programmes, and in addition there is the extra provision in s 17(4) that a photograph of a broadcast or a cable programme or any part of it would be an infringement.

Copying in relation to the typographical arrangement of a published edition means making a facsimile copy of the arrangement (s 17(5)), which includes a copy that is reduced or enlarged in scale (s 178).

7.8 Infringement by issue of copies to the public

In the previous section we have examined how one may infringe the copyright in a work by copying that work. Infringement by copying is the commonest way in which the rights that vest in a copyright work are violated. However, those rights are not limited to preventing copying, they also include the exclusive right to issue copies to the public. This offence is often committed as well, because generally once a work has been copied it will then be issued so as to reap some economic advantage from the expenditure of labour involved in the copying.

Accordingly, by ss 16(1)(b) and 18(1) it is a restricted act to issue copies, in every description of the copyright work, to the public. This is further defined as the act of putting into circulation copies not previously put into circulation in the UK or elsewhere, but does not include any subsequent distribution, sale, hiring or loan of those copies or any subsequent importation of those copies into the UK (s 18(2)(a) and (b)). However, there is a proviso in s 18 which states that in relation to a sound recording, film or computer program the restricted act includes any rental of copies to the public. Thus, subject to the proviso, the restricted act is limited to the *first* placing of a work on the market, and subsequent distribution is not caught.

Section 18 dovetails with s 22, which is concerned with the importation of infringing copies. Section 22 requires as an essential precondition in order to make out the offence that the prospective defendant knows, or has reason to believe, that the imported copies are infringing copies. In contrast, under s 18(2)(b) the first importation of a work that has not previously been put into circulation in the UK or elsewhere amounts to an act of primary infringement. There is no requirement for knowledge on behalf of the defendant before liability arises for such an act of primary infringement. Thus, the first importation is treated more strictly than any subsequent importation, and this reflects the potentially greater damage that may be incurred by the copyright owner of the work.

7.8.1 Rental right

The proviso in s 18(2) mentioned above applies to the rental of sound recordings and films. This proviso, then, includes such works as video recordings of films, and so acknowledges the economic reality that few people buy a video, instead most rent one. Accordingly, in order to give the owner of the copyright in the video a just remuneration for his efforts, not only should the first sale be considered, but so should all subsequent rentals of that work. Accordingly, such works are excepted from the usual operation of s 18, and every act of subsequent distribution by way of rental is covered. Rental is defined in s 178 as meaning any arrangement under which a copy of a work is made available

- for payment (in money or money's worth); or

- in the course of a business, as part of services or amenities for which payment is made, on terms that it will or may be returned.

Section 18 applies equally to public libraries, but the requirement that the arrangement be for money under s 178 does not apply (Schedule 7 para 8). Accordingly, lending not for profit of a video falls outside the provision of s 18, except when done by a public library.

At present, s 18 protects the position of the owner of the copyright in the type of works listed in the proviso, but not the authors of the underlying copyright works, eg the literary or musical works. This will change when the UK implements Council Directive 92/100/EEC on Rental Rights and Lending Rights. These provisions should have come into force by 1 July 1994 (Article 15(1)). This Directive confers rental rights on authors and performers as well as on the producers of films (Article 2(1)). The Directive confers an unwaivable right to equitable remuneration for rental (Article 4(2)).

In addition to the above schemes, there is a public lending right, whereby the copyright owners of literary works receive remuneration from the Central Fund for their works that are lent out by public libraries (Public Lending Right Act 1979). This has been in force since 1 March 1980.

Under s 19(1) it is a restricted act to perform in public a literary, dramatic or musical work. Performance is further defined in s 19(2)(a) and (b), to include the delivery of a lecture, address, speech or sermon and, in general, includes any mode of visual or acoustic presentation, including a presentation by means of a sound recording, film, broadcast or cable programme. Furthermore, the playing or showing in public of a sound recording, film, broadcast or cable programme is a restricted act (s 19(3)). However, by s 19(4), where the copyright in a work is infringed by it being performed, played or shown in public by means of an apparatus that is capable of receiving visual images or sounds conveyed by electronic means, eg a television in a public house, then the person by whom the visual images or sounds

7.9   Infringement by performance, showing, or playing of a work in public

are sent shall not be regarded as responsible for the infringement, nor shall the performers themselves be regarded as responsible. Hence, the person who is responsible for this type of primary infringement is the person who actually operates the apparatus that receives the visual or sound signals (*Performing Right Society Ltd v Hammond's Bradford Brewery Co Ltd* (1934)).

It is a question of fact whether a performance is in public or private. The relationship between the audience and the owner of the copyright (rather than with the performer) is of primary importance in deciding whether or not a performance is in public. If the audience would normally have paid to be present at the performance, then this provides strong evidence that the performance is to be treated as a public one (*Performing Right Society Ltd v Rangers FC Supporters Club* (1975)). It has been held that the playing of music while a telephone caller is waiting on the 'hold' facility of a telephone exchange system is not a public performance (*Australasian Performing Right Society Ltd v Testra Group Corporation Ltd* (1994)).

7.10	**Infringement by broadcasting or inclusion in cable programmes service**	As we have seen, s 19 imposes a liability on a person who is in control of the apparatus receiving a copyright work. The person who is responsible for the contents of the broadcast, or the actual arrangements for the signal being sent in the first place, is caught under s 20. This imposes liability for the broadcasting or inclusion in a cable programme of a literary, dramatic, musical or artistic work (s 20(a)); or a sound recording or film (s 20(b)); or a broadcast or cable programme (s 20(c)).
7.11	**Infringement by making an adaptation**	It is a restricted act to make an adaptation of a literary, dramatic or musical work (s 21(1)). The adaptation is taken to have been made when it is recorded (s 21(1)). However, if any of the acts that are restricted by copyright in the underlying work, such as copying, performance in public and so on, are done with the adapted work, then there is no need for the adaptation to have been recorded for that act to constitute a primary infringement of the original work (s 21(2)). Thus, for example, if an adaptation of a play is written down then that would, in of itself, amount to an infringement; furthermore, if the adaptation was performed, even without having been recorded in any manner, then that would still be an infringement.

The Act further defines adaptation in relation to literary and dramatic works to mean a translation of the work (s 21(3)(a)(i)); the conversion of a dramatic work into a non-dramatic work and *vice versa* (s 21(3)(a)(ii)); or the conversion of a story into a series of pictures for reproduction in a newspaper or such like, ie a strip cartoon (s 21(3)(a)(iii)).

Translation is not further defined in the CDPA 1988, save for computer programs, but the usual dictionary meaning of 'conversion of a literary work from one human language to another' would be appropriate.

The authorisation of an act of primary infringement is a restricted act (s 16(2)). A person is vicariously liable for any act of infringement committed by his servant or agent in the course of that person's employment, even if the employer explicitly prohibited the acts that constitute the infringing acts (*Performing Right Society Ltd v Mitchell and Booker (Palais de Danse) Ltd* (1924)). The employer would not be liable, however, if the employee was on a 'frolic of his own'. However, if the person who committed the act of infringement is not his servant or agent, ie anyone who is not an employee, then liability only arises if there has been authorisation, and this a matter of fact that has to be decided by the trial judge (*Australasian Performing Right Association Ltd v Koolman* (1969)).

Authorisation is given a wide meaning in copyright law. For example, 'authorises' has been held to mean, *inter alia*, 'sanctions, approves or countenances' (*Falcon v Famous Players Film Co* (1926)). Over the years, however, this wide definition has been somewhat narrowed. In *CBS Songs Ltd v Amstrad Consumer Electronics plc* (1988), which concerned the sale of hi-fi systems fitted with a high-speed dubbing facility for cassette tapes, the House of Lords agreed with the Court of Appeal in *Amstrad Consumer Electronics plc v British Phonographic Industry Ltd* (1986), that 'authorise' means 'a grant or purported grant, which may be express or implied, of the right to do the act complained of'. As a consequence, it was held that the sale of the twin cassette machine was not an act of authorising the infringement of copyright, because Amstrad plc had not granted, either explicitly or implicitly, the consumer to copy other people's cassettes, for it had no standing with the consumer whereby such a grant could be conferred.

Whitford J in *CBS Inc v Ames Record & Tapes Ltd* (1982) said that:

'Any ordinary person, would, I think, assume that an authorisation can only come from somebody having or purporting to have authority and that an act is not authorised by someone who merely enables or possibly assists or even encourages another to do that act, but does not purport to have any authority which he can grant to justify the doing of the act'.

7.12   Infringement by authorisation

In this case the defendant lent out records from its library, and simultaneously sold blank cassettes at a discount, but this was held not to be an act of authorisation, because the person doing the actual copying, ie the purchaser, was not controlled by, or in any way bound to, the seller in a manner that would indicate that the latter could authorise an act of the former.

In *Keays v Dempster* (1994) the plaintiff owned the copyright in a photograph which was reproduced in a book written by the defendant. The defendant selected some photographs, and then it was up to the publisher to procure the right to reproduce the photographs which he has chosen from many thousands. It was held that the defendant had not authorised the publisher to reproduce the photograph, he merely selected the ones he wanted, and it was up to the publisher to pay the appropriate fees and secure the necessary licences.

In Australia, the Courts have followed a slightly different route. The emphasis has been placed upon whether control is maintained over the *apparatus* which will be used to do the act of infringement. In *Moorhouse v University of New South Wales* (1976)), it was held that:

> '... a person who has under his control the means by which an infringement of copyright may be committed – such as a photocopying machine – and who makes it available to other persons, knowing, or having reason to suspect, that it is likely to be used for the purpose of committing an infringement, and omitting to take reasonable steps to limit its use to legitimate purposes, would authorise any infringement that resulted from its use.'

| 7.13 | **Secondary infringement of copyright** | Secondary infringement of copyright is dealt with in ss 22-26. The major distinction between acts of primary and secondary infringement is that in the latter case the defendant must know, or have reason to believe, that the articles in which he is dealing are 'infringing copies'. Furthermore, unlike acts of primary infringement, it is not possible to authorise an act of secondary infringement. |

The various acts that may amount to secondary infringement are:

- importing an infringing copy;

- possessing or dealing with an infringing copy;

- providing the means for making an infringing copy;

- permitting the use of premises for an infringing performances; and,

- providing apparatus for an infringing performance.

It will be noticed that the first three offences involve what is called 'an infringing copy'. First, though, the concept of 'knowledge' in secondary infringement is examined as this is a pre-requisite for all classes of secondary infringement.

Actual, as opposed to constructive, knowledge is required (*Hoover plc v George Hulme Ltd* (1982)); yet it has been held that the defendant may be assumed to have the 'ordinary understanding expected of persons in his line of business' (*RCA Corporation v Custom Cleared Sales Pty Ltd* (1978)). *A fortiori*, wilful blindness will not provide a defence (*Ross v Moss* (1965)). Nor is it a defence, if the defendant knew all the relevant facts, but believed, mistakenly, that as a matter of law the article did not infringe, even if his belief was based upon legal advice (*Sillitoe v McGraw-Hill Book Co Ltd* (1983)).

7.13.1   Knowledge

In all cases the defendant must be given a period of grace once he has become aware of the facts before he is fixed with having the prerequisite knowledge. Each situation depends on its facts, for example, if only a few, simple inquiries are needed to ascertain the true position, then the period of grace will only be a few days; whilst, if ascertaining the true situation is fraught with difficulty, then a longer period, of say 21 days, may be allowed by the courts (*Monsoon Ltd v India Imports of Rhode Island Ltd* (1993)). If a defendant stops doing the offending acts during the grace period, then because he has not been fixed with knowledge until the end of that period, an essential element of the tort of secondary infringement will not be present. As a consequence, no liability will arise for those acts done before and during the grace period.

Section 22 provides that the copyright in a work is infringed by a person who, without the licence of the copyright owner, imports into the UK, otherwise than for his private and domestic use, an article which is, and which he knows or has reason to believe is, an infringing copy of the work. This provision is not designed to impose liability upon the overseas manufacturer of the infringing articles, but rather the third party importers (*Paterson Zochonis Ltd v Merfarken Packaging Ltd* (1983)). In a case which involved the infringement of Barbie dolls being imported into Hong Kong, the word 'import' was held to have its normal meaning of 'bringing into' (*Mattel Inc v Tonka Corporation* (1992)).

7.13.2   Importing infringing copies

An 'infringing copy' is defined as an article which has been, or is proposed to be, imported into the UK, and which had it been made in the UK would have constituted an infringement of the copyright in the work in question, or would have been a breach of an exclusive licence agreement relating to that work (s 27(3)). Note that the section uses the word 'article' and not 'work' in defining an infringing copy.

Nothing, however, in subsection 27(3) is to be construed as applying to an article that may lawfully be imported into the UK by virtue of any enforceable Community right within the meaning of s 2(1) of the European Community Act 1972 (s 27(5)). Thus, if an article is in free circulation within the European Union, then its importation will not be an infringing act, because of the doctrine of exhaustion of rights (*Deutsche Grammophon GmbH v Metro-SB-Großmärkte GmbH & Co KG* (1971) and *Warner Brothers Inc v Christiansen* (1991)).

It is irrelevant, when considering the question of whether or not an article is an infringing copy, that the imported article in question was purchased legally in a country outside of the EU Member States without any restriction on the resale of that article. This is because there is no implied licence that such an article may then be imported and resold within the United Kingdom (*Penguin Books Ltd v India Book Distributors* (1985)). If the works have been placed on the market within the EU with the consent of the copyright owner, he would thereafter be prevented from stopping the importation of the works into another EU Member State such as the UK. However, if no consent had been given, even if the works had been legally produced, then the importation could be stopped (*EMI Electrola GmbH v Patrica Im-Und Export Verwaltungsgesellschaft mbH* (1989)). The mere fact that a copyrighted article was sold, and that the copyright owner did not prevent that sale, does not mean that the copyright owner consented to the sale (*EMI Records Ltd v The CD Specialists Ltd* (1992)). Accordingly, so long as an article was sold within the EU with the consent of the copyright owner, then that article may be imported into the UK (s 27(5)).

7.13.3	Possessing or dealing with infringing copies	The copyright in a work is infringed by a person who, without the licence of the copyright owner, possesses in the course of business (s 23(a)); or sells or lets for hire, or offers or exposes for sale or hire (s 23(b)); or in the course of business exhibits in public or distributes (s 23(c)); or distributes otherwise than in the course of a business to such an extent as to affect prejudicially the owner of the copyright (s 23(d)), an article which is, and which he knows or has reason to believe is, an infringing copy of the work. Business is defined to include a trade or profession (s 178). The business must be one which deals in the type of articles of which the infringing article is an example, and must not simply be a business *per se* which has, for some other accidental reason, an infringing article (*LA Gear Inc v Hi-Tech Sports plc* (1992)). Thus, this section is designed to prevent people from trading in infringing copies.

The copyright in a work is infringed by a person who, without the licence of the copyright owner makes (s 24(1)(a)); or imports into the UK (s 24(1)(b)); or possesses in the course of business (s 24(1)(c)); or, sells or lets for hire, or offers or exposes for sale or hire (s 24(1)(d)), an article specifically designed or adapted for making copies of that work, knowing or having reason to believe that it is to be used to make infringing copies. This section prohibits the making of dies and other such instruments of manufacture designed to reproduce specific copyright works, rather than preventing the distribution of, for example, twin cassette deck tape recorders of photocopying machines.

There is a further new provision that states the copyright in a work is infringed by a person who, without the licence of the copyright owner, transmits the work by means of a telecommunications system (otherwise than by broadcast or inclusion in a cable programme service), and who knows or has reason to believe that infringing copies of the work will be made by means of the reception of the transmission in the UK or elsewhere (s 24(2)). This provision would catch the person who puts a copy of a computer program, in which copyright vests, on a computer bulletin board with the expectation that copies would be downloaded by users of that facility.

7.13.4 Providing the means for making infringing copies

Section 25(1) provides that where the copyright in a literary, dramatic or musical work is infringed by a performance at a place of public entertainment, any person who gave permission for that place to be used for the performance is also liable for the infringement unless, when he gave permission, he believed on reasonable grounds that the performance would not infringe copyright. 'Place of public entertainment' is further defined to include premises which are occupied mainly for other purposes, but which from time to time are made available for hire for the purpose of public entertainment (s 25(2)).

Permission is not given if there is no knowledge of what particular work will be performed (*Performing Right Society Ltd v Ciryl Theatrical Syndicate Ltd* (1924)). Accordingly, the person who granted the permission to use the venue in such circumstances would not be liable for any infringement. However, it must be remembered that wilful blindness will not provide a defence, and further that the defendant will be assumed to have the ordinary awareness of someone in his line of business.

7.13.5 Permitting the use of premises for infringing performances

Where copyright in a work is infringed by a public performance of the work, or by the playing or showing of the work in public, by means of apparatus for playing sound

7.13.6 The provision of apparatus for infringing performances, etc

recordings (s 26(1)(a)); or showing films (s 26(1)(b)); or receiving visual images or sounds conveyed by electronic means (s 26(1)(c)), the following persons are also liable for the infringement. First, the person who supplied the apparatus (s 26(2)(a)); secondly, an occupier of premises who gave permission for the apparatus to be brought onto the premises (s 26(3)); and, thirdly, a person who supplied a copy of a sound recording or film used to infringe copyright (s 26(4)).

The actual performer of the infringing acts would be committing an act of *primary* infringement (s 19(1)).

There are further provisions in ss 297-299 that concern the fraudulent reception of transmissions. For example, it is an offence to sell an unauthorised decoder (s 297A inserted by the Broadcasting Act 1990 s 179(1)). Furthermore, the sale of unauthorised decoders for use abroad is prohibited (*BBC Enterprises Ltd v Hi-Tech Xtravision Ltd* (1992)). It is to be noted that this right is not really a 'copyright' at all, but rather a new *sui generis* right that prevents the sale of equipment that is capable of dealing with encrypted copyright works. The exact ramifications of such a right are, as of yet, not fully known.

7.14 Date of the potential infringement	All acts of potential infringement that occur after the commencement of the 1988 Act, ie 1 August 1989, are governed by the new Act; while any potentially infringing act done before that date is governed by the provisions of the 1956 Act (CDPA 1988 Schedule 1 para 14(1)). An infringement of copyright is a tortious wrong. There may be a number of separate acts of infringement by the defendant, each of which will constitute a separate offence (*Ash v Hutchinson & Co (Publishers) Ltd* (1936)). However, there must be a full trial of the action in order for the court to determine whether the separate acts of manufacture, distribution and sale of an allegedly infringing copy constitute one continuing cause of action, or whether, in contrast, each act forms a separate act of infringement. This issue cannot be resolved at the interlocutory stage of an action (*Banks v CBS Songs Ltd* (1992)).

It is standard practice in intellectual property matters to decide the issue of infringement by reference to sample acts of purported infringement. If infringement is found in these cases, then damages would be assessed on all acts of infringement, including those that occurred after the issue of the writ (*Banks v CBS Songs Ltd* (1992)).

Copyright: Infringement

It is a pre-condition to a successful action for copyright infringement that the groundwork has been laid correctly, ie the subject matter is a copyright work and the title of which vests with the prospective plaintiff, ie 'First, we got to get all our ducks in a row …'.

Introduction

Classically, copyright protects the expression and not the idea (*Kenrick & Co v Lawrence & Co* (1890)). However, if the idea is expressed in enough detail then the idea will also be protected (*Ibcos Computers Ltd v Barclays Mercantile Highland Finance Ltd* (1994)).

Essence of copyright protection
Protection of a particular expression

There must be a causal link between the original work and the derived work (*Billhöfer Maschinenfabrik GmbH v Dixon & Co Ltd* (1990)). It is necessary for copyright to subsist in the original work (*Purefoy Engineering v Sykes, Boxall* (1955)). However, it is *not* necessary for copyright to subsist in each and every link in the chain of causation (s 16(3)).

Causal link

Copying is essentially inferred by the courts from the similarity of the work and the purportedly derived work (*Antocks Lairn Ltd v I Bloohn Ltd* (1971)). Evidence of similar mistakes in both works, lends credence to the allegation of copying (*Ibcos Computers Ltd v Barclays Mercantile Highland Finance Ltd* (1994)).

Evidence of copying

Indirect copying is usually used to indicate that a change of format has occurred in the chain of causation, eg the dolls of Popeye the Sailor derived from drawings in strip-cartoons (*King Features Syndicate v Kleeman* (1940)). It is also possible for one link to be a detailed verbal description (*Plix Products Ltd v Frank M Winstone (Merchants) Ltd* (1986)).

Indirect copying

In *Francis Day & Hunter Ltd v Bron* (1963) it was held possible that liability could arise even though the defendant was not consciously aware that he had copied an earlier work.

Subconscious copying

Copyright is only infringed if a *substantial* proportion of the original is misappropriated. Substantiality is judged qualitatively and not quantitatively (*Ladbroke (Football) v*

Substantiality of material copied

William Hill (Football) (1964)). However, Petersen J in *University of London v University Tutorial* (1916) said that 'what is worth copying is *prima facie* worth protecting'.

Primary and secondary infringement

Copyright infringement may be divided into primary acts, which are dealt with in ss 16-21, and secondary acts, which are dealt with in ss 22-26. Only in the case of secondary acts of infringement is there a necessary pre-condition for a *mens rea* element by the defendant.

Primary acts of infringement

The owner of the copyright in a work has the exclusive right, *inter alia*, to copy the work, issue copies to the public and to make adaptations (s 16(1)). Thus, it is a primary act of infringement for anyone, without the licence of the copyright owner, to do or authorise anyone else to do, any of the restricted acts (s 16(2)).

Infringement by copying

The unauthorised copying of a work is an act restricted for every description of the work (s 17(1)). This is probably the commonest form of copyright infringement.

Literary works

If the original is reproduced in any material form then the copyright will have been infringed.

Dramatic works

There is no infringement if only the bare plot has been copied (*Sutton Vane v Famous Players Film Co Ltd* (1928-35)). However, if the detailed plot has been appropriated, then there may be infringement. There is also infringement when a dramatic work is converted into a non-dramatic work and *vice versa* (s 21 (3)(a)(ii)).

Musical works

For musical works, similarity is tested by the impression upon the ear (*Austin v Columbia Gramophone Co Ltd* (1917-23)).

Artistic works

For very simple diagrams, the derived work must be almost a facsimile copy before liability will arise (*Politechnika v Dallas Print Transfers* (1982)).

For artistic works, similarity is judged by the impression upon the eye (*Spectravest Inc v Aperknit Ltd* (1988)).

The visual significance of the elements of the drawing are to be judged by the appropriate target audience (*Billhöfer Maschinenfabrik GmbH v TH Dixon & Co Ltd* (1990)).

Other copyright works

Generally, the usual provisions apply to all other copyright works.

This involves making public that which was previously not public (*Infabrics v Jaytex Shirt* (1981)). Generally, subsequent distribution after the first sale is not an infringement, save in the special case of sound recordings, films and computer programs.

Infringement by issue of copies to the public

Council Directive 92/100/EEC confers rental rights on authors and performers.

Rental right

This places a liability on the person who operates the apparatus that receives the infringing work (*PRS v Hammond's Bradford Brewery* (1934)). Whether an audience amounts to the public is always a question of fact. The 'hold facility' on a telephone system was held not to amount to a public performance (*Australasian PRS v Testra Group Corporation* (1994)).

Infringement by performance, showing, or playing of a work in public

The person responsible for the broadcast or cable service is liable (s 20).

Infringement by broadcasting service

An unauthorised adaptation will infringe a copyright work (s 21). Taking detailed and extensive quotes from a work amounts to an adaptation (*Sillitoe v McGraw-Hill Book Co (UK) Ltd* (1983)).

Infringement by making an adaptation

Authorisation means the grant, express or implied, of the right to do an act (*CBS Songs Ltd v Amstrad plc* (1988)). However, the authorisation must come from a person in authority and not just anyone (*CBS Inc v Ames Record & Tapes Ltd* (1982)).

Infringement by authorisation

It is an essential pre-condition for secondary infringement that the defendant knows or has reason to believe that he is dealing in infringing copies. Another difference from primary infringement is that one cannot authorise an act of secondary infringement.

Secondary infringement of copyright

There is a period of grace after becoming aware of the facts and being fixed with knowledge for the purpose of secondary infringement, in order to allow the defendant to check the truth of the facts (*Monsoon Ltd v India Imports* (1993)).

Knowledge

'Importing' is given its natural meaning of 'bringing into' (*Mattel Inc v Tonka Corporation* (1992)). There is the usual principle of exhaustion of rights that operates in the EU (*Warner Brothers Inc v Christiansen* (1990)). However, this does not operate outside the EU, and furthermore no such term

Importing infringing copies

may be implied (*Penguin Books Ltd v India Book Distributors* (1985)).

Possessing or dealing with infringing copies

The business must be in the same field of activity as would that in the infringing copy (*LA Gear Inc v Hi-Tech Sports plc* (1992)).

Providing the means for making infringing copies

The prohibition extends only to articles designed especially to infringe particular works, eg screen prints or printing dies.

Permitting the use of premises for infringing performances

The defendant must have knowledge of work that is to be performed; however, 'wilful blindness' will not constitute a defence (*PRS v Ciryl Theatrical Syndicate* (1924)).

Provision of apparatus for infringing performances, etc

It is an offence to sell unauthorised decoders (s 297A). This right is *sui generis,* and not really a 'copyright' *per se.*

Date of the potential infringement

All infringements after 1 August 1989 governed by the CDPA 1988. Each act of infringement is a separate tortious act (*Ash v Hutchinson & Co (Publishers) Ltd* (1936)).

Chapter 8

Copyright: Permitted Acts and Defences

In the last chapter, we examined those acts that amount to an infringement of copyright in a work. These 'infringing acts' are detailed in ss 16-26. Principal amongst them were the primary acts of infringement of copying and issuing to the public, and the secondary act of infringement of importing infringing copies. It is readily apparent that these provisions are very broad in their application. In fact, the provisions are so broad that if there were no checks upon their operation, then the smooth running of society would be hindered. Hence, the legislature has made extra provisions that allow certain activities to occur without attracting liability for copyright infringement. These 'permitted acts' thus form a limitation on the rights of the copyright owner. The permitted acts are contained in ss 28-76. Each section deals with a very limited activity that Parliament has thought necessary to exclude from the ambit of copyright. The protection conferred on the person who, save for the operation of that section, would be infringing copyright, is very tightly drawn. This is to ensure that only those activities that are strictly necessary for the smooth running of society are permitted, and that no general licence is given to the general public that could seriously damage the rights of the copyright owner. By and large, the permitted acts cover educational or public administrational matters, and incidental uses of copyright material.

8.1 Introduction to permitted acts

Sections 29-76 contain the detailed provisions relating to the permitted acts. Section 28 is of a more general nature, and it applies to all the other sections.

8.2 General provisions

Section 28(1) provides that the provisions of Chapter III, ie the permitted acts in ss 29-76, specify various acts that may be done in relation to copyright works notwithstanding the subsistence of copyright in those works. The sections only relate to the question of infringement of copyright and do not affect any other right or obligation that may restrict the doing of any of the specified acts. For example, an activity which would otherwise be allowed by virtue of the operation of a section within Chapter III may be proscribed between two parties by reason of a contractual arrangement. As a consequence, then, any breach of such a term would amount to a breach of contract, but not an act of infringement of copyright.

Where no particular description of the work is given that limits the permitted act to a certain type of work, then the permitted act applies to all classes of copyright work (s 28(2)). No inference may be drawn from the descriptions of acts permitted by ss 29-76 as to the scope of copyright protection (s 28(3)). Furthermore, the provisions are to be construed independently of each other, so that the fact that an act does not fall within one provision does not mean that it is not covered by another provision (s 28(4)). By virtue of s 76, the acts permitted apply equally not only to an underlying literary, dramatic, or musical work, but also to any adaptation of that work.

The defences apply to acts done after 1 August 1989. Before that date the provisions of the CA 1956 apply (CDPA 1988 Schedule 1 para 14(1)).

8.3	**Fair dealing and incidental inclusion**

Sections 29-31 provide that some acts of a general nature are not to be considered an infringement of copyright. These include private study, criticism and incidental inclusion. There seems to be a dual justification for allowing these acts. The first is that the members of society should not be fettered by copyright restrictions when conducting private study or research. Similarly, society benefits from the availability of criticisms and reviews of other people's work. The second justification is that, so long as only a small amount of material is used so that the rights of the copyright owner are not prejudiced, then by necessary implication this would amount to *de minimis* use that would be impossible to regulate fully in anything other than a totalitarian regime.

8.3.1	Research and private study

There is no infringement in fair dealing with a literary, dramatic, musical or artistic work if done for the purpose of research or private study (s 29(1)). As this section can only come into operation once infringement has been shown, ie a substantial amount of the copyright work has been appropriated, it has been suggested that there can never be a situation in which the work has been dealt with fairly (*Independent Television Publications Ltd v Time Out Ltd* (1984)). However, this would mean that Parliament had enacted a purely nugatory provision, which, as a matter of principle, is unsound.

The fact that a work has to be reproduced for research or private study is a necessary, but not sufficient condition for this provision to operate (*University of London Press Ltd v University Tutorial Press Ltd* (1916)). The use must also be 'fair'. This issue of 'fairness' is present in both s 29 and s 30 (which concerns fair dealing for the purpose of review or criticism).

Similar considerations should apply in each case, and so this issue will be considered next, illustrated by cases that have involved either s 29 or s 30.

What amounts to fair dealing will depend upon the particular facts of the case (*Hubbard v Vosper* (1972)). Relevant factors include the amount of the work used (*Hubbard v Vosper* (1972)); the number of people to whom the copies have been shown (*British Oxygen Co Ltd v Liquid Air Ltd* (1925)); whether the treatment of the work will adversely affect the normal exploitation of the work (Berne Convention Article 9(2)); whether the work was previously unpublished, and has now been leaked to the press (*Beloff v Pressdram Ltd* (1973)); whether the copyist intended the new work to be really a review or criticism (*Associate Newspaper Group plc v New Group Newspapers Ltd* (1986)); whether the true intention of the reviewer was to damage the author of the original work rather than to review the work itself (*Hubbard v Vosper* (1972)); and, whether the copy was made for the economic benefit of the reviewer (*Sillitoe v McGraw-Hill Books Co (UK) Ltd* (1983)).

Section 29(4) (as inserted by the Copyright (Computer Programs) Regulations 1992 reg 7) explicitly states that it is not fair dealing for the purposes of research or private study to convert a computer program expressed in a low level language into a version expressed in a high level language, nor it is fair, incidentally in the course of converting the program, to copy it. However, such acts may be permitted if done in accordance with s 50B, but this section is concerned with making back-up copies of computer programs, and has nothing to do with fair usage *per se*.

It is not an infringement of copyright to deal fairly with a work for the purpose of criticism or review, so long as sufficient acknowledgement is given (s 30(1)). Such a provision is necessary to allow members of society to comment publicly on the works of others.

Fair dealing with a work (other than a photograph) for the purpose of reporting current events is permitted so long as sufficient acknowledgement is given (s 30(2)), but no acknowledgement is needed if the current event is reported by means of a sound recording, film, broadcast or cable programme (s 30(3)). In *British Broadcasting Corporation v British Satellite Broadcasting Ltd* (1991) it was held by Scott J that this provision was available in the situation where one television company wished to use excerpts from another company's programmes, which, in this case, concerned football matches played in the World Cup. The copyright work need not itself

8.3.2   Fair dealing

8.3.3   Criticism, review and news reporting

be current, so long as its use is reasonably necessary for the reporting of the current events (*Associated Newspapers Group plc v News Group Newspapers Ltd* (1986)).

8.3.4	Sufficient acknowledgement	For the purposes of review or criticism, the use will only be fair if there has been sufficient acknowledgement. This is the *quid pro quo* of being allowed to use the work. Sufficient acknowledgement is defined in s 178 as meaning that the work in question is identified by its title and its author.

The requirement for sufficient acknowledgement under the CA 1956 s 6(10) was slightly, yet significantly, different, in that the author could have previously agreed that no acknowledgement of his name should be made. Furthermore, it should be noted that the author, and not the copyright owner, must be identified (*Express Newspapers plc v News (UK) Ltd* (1990)).

8.3.5   Incidental inclusion

By s 31(1) copyright in a work is not infringed by its incidental inclusion in an artistic work, sound recording, film, broadcast or cable programme. If there was no such provision, then it would be an almost impossible task to produce any work that did not infringe someone's copyright. Thus, this provision is purely pragmatic in nature. However, a musical work, words spoken or sung with music, or as much of a sound recording, broadcast or cable programme as includes a musical work or such words, shall not be regarded as incidentally included in another work if it is deliberately included (s 31(3)). The exception for deliberately included material is entirely reasonable, for, presumably, it was included to enhance the new work, and so if the author of the new work receives some benefit, then the author of the included work should as well.

8.4   Educational usage

The guiding principle when dealing with copyright works for use in educational establishments is that so long as only those *directly involved* in the educational process reproduce the material *manually*, then there is no infringement. This represents a compromise between prejudicing the economic interests of authors, whose material has educational value, and facilitating the ready access of students to valuable source material.

8.4.1   Instruction

Thus, copyright in a literary, dramatic, musical or artistic work is not infringed by its being copied in the course of instruction or of preparation for instruction, provided that the copying is done by a person giving or receiving instruction and is not by means of a reprographic process (s 32(1)). Reprographic process is further defined in s 178 as meaning a process for making facsimile copies or involving the use of an appliance for making multiple copies, but does not include the making of a film or sound recording. So, a teacher may reproduce an otherwise infringing copy of a work on an overhead projector sheet, and a pupil may reproduce such material in an examination answer, but photocopies of a play may not be made and then handed out to the class.

The performance of a literary, dramatic or musical work before an audience consisting of teachers and pupils at an educational establishment and other persons directly connected with the activities of the establishment by a teacher or pupil in the course of the activities of the establishment or at the establishment by any person for the purpose of instruction is not a public performance for the purposes of infringement of copyright (s 34(1)). Nor is the playing or showing of a sound recording, film, broadcast or cable programme before a similar audience for similar purposes an infringement (s 34(2)). However, a person is not to be taken as being directly connected with the activities merely on account of being a parent of a pupil (s 34(3)).

8.4.2   Performance of works in an educational establishment

This, then covers for example the recital of a play within an English lesson, or the watching of a video recording of, say, a 'Horizon' programme in a science lesson. However, the school play performed in front of parents, whether or not they have paid for the privilege, is not included within the scope of this provision. Such an activity could, thus, be caught by the primary act of infringement of performing a work in public (s 19).

A recording of a broadcast or cable programme, or a copy of such a recording, may be made by or on behalf of an educational establishment for the educational purposes of that establishment without thereby infringing the copyright in the broadcast or cable programme, or any work included in it (s 35(1)). Thus, a television programme may be video-taped so that it may be shown later in class.

8.4.3   Recording of programmes by educational establishments

However, this provision does not apply if there is a licensing scheme certified for this purpose under s 143 (s 35(2)).

It is not an infringement of copyright to reproduce no more than 1%, in any one quarter of the year, of any published literary, dramatic or musical work so long as it was done by, or on behalf of, an educational establishment for the purpose of instruction (ss 36(1) and (2)). However, there is an infringement of copyright if there were licences available, and if the person making the copies knew or ought to have known of their existence (s 36(3)). The limit of 1% is so low, that it is

8.4.4   Reproductive copying by an educational establishment unlikely that such a small amount of material would constitute a substantial amount of the original work in the first place. However, this section does provide protection if the most important 1% is copied for substantiality is judged qualitatively and not quantitatively, eg in *Waterlow Directories Ltd v Reed Information Services Ltd* (1992) infringement was held when the defendant appropriated about 250 names from 12,620. Even allowing for the systematic reproduction of a work, it would take 25 years to copy the whole work, by which time it is likely that it would be out of date.

8.5	**Libraries and archives**

Under ss 37(1), (2) and 38–43 the Secretary of State has made an Order to regulate the activities of libraries and archives (Copyright (Librarians and Archivists)(Copying of Copyright Material) Regulations 1989). These regulations supplement the provisions of ss 38–43. Some of the activities that are regulated by the Order require that the librarian or archivist must be satisfied as to some detail before making or supplying a copy of the work. In such a case, the librarian or archivist may rely on a signed declaration as to that detail by the person requesting the copy, unless he is aware that it is false in a material respect (s 37(2)(a)).

A librarian may supply a copy of an article in a periodical without infringing the copyright therein (s 38 (1)) so long as the copy is supplied only for research or private study, and that only one copy of that article is made, or only one article within the same issue of the periodical is copied, and also that the person who is supplied with the copy is required to pay at least the cost price attributable to the production (s 38(2)).

With regard to either the supply of a copy of an article or part of a published work, the librarian must be satisfied that the request by the person to whom the copy is supplied is not related to a different request by another person for a similar copy (s 40(1) and (2)). This is to ensure that a person cannot, by covert means, obtain two articles from the same journal. In all, these provisions are quite restrictive and if followed strictly impose quite a restraint upon researchers.

8.6	**Public administration**

In order to ensure the smooth running of public administration, there are several provisions that permit the copying of copyright works. Without such provision, the wheels of government, both local and central, would grind to a halt for want of documentary material upon which to base its conclusions.

8.6.1	Parliamentary and judicial proceedings

The principal provision is contained in s 45(1) which provides that copyright is not infringed by anything done for the purposes of parliamentary or judicial proceedings, nor by anything done for the purposes of reporting such proceedings, so long as a work that is itself a published report of the proceedings is not copied (s 45(2)). By s 178 'judicial proceedings' includes proceedings before any court, tribunal or person having authority to decide any matter affecting a person's legal rights or liabilities. However, this provision only applies to specific proceedings that exist when the copy is made (*Auckland Medical Aid Trust v Commissioner of Police* (1976)). Thus, copies cannot be made in anticipation that they would be useful in some later, as yet unknown and unspecified, proceedings.

The Copyright (Computer Programs) Regulations 1992 implemented Council Directive 91/250 EEC, which is concerned with the legal protection of computer programs. This regulation came into force on 1 January 1993, but it applies to computer programs made before that date (C(CP)R 1992 reg 12(1)). This regulation inserted ss 50A-50C within Chapter III of Part I of the CDPA 1988, and extended, for licensed users, the permitted acts with respect to computer programs.	**8.7** **Lawful users of computer programs**
It is not an infringement of copyright for a lawful user of a copy of a computer program to make any back up copy of it which is necessary for him to have for the purpose of his lawful use (s 50A(1)). This amendment now legalises the practice which should be followed by all computer users of ensuring that there is a back up copy of all data and programs that are in use.

Further, where any person has the use of a computer program under an agreement, any term or condition in the agreement shall be void in so far as it purports to prohibit or restrict the making of any back up copies of the program which it is necessary for him to have for the purposes of the agreed use (ss 50A(3) and 296A(1)(a)). | 8.7.1 The making of back-up copies |
| It is not an infringement of copyright for a lawful user of a copy of a computer program expressed in a low level language to convert it into a version expressed in a higher level language or incidentally in the course of so converting the program to copy it (that is, to 'decompile' it), provided that the decompilation must be necessary to obtain the information required to create an independent program that can then be operated with the program decompiled (s 50B). | 8.7.2 Decompilation |
| It is not an infringement of copyright for a lawful user of a copy of a computer program to copy or adapt it, provided that | 8.7.3 Other acts permitted to lawful users |

the copying or adapting is necessary for his lawful use and is not prohibited under any term or condition of an agreement regulating the circumstances in which his use is lawful (s 50C(1)). It may, in particular, be necessary for the lawful user of a computer program to copy it or adapt it for the purpose of correcting errors in it (s 50C(2)). This section does not apply to any copying or adapting permitted under ss 50A or 50B (s 50C(3)).

8.8	**Typefaces**	There was some doubt before the CDPA 1988 was enacted whether of not copyright subsisted in a typeface, even though it had been held that copyright subsisted in a catalogue of typefaces (*Masson Seeley & Co Ltd v Embosotype Manufacturing Co* (1924)). The position was clarified by explicitly enacting the provisions of ss 54 and 55, which detail the permitted use to which a typeface may be put.

Thus, it is not an infringement of copyright in an artistic work consisting of the design of a typeface to use the typeface in the ordinary course of typing, composing text, typesetting or printing (s 54(1)(a)).

Furthermore, if an article is specifically designed to produce material in a typeface in which artistic copyright subsists, then that article may be freely copied after a period of 25 years from the end of the calendar year in which the article was first marketed (s 55(2)), so long as the article was marketed by or with the licence of the copyright owner (s 55(1)). If the article was first marketed before 1 August 1989, then the protection extends for 25 years from 31 December 1989 (CDPA 1988 Schedule 1 para 14(5)).

8.9	**Miscellaneous provisions: literary, dramatic, musical and artistic works**	The previous sections permitted acts of a general nature that facilitate the operation of public administration and other activities common to society, such as education, personal study and the use of computer programs. The remaining sections deal with a multitude of individual situations that, if no provision had been made to exclude them from liability, would cause great inconvenience to society, but not necessarily have disrupted it.
8.9.1	Anonymous or pseudonymous works	There are several provisions that deal with a variety of miscellaneous situations relating to copyright in literary, dramatic, musical and artistic works.

The first such provision provides that copyright is not infringed by an act done at a time when it is not possible by reasonable inquiry to ascertain the identity of the author (s 57(1)(a)), and either it is reasonable to assume that copyright has expired (s 57(1)(b)(i)), or that the author died 50 years or more before the beginning of the calendar year in which the act is done (s 57(1)(b)(ii)). This provision does not apply in relation to a work in which Crown copyright subsists (s 57(2)(a)), or a work in which by virtue of s 168 copyright vests in an international organisation for more than 50 years (s 57(2)(b)).

Where an article on a scientific or technical subject is published in a periodical and it is accompanied by an abstract which indicates the contents of that article, then there is no infringement of the copyright in either the abstract, or the article, to copy the abstract and issue copies to the public (s 60(1)), unless there is a licensing agreement under s 143 (s 60(2)).

8.9.2   Abstracts

Thus, even though much work may have been expended by the writer of the abstract so as to succinctly convey the meaning of the article, Parliament has felt that society will be benefit by the dissemination of the abstracts and the concomitant spread of knowledge, and this benefit is greater than any prejudice that may be experienced by the author of the abstract.

The copyright in a building (s 62(1)(a)), or a sculpture, model for a building and works of artistic craftsmanship, if permanently situated in a public place or in premises open to the public (s 62(1)(b)) is not infringed by the making of a graphic work representing it (s 62(2)(a)), or making a photograph or film of it (s 62(2)(b)), or broadcasting or including in a cable programme service a visual image of it (s 62(2)(c)). Thus, there is no infringement of the copyright in a building when a photograph is taken that contains the building as a backdrop. However, the taking of a photograph of a sculpture that is on display in a place open to the public may be restricted by the contracted conditions when admission was granted (*Sports and General Press Agency Ltd v 'Our Dogs' Publishing Co Ltd* (1916)).

8.9.3   Artistic works on public display

It is not an infringement of copyright in an artistic work to copy it, or to issue copies to the public, for the purpose of advertising the sale of the work (s 63(1)). However, in any subsequent dealing with such a copy, which save for action of s 63(1) would have been an infringing copy, then the copy shall be treated as an infringing copy (s 63(2)). Thus, for example, Christie's Contemporary Art Club issues very fine glossy reproductions of the works that they are trying to sell, in order to assist in the advertisement of the principal work of art. Yet these reproductions may not knowingly be subsequently sold or exhibited in public or otherwise

8.9.4   Advertisement of sale of an artistic work

distributed since then they would be treated as infringing copies, and this would amount to an act of secondary infringement (s 27(6)).

| 8.9.5 | Subsequent works of art by the same artist |

An artist does not infringe the copyright in one of his earlier artistic works, so long as he does not repeat or imitate the main design of the earlier work (s 64). This section only applies if he does not own the copyright, for if he did then the issue of infringement would not arise. Thus, an artist may produce a series of artistic works all of which carry his individual stamp, without fear that he will be liable for infringement of his earlier works.

| 8.10 | **Miscellaneous provisions: sound recordings, films and computer programs** |

Sections 66 and 67 make provisions for various miscellaneous permitted acts with respect to the principal derived works. Thus, it is not an infringement of the copyright in a sound recording to play it as part of the activities of, or for the benefit of, a club, society, or other organisation (s 67(1)), so long as the organisation is not established or conducted for profit and its main objects are charitable, or are otherwise concerned with the advancement of religion, education, or social welfare (s 67(2)(a)), and that the proceeds of any charge for admission are applied solely for the purposes of the organisation (s 67(2)(b)). Thus, it would not be an infringement of the copyright in a sound recording to play a record so as to provide the musical accompaniment for a church congregation as sometimes occurs at small rural churches; nor would it amount to an infringement when the Women's Institute play Jerusalem at the commencement of their soirées.

| 8.11 | **Miscellaneous provisions: broadcasts and cable programmes** |

Sections 68-75 make provisions for various miscellaneous permitted acts with respect to the more recently developed derived works.

Thus, for example, s 70 provides that the making for private and domestic use of a recording of a broadcast or cable programme solely for the purpose of enabling it to be viewed or listened to at a more convenient time does not infringe any copyright in the broadcast or cable programme or in any work included in it. Thus, this section allows a person to record on a video cassette a film shown on television so long as it is for purely private and domestic use. This practice is called time-shifting.

| 8.12 | **Broadcast and cable programme listing** |

The *Radio Times* and the *TV Times* had a monopoly on the publication of comprehensive information that related to the future airing of television broadcasts on the BBC and the independent television channels. Other publications, such as newspapers and magazines, were only allowed to print the television listing one day ahead for weekdays, and two days ahead for the weekend. The weekly entertainment magazine *Time Out* wished to publish a weekly television listing and so it sought permission to do this, but was denied. The courts held that as the television listings could be protected as a literary work, the copyright owners could prevent *Time Out* from publishing a weekly television guide (*Independent Television Publications Ltd v Time Out Ltd* (1984)).

The Monopolies and Mergers Commission decided not to interfere on the ground that any proposed solution would probably be worse than the problem (British Broadcasting Commission and Independent Television Publications Ltd Report (1985)). Three cases then went before the Court of First Instance in which it was argued that such a situation was a breach of Article 86 of the Treaty of Rome 1957, ie an abuse of a dominant position in that the copyright owners refused to grant licences to potential competitors (*Independent Television Publications Ltd v Commission of the European Communities* (1991), *Radio Telefis Eireann v Commission of the European Communities* (1991), (the '*Magill*' case, so named after the Irish publisher), and *British Broadcasting Corporation v Commission of the European Communities* (1991)). It was held at first instance that there was no abuse. The '*Magill*' case then went before the ECJ, where in the Advocate-General's opinion there was no abuse under Article 86. On 6 April 1995 the judgment of the ECJ was handed down, and it upheld the decision of the Court of First Instance, and so did not follow the Advocate-General's opinion. Thus, the exercise of the copyright in the TV listings and the refusal to grant licences has been held to breach Article 86.

However, the Government had already decided to alter the law within the UK to enable other interested parties the right to publish the television information on a weekly basis.

Part I, Chapter III of the CDPA 1988 contained provisions for permitted acts in ss 28-76. As originally published there were no provisions within this Part which allowed third parties to publish programme listings for broadcasts or cable programme services. In accordance with the Paris revision of the Berne Convention which the UK ratified on 2 January 1990, changes were introduced. The exact nature of these changes was somewhat unusual in that instead of simply amending the CDPA 1988, the Broadcasting Act 1990 made provisions that were to be considered as to be included in Part I, Chapter III of the CDPA 1988, ie permitted acts (BA 1990 Schedule 17 para 7(1)), and yet remained contained within the BA 1990 s 176

8.12.1   The provisions in the Broadcasting Act 1990

and Schedule 17, and so this Act did not formally insert any supplementary sections into the CDPA 1988.

The new provisions effect not only existing works, but also works which have yet to come into existence (BA 1990 Schedule 17 para 7(3)). The provisions came into effect on 1 March 1991, save that for listings which relate to programmes which are to be aired on or after that date then the provisions had effect from 1 January 1991 (Broadcasting Act 1990 (Commencement No 1 and Transitional Provisions) Order 1990 Article 5).

8.12.2   The duty to provide advance information about programmes

The person who provides a programme service (BA 1990 s 176(7)) must provide certain information to a person who wishes to publish that information (s 176(1)). This information includes the title of the programmes, and the time of transmission (s 176(2)), but does not apply to advertisements (s 176(8)). The scheme operates by way of a compulsory licence which the publisher must be granted by the provider of the programmes service (Schedule 17 para 2), regardless of whether that provider has assigned the copyright in the works which contain the programme information (Schedule 17 para 1). A prospective publisher must give reasonable notice to the provider of the service (Schedule 17 para 3). If the provider of the service refuses to grant a licence, or only offers one on terms which the prospective publisher considers unreasonable, then, after the expiry of the notice period given by the publisher, he may still publish without infringing copyright so long as he pays what the publisher considers to be a reasonable royalty (Schedule 17 para 4). Any dispute is to be settled by the Copyright Tribunal (Schedule 17 para 5 and 6).

8.13   The right to use sound recordings in broadcasts and cable programmes

The Broadcasting Act 1990 amended the CDPA 1988 in another extensive manner by inserting seven sections within Part I Chapter VII, that are concerned with copyright licensing. The new sections are 135A-135G and concern the use as of right of sound recordings in broadcasts and cable programme services. These new provisions came into force on 1 February 1991 (Broadcasting Act 1990 (Commencement No 1 and Transitional Provisions) Order 1990 Article 4).

The Phonographic Performance Ltd (the 'PPL') imposed certain constraints on the amount of time that a sound recording could be used in a broadcast or cable programme (the 'needletime'). The Monopolies and Mergers Commission reported on the issue (Collective Licensing 1988), and recommended that the needletime restrictions be removed and that a licence system similar to that proposed for the advance publication of television listings be instigated. Broadly, these recommendations have been incorporated into the CDPA 1988 as ss 135A-135G by the BA 1990 s 175, and follow the same format as the provisions contained in the BA 1990 Schedule 17.

There are no statutory defences to copyright infringement under the CDPA 1988. Under the CA 1956 there was only one, which was contained in s 9(8). However, case law has developed a number of common law defences to copyright infringement.

8.14   Introduction to defences

The principal common law defence concerns the principle of non-derogation from grant, which was developed in *British Leyland Motor Corporation Ltd v Armstrong Patents Co Ltd* (1986). This states that a copyright owner cannot derogate from the grant of his licence to a purchaser in such a way that the use of the copyrighted article is restricted so as to reduce the efficacy of that article.

Another common law principle concerns those works which are denied protection because of public policy. The CDPA 1988 makes explicit provision that nothing in Part I of the CDPA 1988 affects any rule of law preventing or restricting the enforcement of copyright on the grounds of public interest or otherwise (s 171(3)).

Section 97(1) provides that where in an action for copyright infringement it is shown that at the time of the infringement the defendant did not know, and had no reason to believe, that copyright subsisted in the work to which the action relates, the plaintiff is not entitled to damages against him, but this is without prejudice to any other remedy, ie an injunction. From the wording of this section, it would appear that an account of profits could be awarded against such an innocent defendant. This, though, would seem to go against the spirit of the section that the defendant should not suffer any financial penalty for his wrong-doing. Thus, in such a case the court is likely, in the exercise of its discretion, not to award an account of profits. To avail himself of this section, a defendant has to show that he had no reason to believe copyright subsisted in the allegedly infringed work. This is a high hurdle to overcome because, in any commercial setting, a defendant would be expected to be aware of the existence of copyright and hence he could reasonably be expected to check specifically for any article about which he did not definitely know.

The reverse side to excusing an innocent defendant from damages is contained in s 97(2), which states that if the infringement is 'flagrant' then additional damages may be imposed on the defendant.

8.15 Subject matter not protected on the grounds of public policy

The courts themselves have on a few occasions denied relief to a plaintiff when the subject matter of the dispute was held to be libellous, immoral, obscene, scandalous or irreligious, or that the work involved the deception of the public. Thus, copyright subsists, but the courts will decline to help the aggrieved party on the grounds of public policy (*Attorney-General v Guardian Newspapers (No 2)* (1988)).

The bulk of the cases arose in the 19th century when the judiciary were more protective of the sensibilities of the public. For example, the irreligious poem *Cain* by Lord Byron was denied protection (*Murray v Benbow* (1822)), as was a book of memoirs which was held to be both libellous and obscene (*Stockdale v Onwhyn* (1826)). The last work concerned the memoirs of Harriette Wilson, the celebrated courtesan, the opening sentence of which read 'I will not say how, or why, I became at 15 the mistress of the Earl of Craven'! The Earl later became the Duke of Wellington, and it is of this work that His Grace said 'Publish and be damned'.

Nowadays, the work would have to be considered grossly immoral before the courts would refrain from assisting a wronged plaintiff (*Stephens v Avery* (1988)). In *Whitehouse v Lemon* (1979), which concerned an alleged blasphemous libel, it was held that one could attack a religion so long as it was not done in an offensive manner.

The early case law reflected the views of Lord Eldon, who thought it best to deny protection to works that contained antisocial material. Thus, for example, the owner of the copyright of the allegedly libellous poem 'Wat Tyler' was denied both damages and an injunction when the poem was plagiarised (*Southey v Sherwood* (1817)). This led to the rather unfortunate consequence that cheap copies of the poem were circulated unrestrained all over the country. It would seem more appropriate to deny the plaintiff of such a work damages, and so demonstrate the displeasure of the court in the work, but to grant an injunction in order to prevent the work becoming freely available.

A different facet of public policy for denying relief is where the plaintiff has deceived the public. In the case of *Wright v Tallis* (1845) the plaintiff falsely claimed that the work was the translation of an eminent German scholar in order to enhance the sales of his work. His action failed against the defendant who successfully pleaded the fraud on the public as a defence. In *Slingsby v Bradford Patent Truck and Trolley Co* (1905) the plaintiff had issued a brochure to the public that contained illustrations of various trucks, trolleys and barrows. The brochure prominently indicated that he held valid patents on the items in question. In fact the plaintiff did not hold any English patents for the articles in question. When the defendant copied the brochure, the plaintiff was refused an injunction on the grounds that he had intended to deceive the public.

Infringement only occurs if a restricted act is performed without the licence of the copyright owner (s 16(2)). Any licence made before 1 August 1989, will continue to have like effect after that date (Schedule 1 para 25(1)). It is for the plaintiff to prove that the act was done without a licence Normally, in order to avoid liability, a licence is taken explicitly, for example, the licence that accompanies a computer program which allows the purchaser to use the program.

8.16   Licence

On occasions the licence that accompanies the product is plain and purports to restrict the activities of the purchaser. However, some such terms and conditions are void. For example, any term or condition that purports to prohibit a purchaser of a computer program from using any device or means to observe, study or test the functioning of the program in order to understand the ideas and principles which underlie any element of the program is void (CDPA 1988 s 296A(1)(c) as inserted by Copyright (Computer Program) Regulations 1992 reg 11). In such a case, the offending term is struck out and in its place there will be an implied term which will allow such activities by the purchaser.

In other circumstances there may be no licence agreement at all when the work is purchased. For example, in the case of a knitting pattern, it is suggested that there is an implied licence that the pattern may be worked domestically so as to produce the knitted garment, but that it cannot be worked commercially so as to produce large numbers of knitted garments corresponding to that pattern (*Roberts v Candiware* (1980)).

It has been held arguable that there is an implied licence for quotations from third parties printed in one newspaper to be reproduced by another newspaper (*Express Newspapers (UK) Ltd v News (UK) Ltd* (1990)). There is an implied licence from the author of a letter to the Letters Editor of a newspaper to publish the letter. This is necessary to give business efficacy to the arrangement, for publication is the purpose for which the letter was written.

Generally, if a work is produced in response to a request and the agreement is such that the copyright remains with the creator and does not pass to the commissioner, then there is an implied licence that the commissioner may use the work in a manner to give effect to the understanding between the parties at the time of the contract (*Ironside v HM Attorney-General* (1988)). The acts that may be performed under the licence depend upon the circumstances of the particular case. For example, where an architect is commissioned to produce some plans for a building, and yet retains the copyright, there is an implied licence that the commissioner and his successors in title may construct a building in accordance with the plans (*Blair v Osborne & Tomkins* (1971)).

8.17 Non-derogation from grant

By analogy with patent law, it was assumed that the owner of an object in which copyright subsisted, yet which he himself did not own, was nevertheless entitled to reproduce spare parts so that the original object could be repaired. This operated by way of an implied licence from the copyright owner. The purchaser could not remake the item totally (*Sirdar Rubber Co Ltd v Wallington, Weston & Co* (1907)). However, he could replace parts to prolong the useful life of the purchased article (*Solar Thomson Engineering Co Ltd v Barton* (1977)). Not only could the purchaser make the spare parts himself, but he could engage someone else to make them, so long as the spare parts were not copied from the original plans, but rather that they were the product of reverse engineering, that is to say that the spare part was designed by the repairer so as to fit in with the rest of the article (*Weir Pumps Ltd v CML Pumps Ltd* (1984)). Furthermore, a small stock of spare parts could be made at any one time in order to provide for future needs of the repairer (*Hoover plc v George Hulme Ltd* (1982)).

However, there were limits on what could be done in anticipation of the needs of the general public for spare parts that would need replacing. Thus, this implied licence did not allow an independent third party to make spare parts purely to supply the replacement needs of those people who had purchased the item (*British Leyland Motor Corporation Ltd v Armstrong Patents Co Ltd* (1986)). The implied licence concept posed obvious problems when there was no privity of contract between the copyright owner and the purchaser of the item which required the spare part. Furthermore, even between contracting parties, an implied term may be superseded by an express term to the contrary. Thus the mechanism of an implied term was dropped by the House of Lords in *British Leyland Motor Corporation Ltd v Armstrong Patents Co Ltd* (1986), and in its place, the novel idea was proposed of the concept of non-derogation from grant. This idea was imported from land law, and is a common law principle by which the grantor may not act so as to frustrate the essence of the licence which he has granted. Thus, in this case, British Leyland, as the copyright owner of the drawings that embodied the design for car exhausts, could not use this property right to create a monopoly upon the provision of spare exhaust systems by third parties, which were in business to satisfy the legitimate needs of car purchasers.

This illustrates the classic conflict between monopoly rights and free trade, and in this case the House of Lords felt that, even though an infringement of the drawings was committed by Armstrong Patents Co Ltd, no liability should result.

Under the Treaty of Rome 1957, there are various provisions that potentially are relevant to the exercise of IPRs in the UK. These provisions are Articles 30-36, which relate to the free movement of goods, Article 85, which prohibits anti-competitive agreements that distort the market, and Article 86, which prohibits the abuse of a dominant market position. These are commonly referred to as 'Euro-defences'.

8.18   Defences available under the Treaty of Rome 1957

The most notable case concerning a Euro-defence in a copyright matter is *Radio Telefis Eireann v Commission of the European Communities* (1991) (the '*Magill*' case). There must be a connection between the alleged abuse and the jurisdiction of the UK court. In *Ransburg-Gema AG v Electrostatic Plant Systems Ltd* (1989), Aldous J stated:

> 'The nexus required is therefore that the exercise of the exclusive right as sought by the plaintiff in the pleadings would involve a breach of the Treaty. Thus, for there to be a defence under Article 86, it must be pleaded that the plaintiff is in a dominant position, and that the relief claimed would involve an abuse of that dominant position affecting trade between Member States. If such is pleaded properly and proved, the court is precluded from granting the relief, because to do so would produce a result which could be contrary to the Treaty.'

However, in *Pitney Bowes v Francotyb-Postalia GmbH* (1991), Hoffmann J said 'there is, so far as I know, no English case in which a defence under Article 86 to an action asserting intellectual property rights has actually succeeded.' In practice, the common fate of a Euro-defence is for it to be struck-out (*Digital Equipment Corp v LCE Computer Maintenance Ltd* (1992)).

It is possible in principle to refuse to grant a plaintiff an interlocutory injunction on the grounds that he is in breach of the Treaty (*Quantel Ltd v Electronic Graphics Ltd* (1990). However, in practice, such a course of action is nearly always refused (*Leyland Day Ltd v Automotive Products plc* (1993)).

Hence, to date Euro-defences have not provided a useful shield to a defendant in an IP matter, let alone a copyright matter.

Copyright: Permitted Acts and Defences

There are 49 sections which deal with permitted acts (Part I Chapter III (ss 28-76)) ie acts that save for these provisions would otherwise be an infringement of copyright.

Introduction to Permitted Acts

Chapter III only relates to the question of infringement (s 28(1)). The provisions are to be construed independently of each other (s 28(4)). Furthermore, the provisions apply equally to any adaptation of the work (s 76). It is for the defendant to show that he falls within one of the provisions in order to escape liability.

General provisions

The fair dealing of copyright material for the purpose of research or private study is permitted (s 29). What amounts to 'fair dealing' is always a matter of fact and impression (*Hubbard v Vosper* (1972)). One of the relevant considerations is whether damage to the copyright owner is likely (*Sillitoe v McGraw-Hill Books Co* (1983)).

Fair dealing and incidental inclusion

The fair dealing of copyright material for the purpose of criticism, review and news reporting is permitted, so long as there is sufficient acknowledgement (s 30(1)). The work in question may be old, but its inclusion must be necessary for the review in order to qualify (*Associated Newspapers Group plc v News Group Newspapers Ltd* (1986)).

Sufficient acknowledgement means that the work in question is identified by its title and its author (s 178).

Incidental inclusion is permitted (s 31(1)) so long as the work was not deliberately included if it was a musical work (s 31(3)).

Permitted acts with respect to educational activities are covered in ss 32-36.

Educational usage

Generally, if part of an educational instruction and the work was reproduced manually, then it is allowed (s 32(1)).

A performance before teachers and pupils is permitted (s 34(1)), but if parents are there, then probably not allowed.

Recordings of broadcasts or cable programmes are allowed (s 35(1)), so long as there is no licensing scheme under s 143 in place (s 35(2)).

1% of a work may be reproduced in any one quarter for the purpose of instruction (ss 36(1) and (2)). This allows even the most important 1% to be copied and so avoids the problem of substantiality.

Libraries and archives

The activities of libraries and archives is governed by ss 37-44, and the Copyright (Librarians and Archivists) (Copying of Copyright Material) Regulations 1989.

Copies of articles may be supplied for research or private study (s 38 (1)). Furthermore, the whole or part of a published edition may be supplied to other libraries (s 41(1)). It is permissible to copy a work in order to preserve or replace it (s 42(1)), but only if it could not be purchased (s 42(2)).

Public administration

To ensure the smooth running of government, provisions are contained in ss 45-50 that all necessary documentation is freely available. These works may be copies for the purpose of parliamentary or judicial proceedings, or reporting such proceedings (s 45).

Lawful users of computer programs

The Copyright (Computer Programs) Regulations 1992 inserted ss 50A-50C into Chapter III of the CDPA 1988. These sections implement Council Directive 91/250 EEC. Thus, it is permissible to make back-up copies by a lawful user (s 50A(1)), and this right cannot be excluded by contract (ss 50A(3) and 296A(1)(a)). Furthermore, decompilation is permissible (s 50B(1)). It is also permissible to make adaptations if necessary for lawful use (s 50C(1)), for example, to correct an error (s 50C(2)).

Typefaces

Prior to the CDPA 1988, there was doubt if copyright subsisted in a typeface *per se*, even though it had been held that copyright did subsist in a catalogue of typefaces (*Masson Seeley & Co Ltd v Embosotype Manufacturing Co* (1924)). So long as the use is in the ordinary course of typing, then it is permissible (s 54).

Miscellaneous provisions: literary, dramatic, musical and artistic works

Various miscellaneous provisions relating to primary works of copyright are contained in ss 57-65. If it is a reasonable assumption that copyright has expired in an anonymous or pseudonymous work, then it may be copied (s 57).

The abstract accompanying an article in a journal may be copied and the copy issued to the public (s 60(1)), unless there is a licensing agreement under s 143 in place (s 60).

Subsequent works of art by the same artist will not infringe previous works of his so long as he does not reproduce the main design of the earlier work (s 64).

Rental agreements (s 66) may be determined by the Copyright Tribunal. The playing of sound recordings at non-profit making societies, eg churches and WIs, is allowed (s 67).

Miscellaneous provisions: sound recordings, films and computer programs

The copyright owners of the weekly television listings prohibited others from using that information (*Independent Television Publications Ltd v Time Out Ltd* (1984)). Parliament amended the law so that there is now a duty to provide advance information about programmes (BA 1990 s 176(1) and Schedule 17). This became effective from 1 March 1991.

Broadcast and cable programme listing

Similar provisions were made for using sound recordings in broadcasts and cable programmes (CDPA 1988 ss 135A-135G inserted by the BA 1990 s 175). These provisions were effective from 1 February 1991.

The right to use sound recordings in broadcasts and cable programmes

There are no statutory defences to copyright infringement under the CDPA 1988, only common law defences.

No damages will be awarded against an infringer who did not know, or had reason to believe, that copyright subsisted in the work copies (s 97(1)).

Introduction to defences

Copyright may not be protected on the grounds of public policy; however, the copyright in the work subsists, it is just not enforced (*AG v Guardian Newspapers (No 2)* (1988)). Examples of works where the copyright was not protected include the irreligious poem 'Cain' by Lord Byron (*Murray v Benbow* (1822)); and a courtesan's indecent memoirs (*Stockdale v Onwhyn* (1826)). For a work not to be protected nowadays, it must be grossly immoral (*Stephens v Avery* (1988)).

If a work practises a deception upon the general public, then it will be deprived of protection (*Wright v Tallis* (1845)).

Subject matter not protected on the grounds of public policy

Licences made before 1 August 1989 continue to have effect (Schedule 1 para 25(1)). It is for the plaintiff to prove the lack of a licence.

An implied licence may exist, eg to reproduce a knitwear pattern domestically (*Roberts v Candiware* (1980)).

The implied licence gives effect to the understanding between the parties (*Ironside v HM Attorney-General* (1988)). An

Licence

implied licence may devolve to heirs and successors in title if that is necessary to give efficacy to the contract (*Blair v Osborne & Tomkins* (1971)).

Non-derogation from grant

By analogy with patent law, the principle of non-derogation from grant ensures the efficacy of the copyrighted article in the hands of the purchaser. There are limits: thus one cannot remake an item totally (*Sirdar Rubber Co Ltd v Wallington Weston & Co* (1907)), but one may prolong the item's useful life (*Solar Thomson Engineering Co v Barton* (1977)). The spare parts should be reverse engineered and not copied from the original drawings (*Weir Pumps Ltd v CML Pumps Ltd* (1984)). A small stock of spare parts may be accumulated (*Hoover plc v George Hulme Ltd* (1982)). It is even permissible for an independent third party to manufacture the parts in anticipation of the needs of others (*British Leyland Motor Corporation v Armstrong Patents* (1984)).

Defences available under the Treaty of Rome 1957

It is possible to plead that an act breaches an Article of the Treaty of Rome, eg the *Magill* case in which it is alleged that Article 86 is breached (*Radio Telefis Eireann v Commission of European Communities* (1991)). However, Euro-defences are treated with great sceptism in UK courts and are usually unsuccessful (*Pitney Bowes v Francotyb-Postalia GmbH* (1991)).

Chapter 9

Moral Rights

Moral rights aim to protect the reputation of an author of a creative work and also the integrity of that work. They are based upon the belief that the value of a creative work is both aesthetic in nature as well as commercial. The Court of First Instance in the combined *Magill* cases held that the essential function of copyright was 'to protect the moral rights in the work and ensure a reward for creative effort' (*Radio Telefis Eeireann v Commission of the European Communities* (1991)).

This topic of moral rights reflects the fundamentally different of approach between the legislature in the UK and those that exist on the continent that has historically been adopted concerning works in which copyright subsists. In the UK, the principal concern of the legislature is the economic exploitation of the work, and the corresponding interplay between the conflicting commercial interests of the author, other business people and the general public. On the continent, in contrast, of major importance is the acknowledgement of the creative element in the work, and the protection of the integrity of that creation. Thus, the formulation of the concept of moral rights of an author in a work preceded the development of a framework that allowed the commercial exploitation of that work. In France, these moral rights are both inalienable and perpetual; while the economic rights, which are concerned with the commercialisation of the work, may be assigned and are of limited duration. In Germany, the moral and economic rights have been formulated along the same lines so that the moral rights last as long as the economic rights. This latter situation is the minimum requirement under Article 6*bis* of the Berne Convention.

The absence of explicit legislation prior to the CDPA 1988 providing for a system of moral rights in the UK did not necessarily mean that an author was without any protection against the degradation of the integrity of his work: rather if he sought protection it had to be based upon a different cause of action.

For example, it is possible to make contractual provisions between an author and his publisher in order to safeguard the creative integrity of his work. In *Frisby v British Broadcasting Corporation* (1967), the plaintiff successfully prevented the defendant from removing a single line from his play since this amounted to a breach of the term of the contract not to make

9.1 Introduction

structural alterations to the play. The author considered the line that the defendant proposed to remove was crucial to the whole plot, and was in a sufficiently secure position to insist upon the retention of the line. However, while an established author may be able to negotiate terms that are favourable to himself, that degree of bargaining power is not available in practice to the newcomer, who is often offered a contract on a 'take it or leave it' basis.

The law of defamation has been successfully invoked to compensate an authoress for the unlicensed serialisation of her novel, in which the plot was abridged and other elements were added in order to entice readers to purchase the next edition (*Humphreys v Thomson & Co Ltd* (1905-1910)).

A film of a well-known review sketch was held to amount to passing-off, because the defendant wrongly claimed that the sketch had been written by the plaintiff (*Samuelson v Producers Distributing Co Ltd* (1931)).

It is also possible to use other causes of action such as malicious falsehood, breach of confidence, and interference with contract. Furthermore, there used to be the tort of misattribution which was introduced by the CA 1956 s 43.

9.2   Current legislation

The CDPA 1988 introduced a comprehensive system of moral rights for the first time in the UK, namely the various rights themselves (Chapter IV ss 77-89); transmission (Chapter V ss 94-95); infringement (Chapter VI s 103); and, lastly, the transitional provisions (Schedule 1 paras 22-24). These rights are often referred to by their French titles. Collectively, they are known as *les droits moraux*. The principal amongst them are *le droit de paternité* (the right of paternity, or the right to claim authorship) and *le droit au respect de l'oeuvre* (the right of integrity, or the right to object to derogatory treatment). The recognition of these two rights is required by the Berne Convention as incorporated by the Rome revision in 1928. The CDPA 1988 goes further and makes provisions for the right to prevent false attribution of a work, and the right to privacy in certain private photographs and films that have been commissioned.

In each case the right is inalienable, ie it cannot be assigned to another person (s 94). However, on the death of the author *le droit de paternité, le droit au respect de l'oeuvre* and the right to privacy in photographs may be transmitted to any specific person (s 95(1)(a)) or if there is no specific intention, then the right flows with the copyright work (s 95(1)(b)). When a work is left jointly to several heirs, then the court may appoint an administrator of the estate if the heirs cannot agree between themselves (*Maria Widmaier v Spadem* (1993)). The right to object to false attribution after the author's death is actionable by his personal representatives.

Broadly, the moral rights that have been conferred are limited to protecting the reputation of authors of literary, dramatic, musical, artistic works or directors of films. The coverage does not extend to such works as sound recordings, broadcasts, cable programmes or the typographical arrangement of a published edition in which copyright may subsist.

An infringement of a moral right is actionable as a breach of statutory duty owed to the person entitled to the right (s 103(1)).

Le droit de paternité (the right of paternity) is the principal moral right. It ensures that the author of a literary, dramatic, musical or artistic work in which copyright subsists has the right to be identified as the author (s 77(1)).

9.3   *Le droit de paternité*

This right is also extended to the director of a film in which copyright subsists, despite the fact that the director is not normally the person who is deemed to be the author of the work. The person who is deemed to be the author is the person who makes the necessary arrangements for the making of the film, and this is normally the producer, not the director, of the film (s 9(2)(a)). However, under Council Directive 93/98/EEC of 29 October 1993 the principal director of a cinematographic or audiovisual work shall be considered as its author or one of its authors (Article 2(1)).

The right of paternity applies also to adaptations of the work. In such a case, the author of the underlying work must be identified as such.

The right to identification includes not only the author's or director's real name, but also extends to the use of a pseudonym or some other particular form of identification (s 77(8)).

The author of a literary work (other than words intended to be sung or spoken with music) or a dramatic work has the right to be identified as the author whenever the work is published commercially, performed in public, broadcast or included in a cable programme service (s 77(2)(a)); or copies of a film or sound recording that include the work are issued to the public (s 77(2)(b)). The restriction to commercial publication ties the assertion of authorship to the economic exploitation of the work in question. Thus, in the UK, the moral rights have not been elevated to a point of overriding importance, and

9.3.1   When the right may be acknowledged

independence of, the economic exploitation of the work as is the case in other jurisdictions such as France.

The right similarly extends to adaptations of the original work. However, the right does not extend to public performances, broadcasting or the inclusion of the work in a cable service.

The rights conferred to the author of an artistic work are similar, and also include the situation when the work is exhibited in public (s 77(4)). However, the right does not extend to the making of an adaptation of an artistic work, because such an act *per se* is not an infringement (s 21(1)).

The author of a work of architecture in the form of a building also has the right to be identified on the building as constructed (s 77(5)). The use of the preposition 'as' is not entirely without ambiguity. The most sensible meaning is that so long as the building corresponds substantially to the architect's plans, then he should receive recognition for the building for the life-time of that building.

The director of a film has the right of paternity whenever the film is shown in public, or copies of the film are issued to the public (s 77(6)).

In all cases the assertion of authorship must be done in a clear and reasonably prominent manner so that each and every person who comes into contact with the work is likely to notice the assertion (s 77(7)).

| 9.3.2 | The right must be asserted originally |

Apart from the general requirement that the right may only be asserted when the work is being exploited commercially, the other major requirement is that the author or director must have asserted his right to be identified as the author or director as is appropriate (s 78(1)). This may be done generally or in relation to any specified act or description of acts when the copyright is assigned by including a statement to that effect (s 78(2)(a)); or by a separate instrument in writing signed by the author or director (s 78(2)(b)). The right may also be asserted in relation to the public exhibition of an artistic work by securing that the author is identified on the work, or on a frame, mount or such like (s 78(3)(a)). In all cases everyone is bound regardless of whether or not he or she has notice of the assertion, and regardless of whether or not the identifying mark is still present or visible (s 78(4)). The moral right may be asserted at any time during the duration of the right, and will be retroactive in effect. However, it is likely that any damages for infringement during the period before the right was asserted will be reduced since the court has the discretion to take into account any delay in the assertion (s 78(5)).

Even though *le droit de paternité* is generally applicable to all literary, dramatic, artistic or musical works in which copyright subsists, Parliament has limited the exact nature of the works for which it is appropriate (s 79(1)). Thus, the right does not apply in relation to computer programs, designs of a typeface, or a computer generated work (s 79(2)). In the case of computer programs it could be of great economic importance for the author that he is recognised as such. However, in a computer program of any size, it could be difficult to ascertain who wrote what.

The right does not apply to anything done by or with the authority of the copyright owner in situations where either the copyright originally vested with the author's employer, because the work was produced in the course of employment (s 79(3)(a)); or where the copyright originally vested in the employer of a director of a film (s 79(3)(b)). Moreover, s 79(3) has the effect of preventing discontented ex-employees from causing problems.

Furthermore, the right is not infringed if by an act which by virtue of a number of the sections provides that copyright is not infringed. These acts include certain of the permitted acts that relate to a copyright work such as fair dealing under s 30 (s 79(4)(a)).

These provisions are purely pragmatic in nature, as the assertion of authorship in such cases would be an undue burden on the person who is doing the permitted act, and be of little value to the author. Similarly, the right does not apply in relation to any work made for the purpose of reporting current events (s 79(5)).

In addition to the right to be acknowledged as the author of a work, the other principal moral right is the right to object to the derogatory treatment of the work (s 80(1)). There is no need to assert the second right before it may be invoked, unlike the previous right to be identified as the author, which must be asserted before it can be invoked.

For the purpose of this right, 'treatment' of a work means any addition to, deletion from, alteration to, or adaptation of, the work (s 80(2)(a)). There are, however, a number of exceptions, eg a translation of a literary or dramatic work (s 80(2)(a)(i)).

The treatment of a work is derogatory if it amounts to distortion or mutilation of the work or is otherwise prejudicial to the honour or reputation of the author or director (s 80(2)(b)). This rather broad and general provision follows the European approach to legislation. However, even though

9.3.3   Exceptions to the right

9.4   *Le droit au respect de l'oeuvre*

the provision may be considered rather broad, it is actually narrower than the corresponding provision in the Berne Convention (Article 6*bis*) that defines derogatory treatment to include 'distortion, mutilation or other modification of, or other derogatory action in relation to the work'.

Thus, under English law it would not be derogatory to place an unaltered work in a setting in which it would be scorned and subjected to contempt that would be prejudicial to the honour or reputation of the author, while under the Berne Convention such an action would infringe the author's moral rights. A potential example would be the hanging of a work of art by a well known Jewish artist in a gallery devoted to Nazi glorification of the Aryan race. This act would not amount to a *treatment* of the work and so fall outside s 80(2); however, it would amount to an *action* done in 'relation to the work' and so fall within Article 6*bis* of the Berne Convention.

| 9.4.1 | Infringement of the right |

The right to object to derogatory treatment of a literary, dramatic or musical work is infringed by a person who publishes commercially, performs in public, broadcasts or includes in a cable programme service a derogatory treatment of the work (s 80(3)(a)); or who issues to the public copies of a film or sound recording of, or including, a derogatory treatment of the work (s 80(3)(b)).

In the case of an artistic work, the right is infringed under similar circumstances, with the additional protection that a derogatory treatment of a work may not be exhibited in public nor may copies of the graphic representation of the derogatory treatment of the work be issued to the public (s 80(4)).

There is a similar provision enshrined in Canadian law. Prohibited acts include any distortion, mutilation or other modification of the work. The author of a statue, which comprised a group of 60 geese known as *Flight Stop*, objected to the addition of red ribbons to the necks of the birds. The ribbons had been attached by the owners of the statue (a shopping precinct management company) as part of the Christmas decorations. It was held that the ribbons did distort or modify the work, and that the plaintiff's belief that they made his naturalistic composition look ridiculous was reasonable under the circumstances, and hence it was prejudicial to his honour or reputation (*Snow v The Eaton Centre Ltd* (1982)).

An architect, whose building is being subjected to derogatory treatment, has the right to require that whatever identifies him as the author be removed (s 80(5)). This could cause problems if the form of identification was central to the structure of the building, for example, if the architect's initials formed a structural component. There is an increasing prevalence for the foray of large new buildings to contain a large work of art. This, however, may lead to hitherto unforeseen problems. For example, the owner of a building was prohibited from removing an unfinished sculpture which had been built into the fabric of the lobby of the building, because the process of removal would necessarily destroy parts of the work (*Carter v Helmsley-Spear Inc* (1994)).

In the case of a film, the right is infringed if the derogatory treatment of the work is shown in public or copies are issued to the public (s 80(6)). The authors of a film about the Vietnam War successfully prevented the distributor from inserting a notice which purported to explain the interpretation given in the film. The director had previously expressly forbidden the inclusion of such an explanatory notice (*SA Argos Films v Ivens* (1992)).

There are number of exceptions to the right to object to the derogatory treatment of a work (s 81(1)). The first among these, is that there is no protection for computer programs or computer generated works (s 81(2)). In the case of the latter type of work, because this, by definition, has no identifiable *human* author, and so no human feelings could be hurt by a derogatory treatment.	9.4.2 Exceptions to the right

The remaining exceptions follow similar categories to those that were excluded from the right to identification of authorship.

The right to object to derogatory treatment is not conferred on works in which the copyright originally vested with the author's or director's employer (ss 82(1)(a), unless the author was identified at the time of the relevant act (s 82(2)(a)) or had been previously identified in or on published copies of the work (s 82(2)(b)). If the right does apply, because the author was so identified, then it is not infringed if there is a sufficient disclaimer (proviso to s 82(2)).	9.4.3 Restriction to certain types of work

This is similar to secondary infringement of copyright, because there is a requirement that the person is only liable if he knows or has reason to believe that the article in which he is dealing is an infringing article (proviso to s 83). An infringing article is one that has been subjected to derogatory treatment, and has been, or is likely to be, the subject of any of the prohibited acts that are appropriate to the type of work in question.	9.4.4 Infringement of the right by dealing with an infringing article

The further acts that amount to an infringement of the right to object to derogatory treatment are (so long as the person has the requisite knowledge or belief) include, for example, possessing in the course of business (s 83(1)(a)) and, in the course of business, exhibiting in public (s 83(1)(c)).

If there has been an infringement of this right, then an injunction may be obtained to prevent the further dissemination of the adulterated work. However, if the defendant offers to insert a disclaimer that disassociates the author from the treatment of the work, then the court may refuse to grant the injunction (s 103(2)). In such a case the distribution of the altered work with the disclaimer is not prevented.

9.5   False attribution of a work

This right is the obverse to that of being identified as the author of a work. This is the only moral right that explicitly existed under the Copyright Act 1956 (namely s 43). This right is similar in many respects to the protection conferred by the tort of passing-off.

A person has the right not to have a literary, dramatic, musical or artistic work falsely attributed, either explicitly or implicitly, to him as the author (s 84(1)(a)). The same applies to the false attribution of a person as the director of a film (s 84(1)(b)).

The right is infringed by a person who issues copies to the public of a work that contains such a false attribution (s 84(2)(a)), or exhibits in public an artistic work, or a copy of it, in or on which there is a false attribution (s 84(2)(b)).

In the case of an artistic work, the right is also infringed by a person who, having the requisite knowledge or belief, in the course of business deals with a work that has been altered after the author parted with possession of it, and yet claims that the work is an unaltered work of the author (s 84(6)(a)); or deals with a copy of such a work as being a copy of the unaltered work of the author (s 84(6)(b)). Such an act would also amount to passing-off.

Not only does this right apply to the false representation that a work is by the author, but it also applies to a literary, dramatic or musical work that is falsely represented as being an adaptation of the work of a person (s 84(8)(a)); and to a copy of an artistic work that is falsely represented as being a copy made by the author of the artistic work (s 84(8)(b)).

This right is also infringed by any false statement as to the authorship of a work of joint authorship, and by the false attribution of joint authorship in relation to a work of sole authorship, and such a false attribution infringes the right of every person to whom authorship of any description is, whether rightly or wrongly, attributed (s 88(4)). Thus, if a person is described as a sole author of a work, when in fact he is a joint author, then both he and the unacknowledged co-author may sue for infringement of moral rights.

This is the first example of a genuine privacy law in the UK. Its ambit is, however, strictly limited. In the case of a photograph, the author is the person who created it (s 9(1)), which is the actual photographer. There are many domestic occasions where a professional photographer may be commissioned to record the event for the family, eg a wedding or graduation. In these circumstances the interests of the copyright owner may conflict with those of the commissioner, especially if the latter is famous. This right is intended to regulate this conflict.

The right lasts so long as copyright still subsists in the photograph, which may be after the death of the commissioner, in which case the right may be exercised by his personal representatives, or to another person explicitly nominated (s 95(1)).

Section 85 delineates this limited right of privacy for photographs. When the taking of a photograph, or the making of film, was commissioned for private and domestic purposes, then the commissioner has the right to stop copies of the resulting work being issued to the public (s 85(1)(a)); or being exhibited or shown in public (s 85(1)(b)); or being broadcast or included in a cable programme service (s 85(1)(c)).

There are various exceptions that are provided for by subsection 85(2). They, in essence, tie the right to privacy to the copyright that may subsist in the work. So, the performance of some of the permitted acts provided for by Part I Chapter III of the CDPA 1988 does not constitute an infringement of the right to privacy.

However, this right does not protect a person against the misuse of all photographs of him. Thus, when two well known actors had had photographs of their faces superimposed on photographs of scantily clad bodies positioned in a pornographic stance, no remedy was available to prevent the publication of the resultant composite picture (*Charleston v News Group Newspapers Ltd* (1994)). The decision rested upon the fact that in the article, which followed the pictures, it stated that they were the unwitting stars of a sordid computer game which was available to their fans and that the plaintiffs themselves knew nothing about it. The addition of the written explanation distinguished the case from *Tolley v JS Fry & Sons Ltd* (1931), in which a caricature in an advertisement of an amateur golfer was published in a manner that indicated that he was being paid for advertising the defendant's products, namely a chocolate bar. In both cases, the issue of defamation was important. However, the former case of *Charleston v News Group Newspapers Ltd* (1994) illustrates the limitations of s 85, namely that the original photographs must have been *commissioned* before the right comes into operation. In this case, the photographs were the result of a freelance photographer and thus did not fall within the ambit of s 85.

Lastly, in respect of this right, it should be noted that the commissioner of the photograph, ie, the person who can exercise the right, does not have to be the subject of the photograph. This, potentially, could lead to a conflict between the commissioner and the person photographed.

9.7 **Duration of the rights and their application to the work**	The rights to be identified as the author or director conferred under s 77, the right to object to derogatory treatment conferred under s 80, and the right to privacy in certain photographs conferred under s 85 continue to subsist so long as copyright subsists in the work (s 86(1)). However, the right to object to false attribution conferred under s 84 continues to subsist for 20 years after the person's death (s 86(2)). Thus, for literary works and such like, this is shorter than the period for which copyright subsists in the work, but for films it may be longer, especially if the film was made by a director when he was young and he then lived for more than 30 years after it was released (s 13(1)).

Interestingly, the act does not use the expression '20 years after the end of the calendar year in which the person died'. Thus, the exact date of death may be relevant. |
| **9.8** **Consent and waiver of moral rights** | The person entitled to any of the moral rights detailed above may consent to particular acts that would otherwise infringe his rights, and in which case any such acts would not constitute an infringement (s 87(1)).

Furthermore, any of these rights may be waived by instrument in writing signed by the person giving up the right (s 87(2)). The waiver may be specific or general (87(3)(a)), and may relate to present or future works, and may be revocable (s 87(3)(b)).

The general principles of the law of contract and estoppel are explicitly not excluded from the operation of an informal waiver or other transaction in relation to these moral rights (s 87(4)). Thus, even though s 87(2) mentions a signed written instrument, the law of estoppel could operate to provide a defence in the case of a purely oral assurance by the person whose rights are affected, or even by delay or acquiescence.

In the case of joint ownership of photographs, the consent of all the parties must be obtained before an exclusive licence |

agreement may be agreed upon *(Mail Newspapers plc v Express Newspapers plc* (1987)).

The right to be identified as the author under s 77 and the right to privacy of certain photographs or films apply in relation to the whole of the work, or to any substantial part of the work (s 89(1)). Presumably, substantiality will be decided in the same way as it is with the infringement of copyright. However, the right to object to derogatory treatment, conferred under s 80, and the right to object to false attribution apply not only to the whole work, but also in relation to *any* part of the work (s 89(2)). The general principle of *de minimus* must apply, because, taken strictly, if any phrase from a copyright work is taken and then treated in a derogatory manner or not attributed correctly, objection could be taken by virtue of this section.

9.9   Application of moral rights to part of the work

The transitional provisions that concern the exercise of moral rights are contained in Schedule 1 paras 22-24. The Act is not retrospective, and thus no act that takes place before 1 August 1989 is actionable (para 22(1)); however, s 43 of the CA 1956, which is concerned with the false attribution of authorship, continues to have effect with regard to acts that took place before 1 August 1989 (para 22(2)).

9.10   Transitional provisions for the exercise of moral rights

The right to be identified as the author under s 77 and the right to object to derogatory treatment under s 80 do not apply to literary, dramatic, musical or artistic works where the author died before 1 August 1989 (paras 23(1) and 23(2)(a)); nor do they apply in relation to any film produced before that date (para 23(2)(b)). Thus, an old film may be altered in a manner to which the author objects, for example, by cutting scenes or colouring a black and white film. Nor do the rights apply to existing works where the copyright first vested in a person other than the author (para 23(3)(b)).

The right to privacy of certain photographs and films conferred under s 85 does not apply to photographs or films made before 1 August 1989 (para 24).

Apart from these restrictions the moral rights introduced by the CDPA 1988 apply to all relevant works that are in existence on 1 August 1989, and, of course, to all relevant works created after that date.

Moral Rights

Before the introduction into the UK of moral rights by the CDPA 1988 the author of a work was able to gain some protection by means of contract *(Frisby v British Broadcasting Corporation* (1967)): the tort of defamation *(Humphreys v Thompson* (1905-1910)); and the tort of passing off *(Samuelson v Producers Distributing Co Ltd* (1932)). The tort of misattribution of a work already existed in s 43 of the CA 1956, and still applies to old works.

Introduction

The CDPA 1988 introduced three new moral rights in UK law, and continued the exercising of the right against misattribution contained originally in CA 1956 s 43. The rights themselves are detailed in ss 77-89; the transmission of those rights covered in ss 94-95; the infringement of those rights dealt with in s 103; and lastly, the transitional provisions are contained in Schedule 1 paras 22-24.

Current legislation

The rights may be transmitted on death to any specific person (s 95(1)(a)); but if there is no specific intention, then they flow with the copyright work (s 95(1)(b)).

Le droit de paternité (the right of paternity) is contained also in Article 6*bis* (1) of the Berne Convention. In addition to the author of literary, dramatic, musical or artistic work having the right, the principal director of a film is to be considered as its author or one of is authors and so is entitled to this right as well (Article 2(1) of the Council Directive 93/98/EEC.

Le droit de paternité

In a work in which the right to be identified as the author has been asserted, then the author must be acknowledged as such when the work is issued to the public (s 77(2)).

When the right may be acknowledged

The assertion of authorship must be clear and in a reasonably prominent manner (s 77(7)).

The right must be asserted originally before the right may be exercised against a person who has not complied (s 78).

The right must be asserted originally

Computer programs, designs of a typeface, and computer generated works are all excluded from the protection conferred by s 77 (s 79(2)). Furthermore, the right may not be exercised if the copyright was originally vested with the

Exceptions to the right

author's employer (s 79(3)(a)). Moreover, there are a number of permitted acts that also do not infringe the moral right (s 79(4)), nor does reporting current events (s 79(5)).

Le droit au respect de l'oeuvre

Le droit au respect de l'oeuvre (the right of integrity), is the right to object to derogatory treatment (s 80).

Treatment is defined as including an addition to, deletion from or alteration to or adaptation of the work (s 80(2)(a)).

Exceptions include a translation of a literary or dramatic work (s 80(2)(a)(i)).

Infringement of the right

Infringing acts include performance in public (s 80(3)(a)), and issuing to the public (s 80(3)(b)).

The addition of red ribbons to the necks of a group of geese that formed a naturalistic statue entitled *'Flight Stop'* was held to amount to derogatory treatment (*Snow v The Eaton Centre Ltd* (1982)).

The right has been successfully invoked in order to prevent the insertion of an explanatory notice in a film about the Vietnam War (*SA Argos Films v Ivens* (1992)).

Exceptions to the right

There is no protection for computer programs or computer generated works (s 81(2)).

Restriction to certain types of work

The right does not apply if the copyright was originally vested with the author's employer (s 82(1)(a)). Furthermore, there is no infringement of the right if there is a sufficient disclaimer (proviso to s 82(2)).

Infringement of the right by dealing with an infringing article

This is similar to secondary infringement of copyright, because there is a requirement for knowledge, namely the defendant must have reason to believe that the article being dealt in is an infringing article (proviso to s 83). For example, it is an offence to possess a derogatory treatment of a work in the course of business (s 81(1)(a)). An injunction may be refused if a sufficient disclaimer is inserted (s 103(2)).

False attribution of a work

There is a right to prevent the false attribution, either explicitly or implicitly, as the author of a work (s 84(1)(a)). This right is infringed by issuing copies to the public (s 84(2)(a)); or by exhibiting an artistic work (s 84(2)(b)).

False claims of sole or joint authorship are actionable by all parties concerned (s 88(4)).

Copyright in a photograph is owned by the person who created it (s 9(1)). However, the right to privacy of domestic photographs is exercisable by the person who commissioned the photographs (s 85). There are limited exceptions to the exercise of this right, and they relate to permitted acts contained in Part I Chapter III (s 85(2)). Other courses of action may be available, eg defamation (*Tolley v Fry* (1930)). However, this may sometimes be avoided by written disclaimer (*Charleston v News Group Newspapers Ltd* (1994)).

Right to privacy of certain photographs and films

Rights under ss 77, 80 and 85 last so long as copyright subsists in the work (s 86(1)).

The right to object to false attribution, granted under s 84, lasts for 20 years after the person's death (s 86(2)).

Duration of the rights and their application to the work

Consent may be given to particular acts that would otherwise infringe rights, and in such cases there would be no infringement (s 87(1)).

Any of the rights may be waived by an instrument in writing signed by the person giving up the right (s 87(2)). The waiver may be specific or general 87(3)(a)), and may relate to present or future works, and may be revocable (s 87(3)(b)). The general principles of contract and estoppel are explicitly not excluded (s 87(4)).

Consent and waiver of moral rights

Sections 77 and 85 rights apply to the whole, or to any substantial part, of the work (s 89(1)).

Sections 80 and 84 rights apply to whole of the work, or to any part of the work (s 89(2)).

Application of moral rights to part of the work

The CDPA 1988 Act is not retrospective with regard to the moral rights. Thus no act done before 1 August 1989 is actionable (Schedule 1 para 22(1)). However, acts that fall within the CA 1956 s 43 done before 1 August 1989 are still actionable (para 22(2)).

Sections 77 and 80 do not apply where the author died before 1 August 1989 (para 23(1) and 23(2)(a)), or to any film produced before that date (para 23(2)(b)).

Section 85 does not apply to photographs or films made before 1 August 1989 (para 24).

Transitional provisions for the exercise of moral rights

Chapter 10

Rights in Performance

Copyright in a literary, dramatic or musical work does not subsist until that work is recorded in some manner (s 3(2)). Thus, if a musician improvises, for example, at a live stage show, then no copyright work of which he is the author will come into existence. A member of the audience may, however, make a sound recording of that performance, and that person would be the author, and hence first owner, of the copyright which subsists in that recording. This could result in the unsatisfactory situation whereby the musician has no copyright in the work relating to his live performance, while the member of the audience has the copyright in the sound recording, even if that recording was made illicitly.

Prior to the CDPA 1988, the protection that had been granted to performers had been piecemeal in nature. The CDPA 1988 introduced into the UK the first comprehensive scheme of protection. This area of law has also been heavily influenced by European legislation in the form of Council Directive 92/100/EEC on rental and lending rights of certain copyright works. Interestingly, there are no special provisions for joint performances that would marry with the concept of joint authorship in copyright.

The CDPA 1988 s 303(2) and Schedule 8 repealed all the previous legislation that pertained to this area. Entirely new legislation was enacted in Part II of the CDPA 1988 (ss 180-212) and Schedule 2. Section 180(1)(a) confers civil rights on a performer by requiring that his consent is given to the exploitation of his performances; while s 180(1)(b) confers civil rights on the person having the recording rights to a performance; these latter rights extend to recordings made without the consent of the person having the recording right or the consent of the performer. Furthermore, if these rights are violated by dealing with, or using, illicit recordings, then a criminal offence is committed.

In addition to the domestic legislation contained in the CDPA 1988, the Council Directive 92/100/EEC on rental and lending rights in certain copyright works has a great bearing upon the rights of performers. This Directive came into force from 1 July 1994 (Article 15(1)).

10.2.1	Definition of performance and recording	The term 'performance' is defined in Part II to mean a dramatic (which includes dance and mime) or musical performance, or a reading or recitation of a literary work, or a performance of a variety act or any similar presentation, which is, or so far as it is, a live performance given by one or more individuals (s 180(2)). This definition of 'performance' is different from that contained in Part I of the CDPA 1988, which is concerned with primary infringement of copyright by the performance of a work (s 19(2)). The differences may be accounted for by the different functions that the two sections are aiming to achieve. In the case of copyright, 'performance' is being defined for the purpose of infringement; while, in the case of rights in performances, the word needs to be defined in order to delineate the subject matter of the protection conferred.

The term 'recording' is defined to include any film or sound recording made directly from the live performance or made from a broadcast of the performance, or made directly or indirectly from another recording of the performance (s 180(2)).

10.2.2	Rights conferred	The rights conferred are retrospective, ie they apply to performances that took place before 1 August 1989; however, it is not possible to sue for any act done before that date, or even acts done after that date if the later acts were done in pursuance of arrangements made before then (s 180(3)). In essence this is the sum of the transitional provisions.

The rights conferred by Part II of the CDPA 1988 are totally independent from any other right that may subsist in the performance, eg copyright or moral rights (s 180(4)). An infringement of any of the rights conferred by Part II are actionable as a breach of statutory duty (s 194). Furthermore, rights in a performance may arise where there is no copyright in the work; however, it should be noted that the illicit recording of an improvised performance would generate a work in which copyright would subsist, namely the sound recording, the copyright of which would be owned by the person responsible for making the recording.

10.2.3	Council Directive 92/100/EEC	Council Directive 92/100/EEC is concerned with rental and lending rights of certain copyright works. One of its aims is to overcome the piracy of videos and phonograms. The Directive grants the right to authorise or prohibit the rental or lending of originals and copies of copyright works (Article 1(1)). 'Rental' is defined as 'making available for use, for a limited time and for direct or indirect economic or commercial advantage (Article 1(2); while 'lending' is defined as 'making available for

use for a limited period of time and not for direct or indirect economic or commercial advantage, when it is made through establishments which are accessible to the public' (Article 1(3)). These rights shall not be exhausted by any sale or other act of distribution of originals or copies of copyright works (Article 1(4)).

The Directive grants the exclusive right to authorise or prohibit rental and lending to the performer in respect of fixations of his performance (Article 2(1)), but this right may be transferred, assigned or subject to the granting of contractual licences (Article 2(4)). However, where such a transmission of the rights has occurred, the performer shall retain the right to obtain an equitable remuneration for the rental (Article 4(1)), and this right cannot be waived (Article 4(2)).

The Directive grants the exclusive right to performers to authorise or prohibit the fixation of their performances (Article 6(1)); the direct or indirect reproduction of their performances (Article 7(1)); the broadcasting by wireless means of their performances (Article 8(1)); and the distribution of their performances, including copies thereof (Article 9(1)).

Transitional provisions are contained in Article 13, which states that the Directive shall apply without prejudice to any acts of exploitation performed before 1 July 1994 (Article 13(2)).

Even though performance rights are independent of any copyright or moral rights that may accrue, they share certain common features. Thus, there is a need for the performance to be a qualifying performance by virtue of it being performed by a qualifying individual or by virtue of it taking place in a qualifying country (s 181).	**10.3 Qualifying performances**

Section 206(1) defines a qualifying country as meaning the UK, or another member of the European Union; or any other country designated by an Order in Council under s 208. Such an Order in Council has been made which is entitled the Performances (Reciprocal Protection) (Convention Countries) Order 1994. A qualifying individual is a citizen or subject of, or an individual resident in, a qualifying country; while a qualifying person is either a qualifying individual or a body corporate formed under the laws of a qualifying country or having substantial business in a qualifying country. It may readily be appreciated that this definition is similar to that for copyright protection: the wording is not identical, but the import is.

10.4 Infringement of the rights in a performance

The acts that amount to an infringement are delineated in ss 182-184 and 186-188.

10.4.1 Consent required for recording or live transmission

A performer's rights are infringed by a person who, without his consent makes, otherwise than for his private and domestic use, a recording of the whole or any substantial part of a qualifying performance (s 182(1)(a)); or broadcasts live, or includes live in a cable programme service, the whole or any substantial part of a qualifying performance (s 182(1)(b)). If the person believed on reasonable grounds that consent had been given, then he would not be liable for any damages (s 182(2)). If the copies were originally made for private use and thus avoid liability, that protection would be lost once the copies were dealt with commercially. Thus, it is an infringement to barter with copies made for private use (*Helliwell v Piggott-Sims* (1980)).

The acts of infringement described in s 182 are equivalent to primary acts of infringement of copyright, in that there is no requirement for any *mens rea* in order for liability to arise.

There is a similarity between copyright and the rights in a performance, because in each case the whole or a substantial part of the whole must be appropriated by the alleged infringer before liability is imposed. The test of substantiality is likely to be identical to that in copyright actions, and so will not depend on the quantity of what has been taken, but rather the quality. Potentially, this could be as little as one song in a whole show, if that song was sufficiently pre-eminent.

10.4.2 The use of the recordings without consent

A performer's rights are also infringed by a person who, without his consent, shows or plays in public the whole or any substantial part of a qualifying performance (s 183(a)); or broadcasts or includes in a cable programme service the whole or any substantial part of a qualifying performance (s 183(b)) by means of a recording which was, and which that person knows or has reason to believe was, made without the performer's consent.

10.4.3 Dealing with illicit recordings

An illicit recording is a recording of the whole or any substantial part of a performance if it was made, otherwise than for private purposes, without the consent of the performer (s 197(2)).

The recording could have been made anywhere in the world (s 197(6)). If a person knows or has reason to believe that the recording is illicit, he infringes the performer's rights if he imports it into the UK otherwise than for his private and domestic use (s 184(1)(a)); or in the course of business possesses, sells or lets for hire, offers or exposes for sale or hire or distributes an illicit recording (s 184(1)(b)). If the alleged offender innocently acquired the illicit recording, ie he did not know and had no reason to believe that it was an illicit recording (s 184(3)), then the only remedy available against him is damages not exceeding a reasonable payment in respect of the act of which complaint is made (s 184(2)).

The requirement of the requisite knowledge or belief that a recording was illicit before a person is liable under s 184, is akin to the requirement of knowledge or belief that a copy was an infringing copy under the acts that amount to secondary infringement of copyright. Notice that even though there was a *mens rea* element to the offence under s 183, this extended only so far as the lack of consent, and the recording in question need not necessary be an illicit copy as defined by s 197(2).

The role of consent in performance rights is similar to that played by the role of a licence agreement in copyright infringement. In *Rickless v United Artists Corporation* (1987) the defendant had used clips and out-takes from some of the *Pink Panther* films in order to produce a new composite film. The court held that the plaintiff had not consented to this use of the film clippings, but had only agreed to the production of the original films in the form contemplated at the time of the original agreements.

10.5   Consent

Liability under s 183 does, however, depend upon the alleged offender knowing or having reason to believe that the performer has not given his consent. The offence under s 183 may be committed by a person who has acquired a recording from a third party who made that recording without the consent of the performer, but for purely domestic use, and so the making of the recording itself did not fall within s 182(1)(a) initially. Only subsequently, when the recording was played with the requisite knowledge, would an offence be committed under s 183. The burden of proof as to the lack of knowledge or belief that the recording was made without consent rests with the plaintiff, as this forms a component part of the offence that must be alleged and so proved.

Under the old law the person who had the exclusive recording rights for a performer had no rights *vis-à-vis* the person who made a unofficial recording of a performance (*RCA Corporation v Pollard* (1983)). The situation under the CDPA 1988 is different.

10.6   Recording rights

An exclusive recording contract means a contract between a performer and another person under which that person is entitled to the exclusion of all other persons (including the performer) to make recordings of one or more of the

10.6.1   Qualification for recording rights

performances with a view to commercial exploitation of the same (s 185(1)). Recording rights are conferred on a person who is party to an exclusive recording contract to which the performance is subject, or an assignee of such a person, and who is a qualifying person (s 185(2)). If the person party to the exclusive recording contract is not a qualifying person, then the recording right will vest in the licensee of the person, so long as the licence is to make recordings of the performance with a view to commercial exploitation and that the licensee is a qualifying person (s 185(3)).

| 10.6.2 | Infringement of recording rights |

A person infringes the rights of a person having recording rights in relation to a performance who, without his consent or that of the performer, makes a recording of the whole or any substantial part of the performance, otherwise than for his private and domestic use (s 186(1)). Similar to the situation in which the right is conferred on the performer, if the alleged offender believed on reasonable grounds that consent had been given, then no damages may be awarded against him (s 186(2)).

Interestingly, consent may be obtained from either the person having the recording rights or the performer. It is possible that the interests of the two parties may not be in unison on this matter, as is the case of an artist who has fallen out with his recording company. If, in such a situation, the artist authorised the recording of the performance, he may be in breach of his exclusive recording contract with the recording company.

A person also infringes the rights of a person having recording rights in relation to a performance who, without his consent or, in the case of a qualifying performance, that of the performer, shows or plays the whole or any substantial part of the performance (s 187(1)(a)), or broadcasts or includes in a cable programme service the whole or any substantial part of the performance (s 187(1)(b)), by means of a recording which was, and which that person knows or has reason to believe, was made without the appropriate consent. Such consent could be given by either the performer or the person who had the recording rights at that time (s 187(2)). If there was more than one person who had the recording rights relevant to the performance in question, then the consent of all of them must be obtained if the consent of the performer is not obtained. This manner of infringing a person's recording rights is similar to the infringement of a performer's rights.

Lastly, a person infringes the rights of a person having recording rights in relation to a performance when, without his consent or, in the case of a qualifying performance, the consent of the performer, he imports into the UK otherwise than for his private and domestic use, or in the course of business possesses, sell or lets for hire, offers or exposes for sale or hire, or distributes, a recording of the performance which is, and which that person knows or has reason to believe is, an illicit copy (s 188(1)(a)). If the alleged infringer was innocent then the only remedy that is available is damages not exceeding a reasonable payment in respect of the act of which complaint is made (s 188(2)).

Section 191 states that the performance and recording rights continue to subsist in relation to a performance until the end of the period of 50 years from the end of the calendar year in which the performance takes places.

10.7 Duration of performance and recording rights

Neither the performance nor recording rights are assignable (s 192(1)). The recording rights are not transmissible at all (s 192(1)). However, those of the performer are transmissible under certain circumstances. Thus, on the death of a person who is entitled to the performer's right the rights pass to such person as he may specially direct in his will (s 192(2)(a)), or if there is no such direction, then those rights are exercisable by his personal representatives (s 192(2)(b)). The personal representatives may exercise the right independently of each other (s 192(3)).

10.8 Transmission of rights

Section 189 states that those provisions contained in Schedule 2 specify acts that may be done notwithstanding the rights conferred by Part II of the CDPA 1988, and that those acts correspond broadly to certain of those specified in Chapter III of Part I, which relate to the permitted acts regarding works in which copyright subsists. At the end of each provision for a permitted act in Schedule 2, there is commonly a sub-paragraph which states that expressions used in that paragraph are to have the same meaning as those in the corresponding section for the permitted acts with regard to copyright infringement, eg the fair dealing provisions for the purpose of criticism is to be construed similarly to s 30 (Schedule 2 para 2(2)), and so on.

10.9 Permitted acts

The acts that are permitted in relation to performance and recording rights are contained in Schedule 2 paras 1-21 of the CDPA 1988. The provisions specify acts that may be done notwithstanding the rights conferred in Part II, and they only relate to the question of infringement of those rights and do not affect any other right or obligation restricting the doing of any of the specified acts (para 1(1)). No inference is to be drawn from the description of any act which may by virtue of Schedule 2 be done without infringing the rights conferred by Part II as to the scope of those rights (para 1(2)). Furthermore, each of the provisions is to be construed independently of each other (para 1(3)).

Rights in Performance

Copyright in a literary, dramatic or musical work does not subsist until the work is recorded (s 3(2)). Thus, bootleg recordings of live impromptu performances have the first copyright of the material contained in the performance.

Introduction

All previous legislation was repealed (CDPA 1988 s 303(2) and Schedule 8). The civil rights need the consent of a performer before the work is exploited (s 180(1)(a)). In addition, civil rights were created for the person having the recording rights (s 180(1)(b)).

The rental and lending rights of performers is governed by Council Directive 92/100/EEC.

Current legislation

'Performance' means any performance of a literary, dramatic, musical or artistic work (s 180(2)). Recording is defined to include any film or sound recording (s 180(2)).

Definition of performance and recording

The rights are retrospective in that they apply to performances that took place before 1 August 1989.

Infringement is actionable as a breach of statutory duty (s 194).

Rights conferred

In order to qualify, a performance must be performed by a qualifying individual or take place in a qualifying country (s 181).

Qualifying performances

The making of a recording of the whole or any substantial part of a qualifying performance without consent amounts to an infringement (s 182(1)(a)). In addition, it is also an infringement to broadcast live the whole or any substantial part of a qualifying performance (s 182(1)(b)).

It is an infringement to barter with copies made for private use (*Helliwell v Piggott-Sims* (1980)).

Infringement of the rights in a performance

It is an infringement to show or play in public the whole or any substantial part of a qualifying performance (s 183(a)), or to broadcast the whole or any substantial part of a qualifying performance (s 183(b)).

The use of the recordings without consent

Dealing with illicit recordings	Imports of illicit copies (as defined by s 197(2)) into the UK, otherwise than for private and domestic use, amount to an infringement if the importer has the requisite knowledge (s 184(1)(a)). It is also an infringement if, in the course of business, the illicit copies are possessed, sold or distributed (s 184(1)(b)). The illicit recording could have been made anywhere in the world (s 197(6)).
Consent	Consent may be general or particular in nature, and may refer to past or future performances (s 193(1)). The Copyright Tribunal may give the necessary consent (s 190(1)(b)).
Recording rights	There were no rights for the recording company under the old law (*RCA Corporation v Pollard* (1983)).
Qualification for recording rights	An exclusive recording agreement is to the exclusion of all other persons to make recordings for commercial exploitation (s 185(1)). The recording rights are granted to the party to an exclusive recording contract, and so long as he is a qualifying person (s 185(2)). If that party is not a qualifying person, then so long as the licensee of that person is a qualifying person then the rights may be granted (s 185(3)).
Infringement of recording rights	It is an infringement to make a recording of the whole or any substantial part, except for private use (s 186(1)). Consent may be obtained from either the person having the recording rights or the performer. It is also an infringement to show or play the whole or any substantial part of the performance (s 187(1)(a)); or to broadcast the whole or any substantial part of the performance (s 187(1)(b)); or to import into the UK or otherwise deal in illicit copies (s 188(1)(a)).
Duration of performance and recording rights	These rights last for 50 years from the end of the calendar year in which the performance takes places (s 191).
Transmission of rights	Neither the performance nor recording rights are assignable (s 192(1)). The recording rights are not transmissible at all (s 192(1)); however, the performers' rights are transmissible on death (s 192(2)).
Permitted acts	Permitted acts are contained in Schedule 2 paras 1-21 (s 189). They follow those acts permitted for works in which copyright submits.

Chapter 11

Industrial Designs: Copyright Protection

The protection conferred by the subsistence of copyright in an artistic work is usually for the life of the author plus 50 years from the end of the calendar year in which the author died. In the case of a work of art, such as a picture, this period of protection is not unreasonable.

However, if the artistic work is subsequently commercially exploited, then the owner of the copyright would have a disproportionally long period of protection against rival commercial interests.

The most common type of commercial exploitation of an artistic work occurs when an engineering drawing for a machine part is reproduced in three dimensions as the physical component itself. The generic term 'industrial designs' covers all artistic works that are exploited commercially. However, this term is not limited to engineering drawings and their respective machine parts, it also includes drawings for domestic items such as electric plugs, and items of fashion such as designer T-shirts, ie, any commercial exploitation of an artistic work by virtue of it being mass-produced for sale to the general public.

An idea that is capable of protection under the patent law will receive only 20 years protection. Unlike copyright protection, patent protection is an absolute monopoly in that it prevents anyone from producing the same product regardless of whether or not the other person had conceived of the idea totally independently. However, over the centuries a period of about 20 years has been deemed to confer satisfactory protection for a person who wishes to exploit an idea industrially, since this period allows enough time for the inventor to recoup his development costs, and yet does not hinder his commercial rivals unduly in the subsequent exploitation of the market.

Over the years, the legislature has endeavoured to resolve the problem of industrial designs in a number of different ways. None have been entirely satisfactory. Furthermore, the legislation involved has nearly always been rather convoluted in nature which has often resulted in unexpected ramifications. The present solution is no exception, comprising three

11.1 Introduction

11.2 Comparison with the protection afforded to patents

11.3 Early solutions for the reasonable protection of industrial designs

interdigitating systems, namely copyright *simpliciter*, design right and registered design right.

11.3.1   Registered designs

There have been various attempts by the legislative to restrict the term of protection in articles that could be exploited commercially. The design had to be registered, and so this form of protection was called 'registered design'. The protection conferred was similar to patent protection in that an absolute monopoly was granted for the designs. However, this route did not provide a complete answer as some designs are not registrable, because they did not satisfy the qualification criteria. In particular for a design to be registrable it must have 'eye-appeal' (*Amp Inc v Utilux Pty Ltd* (1972)). If a design was merely functional in nature and hence did not appeal to the eye in any aesthetic manner, it could still claim protection under the copyright laws. The result is that purely functional designs received the long term protection under copyright law, while designs that had some aesthetic merit were only granted the shorter term of protection under the registered design legislation. This was the opposite of what was desired. Thus, provisions were needed to restrict the protection conferred upon artistic works in which copyright subsisted, and yet were produced commercially.

11.3.2   Approaches under the CA 1911 and CA 1956

Under the CA 1911, artistic works were excluded altogether from having copyright protection, if they were capable of registration under the Patents and Designs Act 1907, except those designs, which though capable of being registered, were not used or intended to be used as models or patterns for industrial production (CA 1911 s 22(1)).

The CA 1956 adopted a different approach. It allowed full artistic copyright to subsist in works that would be industrially produced, but then put limits upon the acts that would constitute an infringement of the copyright when a corresponding design was registered, or if no design was registered when the design was applied industrially (s 10 (before amendment)). The limitations in essence were that after 15 years the owner lost the protection that related to the industrial application of the copyright, but kept those parts of the artistic copyright that allowed protection against non-industrial exploitation (*Dorling v Honnor Marine Ltd* (1964)).

11.3.3   Design Copyright Act 1968

The Design Copyright Act 1968 altered the situation. This Act was intended to improve the position of artistic craftsmen such as jewellery makers. The Act came into force on the 25 October 1968.

This new Act amended s 10 of the CA 1956 in such a way that full artistic copyright was granted for designs for a limited time, even if industrially produced or if a corresponding design was registered. Thus, it was possible to have both copyright and registered design protection for the same article for a limited time period (*Merchant Adventurers Ltd v M Grew & Co Ltd* (1972)).

More fully, the position of an industrially exploited work was if the design could have been registered then it was granted full artistic copyright protection for 15 years, and thereafter it was not an infringement of copyright to do any act that fell within the exclusive right of the copyright owner in the corresponding designs. However, if the design could not be registered then it received the normal full artistic copyright term of protection. If the design was registered, then it was protected under the Registered Design Act 1949, and the protection was limited to a maximum of 15 years (RDA 1949 s 8(2) before amendment).

11.3.4 Consequences of the DCA 1968

This amendment resulted in the bizarre situation where a drawing for an article that did not qualify for design registration was then entitled to full artistic copyright protection even if it was industrially exploited. This scenario arose in the case of *Interlego AG v Tyco Industries* (1988), in which Interlego initially received the benefit of the monopolistic protection afforded by having a registered design for their building bricks. When that registration expired, it then attempted to extend the protection by proposing that the registered design had been improperly granted, and that consequentially it should be entitled to the full term of artistic copyright. This argument failed to sway the court, because the courts held that the Lego building blocks, even though mainly functional in nature, did possess features that appealed to the eye. Thus, the design had been validly registered, and so copyright could not be used to provide an extension of protection.

The CDPA 1988 introduced a new form of protection, called design right, which ran alongside the protection provided by copyright and registered design. Design right is sometimes referred to as unregistered design right in order to distinguish it clearly from registered design right.

11.4 Approach of the CDPA 1988

There is an extensive series of transitional provisions in order to protect the position of the owners of the copyright in drawings that were produced before 1 August 1989. Moreover the transitional provisions dovetail these existing rights with those that would now arise under the three possible heads of protection. The relevant provisions in the CDPA 1988 are ss 51 and 52, and the transitional provisions are contained in Schedule 1 paras 19 and 20.

11.5   CDPA 1988 s 51

Section 51 reads:

'(1)   It is not an infringement of any copyright in a design document or model recording or embodying a design for anything other than an artistic work or a typeface to make an article to the design or to copy an article made to the design.

(2)   ...

(3)   In this section – 'design' means the design or any aspect of the shape or configuration (whether internal or external) of the whole or part of an article, other than surface decoration; and 'design document' means any record of a design, whether in the form of a drawing, a written description, a photograph, data stored in a computer or otherwise.'

11.5.1   Application of s 51

Section 51 applies only to drawings made after 1 August 1989, and it is an attempt to remove the dual protection which existed prior to the passing of the CDPA 1988. The removal of copyright protection is balanced by the introduction of design right which provides for the protection of industrial designs.

Section 51 does not apply to a design insofar as it consists solely of surface decoration. Accordingly, copyright is still the correct protection for things such as wall-paper designs, textiles, and for any other works that consist of surface decoration. It is possible, however, for some of these designs to be eligible for protection under the RDA 1949, but only so far as the design is for an 'article' within the meaning of that Act. It should be noted that, correspondingly, design right does not subsist in surface decoration, since this is explicitly excluded from the ambit of design right protection (CDPA 1988, s 213(3)(c)).

However, the last major exception to the operation of s 51 is for 'anything other than an artistic work'. The term 'anything' must refer to 'any article', because the section is concerned with designs for the shape and configuration of articles. Thus it may be deduced that the principal subject matter of this section is a work where the designer intended the work to be an article. For example, the drawing of a cartoon character, which is later used as the basis for a plastic three dimensional model, would not be a design to which s 51 applies, because a cartoon character is not an article. Thus the original drawing of the cartoon character would be protected by copyright, and there is no need to seek the meaning of 'artistic work'. However, if the design was intended to be for an article, then s 51 applies, unless that article is an artistic work. Accordingly, in this case the meaning of 'artistic work' needs to be examined in order to delineate the scope of this exception to s 51.

If the extensive definition of 'artistic work' contained in s 4 is applied to s 51, then *all* designs would fall within the exclusion of its operation, and so make the whole section redundant. For example, during the 1920s and '1930s, it was common to produce desktop lampstands in the form of human figures. Many of these lampstands were *very* fine sculptures. If a cast was made for a lampstand this would fall within the ambit of s 4, and so be excluded from the operation of s 51. This would be the case even if the lampstand was intended for mass-production, which covers the very scenario that Parliament was attempting to bring within the operation of s 51. Hence this interpretation of what may be meant by the term 'artistic work' in s 51 does not solve the mischief that Parliament expressly wished to overcome.

11.5.2   Artistic work

Thus, in order for this section to have any applicability, the works that are excluded as 'artistic works' must only be those works that were created with no intention of mass-production, but were only subsequently mass-produced. For example, a one-off lampstand that was designed to be unique, but, subsequently, it was mass-produced (probably in a simplified form) because of the critical acclaim that it received while on view. In this case, the one-off lampstand could reasonably be considered as an 'artistic work' and so be entitled to the full term of copyright protection.

Another way of looking at this problem is to say that a design document, regardless of what it portrays, must be an artistic work itself, because it is a drawing. However, the drawing may portray an artistic work, for example, it may be a preliminary sketch for a unique sculpture. In this case the document would be excluded from the operation of s 51.

11.5.3   Design documents

However, if the document portrays the internal workings of a clock, of which many examples were to be made, then the document would fall within the operation of s 51. If that document, however, showed the mechanical parts that were to be hand-crafted by a master clock-maker, it is arguable that the document would be for an artistic work, because the hand-made clock could be considered as a work of artistic craftsmanship, and this would extend to the internal mechanism.

Thus, in order to make the section achieve the desired aim, the intention of the designer must be relevant. Support for this interpretation is found in the use of the word 'for' in the phrase 'a design for anything', which must imply there needs to be an intention on the behalf of the author that the design is for an article, not being an artistic work.

11.6   Transitional provisions to s 51

The transitional provisions that relate to s 51 are contained in Schedule 1 para 19, which reads:

'(1)   Section 51 (exclusion of copyright protection in relation to works recorded or embodied in design document or models) does not apply for 10 years after the commencement in relation to a design recorded or embodied in a design document or model before commencement.

(2)   ...

(3)   In section 237 as it applies by virtue of this paragraph, for the reference in subsection (1) to the last five years of the design right term there shall be substituted a reference to the last five years of the period of 10 years referred to in sub-para (1) above, or to so much of those last five years during which copyright subsists.'

11.6.1   Effect of the transitional provisions

This paragraph has the effect of suspending for 10 years the operation of s 51 to designs that were made before 1 August 1989. Instead the provisions of the design right protection will be applicable. In particular, for the last five years of the protection that is conferred on the work, a licence of right will be available. This will become available for all such works from 1 August 1994 at the latest. The protection for such works will terminate on 1 August 1999 at the latest. A 'licence of right' is a concept introduced in patent legislation. It means that regardless of the wishes of the owner of the right, a person must be granted a licence to produce the article in question.

11.7   CDPA 1988 s 52

Section 52, which concerns the effect of exploitation of a design derived from an artistic work, reads:

'(1)   This section applies where an artistic work has been exploited, by or with the licence of the copyright owner, by –

(a)   making by an industrial process falling to be treated for the purposes of this Part as copies of the work, and

> (b) marketing such articles, in the UK or elsewhere.
>
> (2) After the end of the period of 25 years from the end of the calendar year in which such articles are first marketed, the work may be copied by making articles of any description, or doing anything for the purpose of making articles of any description, and anything may be done in relation to articles so made, without infringing copyright in the work.
>
> (3)-(5) ...'

Section 52 applies directly to all artistic works that were created after 1 August 1989, and were exploited after that date. It also applies to those artistic works that were created before 1 August 1989, but were not exploited until after that date (CDPA 1988 Schedule 1 para 20(2)).

Section 52 applies to artistic works that are industrially exploited. In such a case the copyright is capable of being infringed for a period of 25 years. In this section it is apparent that the artistic work has the meaning given to it by s 4. Thus, even engineering drawings and other documents that are devoid of artistic merit would, by the operation of this section alone, be capable of 25 years copyright protection. However, such documents are excluded by the operation of s 51, and thus do not fall to be considered by s 52.

Instead s 52 is concerned with two broad classes of works. The first is where the design is for the surface decoration of the article. The second class comprises works that are primarily *objet d'art*, but which are subsequently mass-produced.

The function of s 52 is to restrict the term of copyright protection to 25 years, which matches the new extended term of protection for registered designs. This restriction applies to those copyright works that have resulted in the manufacture of articles of any description.

Thus, between them, ss 51 and 52 constitute a complete system which covers the various possible ways in which a drawing in which copyright subsists may be commercially exploited. This may be illustrated as follows. An artist produces a design for a toy dinosaur with the intention that it to be mass-produced. Thus s 51 applies and only design right is available. Alternatively, the artist produces a sketch for a unique sculpture of a dinosaur. In this case, s 51 does not apply. However, subsequently, a limited edition of 250 models is produced. Now s 52 applies. The latter line of reasoning would also apply if the original sketch was later embossed

11.7.1   Application of s 52

into, say, mass-produced sweat shirts. We will now consider the idea of surface decoration in more detail.

| 11.7.2 | Surface decoration |

The question of whether or not a decoration constitutes a surface decoration is usually a straightforward issue to decide. There are, however, a number of examples that are less clear. In *Lerose Ltd v Hawick Jersey International Ltd* (1974), the defendant attempted to argue that a knitted pattern was a three dimensional work, ie not merely a two dimensional reproduction of the 'point pattern'. Whitford J said that:

> ' ... fabrics of this kind which have patterns imposed upon their surface by knitting are ... no more three dimensional objects than would be woven fabrics upon which patterns were printed.'

The consequence of this is that knitted patterns may be considered to be surface decoration, and thus s 52 would be applicable to them.

This, though, does not fully solve the problems raised by knitwear. Clearly, a painted pattern on a plate is a surface decoration, for even though the paint has a finite thickness, it can be excluded by the *de minimu's* principle. Secondly, the paint is applied to the surface of the material forming the plate and does not intermingle with that material to any significant extent. Both of these characteristics are absent in the case of a knitted jumper. The coloured wool, which forms the pattern, is also an integral part of the structure of the jumper. Secondly, the coloured pattern is not applied to the surface, but instead is interlaced throughout the structure of the garment.

Thus, even though the pattern of a knitted jumper may be appreciated as if it were merely a surface decoration, the pattern, in fact, constitutes the very fabric of the garment. If, instead of a multi-coloured knitted jumper, a single-coloured jumper is produced that bears a pattern due to the use of different types of stitches, such as, for example, an Aran sweater. It could now be argued that such a knitted pattern is actually three-dimensional, and so is *not* a surface decoration. In this analysis, it would be possible for the pattern to be protected by the operation of design right. This alternative is considered in the following chapter.

| 11.7.3 | Industrial exploitation |

The Secretary of State has made provisions pursuant to s 52(4), which are contained in the Copyright (Industrial Process and Excluded Articles) (No 2) Order 1989.

The new provisions deem that an article is industrially exploited if more than 50 examples are made (Article 2(a)(i)) so long as those articles do not form part of a set (Article 2(a)(ii)). So, for example, a canteen of cutlery would count as one set, and not as a 100 odd knives, forks *etc*. Also included are goods manufactured in lengths or pieces, not being hand-made goods (Article 2(b)), which would include such items as nuts and bolts, or lengths of curtain railing. Excluded from the scope of this Order are works of sculpture, other than casts or models used or intended to be used as models or patterns to be multiplied by any industrial process (Article 3(1)(a)); wall plaques, medals and medallions (Article 3(1)(b)); printed matter primarily of a literary or artistic character, including book jackets, calendars, certificates, coupons, dress-making patterns, greeting cards, labels, leaflets, maps, plans, playing cards, postcards, stamps, trade advertisements, trade forms and cards, transfers and similar articles (Article 3(1)(c)). Films are explicitly excluded (s 52(6)(a)), and so cartoons are not subject to these provisions. Anything excluded by the operation of Article 3(1) will thus enjoy the full term of copyright.

The transitional provisions that relate to s 52 are contained in Schedule 1 para 20, which reads:

11.8   Transitional provisions to s 52

(1)   Where section 10 of the 1956 Act (effect of industrial application of design corresponding to artistic work) applied in relation to an artistic work at any time before commencement, section 52(2) of this Act applies with the substitution for the period of 25 years mentioned there of the relevant period of 15 years as defined in section 10(3) of the 1956 Act.

(2)   Except as provided in sub-para (1), section 52 applies only where articles are marketed as mentioned in subsection (1)(b) after commencement.'

This paragraph applies to those artistic works that were made before 1 August 1989, and exploited before that date. The substitution of the term of 25 years for 15 years brings the term of protection in line with the new extended term for registered design.

Summary of Chapter 11

Industrial Designs: Copyright Protection

It was possible for certain mass-produced items to enjoy the full term of protection conferred by copyright. This exerted an undue restraint on free trade.

Introduction

Registered designs for mass produced items provides short term monopolistic protection, originally 15 years but now 25 years.

Early solutions for the reasonable protection of industrial designs

CA 1911 excluded artistic copyright if a work was capable of registration under PDA 1907, except for those works not intended for industrial production (CA 1911 s 22(1)). The CA 1956 adopted a different approach.

Approaches under the CA 1911 and CA 1956

Full artistic copyright was granted for a limited period if a corresponding design was registered (CA 1956 s 10). However, restrictions were placed upon what would constitute copyright infringement (*Dorling v Honnor Marine* (1964).

The DCA 1968 amended CA 1956 s 10 with effect from 25 October 1968. Full artistic copyright was granted for designs, but for a limited time. Thus a design could be protected by both copyright and registered design (*Merchant Adventurers v M Grew* (1972)).

Design Copyright Act 1968

If a design was registered or capable of registration, then it was granted only 15 years protection. However, if it did not qualify for registration, then it received the full term of artistic copyright protection. Registerability depended on whether or not a design had eye appeal; if it did then it could be registered under the RDA 1949 (*Interlego AG v Tyco Industries* (1988)).

Consequences of the DCA 1968

A further consequence was that a *purely* functional design received full copyright protection, while a design that was both functional and had eye-appeal only received the protection of RDA 1949. This was the opposite of what Parliament desired.

The CDPA 1988 introduced a new form of protection called design right (or unregistered design right).

The approach of the CDPA 1988

Application of CDPA s 51	Section 51 applies only to drawings made after 1 August 1989. It removes the dual protection that existed under the CA 1956 s 10 (as amended by DCA 1968). Note that design right does not subsist in surface decoration (s 213(3)(c)).
	The term 'anything' must refer to 'any article', and the intention of the author is important.
Artistic work	The full definition in CDPA 1988 s 4 cannot apply. To make sense of s 51, 'artistic works' must mean only those works not intended for mass-production.
Design documents	A design document is one that embodies a design for an article intended for mass-production.
Effect of the transitional provisions	This suspends for 10 years the operation of s 51 for designs made before 1 August 1989. For the last five years of such an old design, a licence of right is available.
Application of CDPA 1988 s 52	Section 52 applies directly to all artistic works exploited after 1 August 1989 (Schedule 1 para 20(2)). An 'artistic work' is as defined in s 4, and includes works with surface decoration, and *objets d'art*.
Surface decoration	A knitted sweater was held to be a two-dimensional work (*Lerose Ltd v Hawick Jersey International Ltd* (1974)).
Industrial exploitation	By virtue of the Copyright (Industrial Process and Excluded Articles) (No 2) Order 1989, industrial exploitation is deemed to have occurred if 50 or more examples are made (Article 2(a)). A work consists of goods manufactured in lengths or pieces, so long as it was not hand-made (Article 2(b)). Printed matter primarily of a literary or artistic character is excluded (Article 3(1)).
Transitional provisions to s 52	(1) Where section 10 of the 1956 Act (effect of industrial application of design corresponding to artistic work) applied in relation to an artistic work at any time before commencement, section 52(2) of this Act applies with the substitution for the period of 25 years mentioned there of the relevant period of 15 years as defined in section 10(3) of the 1956 Act.
	(2) Except as provided in sub-para (1), section 52 applies only where articles are marketed as mentioned in subsection (1)(b) after commencement.

Chapter 12

Industrial Designs: Design Right

Design right was introduced by the CDPA 1988 in order to solve the problem that had arisen under the old law, namely that designs for purely functional articles received the full term of copyright protection even if such articles were mass produced. In contrast, designs that contained both functional and aesthetic elements received the more limited protection conferred by the RDA 1949. Hence, Parliament introduced a new right for functional designs that would be of shorter duration than copyright. This new right is called design right.

12.1 Introduction

Design right can only subsist in designs which came into existence after 1 August 1989 (s 213(7)). Design right subsists in an original design (s 213(1)), which means any aspect of the shape or configuration (whether internal or external) of the whole or part of an article which is not commonplace (s 213(2)). However, design right does not subsist in a method or principle of construction (s 213(3)(a)); nor in the features of shape and configuration which allow the article to be connected to, or placed in, around or against another article so that either article may perform its function (s 213(3)(b)(i)); or any of those features which are dependent upon the appearance of another article of which the article in question is intended by the designer to form an integral part (s 213(3)(b)(ii)); nor does it subsist in surface decoration (s 213(3)(c)).

12.2 Subsistence of design right

The principal exceptions are called 'must fit' and 'must match', and prevent design right protection being conferred upon items such as exhaust systems which must fit the floor-pan of the underside of a given model of a car, or a spare part for a wrought-iron gate which must match the overall style of the remainder of the gate. These categories of exceptions are new, and so there are no parallels in copyright law. However, under the Registered Designs Act 1949 (as amended by the CDPA 1988 Part IV ss 265-273 and Schedule 3) there are now similar provisions.

12.2.1 Principle exceptions

The design must be original, but unlike copyright where this term is not further defined, in the case of design right a partial negative definition is given (s 213(4)). This provides that a design is not original if it is commonplace in the design field in question at the time of its creation. It would appear that a design feature that was commonplace in one area could be

12.2.2 Originality

imported into a different area, where it was unusual, and thereby confer originality.

It has been held by Aldous J in *C & H Engineering v F Klucznik & Sons Ltd* (1992) that the word 'original' should be given the same meaning as in Part I, ie not copied, but rather the independent work of the designer, and thus it should be contrasted with the requirement of novelty that is a prerequisite for a registered design.

12.2.3	Qualification

In order for design right to subsist, the designer or his employer, or the commissioner of the design must satisfy the conditions in ss 218 and 219 (s 213(5)(a)). Otherwise, the person by whom, and the country in which, the articles were first marketed must satisfy the conditions in s 220 (s 213(5)(b)). Furthermore, design right does not subsist unless and until the design has been recorded in a design document or an article has been made to the design (s 213(6)).

12.3 Designer and first owner

The designer, ie the creator (s 214(1)), is the first owner (s 215(1)), unless the design was commissioned or the designer was employed, and produced the work in the course of his employment, in which case the first owner is the commissioner or the employer respectively (s 215(2) and (3) respectively).

If the design does not qualify for protection by any of these means, but does by virtue of s 220, ie the country in which the article was first marketed, then the person who marketed the article will be the first owner of the design right (s 215(4)). These are similar provisions to the first ownership of copyright, except that a commissioner may be the first owner of the design right, but no such provision exists under copyright law.

12.4 Qualification for the subsistence of design right

Broadly, the criteria for qualification are similar to those that exist for copyright to subsist. Thus, a qualifying individual is a citizen or subject of a qualifying country, and a qualifying person is a qualifying individual or a body corporate which is formed under the laws of a qualifying country or has a place of business there which carries on a substantial amount of activity (s 217(1)).

12.4.1	Author or commissioner

A design qualifies for design right if the designer is a qualifying individual (s 218(2)), or if the design was created in pursuance of a commission from, or in the course of employment with, a qualifying person (s 219(1)). Where the design was jointly created, or commissioned, or created in the course of employment, then so long as one of the designers or commissioners or employers was a qualifying person, then the design would qualify. However, only the designer or commissioner or employer who was a qualifying person is entitled to the design right protection (ss 218(4) and 219(3)). Thus, no rights accrue to non-qualifying persons.

If the design does not qualify for protection by virtue of s 217 or s 218, ie the designer, commissioner or the employer, then the design may still receive design right protection by virtue of s 220 which concerns the place of first marketing of an article made in accordance with the design. This provision is similar to that provided under copyright law for the place of first publication of work if it had not already qualified by virtue of the author. Thus, so long as the first marketing is by a qualifying person who is exclusively authorised to put the articles on the market in the UK (s 220(1)(a)), and the marketing takes place in the UK, or the European Union, or any other country as designated under s 255, then the design will qualify for design right protection (s 220(1)(b)).

12.4.2   Place of first marketing

Design right lasts for 15 years from the end of the calendar year in which the design was first recorded in a design document, or an article was first made to the design, whichever occurred first (s 216(1)(a)). However, if the design was made available, ie publicly exploited, within the first five years, then design right only lasts for a further 10 years from the end of the calendar year in which that exploitation first occurred (s 216(1)(b)). The articles may be made available anywhere in the world, so long as it is by or with the licence of the design right owner (s 216(2)).

12.5   Duration of design right

The design right in a work may be infringed by both primary and secondary acts (ss 226 and 227 respectively). Secondary infringement, like copyright, requires the necessary knowledge as an essential element.

12.6   Infringement of design right

The rights of the owner of a design right are phrased in a similar manner to those rights that are conferred upon a copyright owner. Thus, the owner of a design right has the exclusive right to reproduce the design for commercial purposes by making articles to that design (s 226(1)(a)), or by making a design document recording the design for the purpose of enabling such articles to be made (s 226(1)(b)). This arrangement caters for both the formal design of an article whereby a design document is made before the article is made, and also the informal situation in which a designer just makes the article in question without any of the preliminaries of formal documentation (s 213(6)). The second limb of the exclusive right would then still provide protection for an

12.6.1   Protection

article, which was designed without any initial documentation, from a competitor who then produces such drawings in order to reproduce the article in question.

12.6.2 Reproduction	Reproduction means copying the design so as to produce articles that are exactly or substantially to that design (s 226(2)). Thus, the protection conferred is against copying a substantial part, which is similar to copyright protection, and not the monopolistic protection similar to that conferred on patents. Primary infringement occurs when a person, without the licence of the design right owner, authorises another to reproduce the design (s 226(3)). The reproduction may be direct or indirect, regardless of whether any intervening acts themselves infringe (s 226(4)).

Aldous J in *C & H Engineering v F Klucznik & Sons Ltd* (1992) held that the test for infringement is different from that for copyright. In the case of design right there would only be an infringement if the design is copied so as to produce articles exactly or substantially the same as the design. Thus, the test for infringement requires that the alleged infringing article be compared with the design document or article embodying the design. It is an objective test to be decided through the eyes of the person to whom the design is directed and would include not only features that strike the eye, but also ones that are functionally significant. In this case it was held that (on the counterclaim) the plaintiff's pig fenders did not infringe the defendant's design, because even though each had a tubular roll bar to protect the sow's teats from abrasion, the plaintiff's article was flared so as to allow it to be stacked when not in use.

12.6.3 Secondary infringement	Secondary infringement occurs when a person who, without the licence of the design right owner, imports into the UK for commercial purpose (s 227(1)(a)); or has in his possession for commercial purposes (s 227(1)(b)); or sells, lets for hire, or offers or exposes for sale or hire in the course of business (s 227(1)(c)) an article which is, and which he knows or has reason to believe is an infringing article. Thus, there is a requirement for knowledge or reasonable belief on behalf of the potential infringer, which is similar to the requirement for secondary infringement of copyright.
12.7 **Exceptions to rights of design right owners**	The CDPA 1988 makes various provisions in ss 236-245, whereby certain acts do not constitute infringement. These operate in a similar manner to the acts permitted under copyright (ss 28-76). These provisions restrict the ambit of design right, and so the potential defendant must plead, and

prove, the necessary conditions in order to establish protection.

The first provision removes an otherwise possible source of double jeopardy. Where copyright subsists in a work that consists of, or includes, a design in which a design right subsists, it is not an infringement of the design right in the design to do anything which is an infringement of the copyright in that work (s 236). This would cover the situation in which an artistic work is exploited industrially, and thus would be dealt with by the provisions of s 52. Correspondingly, it is not an infringement of any copyright in a design document or model recording or embodying a design for anything other than an artistic work or a typeface to make an article to the design or to copy an article made to the design (s 51(1)). In this case the protection would be that conferred by design right.

12.7.1   Conflict with copyright

Licences of right are available for the last five years of the design right (s 237(1)). Accordingly, once a design has been made available, it is possible to secure a licence of right after five years. Thus, the design right owner may only have an exclusive right in the exploitation of his design for a maximum of five years. This licence of right is available after five years in all cases in which a design right has been conferred.

12.7.2   Licence of right and compulsory licence

In contrast, there may be situations in which there is an abuse of rights conferred by the design right. In such a case, if it is in the public interest, the Monopolies and Mergers Commission may take action (s 238) and take such steps are necessary, which may involve the granting of a compulsory licence, to prevent further abuse occurring. Such action is likely to be taken only in an extreme situation and thus would be a very rare occurrence. It should be noted that this power extends to all cases in which design right subsists, and may be exercised at any time throughout the period of protection conferred. There are similar provisions relating to copyright (CDPA 1988 s 144).

Special rules apply to integrated electronic circuits (colloquially known as 'silicon chips'). Integrated circuits form the basis of the electronic revolution that has characterised the second half of the 20th century. Traditionally, an electronic circuit comprised a collection of individual electronic components such as transistors, resistors and diodes connected together by wires. In an integrated circuit, these individual components are formed from the different interactions of, typically, three layers that form the silicon chip, together with the selective addition of other compounds. It is like a multi-

12.8   Semiconductor topology

layered sandwich with a base layer of semiconductor material, followed by a layer of insulator, which is doped in particular places with various other chemicals so as to form the different electronic components, and all this is then topped with a web of conducting material that links electrically the different parts of the circuit. The whole assemblage is made together, ie each component is integrated one with another. Hence the name.

Originally, integrated circuits could be protected by patents. However, these early patents have now expired and the process is in the public domain. In order to provide further protection, resource was made to the laws of copyright. This is possible because a photographic process is used to produce each integrated circuit. Once a layer of semiconductor has been put in place, then a mask is used to protect various parts of the component while the unprotected parts are etched away. These masks are produced photographically from diagrams in which artistic copyright would usually subsist.

The US, where these rights are known by the name 'mask work rights', introduced the Semiconductor Chip Protection Act in 1984, and the European Community responded with the Council Directive 87/54/EEC 1986 in order to secure reciprocal rights for nationals of Member States.

In the UK, the protection is provided by the Design Right (Semiconductor Topologies) Regulations 1989 which came into force with the CDPA 1988 on 1 August 1989. These Regulations bestow a right called the semiconductor design right which is based upon the unregistered design right, which was also introduced by the CDPA 1988.

12.8.1 Semiconductor design right

According to reg 2(1) a semiconductor design is:

'(a) the pattern fixed, or intended to be fixed, in or upon –

(i) a layer of semiconductor product, or

(ii) a layer of material in the course of and for the purpose of the manufacture of a semiconductor product, or

(b) the arrangement of the patterns fixed, or intended to be fixed, in or upon the layers of a semiconductor product in relation to one another.'

A semiconductor product is defined as:

'... an article the purpose, or one of the purposes, of which is the performance of an electronic function and which consists of two or more layers, at least one of which is composed of semiconducting material and in or upon one or more of which is fixed a pattern appertaining to that or another function.'

The pattern must be original, ie not commonplace within the design field at the time of its creation. The rights which are conferred on the owner are similar to those that accrue to the owner of a design right, save that licences of right are not available for the last five years of the term of protection. However, compulsory licences may be granted at the instigation of the Monopolies and Mergers Commission.

The infringement provisions for the semiconductor design right are the same as for design right as contained in the CDPA 1988 s 226, save that to the extent they are amended by regulation 8 of the DR(ST)R 1989, which introduced a new subsection into the CDPA 1988, namely s 226(1A).

The effect of the amendments is that a competitor's design may be analysed, and then a new design produced to achieve the same ends. This is the heart of 'reverse engineering' of electronic components.

12.9 European developments

Within the Member States of the European Union there is a wide diversity in the protection that is conferred upon designs that are then industrially exploited. In an attempt to remove any distortion that may result from these differences, the European Commission submitted in December 1993 two proposals to the Council of Ministers. The first is a draft Directive on the legal protection of designs (COM (93) 344 final – COD 464), while the second is a draft Regulation on the Community Design (COM (93) 342 final – COD 463). The Community Design would be a common property right which would extend throughout the European Union.

12.9.1 Principal provisions

The draft Directive is concerned with the harmonisation of certain substantive features of the industrial design laws of the Member States, both in relation to one another and in relation to the proposed Regulation on the Community Design. It is proposed, so long as the Directive is adopted, that Member States should implement the necessary legislation by 31 October 1996 (Article 19(1) of the Directive). Once the national laws have been harmonised by the operation of the Directive, it is then proposed that there would be a transitional period in which the Community Design would be introduced. Since the latter actually consists of both a registered and unregistered right, that would mean there would be five possible forms of protection within the UK for the transitional period.

Article 1 of the Directive and Article 3 of the Regulation define a design in similar terms, save that the latter excludes semi-conductor products. However, both exclude computer programs. A design is defined to mean:

'... the appearance of the whole or a part of a product resulting from the specific features of the lines, contours, colours, shape and/or materials of the product itself and/or its ornamentation.'

A product means:

'... any industrial or handicraft item, including parts intended to be assembled into a complex item, sets or compositions of items, packaging, get-ups, graphic symbols and typographic typefaces.'

The design must be new and have individual character (Articles 4 and 5 of the Directive, Articles 5 and 6 of the Regulation). A design shall be considered to have an individual character if the overall impression it produces on the informed user differs significantly from the overall impression produced on such a user by any other design which has been commercialised in the market place or published following registration as a registered Community Design. In order to assess individual character, common features shall, as a matter of principle, be given more weight than differences, and the degree of freedom that the designer had in developing the design shall be taken into consideration.

A design right shall not subsist in a design to the extent that the realisation of a technical function leaves no freedom as regards arbitrary features of appearance (Article 7(1) of the Directive and 9(1) of the Regulation). Thus, wholly functional designs will be denied design right.

Also, design right shall not subsist in a design to the extent that it must necessarily be reproduced in its exact form and dimensions in order to permit the product in which the design is incorporated or to which it is applied to be mechanically assembled or connected with another product (Article 7(2) of the Directive and 9(2) of the Regulation). However, design right may subsist in parts which are mutually interchangeable within a modular system (Article 7(3) of the Directive and 9(3) of the Regulation). This would allow children's building blocks such as 'Lego' to be protected. As presently drafted, design right would be excluded from designs for such articles as stackable chairs or other furniture or articles designed to take up the minimum of space when not in use by utilising the same idea of interdigitation.

The owner of the Community Design property right, which would be obtained by a single application made within 12 months of the initial publication of the design, would be entitled to a monopolistic right to prevent any third party making, selling, importing or exporting any product made to the design. This right would be available upon registration for an initial five year period, which could be renewed for further five year periods up to a maximum of 25 years.

The unregistered community design right, would in contrast, only prevent the unauthorised reproduction of the design for three years from the date of its publication or use anywhere in the world. Thus, it would provide no protection against independently created designs. The longer term of protection and the greater degree of protection which is conferred by the monopoly right is a corollary to the extra work involved in securing registration.

The scope of protection conferred by a design right shall include any design that produces on the informed user a significantly similar overall impression (Article 9(1) of the Directive and Article 11(1) of the Regulation). A range of permitted acts are delineated which include private, non-commercial and educational use.

The thorny issue of spare parts is addressed by the inclusion of a repair clause (Article 14 of the Directive and Article 23 of the Regulation). If a product incorporating a design, or to which the design is applied, is a part of a complex product upon whose appearance the protected design is dependent, ie 'must match', and that the purpose of the use of such a product is to permit the repair of the complex product so as to restore its original appearance and that the public is not misled as to the origin of the product used for repair, then the rights conferred by the design right are limited to only three years. The motorcar producing companies lobbied for an exception to be incorporated. This would have secured the repair market for their exclusive exploitation. However, the manufacturers of spare parts successfully lobbied for the inclusion of a reduction in the term of protection. The result is a compromise between the two interests, which grants a three-year monopoly to the original manufacturer. This, in essence, is a victory to the spare parts manufacturers, because the only parts that will need replacing within the first three years of a model's life are those damaged by accident. The larger market that consists of parts replaced because of old age is open to all.

The Directive and the Regulation are both only in draft form and thus could change substantially before they are adopted. Furthermore, it is possible that the timetable for implementation will be extended.

Industrial Designs: Design Right

The new provisions relating to design right that are contained in ss 213-264 apply after 1 August 1989.

Design right only subsists in designs that come into existence after 1 August 1989 (s 213(7)). The design must be original (s 213(1)). The design may be for the shape or configuration (internal or external) of whole or part of an article (s 213(2)).

However, principles of construction are excluded (s 213(3)(a)). Also excluded are the 'must fit' and 'must match' exceptions (s 213(3)(b) (i) and (ii) respectively). Design right may subsist in surface decoration (s 213(3)(c)).

A design is not original if it is commonplace in the field in question at the time of its creation (s 213(4)).

The designer, employer, or commissioner must satisfied the qualification conditions in ss 218 and 219 (s 213(5)(a)).

Otherwise, the design may qualify if it is first marketed so as to satisfy the conditions in s 220 (s 213(5)(b)).

The design must be recorded in a design document or an article must have been made to the design (s 213(6)).

The designer, ie the creator (s 214(1)), is the first owner (s 215(1)); unless the design is commissioned, in which case the first owner is the commissioner (s 215(2)). Similarly, if the work was produced in the course of employment, then the employer if the first owner (s 215(3)). If a design does not qualify by virtue of the designer, commissioner or employer, then the person who first marketed the article, so long as he qualifies, will be the first owner of the design right (s 215(4)).

The qualification conditions are similar to those for copyright. Thus, a qualifying individual is a citizen or subject of a qualifying country. A qualifying person is a qualifying individual or a body corporate (s 217(1)). Qualifying countries include the UK (s 217(3)(a)); any country designated under s 255 by an Order in Council (s 217(3)(b)); any member State of the European Union (s 217(3)(c)); any country designated under s 256 (s 217(3)(d)).

The designer must be a qualifying individual himself (s 218(2)), or be employed by a qualifying person, or the commission must come from a qualifying person (s 219(1)).

If jointly designed, then only one designer need qualify (ss 218(4) and 219(3)).

Place of first marketing

If the design does not qualify for protection by virtue of s 217 or s 218, then it may still qualify for protection if the place of first marketing of the article, made in accordance with the design, satisfies s 220. The first marketing must take place in the UK or the European Union (s 220(1)(b)).

Duration of design right

The protection conferred lasts for 15 years from when the design was first recorded in a design document, or when an article was first made to the design, whichever occurred first (s 216(1)(a)).

If the design is made available to the public, then only a further 10 years is granted (s 216(1)(b)). The design may be made available anywhere in the world, so long as it is with the licence of the design right owner (s 216(2)).

Infringement of design right Protection

Design right confers the exclusive right to reproduce articles to that design for commercial purposes by (s 226(1)(a)), and the making of a design document recording the design to make such articles (s 226(1)(b)).

Reproduction

Reproduction is copying the design to produce (substantially) identical articles (s 226(2)). Primary infringement involves reproduction, without the licence of the design right owner, of the design (s 226(3)). The reproduction may be direct or indirect (s 226(4)).

Secondary infringement

Secondary infringement occurs when a person, without the licence of the design right owner, imports into the UK for commercial purpose (s 227(1)(a)), or has in his possession for commercial purposes (s 227(1)(b)), or sells, lets for hire, or offers or exposes for sale in the course of business (s 227(1)(c)). An essential element of secondary infringement is that the person must know or have reason to believe that the article is an infringing article.

Exceptions to rights of design right owners

The provisions contained in ss 236-245 delineate certain acts that do not amount to infringement of the design right in a design. For example, it is no infringement of design right to do anything which is an infringement of copyright (s 236).

Licences of right are available for the last five years of the design right (s 237(1). The Monopolies and Mergers Commission may take action in the public interest and grant a compulsory licence if that is necessary to stop the design right owner abusing his position (s 238).

Licence of right and compulsory licences

Special rules for semiconductor topologies are contained in the Council Directive 87/54/EEC 1986. These have been incorporated into UK law by the Design Right (Semiconductor Topographies) Regulations 1989. The DR(ST)R 1989 create a design right in semiconductor topographies. To qualify the design must be original. These rights are similar to unregistered design right; however, there are no provisions for licences of right.

Semiconductor topology

There is a draft Directive (COM (93) 344) and draft Regulation (COM (93) 342). It is intended that these will come into force by 31 October 1996 (Article 19(1)). A design must be new and of individual character. The duration of protection will be for 25 years for a registered Community Design, but only three years for an unregistered design. In the case of repair products, the protection conferred is limited to three years.

European developments

Chapter 13

Registered Designs: Historical Introduction

Copyright *simpliciter* is generally concerned with the protection of works that have some artistic merit, even though there is no explicit requirement for a work to have any such merit, except in the limited case of works of artistic craftsmanship.

There are, however, many articles that are mass-produced that possess little artistic appeal: their main merit is in their value to perform some useful function, ie their utility. An example would be a kettle, the function of which is to boil water. However, it seems to be inherent in human nature that the aesthetic merits of an object will be noticed and appreciated. Hence there is a receptive market for the design and manufacture of kettles that possess some merit in their design that is independent from their function to boil water. Such articles are characterised, and thus distinguished from purely artistic works protected by copyright, by the facts that the utilitarian function is pre-eminent in importance over the aesthetic value, and that such articles are produced in vast numbers. The commercial value of a good design lies in the fact that the article not only performs the function for which it is intended, but it also appeals to the eye of the purchaser, and thus enhances the chance that it will be purchased in favour of some equally efficient, but less pleasant looking, article.

It will be obvious that there is a continuum between the purely functional article, which is devoid of artistic merit, and the purely artistic article, which in turn is devoid of practical use, though whether anything is *completely* devoid of artistic merit or practical use is unlikely: for example, plain building bricks have been displayed in the Tate, while a Henry Moore statue could be used as a park bench.

Intermediate between those articles which merit copyright protection and those ideas which are so novel and inventive so as to merit patent protection is a vast range of articles which are rather more functional in design than artistic, and yet not so inventive as to merit a patent. The protection of this middle ground is achieved by a system of registered and unregistered designs.

Registered design right involves a formal registration system and confers monopolistic protection and so it resembles the patent system in those respects. However, in

13.1   Introduction

contradiction to the patent system, it is designed to protect the *aesthetic*, rather than *functional*, aspects of a work.

13.2 Early history	The legislature has tried to resolve the conflict between conferring some reasonable protection upon the creator of an industrial design, and the limitations that this would impose on an entirely open market in which competitors were free to copy the ideas of other traders. This fundamental conflict is present in all forms of intellectual property law, but, in the field of industrial design, has been particularly vexed, and remains so.

The first statute in this field was the Designing and Printing of Linens, etc, Act 1787, which provided the proprietor of a new and original pattern for linens and similar textiles the sole right of printing the fabric for two months. The title to this right depended on being the first to publish the design by marketing. The protection conferred was very similar to that conferred by copyright for works of some artistic merit.

This first Act was experimental in nature and hence lapsed after one year. However, the experiment was considered to be a success, and so legislation was continued in a piecemeal fashion until 1839.

13.3 Introduction of registration	In 1839, the Copyright of Designs Act 1839 was passed. This new Act was the forerunner of the modern system of registered designs, and it adopted a fundamentally different approach from what had been in existence beforehand. The scope of protection was expanded to include not only printed cloth, but also the shape or configuration of any article of manufacture and also the engraving, or impression or ornamentation on any article of manufacture. The benefits of this new Act could only be obtained if the article in question was registered at the Board of Trade before publication.

A system of registration has several advantages to the commercial community. The foremost of which is the ease with which it is possible to check if any particular design is already in existence, and if so, who is the proprietor of such a design. Such a preliminary check avoids the possibility of a manufacturer setting up a production line, only to find, once the article is on the market, that it infringes someone else's design. Furthermore, registration simplifies the proof of title to the right to the design, and so makes it easier for the owner of such a right to protect it.

There are, however, problems with registration: namely that any system of registration necessitates that the owner incurs the expenses of registration of the design before the design has been proved in the market place. The cost of the system is increased if there is any sort of search required by the Registrar of existing registrations before an application is accepted for a new registration. Such a search procedure maintains the integrity of the register by ensuring that there is no duplication; however, it is expensive and this cost must eventually fall on the consumer.

Over the next 65 years or so, there was a plethora of legislation in which Parliament attempted to reach a satisfactory solution to the problem of protection for works of mixed artistic/functional merit. In particular, the issue of whether or not there ought to be possible dual protection, ie statutory protection under the different rights, for certain works was to vex the legislature during this period.

13.4   The extension of protection for designs

The Copyright of Designs for Ornamenting Articles of Manufacture 1842, also known as the Designs Act 1842, repealed all the previous legislation, and consolidated the statutory framework for design protection. In the forthcoming years, the legislature was often to change its view on the desirability, or otherwise, of an article being capable of securing protection in more than one manner. Under this Act, the legislature decided to exclude the possibility of dual protection for designs of those articles that would be protected by the Sculpture Copyright Act 1814.

By the Copyright of Designs Act 1850, it became possible to register works of sculpture, and thus such articles gained dual protection.

However, dual protection was removed again by the Patents, Designs and Trade Marks Act 1883 s 60, whereby design was defined as:

'... any design applicable to any article of manufacture, or to any substance artificial or natural ... whether ... for the pattern, or for the shape or configuration, or the ornament thereof ... not being a design for a sculpture, or other thing within the protection of the Sculpture Copyright Act 1814.'

This Act also consolidated the previous legislation and formed a unified system for those intellectual property rights that required registration, namely patents, industrial designs and trade marks.

The duration of the protection conferred was extended from five years to a maximum of 15 years by the Patents and Designs Act 1907. The rights conferred upon the proprietor entitled him to stop anyone from making a fraudulent or obvious imitation, and thus the protection conferred paralleled the protection conferred under the copyright legislation.

13.5 The introduction of the requirement for eye appeal

Even though it was possible at this time to register designs for purely functional articles, the courts had refused to confer protection by this route on principles of construction (*Moody v Tree* (1892)). The move by the courts to restrict the scope of protection conferred by registered design rights was a reflection of the general atmosphere prevalent at the time that the protection of industrial property in general was not advantageous to the trading position of the British Empire, and such protection was used by her competitors to the detriment of the UK.

As a result, the Patents and Designs Act 1919 s 19 redefined designs in a more restrictive manner in an attempt to limit the protection that was available for industrial designs. The new definition stated that a design related only to the features of shape, configuration, pattern or ornament applied to any article by any industrial process or means, which, in the finished article, *appeal to and was judged solely by the eye*, but did not include any mode or principle of construction, or anything which was in substance a mere mechanical device.

The introduction of the necessary requirement of 'eye appeal' before an article was capable of protection as a registered design was intended to limit the range of articles that would be eligible for this form of protection. This object was achieved. However, there was an unforeseen consequence in that objects that were not eligible for protection as a registered design became eligible for protection under the copyright laws.

13.6 Copyright Act 1911

Under the Copyright Act 1911 s 22, it was stated that copyright would not subsist in a work that was capable of registration, unless it was not intended that the work should be used as a model or pattern to be multiplied by any industrial process. The intention of the author at the time of the creation of the work was important, and, if he later changed his mind, then the work still qualified for copyright protection (for example, *King Features Syndicate Inc v O and M Kleeman Ltd* (1941), which concerned the subsequent commercialisation as rag dolls of the comic cartoon character Popeye the Sailor). A sculpture, if it was mass produced would not be capable of being protected by copyright; instead, such an object would receive protection only under the registered design legislation if it was made with the intention of producing multiple copies (*Pytram Ltd v Models (Leicester) Ltd* (1930)).

The important consequence that mass-produced designs could not be protected by copyright, lead to the corollary that those designs that did not appeal to the eye and thus were not eligible for registered design protection, could be protected by copyright, so long as at the time of their creation there was no intention of mass-production, rather that the commercialisation was only realised later.

The Registered Designs Act 1949 provided a legislative framework for registered designs which was separate from the patent system. By this Act, a design was defined to mean features of shape, configuration, pattern or ornament applied to an article by any industrial process or means, being features which in the finished article appeal to and are judged solely by the eye, but does not include a method or principle of construction or features of shape or configuration which are dictated solely by the function which the article to be made in that shape or configuration has to perform (s 1(3) (before amendment)). Thus, it continued the exclusion of purely functional aspects of articles from the ambit of registered design protection. A further change transformed the protection conferred into a true monopoly, and thus there was no longer any need to show that the alleged infringement was an imitation.

13.7   Registered Designs Act 1949

The Copyright Act 1956 continued the policy of proscribing the grant of dual protection for designs that were commercially exploited. Thus, s 10 of the 1956 Act (before amendment) read:

13.8   Copyright Act 1956 (unamended)

'(1)   Where copyright subsists in an artistic work, and a corresponding design is registered under the Registered Design Act 1949 (in this section referred to as 'the Act of 1949'), it shall not be an infringement of the copyright in the work

(a)   to do anything, during the subsistence of the copyright in the registered design under the Act of 1949, which is within the scope of the copyright in the design, or

(b)   to do anything, after the copyright in the registered design has come to an end, which, if it had been done while the copyright in the design subsisted, would have been within the scope of that copyright as extended to all associated designs and articles ...'

It is important to note that the word 'copyright' is being used in two contexts. First, 'copyright in the work' refers to copyright proper, and is referred to hereafter as copyright *simpliciter*. Secondly, 'copyright in the registered design' refers to the rights conferred by the RDA 1949, ie 'registered design right' and that is how it will be referred to hereafter. Thus, registered designs, while the design registration was extant, lost copyright protection for those acts that fell within the scope of protection conferred by registration. After the registration had expired, the only protection that was available to the proprietor was based on copyright so far as it was different from the protection that had been available while the design was registered.

The scope of the two different protections conferred in a design, namely copyright *simpliciter* and registered design right, may be likened to two concentric circles, the inner one representing the scope of protection conferred by the registered design right, while the outer one representing the scope of protection conferred by copyright. Thus, while the registered design subsists, the copyright *simpliciter* could not be infringed by any act that came within the inner circle, but that would naturally lead to an infringement of the registered design right. After the expiry of the registered design right, any act falling within the inner circle would still not be an infringement of copyright *simplicier*, and nor would it be an infringement of the registered design right, because that had expired. Only acts that fell within the annulus between the inner and outer circles would amount to an infringement, and then only of the copyright *simpliciter*. An example of an act that falls within this annulus is the right to issue copies to the public, which is conferred by copyright *simpliciter*, but not by registered design right.

If an article was not registered under the Registered Design Act 1949, but copyright subsisted, then subsections 10(2) and 10(3) were applicable.

The result of these subsections, was that if the designer did not register his design (whether or not it was registerable), then naturally he gained no protection for it under the Registered Design Act 1949, but he also obtained no protection for it under the Copyright Act 1956, unless the protection sought was outside the scope of the protection granted to a registered design, ie to acts that occurred within the annulus mentioned above. Furthermore, after a period of 15 years, this loss of protection included all associated designs and not just the original design.

The overall result of these provisions was that a registrable design enjoyed limited copyright protection and if registered could also receive protection under the Registered Design Act 1949. Obviously, if the design was not registered then it could not benefit from the protection conferred by the RDA 1949. Thus there was no possibility of double protection for a design.

The deciding issue was whether or not a design was capable of registration. This capability for registration was considered by the House of Lords in *Amp Inc v Utilux Pty Ltd* (1972). If a customer is likely to be influenced in his purchase of an article, because of the visual appeal of that article, then the design for that article is registrable. This visual appeal need not be aesthetic or artistic; it could, for instance, be bizarre. However, if the appearance of the article merely suggests that it is suitable to fulfil the required function, then the design for that article is not registrable. Thus, their Lordships held that the design for an electrical plug, fitted to a washing machine at the factory and which, when in use, was not visible, had been invalidly registered for its appearance, could not influence the customer. Accordingly, if a design was not capable of registration then the CA 1956 s 10 did not apply, and the design received protection under the copyright law as for any other artistic work.

The direct consequence was the anomalous result that those very articles that the legislature wished to grant protection for only a short period of time, so that trade rivals could freely compete in the market, were actually granted the long duration of protection normally only applicable to literary works.

Section 10 of the CA 156 was amended exclusively by the Design Copyright Act 1968. Subsection 1 of the old s 10 was deleted, subsection 2 was amended, and subsection 3 was completely substituted (DCA 1968 s 1(1)). The remaining subsections were left unchanged.

13.9   Copyright Act 1956 (as amended)

The effect of deleting subsection (1) was to allow full artistic copyright to subsist in designs even if exploited commercially, and even if the design was registered, for a period of 15 years. The immediate result was that the owners of rights in designs began to rely extensively upon the copyright protection that existed, with a concomitant decreased reliance on the registered design rights that existed for industrial designs.

The situation was reviewed by the Whitford Committee, which submitted its Report of Copyright and Designs in 1977. This report proposed that the monopolistic protection granted to industrial designs under the RDA 1949 should be abolished. However, this proposal was not followed in the White Paper of 1986, in which, in contradistinction, it was proposed that not only should the registered design protection be retained, but, in addition, there should be a new design right that did not require registration.

The CDPA 1988, which resulted from the White Paper of 1986, did introduce a new design right that was similar to copyright in that it protected an article from being reproduced. The Act also maintained the monopolistic registered design right; however, the whole of the RDA 1949 was amended so as to dove-tail this registered right with the unregistered right which had been newly created, and in this manner the two rights could attach to different parts of the design of an article.

So it can be seen that the development of a system that confers protection upon designs that are exploited commercially has been tortuous over the last century and a half. The final system with which the United Kingdom is left at present results from many historical threads that reflect a patchwork of special pleadings by interest groups, the xenophobia by the British industrialists and poor statutory drafting. This piecemeal approach continues today, with the EU proposals to introduce new rights (some with and some without the need for registration) to protect industrial designs. Special interest groups, such as car manufacturers, still exert influence of the direction of legislation.

Registered Designs: Historical Introduction

Mass-produced items are generally more utilitarian than copyright protected works, and so the former have less aesthetic merit than the latter.

Introduction

The legislature accordingly considered that such mass-produced items deserved less protection than copyright works.

The Designing and Printing of Linens, etc, Act 1787 was the first Act to grant protection to industrially-produced goods. It granted two months' protection for fabric designs. This experiment of granting such rights was considered successful and so further legislation was passed. The Copyright of Designs Act 1839 introduced a registration system for industrial designs.

Early history

The Copyright of Designs for Ornamenting Articles of Manufacture 1842 (aka the Designs Act 1842) excluded dual protection for industrial designs, ie no overlap with the protection conferred under the Sculpture Copyright Act 1814.

The extension of protection for designs

By the Copyright of Design Act 1850 dual protection became possible. However, the Patents, Designs and Trade Marks Act 1883 s 60 removed the possibility of dual protection for a design, ie both copyright *simpliciter* and registered design right.

The Patents and Designs Act 1907 extended the period of protection to 15 years. The Patents and Designs Act 1919 s 19 introduced the requirement for eye-appeal.

Copyright *simpliciter* would not subsist in a work that was capable of registration, unless it was not intended that the work should be used as a model or pattern to be multiplied by an industrial process. The intention of the author at the time of the creation of the work was important, and, if he later changed his mind, the work still qualified for copyright protection (*King Features Syndicate Inc v O and M Kleeman Ltd* (1941)).

Copyright Act 1911

This Act introduced the requirement that those features of a design capable of registration must appeal to and be judged solely by the eye (s 1(3) before amendment).

Registered Designs Act 1949

Copyright Act 1956 (unamended)	If a design was registered, then there was no dual protection for that design while it was so registered. Once the registration lapsed, the only protection remaining was that conferred by copyright, unless the act would have been proscribed by the registered design right, in which case no protection survived. If a design was eligible for registration, but was not so registered, the only protection conferred was the same as the situation when there had been a registration, but it had lapsed. Then there was no dual copyright/registered design protection at any time in an industrial design. The consequence of this legislation was that purely functional aspects of a design received protection by copyright, while a design for a functional object that incorporated some feature with eye-appeal that would influence a potential purchaser would qualify for registration (*Amp Inc v Utilux Pty Ltd* (1972)).
Copyright Act 1956 (as amended)	The Design Copyright Act 1968 amended the CA 1956 s 10. The amended s 10 conferred full artistic copyright to designs even if they were exploited commercially, but the period of protection was limited to 15 years.

Chapter 14

Registered Designs: Qualification

Designs that are capable of registration are governed by the Registered Designs Act 1949, as amended by the CDPA 1988 ss 265-273 and Schedule 3. The complete amended text of the RDA 1949 is reproduced as Schedule 4 to the CDPA 1988.

Sections 265-271 of the CDPA 1988 came into force on 1 August 1989. Section 272 concerns the minor amendments contained in Schedule 3, of which paras 1-20 and 22-38 also came into force on the 1 August 1989 (Copyright, Designs and Patents Act 1988 (Commencement No 4) Order 1989). Section 273, which relates to Schedule 4 with the full text of the amended RDA 1949, came into force on the 13 August 1990, along with para 21 of Schedule 3 (Copyright, Designs and Patents Act 1988 (Commencement No 5) Order 1990). There is a new series of Rules that govern the registration of registered designs, namely the Registered Designs Rules 1989.

The CDPA 1988 replaced the confusing terminology of the unamended RDA 1949 of 'copyright in a design' with the less confusing term of 'right in a registered design'. This is to be welcomed, because registered design rights are quite dissimilar from rights in works in which copyright subsists.

14.1 Current statutory framework

Section 1 of the RDA 1949 as amended defines a design to mean:

'features of shape, configuration, pattern or ornament applied to an article by any industrial process, being features which in the finished article appeal to and are judged by the eye, but does not include -

(a) a method or principle of construction, or

(b) features of shape or configuration of an article which -

(i) are dictated solely by the function which the article has to perform, or

(ii) are dependent upon the appearance of another article of which the article is intended by the author of the design to form an integral part.

14.2 The definition of a design capable of registration

| 14.3 | Shape, configuration, pattern or ornament | The four types of features, namely shape, configuration, pattern or ornament, are usually separated into two groups of two, namely shape and configuration as one group, and pattern and ornament as the other. |

14.3 **Shape, configuration, pattern or ornament**

The four types of features, namely shape, configuration, pattern or ornament, are usually separated into two groups of two, namely shape and configuration as one group, and pattern and ornament as the other.

14.3.1 **Shape or configuration**

It is not immediately clear how a shape or a configuration may be applied to an article. The point was elucidated by Lindsay LJ in *Clarke v Sax & Co Ltd* (1896), in which His Lordship stated:

> 'Again, the Act does not apply to the things to which a design is applied; the Act applies to the design applied to them. The distinction is obvious enough when the design is for a pattern or ornament; but when, as in this case, the design is for the shape of a thing, the distinction is reduced to the difference between the shape of a thing and a thing of that shape. A design applicable to a thing for its shape can only be applied to a thing by making it in that shape.'

A practical example would be the characteristic shape that a manufacturer designs for a kettle. The functional ability to boil water is little altered, while the aesthetic appeal of one shape over another may be large.

14.3.2 **Pattern or ornamentation**

It is clearer how a pattern or an ornament may be applied to an article. However, not all graphic works that are applied to an article will be capable of registration. For example, words and numerals that do not form an integral part of the design, will not be capable of registration (*United Africa Co Ltd's Application* (1959)).

14.3.3 **Shape/configuration and pattern/ornamentation dichotomy**

Even though the courts have readily distinguished between features of shape and configuration on the one hand, and features of pattern and ornamentation on the other, they have normally not distinguished between the pattern or ornament of an article, nor between the shape and the configuration of an article (*Kestos Ltd v Kempat Ltd and Vivian Fitch Kemp* (1936)).

However, in *PB Cow & Co Ltd v Cannon Rubber Manufacturers Ltd* (1959), which concerned closely spaced diagonal ribbing on a hot water bottle, Lord Evershed MR did attempt to distinguish between shape and configuration, when he said:

> 'I would have thought it right to say that the ribbing is so marked a feature of the bottle as a whole as to be entitled to be described as a feature of its configuration. It may not be "shape", but I think it is "configuration".'

The argument by the defendants that the ribbing was pattern or ornament failed.

Similarly, in *Sommer Allibert (UK) Ltd v Flair Plastics Ltd* (1987), it was held at first instance by Whitford J, that the moulded grooves in the seat and back of a plastic garden chair constituted part of the configuration of the design. Slade LJ in the Court of Appeal held that the grooves were neither pattern nor ornament, but rather were part of the shape or configuration of the design; however, Slade LJ did not attempt to limit further the features to being either shape or configuration.

For a design to be registered, it cannot exist in isolation, it must be associated with an article which must be specified in the application. What constitutes an 'article' for the purposes of the RDA 1949 is not entirely straightforward.

14.4   What constitutes an article for registration

The interpretation section (RDA 1949 s 44(1)), defines an article as meaning 'any article of manufacture and includes any part of an article if that part is made and sold separately'. However, pursuant to s 26 of the RDR 1989 printed matter primarily of a literary or artistic character is excluded from registration.

14.4.1   Statutory provisions

Computer fan-feed paper, which contains alternating horizontal bands of white and light green, designed to facilitate the checking of a computer read-out, was held not to be incapable of registration merely because matter of a literary nature was printed onto it; however, the registration was refused on other grounds (*Lamson Industries Ltd's Application* (1978)). Whitford J observed that the computer paper could not sensibly be described as printed matter in the sense in which that word was apparently used in r 26. In contrast a plastic cushion on which was printed advertising material was held to be primarily of a literary or artistic character (*H Klarmann Ltd v Henshaw Linen Supplies* (1960)). In *Littlewoods Pools Ltd's Application* (1949), application for the registration of a football pools coupon was refused on the grounds that the paper upon which the design was printed did not constitute an article, but was merely the support for the information contained within the coupon. In contrast, wall-paper serves a function regardless of the pattern which is applied to its surface and thus is an article capable of registration.

14.4.2   Examples

Registration is denied to those individual components that form an integral part of a larger article, but are not sold separately from that larger complete article. This has lead to some problems of interpretation by the courts of what is, or is not, meant by an 'article'. This dilemma of what constitutes an article in its own right is of great practical consequence to manufactures who wish to register all the possible spare parts to their finished articles so as to exercise control over the spare parts market.

14.4.3   Integrated parts of a larger article

The House of Lords in *R v Registered Design Appeal Tribunal, ex p Ford Motor Co Ltd* (1994) held that a motor vehicle part which had no independent life as an article of commerce and as such was merely an adjunct to a larger item was not capable of individual registration. Lord Mustill stated that:

> 'The purpose of the words ['... if that part is made and sold separately'] was to distinguish between, on the one hand, an item designed for incorporation, whether as a spare part or as an original component, in a particular article or range of articles made by the manufacturer of the component, and on the other hand an item designed for general use, albeit aimed principally at use with the manufacturer's own artefacts.'

For example, a wing panel has no independent existence, but is used only to replace a damaged wing panel, and thus it could not be registered separately. In contrast, articles such as wing mirrors, wheels, seats or steering wheels comprised parts which, while *in situ* contribute to the appearance of the vehicle, are subsidiary to its essential shape and are thus eligible for registration.

14.5   Eye appeal

The purpose of registered designs is to protect those parts of an article that attract the eye of the customer and thus give a competitive advantage to the manufacturer. A new invention would be protected by the patent legislation, the value lying not in any aesthetic appeal but in the functional advance of the invention. Under the unamended RDA 1949 s 1(3) the features of a design had to appeal to and be judged solely by the eye. The omission of the word 'solely' in the amended Act implies a change in the substantive law to allow other features to be registered that previously could not be registered. This would include, for instance, a feature that appealed to the sense of touch, rather than the eye, for example, a very delicate *basso* or *alto* relief that, under normal conditions, cast no shadow, and thus could not be detected by the eye.

There is no requirement that the article be objectively of any artistic or aesthetic merit, which is similar in this respect to the lack of a requirement for literary merit in order for copyright to subsist in a work. The article must appeal to the eye of the potential customer, and the view of the designer is not decisive on the matter.

14.5.1   Contrasted with functionality

In *Amp Inc v Utilux Pty Ltd* (1972), which concerned the electrical terminal fixings for washing machines, the House of Lords held that an article that was purely functional in nature could not be registered, because in such a case there was no feature that could appeal to the eye.

In contrast to articles whose features are purely functional, many articles have features that serve a dual role by being both functional and aesthetic in nature. The issue of whether or not features of an article which served this dual role are capable of registration was considered by the Privy Council in *Interlego AG v Tyco Industries Inc* (1988). It was held, notwithstanding the purely functional nature of those bumps and interdigitating tubes that allowed the Lego building blocks to interconnect, that the exact dimensions had been chosen so as to produce a pleasing effect upon the eye. Thus, a feature which is functional, but not exclusively so, may contain sufficient design input to merit qualifying for registration.

The eye appeal of the article need only feature in the finished article, and there is no requirement that the features should be judged at the time when the article was bought, so long as the feature does at some stage appeal to and is judged by the eye of the purchaser. Thus, the contrasting shades of the external and internal layers of a chocolate egg that are only revealed during its consumption, which is the natural fate of such a confectionery, is a feature which appeals to the eye and so may qualify for registration (*P Ferrero and CSpA's Application* (1978)). There is no requirement that the features which appeal to the eye be visible when the article is finished, or even when it is in use, so long as they are features which do appeal to the eye of the consumer. Thus, the design for the underside of a shower tray was capable of registration (*Gardex Ltd v Sorata Ltd* (1986)). In this case there was evidence from the designer that he had intended the underside, as well as the topside, of the shower tray to have an aesthetic appeal.

The second substantive change that was introduced by the CDPA 1988 into the RDA 1949 as a pre-condition for registrability was the requirement that the appearance of the article was of material importance to the customer s 1(3).	14.5.2 Material importance to the purchaser

Hence, the article must not only contain some feature of eye appeal, but that this feature is of importance in persuading the customer to purchase the article. The operation of this exclusion would, it is submitted, ensure that design for the underside of the shower tray would be refused registration, thus overruling *Gardex Ltd v Sorato Ltd* (1986).

A design must be new in order to qualify for registration (s 1(2)). The registrar may make such searches, if any, as he thinks fit, in order to determine whether or not an application for registration is new (s 3(3) (as amended by the CDPA 1988 s 272, Schedule 3 para 1)). Furthermore, a statement of novelty needs to be lodged with the application which should specify	**14.6 Requirement of novelty of the design**

those features that are claimed to be novel (RDR 1989 r 15). It is the practice of the Registry to register one application for a design that contains novel features of pattern or ornament, and a separate application for the novel features of configuration or shape (*Evered & Co Ltd's Applications* (1961)). The reason for this practice is that the statement of novelty determines not only the validity of the registration, but has a bearing on the question of infringement.

14.6.1	Date for determining novelty

Usually the question of novelty is determined with reference to the date of the application for registration. However, this date may be displaced in favour of either a later or an earlier date (s 3(4) (as amended)). Thus, if an application has been amended so that the appearance of the design has been altered significantly, the date of the amendment is used to assess novelty (RDR r 34(1)(a)). In contrast if the original application disclosed more than one design, and the application has been amended so as to contain only one new design, the issue of novelty for the other (excluded) new designs will be decided by reference to the original application date (RDR r 34(1)(b)).

14.7 Novelty and originality

What decides if an article is new or not? The CDPA 1988 has introduced a change in the test: under the original RDA 1949, the test was whether or not the article was 'new or original' (RDA 1949 s 1(2)). In the amended RDA 1949, the test became whether or not the article was 'new' (s 1(2)). The words 'or original' have been dropped. Thus, it is necessary to examine the old case law in order to determine whether anything turns on the omission of these two words, for *prima facie* a change in wording means a change in the law.

14.7.1	Difference between novelty and originality

The difference between the terms 'novelty' and 'originality' was considered by Buckley LJ in *Dover Ltd v Nürnberger Celluloidwaren Fabrik Gebrüder Wolff* (1910), in which His Lordship said:

'If the Design be new, it may be registered under that expression; but the Act, by Section 49, seems to contemplate that it may be registered even if it be not new provided that it be original. The explanation of this lies possibly in the fact that the novelty may consist not in the idea itself but in the way in which the idea is to be rendered applicable to some special subject matter. The word 'original' contemplates that the person has originated something, that by the exercise of intellectual activity he has started an idea which had not occurred to anyone before, that a particular pattern or shape or ornament may be rendered applicable to the particular article to which he suggests that it shall be applied. If that state of things be satisfied, then the Design will be original, although the actual picture or shape or whatever it is which is being considered is old in the sense that it has existed with reference to another article before.'

On balance, the judiciary has considered that the terms 'novelty' and 'originality' may impart different connotations, but the exact ambit is not clearly defined. As a consequence, the change introduced by the CDPA 1988 with the omission of the words 'or original' is a change in the law, but one of unclear ramifications.

14.7.2   What constitutes novelty?

Thus, novelty may reside in the design *per se* being new, and also in the first application of a particular design to any given type of article (*Saunders v Wiel* (1893)). However, for the latter type of novelty, the subsequent type of article must be substantially different in nature from the first type of article. In *Sebel & Co Ltd's Application (No 1)* (1959) a registration for a rocking horse was rejected on the grounds that even though the particular design of horse had not been used in conjugation with the particular design of stand, the overall effect was not sufficiently novel to warrant the design being admitted onto the register.

Generally, variations in colour have not been sufficient to confer novelty on an article, for example, a range of colours used for the pellets of a drug contained within a transparent sheath (*Smith, Kline and French Laboratories Ltd's Application* (1974)). However, in principle, it seems that a particularly striking combination of colours could confer novelty. In the case of a football jersey in red, white and blue strips, Whitford J allowed the application to proceed, partly on the grounds that if problems arose at a later date, then all the relevant issues could be discussed at any subsequent trial (*Cook and Hurst's Application* (1979)).

Section 1(4) states that: 'a design shall not be regarded as new for the purpose of the Act if it is the same as a design -

(a)   registered in respect of the same or any other article in pursuance of a prior application, or

(b)   published in the United Kingdom in respect of the same or any other article before the date of the application, or if it differs from such a design only in immaterial details or in features which are variants commonly used in the trade.'

14.8   **Qualities excluded from conferring novelty**

A prior application need not have reached registration in order for it to block the registration of the second and subsequent applications (*Shallwin Ltd's Application* (1961)). However, if the

14.8.1   Prior registrations and applications

prior application fails for any reason, then it is no longer relevant in *this* context, because any such application is deemed never to have had effect (s 20(5)(c)). However, such an application may be relevant to the issue of *prior publication*.

14.8.2   Prior publication

Under s 1(4)(b) prior publication in the United Kingdom of an article may prevent the subsequent registration of a design. It is likely that publication with regard to designs has a similar meaning to that found in the patent legislation, because in each case a statutory monopoly is being granted. The policy underlying this restriction in registration is that it would be iniquitous to grant a monopoly that covered information already in the pubic domain. Accordingly, there is prior publication if the relevant information is contained within a document that was freely available to the general public, regardless of whether or not it was ever actually read by anybody.

While it is not necessary that the prior disclosure be in writing, a merely oral disclosure is insufficient (*Rosedale Associated Manufacturers Ltd v Airfix Products Ltd* (1957)). If a prior publication contains 'clear and unmistakable directions' so that the proposed design could be produced, then that will be sufficient to anticipate the design (*Flour Oxidizing Co Ltd v Carr & Co Ltd* (1908)).

14.8.3   Immaterial or trade variants

By virtue of the proviso to s 1(4), a design is not to be considered novel 'if it differs from [a prior registered design] only in immaterial details or in features which are variants commonly used in the trade'. Only an application or publication that anticipates the design in question is of concern. It is a question of fact whether any variations between the old and the new designs are immaterial or not. This issue is for the court to decide after having received all the evidence, which may include experts in the particular field. Historically, the matter is to be judged by the effect upon the eye of the judge, and so even small variations in detail that result in a great change in the visual impression may amount to a material variation and so confer novelty (*Rollason's Registered Design* (1898)).

14.9   **Designs that are excluded from registration**

Section 43(1) states that:

'Nothing in this Act shall be construed as authorising or requiring the registrar to register a design the use of which would, in his opinion, be contrary to law or morality.'

An anatomically correct doll wearing a kilt was not denied registration, even though it was held that the design was capable of offending part of the population (*Masterman's Design* (1991)).

Section 3(5) (as amended) gives the registrar a general discretion to refuse to register an application (*Leara Trading Co Ltd's Designs* (1991)).

A method or principle of construction is excluded from design protection (s 1(1)(a)). The correct approach to secure protection for such an idea is a patent. If, however, the statement of novelty, which must accompany any application for registration, is so widely drafted that it appears to encompass a method of construction, it will only be held valid if the design is limited to the specific example cited in the specification. So, for example, in *Pugh v Riley Cycle Co Ltd* (1912), the registered design could have been interpreted as a principle of construction for a spoked wheel. This *per se* would have been invalid, and as a consequence the registration was limited to the particular example disclosed.

If the article is built, in the normal sense of the word, on site, such as, for example, a petrol filling station, then the design for such a building is not capable of registration (*RH Collier & Co Ltd's Applications* (1937)). Similarly, in *Concrete Ltd's Application* (1940) the construction of an air-raid shelter from pre-formed concrete blocks was refused registration on the grounds that such an operation did not constitute the application of a design to an article. However, in this case it was explicitly held that articles that were transported to the customer's premises for assembly were not in all cases excluded from registration. The key point being whether the final structure should be considered as having been constructed on site, or whether it was manufactured elsewhere and merely assembled on site.

14.9.1 Principles of construction

Section 1(1)(b)(i) excludes from registration features of shape or configuration of an article that are dictated *solely* by the function the article has to perform. This exception does not apply to exclude any features of pattern or ornamentation.

In *Interlego AG v Tyco Industries Inc* (1988), it was held that even though the bumps and hollow tubes were functional in nature, the exact choice of the dimensions of those features imported a visual appeal. As a consequence, the bumps and tubes played a dual role, ie both functional and aesthetic, and so these features were not excluded from registration.

14.9.2 Features dictated by functionality

The CDPA 1988 introduced a substantive change in what was exempt from registration when it inserted the 'must match' exception. This was inserted as a direct result of the 1985

14.9.3 'Must match' exception

Monopolies and Mergers Commission's report on the Ford Motor Company's refusal to grant licences for the manufacture or sale of replacement body parts for Ford vehicles.

The RDA 1949 s 1(1)(b)(ii) (as amended) reads that 'features of shape or configuration of an article which are dependent upon the appearance of another article of which the article is intended by the author of the design to form an integral part' are excluded from the definition of an article that may be capable of registration. This follows the wording of the same exclusion from design right contained in the CDPA 1988 s 213(3)(b)(ii), and as such a spare part that falls within this exception will not receive protection by either registration of the design or unregistered design right. This effectively curtails the monopoly that car manufacturers previously held over the supply of spare parts for the body panels and such like of a car. The direct result of this will be an increase in competition from the spare part manufacturers.

In *Vales Vision SA v Flexible Lamps Ltd* (1994), Aldous J held that when two articles are designed to fit together, it is irrelevant which one was designed first.

14.10   Novelty subject to the effect of the RDA 1949, ss 4, 6 and 16

Subsection 1(4) of the RDA 1949 as amended takes effect subject to the provisions of ss 4, 6 and 16 of the Act (proviso to s 1(4)).

Principal among these provisions is s 4 which allows the registration of the same design in respect of other articles, or designs with immaterial variations in respect of the same article, if the subsequent application is made by the proprietor of the first registered design, so long as the right in any design registered by virtue of this section does not extend beyond the end of the period for which the right subsists in the original registered design. This provision allows a manufacturer to extend the range of articles based upon a proven registered design without encountering problems of lack of novelty, because of the existence of the previous articles.

Section 6(1) states that a design shall not be refused registration merely because it has been imparted under a duty of confidentiality to another person, even if that other person reveals the design in breach of his duty to the prospective proprietor. Section 6(2) states that an application for registration is not to be refused for lack of novelty if the design was displayed, with the consent of the proprietor, at an exhibition certified by the Secretary of State. The certification of the Secretary of State needs to be obtained before the design is displayed. This subsection only provides a grace period of six months from the opening of the exhibition. Within that period, the application must be lodged (proviso to s 6(2)).

If an artistic work is subsequently used as the basis for an application for a registered design, by or with the consent of the copyright owner in the artistic work, then no regard with be paid of any previous use made of the artistic work when the question of the novelty of the design falls to be considered (s 6(4)). However, this exclusion from the consideration of novelty does not apply if the previous use consisted of, or included, the sale, letting for hire, or offer or exposure for sale of articles to which had been applied industrially the design in question or a design differing only in immaterial details or in features which are variants commonly used in the trade, and that the previous use was made by or with the consent of the copyright owner (s 6(5)). The terms that involve consideration of the copyright have the meaning contained in the CDPA 1988 (RDA 1949 s 44(1)).

Section 16 allows the Secretary of State to make special rules to deal with emergency situations such as war.

Registered Designs: Qualification

The current statutory framework is contained in the Registered Designs Act 1949, as amended by the CDPA 1988 ss 256-273 and Schedule 3. The complete amended text of the RDA 1949 is reproduced as Schedule 4 to the CDPA 1988. The majority of the provisions came into force on 1 August 1989. There is also a new set of rules that govern the registration procedure contained in the Registered Designs Rules 1989.

Current statutory framework

Features of shape, configuration, pattern or ornament, that are applied to an article by any industrial process, and which appeal to and are judged by the eye (s 1).

The definition of a design capable of registration

Clarke v Sax & Co Ltd (1896) contains the classic definition.

Shape or configuration

Usually neither words nor numerals may be included as features of patterns or ornamentation (*United Africa Co Ltd's Application* (1959).

Pattern or ornamentation

Usually the court would not distinguish between shape and configuration, nor between pattern and ornament (*Kestos Ltd v Kempat Ltd and Vivian Fitch Kemp* (1936)).

However, the ribs on a hot water bottle were held to be configuration (*PB Cow v Cannon Rubber Manufacturers* (1959)), and so were the grooves in the backs of plastic chairs (*Sommer Allibert (UK) Ltd v Flair Plastics Ltd* (1987)).

Dichotomy between pattern/ornamentation and shape/configuration

To qualify an article must be made and sold separately (s 44(1)). Literary and artistic works are excluded (RDR 1989 r 26).

What constitutes an article for registration

Fan-fold computer paper, which had horizontal green lines, was held not to be literary work (*Lamson Industries Ltd's Application* (1978)). However, printed cushion covers were held to be a literary work (*Klarmann Ltd v Henshaw Linen Supplies* (1960)).

Football coupon forms were held not to be an article (*Littlewoods Pools Ltd's Application* (1949)).

Examples

Excluded articles which form an integrated part of a larger article	In *R v Registered Design Appeal Tribunal, ex p Ford Motor Co Ltd* (1994), the House of Lords considered the question of spare parts for cars.
Eye appeal	A registrable article must appeal to and be judged by the eye (s 1(1)).
Contrasted with functionality	Purely functional articles cannot be registered (*Amp Inc v Utilux Pty Ltd* (1972)). However, an article that combined functionality with eye-appeal could be registered (*Interlego AG v Tyco Industries Inc* (1988)).
	Eye-appeal is to be judged at the time of use, and not purchase (*P Ferrero and CSpA's Application* (1978)).
	The intention of the designer has been held to be relevant, but this is to be doubted (*Gardex Ltd v Sorata Ltd* (1986)), because now the aesthetic considerations must be considered to a material extent by consumer (s 1(3) as amended).
Requirement of novelty of the design	A design must be new (s 1(3)). The applicant must lodge a statement of novelty (RDR 1989 r 15). In an application, it is usual to separate the novel features of shape/configuration from those of pattern/ornament (*Evered's Application* (1961)). The usual date for determining the novelty or otherwise of a design is the date of the application (s 3(4)).
Novelty and originality	The classic statement of the difference between 'novelty' and 'originality' is contained in *Dover Ltd v Nürnberger Celluloid-waren Fabrik Gebrüder Wolff* (1910).
What constitutes novelty?	Novelty may reside in the design *per se*, or in its novel application to the article in question (*Saunders v Wiel* (1893)).
	Usually colour is insufficient to confer novelty (*Smith, Kline and French Laboratories Ltd's Application* (1974)), but if it is particularly striking it may (*Cooks and Hurt's Application* (1979)).
	Qualities excluded from conferring novelty are contained in s 1(4).
Prior registrations and applications	A prior application is sufficient to destroy novelty; there is no need for it to be actually registered (*Shallwin Ltd's Application* (1961)).
Prior publication	So long as the publication is publicly available, then that amounts to prior publication.

Oral disclosure is insufficient (*Rosedale Associated Manufacturers Ltd v Airfix Products Ltd* (1957)).

It is the visual effect of the variation that must be considered when determining whether or not the variation is immaterial (*Rollason's Registered Design* (1898)).

Immaterial or trade variants

There is a discretion to refuse registration of immoral designs or those which would be contrary to law (s 43(1)). However, it was held that an anatomically correct doll wearing a kilt was not immoral (*Masterman's Design* (1991)). There is in addition a general discretion to refuse registration (s 3(5)) (*Leara Trading Co Ltd's Designs* (1991)).

Designs that are excluded from registration

A method or principle of construction is excluded from design protection (s 1(1)(a)). Thus a design for a spoked wheel was limited to the specific example registered (*Pugh v Riley Cycle Co Ltd* (1912)).

Principles of construction

In an article is built on site, then generally it cannot be registered, eg a petrol station (*RH Collier & Co Ltd's Applications* (1937)).

Articles dictated solely by the function may not be registered. (s 1(1)(b)(i)).

Features dictated by functionality

Similarly designs that 'must match' are excluded from registration (s 1(1)(b)(ii)). This is similar to the design right exclusion.

'Must match' exception

A range of similar articles may be registered by same proprietor (s 4).

Novelty subject to the effect of ss 4, 6 and 16

Display at a recognised conference is permissible without destroying novelty (s 6(2)).

Emergency provisions to deal with times of war etc are contained in s 16.

Chapter 15

Registered Designs: Ownership, Duration and Infringement

Only the person who claims to be the proprietor of the design may apply for registration of that design (s 1(2)). Furthermore, an application for the registration of a design in which design right subsists shall not be entertained unless made by the person claiming to be the design right owner (s 3(2)). Thus, the rights in the registered design and the unregistered design cannot be split at the application stage. It is possible to assign rights in a registered design, and in such a case, the new proprietor must register his interest (s 19(1)).

15.1 Registration by the proprietor

If design right subsists in a registered design, and the proprietor of the registered design is also the design right owner, then an assignment of the design right shall be taken also to be an assignment of the right in the registered design, unless a contrary intention appears (s 19(3B)). Thus, it seems possible, as a matter of law, that the design right and the right in the registered design in a design may be separated. However, the Registrar will not register a transfer of interest in a registered design, unless he is satisfied that the applicant is also entitled to the interest in the corresponding design right (s 19(3A)), and thus such a separation of rights would seem to be of limited value.

15.2 Separation of rights in registered design and design right

The original proprietor of a design, for the purposes of the RDA 1949 (as amended), is the author of the design (s 2(1)) subject to two provisos, the first of which states that where a design is created pursuant to a commission for money or money's worth, the person commissioning the design shall be treated as the original proprietor of the design (s 2(1A)). Similarly, provision is made for the commission of an unregistered design (CDPA 1988 s 215(2)).

15.3 Original proprietor of the registered design

The second proviso states that where, in a case not falling within subsection 2(1A), a design is created by an employee in the course of his employment, his employer shall be treated as the original proprietor of the design (s 2(1B)). By s 44(1), the terms 'employee', 'employment' and 'employer' refer to employment under a contract of service or of apprenticeship. The definition of employment and the consequential ownership by the employer is to the same effect as that contained in the CDPA 1988 ss 11(2) and 178.

Rather peculiarly there are no provisions to deal with the situation of joint authorship as are found in the copyright, design right and patent legislation. Nor are there any provisions to cover ownership rights in applications for registered designs.

15.4 Authorship of a design

The author of the design is the person who created it (s 2(3)). In the case of a design generated by a computer in circumstances in which there is no human author, then the person by whom the arrangements necessary for the creation of the design are made shall be taken to be the author (s 2(4)). A design that is produced by a human who uses a computer merely as a tool would not fall within s 2(4).

15.5 Duration of the right in a registered design

Under the original RDA 1949 s 8, the initial period of registration for a design was five years, to which two further periods of five years could be added. Thus, under the old RDA the total possible period of protection was 15 years.

Under the amended RDA 1949s 8(1), the initial period is still five years. However, by s 8(2) it is now permissible to extend the registration for a further *four* periods of five years, which brings the total possible permitted duration of protection to 25 years. The period of protection runs from the date of the application for registration and not the date of the certification of the registration (s 3(5)). Thus, the slower the registration process, the shorter the time period the article will benefit from protection in the market place.

By the operation of the CDPA 1988 s 269(2), the extended period of protection does not apply to any design that was registered before 1 August 1989, and so old designs will receive 15 years protection at the most.

If the registered design is based upon an artistic work in which copyright subsists, then if the copyright ends while the registered design right is still extant, the registered design right will also lapse at the same time, and it cannot be renewed (s 8(5)).

If a design has been registered only by virtue of the operation of s 4, which allows the registration of closely related articles that would otherwise not be allowed registration because the original article would have anticipated the design, then all the registrations expire at the same time as the original registration expires (s 4(1)).

15.6 Transitional provisions

The overall intention of Parliament on amending the RDA 1949 by the CDPA 1988 was to restrict the scope of designs which would receive protection, in particular by the operation of the 'must match' exclusions. In order to foil any attempts by prospective proprietors who wished to submit an application for a design which would be allowed under the original RDA, but which would be excluded by the amended RDA, special transition provisions were enacted and are contained in the CDPA 1988 s 266.

These special provisions pertain to applications for designs filed between 13 February 1988 and 1 August 1989. They are contained in CDPA 1988 s 266, which by subsection (8) are to be construed as one with the Registered Design Act 1949 as amended, but do not form part of the amended Act. The right in any design to which this section applies, expires on 1 August 1999, if it has not already expired (s 266(1)(a)). Furthermore, anyone is entitled to a licence as of right from 1 August 1989 in an applicable design (s 266(1)(b)). The section only applies to those designs that qualified for registration under the old s 1, but would not do so under the new s 1 of the RDA 1949 as amended. Broadly, these provisions place the proprietor of a registered design registered during this period in a similar position to the owner of an unregistered design right.

Registered design protection had its origins in copyright, and so naturally there was an original requirement that the allegedly infringing design was copied from the registered design, ie some chain of derivation was needed. This requirement for copying was finally removed in the RDA 1949, which thus created a proper monopolistic right (*Gaskell & Chambers Ltd v Measure Master Ltd* (1993)).	**15.7 Introduction to infringement**

A design is taken as being registered as of the date on which the application was made or is to be treated as having been made (s 3(5)). However, no proceedings shall be permitted in respect of an infringement committed before the date on which the certificate of registration of the design is granted (s 7(5)). If, however, there is a design right or copyright present in the design as well as a registered design, then an action may be brought for the infringement of those rights before the certificate of registration has been granted.

The registration of a design under the RDA 1949 gives the registered proprietor the exclusive right:	**15.8 Rights conferred by registration of a design**

- to make or import for sale or hire, or use for the purposes of a trade or business; or

- to sell, hire or offer or expose for sale or hire, an article in respect of which the design is registered and to which that design or a design not substantially different from it has been applied (s 7(1)).

15.8.1   Direct and enabling infringement

The right in the registered design is infringed by a person who without the licence of the registered proprietor does anything which by virtue of subsection 7(1) is the exclusive right of the proprietor (s 7(2)). This corresponds to direct infringement of the registered design. It is not an infringement merely to possess an otherwise infringing article, even in the course of trade; nor is it an infringement to do any of the otherwise infringing acts if done purely for domestic, as opposed to commercial, purposes. However, it is still an infringement to make the articles in question during the monopoly period, with an intention to sell them after the period has expired (*M'Crea v Holdsworth* (1848)).

The right in the registered design is also infringed by a person who, without the licence of the registered proprietor, makes anything for enabling any such article to be made, in the UK or elsewhere, as mentioned in subsection 7(1) (s 7(3)). This corresponds to enabling infringement to occur.

The making of the device that enables any registered design to be made must occur in the UK. In contrast, the actual fabrication of the article in accordance with the registered design may occur anywhere in the world. It should be noted that a registered design does not confer the exclusive right merely to make an article to which the registered design is applied, rather the making must be for one of the purposes specified in s 7(1), ie for essentially *commercial* purposes. Thus in *Dorling v Honnor Marine Ltd* (1965), Harman LJ observed that 'the private maker who is the chief purchaser of the kits of parts will not be within the section [the old RDA 1949 s 7(1)] because he does not make the article for sale but for his own use'.

15.8.2   General considerations

Subsection 7(4) extends the rights in a registered design for an article to the kit component parts of a registered design. For this purpose 'kit' means a complete or substantially complete set of components intended to be assembled into an article.

Note that the rights are conferred only in respect of articles for which a design has been registered (s 1(2)), and such articles need to be specified in the application. Thus, if the design is applied to articles that are different from those for which the registration was secured then no infringement will have occurred (*Bourjois Ltd v British Home Stores Ltd* (1951)). This has the practical consequence that if a proprietor wished to protect a particular design for a wide range of goods, then the total cost of all the necessary applications becomes large.

Wide protection is often sought when exploiting the merchandising possibilities in characters, for example cartoon characters, which for a season may appear on everything from duvet covers to wrist watches.

In proceedings for the infringement of the right in a registered design, damages shall not be awarded against a defendant who proves that at the date of the infringement he was not aware, and had no reasonable ground for supposing, that the design was registered. A person shall not be deemed to have been aware or to have had reasonable grounds for supposing that the design was registered merely by reason of the marking of an article with the word 'registered' or any abbreviation thereof, or any word or words expressing or implying that the design applied to the article has been registered, unless the number of the design accompanied the word or words or the abbreviation in question (s 9(1)). Nothing in this section shall affect the power of the court to grant an injunction in any proceedings for infringement of the right in a registered design (s 9(2)). The test is an objective one which is to be judged in the light of all the circumstances at the time of the infringement (*Lancer Boss Ltd v Henley Forklift Co Ltd* (1975)).

15.8.3   Innocent infringers

The inclusion of this section significantly reduces the value of a registered design to its proprietor. Furthermore, it derogates from the principle that once a registration has been placed upon a public register, then the public at large is deemed to know of its existence. There are similar restrictions on the amount of damages for patent infringement (PA 1977 s 62). The legislature seems to have adopted the view that in cases where a monopoly has been granted, the public should be protected from false, and incomplete, claims that relate to the rights. Thus, only if the appropriate registration number is included, will the court award damages, because in such a situation any potential defendant could have easily checked the claims of the plaintiff before embarking on the offending acts.

If the specification of novelty contains a precise statement of what is being claimed as new, then for an infringement of that registered design to have occurred the alleged infringing article must contain all of the specially claimed novel features. The omission of only one such claimed novel feature will ensure that no liability arises. In *Portable Concrete Buildings Ltd v Bathcrete Ltd* (1962), in which novelty had been claimed in a design for the front and rear of a garage, it was held that there was no infringement, because even though the front end was identical, the rear end of the offending article was different.

15.9   **The scope of the protection granted by a registered design**

The right in a registered design is not infringed by the reproduction of a feature of the design which, by virtue of s 1(1)(b), has been omitted in determining whether or not the design is registrable (s 7(6)).

15.10 Who may commence an action for infringement?

Normally, the proprietor of the registered design will initiate infringement proceedings, because he is the person to whom the rights under the statute have been granted. However, on occasion it is possible for a licensee to sue in his own name if suitable provisions have been made in the licence agreement.

15.10.1 Registered proprietor

The rights conferred by the RDA 1949 as amended appertain to the registered proprietor, who is the person or persons for the time being entered on the register of designs as proprietor of the design (s 44(1)). Thus, it would appear that if a registered design is assigned, then before an action for infringement may be initiated, the new proprietor must be entered upon the register.

15.10.2 Licensee

An exclusive licensee does not have any separate right to sue in his own name. In *Heap v Hartley* (1889), Fry LJ said:

> 'A licence may be, and often is, coupled with a grant, and that grant then may convey an interest in the property, but the licence pure and simple, and by itself, never conveys an interest in property. It only enables a person to do lawfully what he could not otherwise do, except unlawfully. I think, therefore, that an exclusive licensee has no title whatever to sue.'

However, this may be circumvented by drafting the licence agreement in such a manner as to grant the licensee the right to sue in the name of the registered proprietor.

15.11 Compulsory licences and licences of right

A compulsory licence may be granted to an interested person if the registered design is not being worked in the UK (s 10). However, this section has been little used. The rather fuller provisions under the PA 1977 s 48 have merited much judicial consideration, that in essence come to the conclusion that the corresponding patent provisions may be in conflict with the Treaty of Rome (eg *Re Compulsory Patent Licences: EC Commission v United Kingdom* (1993)).

Licences of right may be granted after a report from the Monopolies and Mergers Commission (s 11A), or as a consequence of an undertaking by a defendant to take such a licence once a plaintiff has issued infringement proceedings (s 11B), or in respect of a registered design for which an application was made between 12 January 1988 and 1 August 1988, under CDPA 1988 s 266.

The issue of infringement depends upon whether or not the offending article has a 'design not substantially different from' the registered design (s 7(1)).

The degree of difference required so as to be 'substantially different from' varies from design to design. Thus, if a design is vastly different from the prior art, the corresponding monopoly will be large and so an allegedly infringing article would have to be more different from the registered design than would otherwise be the case. The converse is true as well, in that if the registered design is only slightly different from the prior art, then the exclusive monopoly will enjoy a smaller sphere of influence, and so an allegedly infringing article need only differ slightly in order to escape liability (*Simmons v Mathieson & Co Ltd* (1911)). As the right conferred is monopolistic in nature, the issue of derivation is irrelevant to the question of infringement.

If a design is registered in which novelty is claimed in both the features of the ornamentation and pattern and in the features of the shape and pattern, then such a registered design will only be infringed if both sets of features are found in the purported infringement.

The Court of Appeal in *Benchairs Ltd v Chair Centre Ltd* (1974) held that it was proper to regard the plaintiff's exhibited article as a visual representation of the subject matter of the plaintiff's registered design. However, Aldous J in *Gaskell & Chambers Ltd v Measure Master Ltd* (1993), a case which concerned a spirit measure dispenser, stated that:

'The comparison that has to be made is between the representations registered and the alleged infringements. It is necessary in particular to compare the whole of the shape and configuration of the dispenser shown in the representations of the registered design with the alleged infringements. This is particularly relevant in this case as the registered design only contains a front perspective view from above and a front perspective view from below which results in the back not being shown and only certain features of the side being clearly visible.'

This approach must be logically correct, because the monopoly is granted for the registered design and not the physical article which is made from it.

The issue of substantive difference is to be determined by the court, guided by expert evidence if appropriate. The differences are to be judged by the eye of a customer who is interested in the design of the article that is to be purchased. However, such a person is not assumed to have a photographic memory, thus the 'imperfect recollection' test that is

15.12 The question of infringement

15.12.1 Correct comparison

15.12.2 Substantial difference

used in the comparison of trade marks is useful in answering the question of infringement of registered designs (*Sommer Allibert (UK) Ltd v Flair Plastic Ltd* (1987)).

Aldous J summarised this test in *Gaskell & Chambers Ltd v Measure Master Ltd* (1993) in which he stated that:

> 'It is settled law that the comparison must be made between the registered design and the alleged infringement side by side and also upon an assumption of 'now and then', namely upon the assumption that the two designs are compared side by side and, thereafter, the interested addressee goes away and comes back later to the alleged infringements. It is in that way that the court can conclude which features of the design would in reality appeal to and be noticed by the eye and then decide whether the designs are or are not substantially different.'

In particular, it is relevant if any striking feature of the registered design has been omitted or included in the alleged infringement (*Dunlop Rubber Co Ltd v Golf Ball Developments Ltd* (1931)). The absence of such a striking feature will be strong evidence in support of the fact that there is no infringement. Accordingly, not only must the offending article contain all of the features in which novelty is claimed, but in practice it must also contain all the striking features as well, otherwise it is likely that a court will hold that there has been no infringement. Thus, it was held that there was no infringement of the registered design for a kettle, in which the defendant's design had a similar handle and body, but the spout was different (*Best Products Ltd v FW Woolworth & Co Ltd* (1964)).

Registered Designs: Ownership, Duration and Infringement

Only the person who claims to be the proprietor may apply for registration (s 1(2)). The applicant must also be design right owner, if applicable (s 3(2)). The transmission of registered design rights, is governed by s 19.

Registration by the proprietor

An assignment of design right, implies the assignment of any corresponding registered design (s 19(3B)). It appears to be a legal possibility that the unregistered and registered design rights may be separated. However, for registration, both rights must be held by the same person (s 19(3A)) and so such a separation would be of limited value.

Separation of rights in registered design and design right

The first owner of the design is the author, ie the person who created the work (s 2(1)), with only two exceptions. First, if the work was commissioned, then the commissioner is the first owner (s 2(1A)). Secondly, if the work was produced by an employee in the course of his employment, then the employer is the first owner (s 2(1B)). Employment is defined in s 44(1), and is given a similar meaning as in copyright law (CDPA 1988 ss 11(2) and 178).

Original proprietor of the registered design

The creator of the design is the author (s 2(3)). For computer generated designs, the person who makes the arrangements necessary for the creation of the design is the author (s 2(4)).

Authorship of a design

Under the unamended RDA 1949, 15 years was the maximum possible. Now there is an initial five year period, renewal possible for a further 20 years (s 8(1)). The period of protection is effective from date of application (s 3(5)). This extended period of protection only applies to new designs (CDPA 1988 s 269(2)).

If registration is based on an artistic work, the protection expires with that work (s 8(5)). If the registration is based on s 4, ie associated with the related designs, then the right expires with principal design (s 4(1)).

Duration of the right in a registered design

For designs filed between 13 February 1988 and 1 August 1989, protection expires on 1 August 1999, if it has not already done so (s 266(1)(a)). Licence as of right in such designs may be granted from 1 August 1989 (s 266(1)(b)). These designs must have satisfied the old definition, but not the new.

Transitional provisions

Introduction to infringement	There is now a 'true monopoly' in a registered design, and so there is no need for the offending article to have been copied from the original. No infringement proceedings may be commenced until the certificate of registration has been issued (s 7(5)).
Rights conferred by registration of a design	Direct infringement is regulated by s 7(1), while enabling infringement is governed by s 7(3). The protection only covers articles that are actually specified in the registration (*Bourjois Ltd v British Home Stores Ltd* (1951)).
Innocent infringers	No damages may be awarded against innocent infringers (s 9(1)); however, an injunction may be granted (s 9(2)). Innocence is an objective test (*Lancer Boss Ltd v Henley Forklift Co Ltd* (1975)).
The scope of the protection granted by a registered design	The offending article must contain all the novel features claimed in the registration before it can be held to be an infringement (*Portable Concrete Buildings Ltd v Bathcrete Ltd* (1962)). There is no infringement if the features excluded under s 1(1)(b) have been copied (s 7(6)).
Who may commence an action for infringement	Usually the registered proprietor will be the plaintiff. However, it is possible for a licensee to sue in the name of the registered proprietor if the licence agreement is so drafted.
Compulsory licences and licences of right	A compulsory licence may be obtained (s 10). However, it is likely that there may be a conflict with European legislation (*Re Compulsory Patent Licences: EC Commission v UK* (1993)). A licence of right may be obtained after a MMC report (s 11A), or if granted as a consequence of undertakings being given by the defendant in infringement proceedings (s 11B). These are also available for designs registered between 12 January 1988 and 1 August 1989 (CDPA 1988 s 266).
The question of infringement	The degree of difference between the registered design and the prior article determines the scope of monopoly conferred on the registered design (*Simmons v Mathieson & Co Ltd* (1911)).
Correct comparison	The offending article should only be compared with the registered design itself (*Gaskell & Chambers Ltd v Measure Master Ltd* (1993)).
Substantial difference	It is valid to use the imperfect recollection test developed in trade mark law (*Sommer Allibert (UK) Ltd v Flair Plastic Ltd*

(1987)) and this should be coupled with a side by side comparison.

The inclusion or omission of any particular striking element of a novel feature will be significant (*Dunlop Rubber Co Ltd v Golf Ball Development Ltd* (1931)).

Chapter 16

Patents: Historical Introduction

Patents have a long and distinguished history in the UK. Originally, a patent was granted by the Crown as an exercise of the Royal prerogative. This was similar in nature to the grant of printing licences which were the predecessor to copyright. The 'Letters Patent' consisted of a Royal Proclamation to the public that the bearer of the 'Letters' had the authority of the Crown to do whatever was specified within the Letters Patent. The Royal Seal was affixed to the bottom of the Letters, so that the contents could be read without breaking the Seal. The word 'patent' comes from the Latin, 'patere', which means 'to lie open', ie the Royal grant was open for all to see. The Royal nature of the grant was reflected in the fact that originally an action to enforce a patent was based upon the offence of disobedience to the Royal command contained in the grant.

16.1 Grant of Letters Patent

Patents were not originally concerned with rewarding an inventor, but rather with rewarding a merchant who introduced a new product into the UK. In this way the patent was more akin to a trading monopoly granted in return for introducing new technology into the country and instructing English workers in the use of that technology, rather than a monopoly granted as a reward for inventing something *ab initio*.

Elizabeth I, however, rather than just granting patents to merchants who had introduced new and useful products or techniques into this country, also started granting patents for basic commodities. This, naturally, led to the rise in price of these commodities, which ultimately led to Parliament exerting pressure upon the Monarch to cease issuing patents in such cases. Shortly after the death of Elizabeth I, the courts held that the monopoly granted by the old Queen in favour of a merchant for the exclusive right to import playing cards was invalid at common law (*Darcy v Thomas Allin* (1602)). This is generally taken to be the first patent case recorded in the English law reports.

16.2 System under Elizabeth I

The Statute of Monopolies 1623 attempted to regulate the position of the grant of monopolies to the populace. Section 6 permitted a monopoly to be granted for 14 years for any manner of new manufacture. The period of 14 years

16.3 Statute of Monopolies 1623

corresponds to two cycles of apprenticeships; a sufficiently long time to introduce the new technology and train the workforce. The underlying justification for the patent system was that technological innovations were put to work for the benefit of the country's economy. The patent could be granted to the true and first inventor. This, however, was interpreted widely to include not only the creator of the invention, but also the person who first introduced the invention into the country. It was explicitly stated within the Act that the patent was not to be 'contrary to the law nor mischievous to the state, by raising in price of commodities at home, or hurt of trade, or generally inconvenient'.

16.4 Developments during the 19th and early 20th centuries

The Patents Law Amendment Act 1852 marks the beginning of the modern practice in patent law. This Act set up the Patent Office and the Register of Patents, and established a procedure whereby only one patent application was needed to be filed for England, Scotland and Ireland, which resulted in one patent that covered all these countries. More importantly, this Act also required that a specification (which could be provisional) be included with the patent application. The point of the specification was to set out fully the nature of the invention, and how best it could be put into practice.

The Patents, Designs and Trade Marks Act 1883 required that the full specification be filed and that it be examined by the Patent Office before a patent would be granted. There followed several Acts that made minor amendments. The Patents Act 1902 introduced the requirement that previously published specifications be searched in order to determine whether or not the invention revealed in the patent application had been previously published, ie a search to ensure that the patent was novel. This official searching commenced in 1905, and extended to the specifications that had been granted in the previous 50 years. The search was not concerned with the issue of obviousness, but only with the question of novelty.

16.5 The claims of a patent

The first patents that were granted did not even include a specification that revealed in detail how the patented invention worked, nor did they include a separate section in which the inventor claimed what he thought was new and patentable. When patent actions were heard before a jury it was for the jury to decide what was in essence claimed by the patentee, and thereby determine the scope of the invention.

The PDTMA 1883 s 5(5), required that a 'distinct statement of the invention claimed' must be included, and thus it became mandatory for the patentee to include in his application a statement of the claims that he made for the invention.

However, even after the passing of this Act, it was not clear that the claims were to be taken as determining the scope of the invention as the inventor thought fit, until this point was settled in *Nobel's Explosive Co Ltd v Anderson* (1894). Following this case it was no longer possible for the inventor to claim that the patent extended to different embodiments that were outside the scope of the claims, yet were contained within the specification. This marks the beginning of the practice that the claims are to mark the boundary of the patent, ie the 'fence-posts', rather than being indicative of the general nature of the invention, ie 'guide-posts'.

The Patents and Designs Act 1919 introduced a provision whereby, if a patent contained some invalid claims, then the remainder of the claims could still be held to be good. Thus, the inclusion of invalid claims no longer invalidated the whole patent.

The Patents Act 1949 substantially rewrote the laws that related to patents. The definition of invention was widened, as were the grounds of opposition to the grant of a patent. The restrictions on the patenting of chemical substances, drugs and food-stuffs were abolished.

16.6   Patents Act 1949

Ever since the first patents were granted as an exercise of Royal Prerogative, patents have had an effect on the trade between nations.

One of the areas of great divergence amongst different countries is the degree to which an application is subjected to any sort of scrutiny before the patent is granted. In countries such as Italy, which operates a registration system, the patent application is not subjected to any search or examination at all. In other countries, for example, Switzerland, there is a system whereby the patent application is extensively examined and interested third parties are allowed to intervene with their own observations.

Even though there are great differences in how a patent may be obtained in different countries, it was soon realised that it would be advantageous to the economy of the country if foreigners were accorded the same rights in this respect as native-born people.

16.7   International Patent Conventions

The first international agreement that concerned the reciprocal rights in the field of intellectual property law was the Paris Industrial Property Convention of 1883 (the 'Paris Convention'). The basic formula for the reciprocation of rights is that the nationals of any one of the Member States would be accorded the same rights in another Member State as would

16.7.1   Paris Industrial Property Convention 1883

the nationals of that second Member State be accorded by that second Member State within that second Member State. This formula allows countries to join that have little or no patent system of their own, and yet secures for them and their nationals, rights in their fellow Member States that do have a patent protection system. The idea is that in this way such States may be encouraged to develop a patent protection system for themselves.

The Paris Convention also established a system of priority, whereby an application made in one of the Member States gives a period of grace (currently 12 months) in which the applicant may apply for a patent in other Members States, without the application being held being held invalid for want of novelty as a result of the prior publication in the first Member State. The final granted patents will all bear the priority date of the first application.

The Convention's main aim is to allow entry for foreigners to each country's patent system; it does not produce an international patent system *per se*.

| 16.7.2 | Patent Co-operation Treaty 1970 |

The Patent Co-operation Treaty of 1970 (the 'PCT') came into force on 1 June 1978. It is administered by the World Intellectual Property Organisation ('WIPO') based in Geneva. There are two separate parts to the PCT, Chapters 1 and 2. Chapter 1 provides for an international search facility which is designed to discover whether or not the subject matter of the new application has been patented before. The second chapter is a preliminary examination procedure, which, even though not based upon any international agreement about the grounds for validity of a patent, produces a report which is concerned with certain basic questions such as novelty, inventive step and subject matter. The purpose of such a report is that the individual Member States may then apply the local law to the information that has already been gathered, and then grant (if appropriate), on an individual basis, nationally based patents. The advantage of using the PCT for a prospective patentee is that instead of there being a search in each and every country in which a patent is sought, a single search is performed and this will suffice for all the convention countries, with a corresponding saving in cost to the applicant.

| 16.7.3 | European Patent Convention 1973 |

On 1 June 1978, a European system also came into operation. This was the European Patent Convention (the 'EPC'). The EPC is administered by the European Patent Office (the 'EPO') based in Munich. This convention operates along similar lines to the PCT, in that a single application may be made to the EPO, which then makes a search and preliminary examination of the patent. After this stage the patent application is passed

to the individual countries which will grant, or refuse to grant, as the case may be, a patent for that country.

In addition to the EPC, the EEC Member States also set up the Community Patent Convention (the 'CPC'). This provides that after the search and examination of a patent application by the EPO, instead of the application then being referred to the Member States for the granting of a bundle of national patents, a single community-wide patent may be granted. This Convention has been revised in 1985 and 1989. There are, however, procedural and political problems with the implementation of this Convention, and as a consequence this system is not yet operational. Once the system is working, then a community patent will be unitary, ie it will be granted, revoked or allowed to lapse only in respect of the whole community and not on a country by country basis as is the case with patents granted under the EPC.

16.7.4   Community Patent Convention 1975

Under the PA 1949 s 22(3), the term of protection for a patent in the UK was only 16 years. It could, however, be increased by up to 10 further years if the patentee could show that he had not received adequate remuneration from the exploitation of the patent or there had been loss due to war (PA 1949, ss 23 and 24 respectively).

16.8   Duration of patent protection

Currently, the term of protection afforded by a patent is 20 years. Transitional provisions deal with those patents that had been granted under the old law, but now have the extended protection period. Thus, certain old patents are entitled to the increased twenty-year period of protection, but for the last four years the patent is marked 'licence of right' (PA 1977 Schedule 3, paras 4 and 5).

The pharmaceutical industry has lobbied Parliament that this period of protection is too short in which to recoup the investment required to develop a drug, because a significant proportion of these 20 years must be spent in satisfying the safety tests that have been laid down before a new drug may be released onto the market. In order to deal with this situation, Council Regulation 1768/92 has been introduced which extends the period of protection for a patented medicine. The amount of the extension equates to the period between the application for the patent and the granting of the first permission to market the drug anywhere in the EU, less five years, and up to a maximum of five years. This extra protection is called a supplementary protection certificate. Furthermore, old pharmaceutical patents no longer have to be marked 'licence of right' as is the case with non-pharmaceutical patents (PA 1977 Schedule 1 para 4A and 4B as amended by the CDPA 1988 ss 293 and 294).

16.9   Patents Act 1977

The law that regulated patents in the UK was fundamentally altered by the Patents Act 1977. This Act, in essence, repealed all the previous patent legislation in the UK. The PA 1977 came into force on 1 June 1978. All old patents with more than five years unexpired have a lifetime of 20 years, but with special provisions for licences of right in their last four years of life. These provisions will all be spent by 31 May 1998.

The 1977 Act represents a fundamentally different approach to patent legislation from that which went before it. This Act incorporates into domestic law the EPC and the CPC. The preliminary examination now includes a consideration of inventiveness and not just novelty. Furthermore, the definition of infringement has been widened so that acts that were previously only actionable as procuring an infringement are now actionable directly. Lastly, the European doctrine of 'exhaustion of rights' has been introduced.

Patents: Historical Introduction

Letters Patent were originally an open letter from the Monarch to the people.

Grant of Letters Patent

The system was akin to a trading monopoly. There was no need for the subject matter to be novel or inventive. However, the patent had to be worked within the UK, so as to benefit the economy. Elizabeth I also granted patents for stable commodities. The monopoly in importing playing cards was held to be unlawful at common law (*Darcy v Thomas Allin* (1602)).

System under Elizabeth I

During the reign of James I, there was a move towards increased competition by allowing more for free trade. The Statute of Monopolies 1623 s 6 introduced a 14 year period of protection for patents so long as they did not harm society.

Statute of Monopolies 1623

The Patents Law (Amendment) Act 1852 set up the Patent Office, and a unified system for the whole of the UK. The inclusion of a specification was introduced as a mandatory requirement.

    The Patents, Designs and Trade Marks Act 1883 introduced the requirement that a full specification was included on filing. Furthermore, the specification was now examined. A proper novelty search was introduced from 1905 by the Patents Act 1902.

Developments during the 19th and early 20th centuries

The PDTMA 1883 s5(5) introduced the requirement for claims to be included. These claims limited the scope of the monopoly conferred by the patent (*Nobel's Explosive Co v Anderson* (1894)).

    By the Patents and Designs Act 1919 the inclusion of an invalid claim no longer jeopardised the whole patent.

Inclusion and role of the claims of a patent

The definition of what may be patented was widened. Correspondingly, the grounds for opposition were widened.

Patents Act 1949

Introduced the basic principle of reciprocal rights, and a priority system, whereby an application in one Member State would not invalidate an application made later elsewhere, so long as it was made within 12 months

Paris Industrial Property Convention 1883

Patent Co-operation Treaty 1970	Came into force on 1 June 1978 and is administered by WIPO. Chapter 1 is concerned with international search facilities, while Chapter 2 deals with an initial examination procedures. The result is a bundle of national patents.
European Patent Convention 1973	Came into force on 1 June 1978 and is administered by the EPO. The result is a bundle of national patents being granted.
Community Patent Convention 1975	This Convention is not yet in force. The result would be a single unitary patent, which covers the whole of the EU.
Duration of patent protection	Previously, under the PA 1949, the term of protection was 16 years. Under the PA 1977, it is 20 years, which is in line with the rest of Europe. There are transitional provisions for old patents and special allowances for pharmaceutical patents.
Patents Act 1977	Came into force from 1 June 1978. It incorporates the CPC and the EPC. There is a preliminary search for both inventiveness and novelty. The doctrine of 'exhaustion of rights' has been introduced.

Chapter 17

Patents: Specification

A patent that has effect within the UK may have been obtained by one of two routes. Either it is a purely domestic patent which has been granted by the Patent Office; or else, it is a European (UK) patent obtained through the EPO. In the latter case, the patent is said to have the UK as one of its designated countries. More than likely, there will be corresponding patents designated for other EU States. A European (UK) patent is treated in the Courts of England and Wales as if it had been granted by the Patent Office (PA 1977 s 77).

There are no restrictions based upon nationality concerning who may apply for a patent at either the EPO or the British Patent Office. Thus, any person may make an application for a patent, either alone or jointly with another (s 7(1)). The only restriction is that the person who makes the application should be the inventor or joint inventor (s 7(2)(a)). There is one major exception, whereby in preference to the inventor, any person who at the time of the making of the invention was entitled to the property in the patent (other than an equitable interest) in the UK (s 7(2)(b)), or any successors in title (s 7(2)(c)) may apply for the patent. The most likely person to qualify under s 7(2)(b) is the employer of the inventor.

For these purposes, the inventor is the actual devisor of the invention (s 7(3)).

Except so far as it is proved, a person who makes an application for a patent shall be taken to be the person entitled to make the application (s 7(4)).

The central documentation in a patent application is the patent specification itself. This consists of the title, the name of the inventor, a description of the invention (which may include drawings), and the claims. There is usually an abstract, but this is separate and does not form part of the patent itself. The description of the patent must contain sufficient detail for the invention to be performed by a person who is skilled in the appropriate technology, ie it must disclose the invention. The description is sometimes referred to as the body of the patent. The claims mark out the limits of the monopoly rights that are being sought by the applicant. Together, the description and the claims are known as the patent specification.

17.1 Introduction

17.2 Person entitled to apply for a patent

17.3 Patent specification

17.3.1	Initial informal application

Most systems, including the UK's, operate a 'first-to-file' priority procedure, in contrast to a 'first-to-grant' priority system. Generally, the priority date of an invention is the date of filing the application (s 5(1)). However, when a claim specifies more than one invention, each invention may have a different priority date (s 125(2)).

When the first application is made to the Patent Office, there is no need to file a full and completed patent application. Instead, a more informal document may be filed. The purpose of an informal application is to secure an early priority date for the main patent application. In order to do this, the informal application must contain sufficient information to support any claim in the later full specification. Thus, any embodiment of the invention is set out in detail, together with any alternatives that may be worth investigating. It is also common practice to suggest any avenues it is believed that competitors are pursuing. This is to prevent them from later submitting a successful related patent, which could interfere with the commercial exploitation of the initial applicant's patent once it has been granted.

Subsequently, a least one claim, an abstract and a request for a preliminary examination and search must be made (s 15(5)). This must be done within 12 months (Patent Rules 1990 r 25).

17.3.2	Final specification

The final patent specification 'shall disclose the invention in a manner which is clear enough and complete enough for the invention to be performed by a person skilled in the art' (s 14(3)). In addition to the body of the specification which contains a description of the invention disclosing the invention, this description must support the claims which set out the limits of the claimed invention. The claims shall:

- define the matter for which the applicant seeks protection;

- be clear and concise;

- be supported by the description; and

- relate to one invention or to a group of inventions which are so linked as to form a single inventive concept (s 14(5)).

Even though it is a requirement that the claims are clear and concise, it is sometimes advantageous to have claims that are slightly woolly, because, as technology develops, then it is usually easier to stretch vague claims to cover the new material which may potentially infringe a more widely drawn claim.

Generally, the priority date of an invention is the date of the filing of the application (s 5(1)). However, a subsequent application may be deemed to have the priority date of an earlier application if the later one is filed within 12 months of the earlier application, so long as the subsequent application is supported by matter disclosed in the earlier application (s 5(2)(a)).

The earlier application may have been made under the Patent Act 1977, or in any country that is a member of any relevant international convention (s 5(5)). Orders in Council may be made to supplement this list as and when necessary (s 90(1)). Countries declared as convention countries under the Patents Act 1949, remain so for the purpose of the Patents Act 1977 (Schedule 4 para 9).

If a claim specifies more than one invention, then each invention may have a different priority date (s 125(2)). Matter contained in a specification may be accorded an earlier priority date than that of the date of filing if it has been disclosed in an earlier document (s 5(2)(b)). However, for a claim to have an earlier priority it must be supported by an earlier, enabling, disclosure, ie one that made the invention available to the public in such a way as to enable a skilled man to put the claimed invention into effect (*Asahi Kasei Kogyo KK's Application* (1990)). The burden of proof is upon the patentee to establish his *prima facie* entitlement to an earlier priority date if he has sought to rely upon one (*Biogen Inc v Medeva plc* (1995).

The priority date of a patent is the date on which the contents of the patent application are compared with the 'state of the art' in order to determine the issues of novelty and inventiveness.

17.4   Priority date

The whole patent specification comprises two distinct parts: the descriptive body and the claims. Each part serves a different, but related, function. Each is necessary for a patent to be valid.

17.5   Interpretation of the specification

The body of the specification must disclose the invention in a manner that is clear enough and complete enough for the invention to be performed by a person skilled in the art (s 14(3)), and so enable such a person to actually perform the invention in practice. This, in essence, is the consideration that the patentee gives to society in return for the grant of the monopoly. If the body of the patent is insufficient in this regard, then it may be revoked due to invalidity (s 72(1)(c)).

The claims, however, are to define the monopoly that is sought by the patentee (s 14(5)(a)). Each claim may contain a number of integers, which are the individual units that

17.5.1   Relationship between the description and the claims

comprise the whole claim. The construction of the claims, ie their exact meaning, is usually at the centre of any patent dispute.

17.5.2   Wording of a claim

When considering the question of validity of a claim, the patentee will want to put a narrow meaning upon the claims so as to prevent old material anticipating the claims, or making them invalid because they claim something which is obvious. In contrast, a person wishing to attack the validity of a patent will put a wide meaning on the claims for the opposite reasons. Correspondingly, when a patentee is attempting to stop an alleged infringer, he will propose a wide meaning to the claims so as to include within their ambit the activity of the alleged infringer, who will in turn seek to put a narrow meaning upon the claims so as to exclude his activity from the monopoly granted by the patent. In most patent actions, the plaintiff alleges infringement, while the defendant counterclaims by alleging invalidity. Consequently, both parties must steer a course between a wide or narrow construction of the claims that supports his case, but not his opponents.

There are no special rules for the construction of a patent, rather the normal canons of construction should be employed by the court (*Daily v Etablissements Fernand Berchet* (1992)). However, it is permitted for technical items to have a technical meaning (*Unwin v Hanson* (1891)), but the court will take objection to needless 'patent jargon' (*Martin and Biro Swan Ltd v H Millwood Ltd* (1956)).

17.5.3   Ominbus claim

As a matter of practice, claim 1 is usually the principal claim of a patent, and each subsequent claim is built upon that claim; even though there is no reason in law why this should be so. The claims are usually worded in very precise terms so as to delineate the invention claimed. However, the last claim is usually worded in a much more general manner, eg 'as herein described' or 'substantially as described and with reference to, or illustrated by, the diagrams'. This type of claim is called the omnibus claim, and is to be considered as the narrowest claim, and not the widest claim of the patent. Lord Morton in *Raleigh Cycle Co Ltd v H Miller & Co Ltd* (1948), said that:

> 'I think that the reason why such a claim has been inserted is ... [that] ... the patentee fears that his earlier claims may be held invalid, because they cover too wide an area or fail sufficiently and clearly to ascertain the scope of the monopoly claimed ... It is surely more likely that the last claim, referring to the drawings, is intended to be a narrow claim, incorporating the drawings as part of the description, and directed to saving the patent from revocation, if all wider claims are held to be bad.'

The Patents Act 1977 does not directly deal with the question of interpretation of – ie the construction to be placed upon – the claims, but instead states that the invention is specified in a claim of the specification as interpreted by the description and any drawings contained in that specification (s 125(1)). Section 125(3) states that the Protocol on the Interpretation of Article 69 of the EPC applies to s 125(1) as it does to Article 69, which is not surprising because the former was based on the latter.

17.5.4   Statutory position on the interpretation of claims

Article 69 of the EPC states that:

'The extent of the protection conferred by a European patent or European patent application shall be determined by the terms of the claims. Nevertheless, the description and drawings shall be used to interpret the claims.'

The Protocol to the EPC Article 69 states that:

'Article 69 should not be interpreted in the sense that the extent of the protection conferred by a European patent is understood as that defined by the strict, literal meaning of the wording used in the claims, the description and drawings being employed only for the purpose of resolving an ambiguity found in the claims. Neither should it be interpreted in the sense that the claims serve only as a guideline and that the actual protection conferred may extend to what, from a consideration of the description and drawings by a person skilled in the art, the patentee has contemplated. On the contrary, it is to be interpreted as defining a position between these extremes which combines a fair protection for the patentee with a reasonable degree of certainty for third parties.'

The approach that should be adopted in the construction of the claims is a vexed one. In *Catnic Components Ltd v Hill & Smith Ltd* (1982), which was the leading case decided under the PA 1949, the court developed a purposive approach to the interpretation of claims. This case concerned construction joints. The patent claimed that one component was 'vertical' to another. In the alleged infringing article, the component in question was not exactly vertical, but at a slight angle to the vertical. It was held by the House of Lords that this still amounted to an infringement. Further the House held that the court should not be bound by a strict literalistic approach, but rather should find the true purpose of the claim, ie adopt a purposive approach.

Patents: Specification

A patent that has force within the UK may be obtained from either the EPO, or the Patent Office. A European (UK) patent is treated as if it had been granted by the Patent Office (PA 1977 s 77).

Introduction

The person who makes the application should be the inventor (s 7(2)(a)). The most common exception is that the employer of the inventor should be the applicant (s 7(2)(b)). The inventor is the actual devisor of the invention (s 7(3)).

Person entitled to apply for a patent

The description of the invention must be sufficiently detailed to allow it to be worked. The claims delineate the scope of the monopoly.

Patent specification

'First-to-file' systems allow the filing of a preliminary specification to secure priority date. The full specification, with claims, must be filed within 12 months (Patent Rules 1990 r 25).

Initial informal application

The final specification must disclose the invention in a clear and complete manner (s 14(3)).

The claims must define the invention, and they must be clear and concise (s 14(5)).

Final specification

The priority date is the date of the filing of the application (s 5(1)). The priority date determines the date to be used for the 'state of the art' comparisons.

Priority date

The description should disclose the invention, and if it is not sufficient, then the patent is invalid (s 72(1)(c)). The claims define the monopoly that is sought (s 14(5)(a)). The claims consist of integers, which then need to be 'construed' to find their true meaning.

Relationship between the description and the claims

A wide construction of a claim will catch more potential infringements. However, such a wide construction may also include old and obvious material, and so render the claim invalid. There are no special rules for the construction of patents, rather the normal canons of construction should be employed (*Daily v Etablissement Fernand Berchet* (1992)).

Wording of a claim

However, it is permissible for technical terms to have technical meanings (*Unwin v Hanson* (1891)).

Omnibus claim

The omnibus claim is the narrowest, and not the widest claim (*Raleigh Cycle Co Ltd v H Miller & Co Ltd* (1948)).

Statutory position on the interpretation of claims

The purposive approach developed under *Catnic Components Ltd v Hill & Smith Ltd* (1982) is still good law under the PA 1977. The PA 1977 follows the EPC (s 125).

Chapter 18

Patents: Validity

It is commonly said that a weak patent is more powerful in the hands of man with a deep pocket than a good patent is in the hands of a pauper. The justification for this arises from the large cost of running a patent action. In order to reduce the injustice of allowing a weak patent to dominate a market purely because its proprietor is capable of funding litigation, there is a strong argument that patents should not be granted for purported inventions that are later found not to have been worthy of a patent.

18.1   Introduction

The examination procedure introduced under the PA 1977 was designed to accord with the system adopted by the EPO. Accordingly, the patent application is now examined not only with regard to the issue of novelty, but also with regard to the inventiveness of the subject matter. Furthermore, the Patent Office will now search against material gleaned world-wide, rather than just against material of purely British origin.

18.2   Examination of a patent application

The PA 1977 has removed several grounds upon which a patent could be declared invalid under the PA 1949 s 32, namely prior claiming, inutility, false suggestion, illegality of intended use and secret use. The PA 1977 has added one new ground of invalidity, namely that the protection conferred by the patent has been extended by an amendment that should never have been granted.

18.3   Invalidity under the PA 1949 contrasted with that under the PA 1977

There are five grounds, and only five, upon which a patent may be revoked by the courts for invalidity. The grounds for revoking a patent are contained in s 72, which are:

18.4   Grounds for invalidity under the PA 1977

- lack of patentability;

- grant to a person not entitled;

- insufficiency;

- the matter disclosed in the specification extends beyond that disclosed in the preliminary application; and,

- the protection conferred by the patent has been extended by an amendment which should not have been allowed.

Even though, broadly, these heads of invalidity correspond with those that were available under the PA 1949, there was a large change in the detailed wording. This was partly because the PA 1977 was intended to echo the EPC, ie to move from a legislative system that evolved from the common law of England towards a unified continental approach. Thus, *prima facie*, cases decided under the old law will be of little assistance to the courts deciding issues raised under the new legislation. However, even though the wording has altered significantly, some of the underlying concepts, such as novelty and inventiveness, have remained the same, and in practice the courts have not felt compelled to start with a clean slate.

This does not mean though, that the courts can just incorporate the old case law into the new legislation with no regard to the new regime. In particular, if a section is drafted so as to parallel the provisions in the EPC and the PCT, then the court is obliged to pay attention to any cases that may have been decided in foreign courts, and in particular in the ECJ, on the issue. The Court of Appeal in *PLG Research Ltd v Ardon International Ltd* (1995) made an attempt to say that the approach hitherto adopted by the courts in the UK did not conform to the guidelines laid down for the EPC. Furthermore, that greater attention should be taken of decisions in German courts. However, Aldous J firmly rejected these suggestions in *Assidoman Multipack Ltd v The Mead Corporation* (1995), and went on to hold that, on the contrary, the approach in the UK courts was in accord with the guidelines.

Any interested party may commence an action for invalidity. Usually, the person aggrieved is someone whom the proprietor is suing for infringement, and the action for revocation is by way of counterclaim. In this work, only the issue of patentability will be discussed in detail. The other grounds are more appropriate for a practitioner's work.

18.5   Patentable invention: PA 1977 s 1

This is the commonest ground for mounting oppositions to the validity of a patent. Thus, a patent may be revoked if 'the invention is not a patentable invention' (s 72(1)(a)). What constitutes a patentable invention is defined in the opening parts of the Act.

Subsection 1(1) sets out the fundamental requirements of an invention that is patentable. It reads:

'1(1) A patent may be granted only for an invention in respect of which the following conditions are satisfied, that is to say -

(a) the invention is new;

(b) it involves an inventive step;

(c) it is capable of industrial application;

(d) the grant of a patent for it is not excluded by
subsections (2) and (3) below;

and references in this Act to a patentable
invention shall be construed accordingly.'

Subsection 1(2) concerns those things which the Act deems
not to be an invention at all, while subsection 1(3) deals with
those things which are excluded on the grounds of public
policy.

Thus, the first question that needs to be addressed is
whether or not the subject matter of the patent is an invention
within the meaning of the Act, as elaborated in s 1(2).

The Patents Act 1977 does not define inclusively what an
invention is, rather it exemplifies those things which are not to
be considered as an invention for the purposes of the Act.
Section 1(2) states that:

18.6   What is an invention?

'1(2) It is hereby declared that the following (among
other things) are not inventions for the purposes
of this Act, that is to say, anything which consists
of

(a) a discovery, scientific theory or mathematical
model;

(b) a literary, dramatic, musical or artistic work
or any other aesthetic creation whatsoever;

(c) a scheme, rule or method for performing a
mental act, playing a game or doing business,
or a program for a computer;

(d) the presentation of information;
but the foregoing provision shall prevent
anything from being treated as an invention
for the purposes of this Act only to the extent
that a patent or application for a patent relates
to that thing as such.'

In *American Cyanamid Co (Dann's) Patent* (1971), Lord
Diplock said that:

'The only definition of invention contained in the Patents
Act 1949, is by reference to the phrase 'any manner of new
manufacture' in the Statute of Monopolies 1623. This
statute has never been construed as confining the grant of
patents to processes which would have been within the
contemplation of Parliament in the early seventeenth
century as constituting a new manner of manufacture. The
concept of invention as an activity which entitles the
person who undertakes it to a patent monopoly of a

process or its product has been continually changing by applying the social policy which underlay the Statute of Monopolies in the seventeenth century to the changing conditions resulting from advances in technology and the sciences. That policy was to provide a material inducement to persons to undertake whatever effort and expense might be needed to introduce into the UK some useful new process or new product with a view to its becoming generally available for use or manufacture by the inhabitants of the realm.'

His Lordship later said, 'I accept, therefore, the extension of the concept of 'invention' to include antibiotics which are discovered through this kind of research.' This is indicative that the courts have not been hesitant to incorporate new technology as and when it arises.

Section 1 of the PA 1977 is based very closely upon Article 52 of the EPC. In *STERNHEIMER/Harmonic Vibrations* (1989), the technical Board of Appeal of the EPO concluded that those entities that were excluded from being classified as an invention for the purpose of the EPC all showed the common characteristic that they did not use 'technical methods to produce a concrete technical effect'. A similar approach has been promulgated in *Chiron Corporation v Organon Teknika Ltd (No 3)* (1994). We will now look at each of the excluded classes in turn.

| 18.6.1 | Discoveries, theories and mathematical models |

In *Genentech Inc's Patent* (1989), Mustill LJ said:

'You cannot invent water, although you certainly can invent ways in which it may be distilled or synthesised.'

His Lordship later stated:

'Ideas and discoveries have this much in common, that neither is patentable in isolation.'

Thus, the practical application of a discovery may be an invention, while the discovery *per se* cannot be.

A mathematical model *per se* cannot be patented, even if it was used to design a new shape for the propeller of a ship (*Lips' Application* (1959), who, incidentally, designed the propellers for the *Oriana*). Mathematical models are closely related to computer programs which are excluded under subsection 1(2)(c).

| 18.6.2 | Aesthetic creations |

Works of an aesthetic nature have always been held by the courts not to be suitable for patent protection. Instead recourse should be made to the laws of copyright, design right and registered design.

It has been suggested that the proprietor of a patent has abandoned his right to copyright protection in the drawings that accompany his patent application, on the basis that he has elected the monopolistic protection of the patent over the more limited protection, but longer in duration, conferred by copyright (*Catnic Components Ltd v Hill & Smith Ltd* (1978)). This point was not addressed by the Court of Appeal in that case, and has not fallen to be decided by a Court of England and Wales. However, a similar argument has been rejected by the Court of Appeal of Hong Kong (*Interlego AG v Tyco Industries Inc* (1988) and the High Court of Ireland (*House of Spring Gardens Ltd v Point Blank Ltd* (1983)).

Schemes for performing mental acts or playing games are not patentable. Thus, a method for winning at roulette or poker cannot be protected by this means. A claim relating to an expert system was held to be a program for performing a mental act (*Wang Laboratories Inc's Application* (1991)). If the software is hard-wired into the computer, ie made into 'firmware', then the new computer machine consisting of hardware and firmware could be eligible for a patent. However, the mere existence of firmware is not sufficient to ensure patentability. For example, a computer program to find the square root of numbers was not allowed, even though it achieved this aim by using a dedicated 'read only memory' that had been hard-wired to perform this calculation (*Gale's Application* (1991)).

18.6.3   Scheme for performing a mental act

This would include attempts to secure patent protection for packaging that have instructions directing the reader to use the contents (which are not patentable, because they are not new and inventive) in a particular manner (*Ciba-Geigy AG (Dürr's) Application* (1977)). Similarly, a word processor that could handle Chinese characters was denied a patent (*Re the Computer Generation of Chinese Characters* (1993)).

18.6.4   Presentation of information

An invention must be novel in order to qualify for a patent (s 1(1)(a)). The issues of novelty and inventive step, which are required by s 1(1)(b), form the twin principal foundations of a patentable invention.

18.7   Novelty

Novelty is defined in the PA 1977 s 2 as follows:

18.7.1   State of the art

'(1) An invention shall be taken to be new if it does not form part of the state of the art.

(2) The state of the art in the case of an invention shall be taken to comprise all matter (whether a product, a process, information about either, or anything else) which has at any time before the priority date of that invention been made available to the public (whether in the UK or

elsewhere) by written or oral description, by use or in any other way.

(3) The state of the art in the case of an invention to which an application for a patent or a patent relates shall be taken also to compromise matter contained in an application for another patent which was published on or after the priority date of that invention, if the following conditions are satisfied, that is to say -

(a) that the matter was contained in the application for that other patent both as filed and as published; and

(b) the priority date of that matter is earlier than that of the invention.

This section follows the EPC Article 54. 'Published' is defined in section 130(1) as meaning 'made available to the public (whether in the UK or elsewhere) and a document shall be taken to be published under any provision of this Act if it can be inspected as of right at any place in the UK by members of the public, whether on payment of a fee or not and republished shall be construed accordingly'.

18.7.2   General considerations

The state of the art is very widely defined, but broadly it includes all those things that have been disclosed to the public, in contrast to those things that have been kept hidden (*Quantel Ltd v Spaceward Microsystems Ltd* (1990)). Under the PA 1977, there are no territorial limits on the source of the information that may form part of the state of the art, so long as it is available to the public. The general principle is that for a document to anticipate a purported invention, it must contain a clear and unambiguous description of that purported invention. Similarly, if the state of the art includes a pre-dating article that would infringe the claims of the patent, then again such a patent has been anticipated by that article (*Bristol-Myers Co (Johnson's) Application* (1974)). In either case, the test is the same and it is said that there has been an 'enabling disclosure' (*Asahi Kasei Kogyo KK's Application* (1991)).

In *Gillette Safety Razor Co v Anglo-American Trading Co Ltd* (1913), Lord Moulton stated that:

'The defence that the alleged infringement was not novel at the date of the plaintiff's letter patent is a good defence in law, and it would sometimes obviate the great length and expense of patent cases if the defendant could and would put forth his case in this form, and thus spare himself the trouble of demonstrating on which horn of the well-known dilemma the plaintiff has impaled himself, invalidity or non-infringement'.

This is the so-called *'Gillette* defence', and it is still as pertinent today as when it was first formulated (*Merrell Dow Pharmaceuticals Inc v HN Norton & Co Ltd* (1994)).

The bulk of the state of the art will be contained within documents of one type or another. The meaning of 'documents' is very wide indeed. It is not restricted to paper writings, but extends to anything upon which information may be recorded in any manner (*Grant v Southwestern and Country Properties Ltd* (1975)). This would include, for example, computer disks, microfilms, databases, CD-ROMs, and video and sound recordings.

So long as it is permissible for a member of the public to inspect the document, then it forms part of the state of the art, and it is irrelevant whether in fact anyone even knew of its existence, or even read it (*JAPAN STYRENE PAPER/Foam particles* (1991)).

The phrase 'made available to the public' has been held to mean that the information has been added to 'the stock of knowledge which the public either has or can acquire by consulting some source of information open to it' (*Gadd & Mason v Mayor, Aldermen and Citizens of the City of Manchester* (1892)). Strictly, an enabling disclosure to a single person is sufficient (*Humpherson v Syer* (1887)). However, the courts have withdrawn from this logical extreme. Thus, it has been suggested *obiter* that a disclosure to a few scientists pursuing a topic in private is not sufficient to anticipate an invention (*Genentech Inc's Patent* (1989)).

The document may be in any language, thus a single copy of a Japanese publication, which had been received by the Patent Office library just before the priority date, was sufficient to anticipate an invention (*Woven Plastic Products Ltd v British Ropes Ltd* (1970)).

The information contained in a patent application that has been filed before the patent in question, but has not yet been published, may be used when the issue of novelty arises. It will be construed as forming part of the state of the art just prior to the date of the patent in question, and in the light of the common general knowledge at that time (*Genentech Inc's (Human Growth Hormone) Patent* (1989)). The meaning of any term must be understood as it would have been at the time the document was written (*General Tire & Rubber Co v Firestone Tyre & Rubber Co Ltd* (1972)).

It is not permissible to combine the disclosures from several different documents so as to make a mosaic of the information that could then act as an enabling disclosure

18.7.3   Documentary
          disclosure

(*Martin and Biro Swan Ltd v H Millwood* (1956)). However, if other documents are subsumed into a principal document then an enabling disclosure may result.

18.7.4   Prior use disclosure

Prior use is distinct from prior publication. However, both must result in an enabling disclosure. The test for lack of novelty is related to that for infringement. Thus, with regard to prior use, Lord Westbury LC said in *Harwood v Great Northern Railway Ltd* (1865), that:

> 'The true mode of trying the question, of course, would be to reverse the order of time of the two productions, and to inquire whether if anyone had now introduced the [invention], it would or would not have been an infringement of the plaintiff's patent.'

The use of a stove, which was located in a private house, that was shown to visitors, was held to amount to prior use (*Taylor's Patent* (1896)).

Under the PA 1977, the use must be enabling, and, thus, if the invention could not be deduced from the use, then there was no disclosure of the invention (*PLG Research Ltd v Ardon International Ltd* (1995)). Thus, if a prototype is used in public and its workings can be deduced by examination, then the invention will lack novelty (*Lux Traffic Controls Ltd v Pike Signals Ltd* (1993)).

The use of a primitive prototype may be sufficient to amount to prior user; thus, the use of a simple sail-mast attached to a board was held to anticipate the patent for a windsurfer (*Windsurfing International Inc v Tabur Marine (Great Britain) Ltd* (1985)). However, if the prior use is merely to test whether or not the article works, rather than using it to perform its function, then the use may not count against the patentee (*Vax Appliances Ltd v Hoover plc* (1991)).

As the PA 1977 purports to bring the UK patent legislation into line with the Continent, then it may be appropriate to refer to, for example, a commentary on German law in order to assist with the issue of validity (*Prout v British Gas plc* (1992)).

18.7.5   New uses for old ideas

Generally, if the purported invention relies purely upon a novel application for a product or process which in itself is not new, then the patent will fall for want of novelty. Thus, a patent for a method of distributing tobacco evenly using a high speed machine was anticipated by a machine using the same method but at lower speeds, although the method was directed at solving a different problem (*Molins v Industrial Machinery Co Ltd* (1938)).

The collocation of old integers that do not interact to produce a new result will not produce a novel product (*Pugh v*

Riley Cycle Co (1914)). However, if the old integers do interact, then the product may well be novel (*Martin and Biro Swan Ltd v H Millwood Ltd* (1956)). Correspondingly, it is possible for a new patentable invention to arise by the omission of an integer from an old invention (C *Van der Lely NV v Ruston's Engineering Co Ltd* (1985)).

A patent for a new type of socking, which had a tuck in the toe, was anticipated by reason of the fact that some existing machines already produced such tucks, even though it was considered a disadvantage (*Reymes-Cole v Elite Hosiery Co Ltd* (1965)).

In *Esso Research and Engineering Co's Application* (1960) a new use was found for a range of petrol additives. However, one member of that class of compounds had been used previously as a petrol additive, albeit for a different purported purpose which it was unlikely to perform. It was held that the patent for the new use for the range of compounds had to disclaim the previously used member of its class.

Subsection 2(4) concerns those occasions where prior disclosure is deemed not to adversely affect the question of novelty.

Broadly, if the information was obtained by a breach of an equitable duty of confidentiality, then the patent will not be bad for want of novelty (*Saltman Engineering Co Ltd v Campbell Engineering Co Ltd* (1948)). The mere fact that a document is headed 'Confidential' is not conclusive evidence that there was indeed a duty of confidentiality. For example, the facts may show that the document in question was widely circulated in the trade (*JR Dalrymple's Application* (1957)). It is permissible to send samples to a prospective purchaser for comparative testing, so long as the purchaser knew beforehand that the samples had been made available in confidence and were of an experimental and secret nature (*Pall Corporation v Commercial Hydraulics (Bedford) Ltd* (1990)).

By virtue of s 2(6) a substance that has previously been patented may be patented again for a medical use (*John Wyeth & Brother Ltd's Application & Schering AG's Application* (1985)). This provision is, in effect, a relaxation of the normal rules, and arises because such a method is unpatentable as a method under s 4(2). Furthermore, a combination of two or more substances, each of which has been published previously for a medical use, may be patented afresh so long as in combination they act synergically and that the resultant effect is different from the previous effects.

18.7.6	Disclosures that are discounted
18.7.7	Substances used in the treatment of the human or animal body

18.8   Inventive step

Not only must the proposed subject matter of the patent be novel, but it must also be inventive (PA 1977 s 1(1)(b)). Section 3 further elaborates this point:

> 'An invention shall be taken to involve an inventive step if it is not obvious to a person skilled in the art, having regard to any matter which forms part of the state of the art by virtue only of section 2(2) above (and disregarding section 2(3) above).'

This section follows EPC Article 56. Section 2(2), it will be recalled, deals with information that has been made available to the public anywhere in the world. The excluded matter covered in s 2(3) concerns the information contained within patent applications published after the patent in question, but which had been filed earlier and so had an earlier priority date. Accordingly, for the issue of inventiveness material in unpublished patents may not be taken into consideration, unlike the situation when considering the issue of novelty.

18.8.1   Person skilled in the art

The question of obviousness is addressed to the notional 'person skilled in the art'. This mythical person has several characteristics which include an awareness of all the common general knowledge within the relevant sphere of work, that he is competent at the job, but also that he is unimaginative (*General Tire & Rubber Co v Firestone Tyre & Rubber Co Ltd* (1972)). However, he is not so unimaginative that he is a mere automaton. Furthermore, he is interested in the job and the subject matter so that he will consider all the information available to him, and thus make any obvious improvements or developments (*Windsurfing International Inc v Tabur Marine (Great Britain) Ltd* (1985)). For example, it would be obvious to apply new materials as and when they become available to old ideas. Accordingly, it was held to be obvious to coat the thread of a self-pulling type of corkscrew with PTFE in order to ease the penetration of the thread into the cork (*Hallen & Co v Brabantia (UK) Ltd* (1991)).

Originally, the man skilled in the art was taken to be an 'ordinary workman' (*Procter v Bennis* (1887)). Nowadays, this notional person may not even be a single entity. In *General Tire & Rubber Co v Firestone Tyre & Rubber Co Ltd* (1972) it was stated that:

> 'If the art is one having a highly developed technology, the notional skilled reader to whom the document is addressed may not be a single person but a team, whose combined skills would normally be employed in that art in interpreting and carrying into effect instructions such as those which are contained in the document to be construed.'

This has been taken even further in the cases of advanced biotechnological patents where the addressee is to be given the best equipment and to have the training equivalent to a competent doctoral student (*Genentech Inc's Patent* (1989)). In *Chiron Corporation v Organon Teknika Ltd (No 3)* (1994), which concerned a patent for the manufacture of a diagnostic test for Hepatitis C, there were two Nobel Laureates giving expert evidence. The research was conducted by some of the best academics in the world. It may be safely assumed that the skilled addressee in this case was not 'the ordinary worker' of bygone days, but rather a highly trained postgraduate worker with access to the most sophisticated machinery available. In that case, Aldous J stated of the evidence of one of the Nobel Laureates:

'I must be cautious before accepting his evidence as to what would be obvious to the notional skilled addressee ... as it is difficult to draw any inference as to what would be the attitude of such a person from the opinion of a Nobel Prize winner.'

Hoffman LJ in *Société Technique de Pulverisation Step v Emson Europe Ltd* (1993) has observed:

'I am sceptical of the value of the varied cast of imaginary and sometimes improbable people which the law has invented to embody concepts like reasonableness, business efficacy, lack of inventiveness and even parental concern with children proposed for adoption. They may have seemed a folksy way of explaining the law to a jury but I think it is more useful to try to analyse the concepts themselves. I prefer to go back to the language of the statute.'

Thus, there seems to be a judicial move away from hearing the opinion of overly-qualified experts on matters that concern what would, or would not, be obvious to the 'person skilled in the art'.

The term 'mosaic' originated from the phrase a 'mosaic of extracts from annals and treatises' (*Von Heyden v Neustadt* (1881)). The mosaicing of information contained in different documents is not permissible when dealing with the issue of novelty. The opposite stance is adopted when considering the issue of inventiveness. Hence, if it was obvious for the skilled addressee to have before him a number of documents, then he may make a mosaic of all the available information. The caveat is important, for if it required imagination to put the mosaic together in order to arrive at the invention in question, then any product that results from such a mosaic will be inventive (*Mills & Rockley (Electronics) Ltd v Technograph Printed Circuits Ltd* (1972)).

18.8.2   Mosaicing of information

If a literature search would have produced a large number of similar documents, which, if taken together point in no particular direction, it is not permissible to create a selection of the list which *post facto* points in a given direction. Such a selection is called a 'Simkin list' after the person who complied a similar list in *Olin Mathieson Chemical Corp v Biorex Laboratories Ltd* (1970).

The question of inventiveness is one of fact, and thus the issue of whether a previously published document would actually have been considered by the addressee needs to be decided. Thus, if the addressee would not in fact have actually read the document, because, for example, it related to a totally different technological field or was physically unavailable to him, then anything contained within that document could not have been considered by the addressee when considering the issue of inventiveness (*Imperial Chemical Industries Ltd (Pointer's) Application* (1977)). Though, if a document is held to be highly relevant, then regardless of the difficulty of availability, it will still be relevant in considering the question of inventiveness, because the person should have consulted it.

18.8.3	Common general knowledge

Common general knowledge is distinctly different from the information that is contained within the sphere of knowledge that falls to be considered on the issue of novelty. Thus, the information contained in foreign, untranslated journals, which, obviously, has not been widely disseminated, does not form part of the common general knowledge. Instead, common general knowledge comprises the information that a skilled man in the field would have accumulated over the years, and is thus within his contemplation, either consciously or subconsciously, when he reads any particular document (*General Tire & Rubber Co v Firestone Tyre & Rubber Co* (1972)).

18.8.4	Inventive step

The question of the presence of an inventive step, or put another way, whether or not the invention was obvious, is often very hard to ascertain until a full trial of the matter has occurred.

The Court of Appeal in *Windsurfing International Inc v Tabur Marine (Great Britain) Ltd* (1985), laid down four steps that needed to be addressed on the issue of obviousness:

- identifying the inventive concept embodied in the patent;

- imputing to a normally skilled but unimaginative addressee what was common general knowledge in the art at the priority date;

- identifying the differences if any between the matter cited and the alleged invention; and,

• deciding whether those differences, viewed without any knowledge of the alleged invention, constituted steps which would have been obvious to the skilled man or whether they required any degree of invention.

If there is an inventive step between the patent in question and the state of the art preceding the patent application, then regardless of the smallness of that step there has been an invention. A mere 'scintilla' of an invention is sufficient to found a valid patent (*Samuel Parkes & Co Ltd v Cocker Brothers Ltd* (1929)). Whether there has been an inventive step is to be decided objectively and is a question of fact to be decided by the judge (*Johns-Manville Corporation's Patent* (1967)).

The activities of the inventor and any of his competitors at the time of the patent application will produce cogent evidence of the inventive barriers that were actually facing the investigators at the time, rather the opinions of the same investigators looking back on the event with hindsight (*Mölnlycke AB v Procter & Gamble Ltd* (1992)). This is particularly so when the solution appears simple and obvious once it has been stated (*AC Edwards Ltd v Acme Signs & Displays Ltd* (1990)). Thus, the question is not whether the invention is obvious now, with the benefit of hindsight, but rather whether the purported invention was obvious to the people involved in the field just before the patent application.

If the invention involved a step which, in the light of the information then available, was worth a try in the reasonable expectation that something of value might be found, then it would be held to be obvious to try it, and so not inventive (*Johns-Manville Corporation's Patent* (1967)). Thus, the expenditure of laborious and costly effort, even if it amounted to more than the exercise of proficiency, would not amount to an inventive step *per se* (*Genentech Inc's Patent* (1989)).

This is particularly important in the biotechnology areas. Thus in *Biogen Inc v Medeva plc* (1995), which concerned an immunological assay for Hepatitis B, Biogen had adopted a shotgun approach that involved chopping up DNA at random from the Hepatitis B virus (HBV) and then cloning and expressing these random segments to see if anything useful appeared. Hobhouse LJ opined that it was difficult to identify an invention in this case, because Biogen had only made a decision to adopt a course of research that seemed unlikely to succeed. His Lordship then stated:

'A mere commercial decision is not an invention. The product as claimed in claim 1 does not as such disclose any invention. The claimed molecule of recombinant DNA is simply a molecule consisting of an available vector, designed by others, with an undetermined fragment of natural HBV DNA inserted into it at a location designed to receive such an insert ... it does not involve any inventive step.'

In contrast, the courts will hold that an invention may have occurred as the result of 'some sudden or lucky thought, or a mere accidental discovery' (*Crane v Price* (1842)).

Professor Krebs FRS, who discovered the Krebs cycle which is the fundamental metabolic pathway in higher organisms, has said that at any one time there are many possible questions that may be tackled by a research team, however, only a limited number are capable of solution with the technology then available, and even fewer are likely to yield interesting results. Thus, the choice of the right question to study, rather than finding the solution to that problem, is often the most important factor in the advance of a subject. This sentiment has been adopted within patent law. The Court of Appeal in *Beecham Group Ltd's (Amoxycillin) Application* (1980) held that, so long as there was no recognised problem or need that was extant, then the selection of a particular line of research can itself demonstrate that the result was non-obvious.

18.8.5	Long-felt want

If there has been a long-felt want in the industry for a device to fulfil a particular function, and several unsuccessful attempts have been made before the patent in question was proposed, then this will be strong evidence that the patent is inventive (*Non-Drip Measure Co Ltd v Stranger's and FW Woolworth & Co Ltd* (1943)). When the goal of the patent was known to be desirable, any obvious ways of achieving that aim would be expected to have been made before, and so if the goal had not been reached beforehand, then the invention that did reach it must be non-obvious (*Shoketsu Kinzoku Kogyo KK's Patent* (1992)). This may often be demonstrated by the fact that the patented invention is a commercial success (*Unilever plc v Gillette (UK) Ltd* (1989)).

The case of *Parks-Cramer Co v GW Thornton & Sons Ltd* (1966) concerned a system of cleaning the floors between textile machines by means of an adapted vacuum cleaner. This was a problem that many people had attempted to solve, and the new invention was an immediate commercial success. The judge at first instance held that it was obvious to use a vacuum cleaner to remove dust, a fact known to 'every competent housewife'. However, the Court of Appeal held that regardless of the simplicity of the invention, the fact that it was a commercial success, in the face of so many failed attempts, must lead to the conclusion it was not obvious, otherwise it would have been done before. Maybe, one wonders, even though it was obvious to 'every competent housewife', it was not obvious to the (male?) engineer entrusted with solving the problem.

The opposite conclusion is, however, not valid. Thus, just because a patent is not a commercial success does not mean that it is not inventive.

A patent may be granted only for an invention which is capable of industrial application. This requirement accords with the EPC Article 52, and the CPC Article 1(2).

18.9   Capable of industrial application

The use of the word 'capable' restricts the subject matter of valid patents to those inventions that may, in practice, be made or used in industry. Patents are fundamentally concerned with practical innovations, and not hypothetical concepts that have no utility. Thus, even though it is no longer a ground of revocation that a patent lacks utility, the requirement of capacity covers similar grounds.

The requirement of capacity has been used to prevent a perpetual motion machine from being granted a patent (*NEWMAN/Perpetual motion* (1988)). This decision was based upon the accepted idea that such a machine was impossible. However, many innovations have been thought impossible until they were realised in practice. It is questionable whether the patent examiners should be permitted to decide whether or not an innovation is capable of working. Thus, for example, the cold fusion process that has been claimed to occur under certain electrolytic conditions, has been declared impossible by a large sector of the scientific community. However, research is still continuing into the idea. If eventually it is found to be possible, the inventors would merit a patent for their endeavours.

This position is somewhat forced onto the patent examiners because the applications are on paper and not in the form of real examples. For, obviously, an idea that does not work at all in practice is *a fortiori* not capable of industrial application. However, an invention that appears to work regardless that the law of physics say it should not, should not be denied the possibility of protection. Remember, according to the laws of physics puffins and bumblebees should remain earthbound for they are incapable of flight!

The test is whether there is a vendible product (*R v Wheeler* (1819)). This has been widely interpreted. Thus, a patent was granted for a process of converting fog into rain (*Elton and Leda Chemicals Ltd's Application* (1957)).

18.9.1   Industrial application

The product need not be tangible; thus, a method for producing radio waves with certain characteristics was patentable (*Henry Barnato Rantzen's Application* (1947)). However, when dealing with a technical matter, the Patent Office can sometimes come to illogical conclusions. Thus, a patent for the production of visible light was refused (*Philips Electrical Industries Ltd's Application* (1959)). This latter case was distinguished from *Henry Barnato Rantzen's Application* (1947) on the grounds that electricity was an industrial commodity that could be 'laid on' whereas light was not. This, of course, denies that radio waves and visible light waves are both examples of electromagnetic radiation, whose properties may be equally described using Maxwell's equations. Furthermore, each may be 'laid on', eg down a copper wire for electricity and a fibre-optic cable for light.

18.10 Subject matter excluded from patent protection

There are statutory provisions that exclude certain types of work being granted patents. In essence, this is a statutory embodiment of public policy.

18.10.1 Offensive, immoral and anti-social inventions

Subsection 1(3) concerns those things which would, save for the operation of that subsection, be an invention and patentable. It, and subsection 1(4), read as follows:

'(3) A patent shall not be granted -

    (a) for an invention the publication or exploitation of which would be generally expected to encourage offensive, immoral or anti-social behaviour;

    (b) ...

(4) For the purposes of subsection (3) above behaviour shall not be regarded as offensive, immoral or anti-social only because it is prohibited by any law in force in the UK or any part of it.

This broadly follows EPC Article 53. This Article talks about '*ordre public*' which was a new concept for the law of the UK.

These formal provisions prevent an invention that is offensive, immoral or otherwise undesirable from being a patentable invention, and thus capable of protection. This is slightly different to the situation for immoral or scandalous works in which copyright subsists. In those cases copyright subsists, but the courts will not enforce the rights of the copyright holder when such works are infringed.

What is considered immoral changes with the times. Thus, patents for contraceptive devices were once refused the grant of a patent (*Rufus Riddlesbarger's Application* (1936)). However, subsequently, such a patent has been allowed (*Schering AG's Application* (1971)). In the case of *HARVARD/Onco-mouse* (1991), there was an application for a patent for a particular gene line, called the onco-mouse, which was particularly susceptible to developing malignant growths. This gene line would be useful as laboratory models for cancer in the human body. It was likely that the mice would suffer from cancer for the majority of their lives, which would anyway be of a shorter duration that a normal healthy mouse. It was held that it was not immoral for a patent to be granted for these genetically engineered creatures, because the potential advantages to the well-being of humans outweighed the considerations of the suffering of the mice.

In contrast to the position adopted by the EPO, the European Parliament on 1 March 1995 rejected Directive 4/94 on the legal protection of biotechnological invention. This Directive would have permitted human genes and transgenic animals to be patented.

The limitation that the invention must be 'generally expected to encourage' antisocial behaviour ensures that innovations that could be put to good use, even though they have some adverse side-effects, may still be patentable. Thus, inventions for weapons may be patented, even if these involve human suffering. For example, in *Palmer's Application* (1970), a patent was granted for:

> 'A method of defence by a human against a human attacker comprising the steps of puncturing the skin of the attacker and injecting a sub-lethal dose of a chemical irritant substance into the body of the attacker so as to cause sufficient temporary pain to the attacker to cause him to break off the attack but wherein the pain will cease during a discrete interval of time because of the dissipation of the irritating substance and the attacker will suffer no permanent ill-effects.'

Under the PA 1977, subsection 1(3)(b) reads:

18.10.2   Animals and plants

> 'A patent shall not be granted for any variety of animal or plant or any essentially biological process for the production of animals or plants, not being a micro-biological process or the product of such a process.'

Under the PA 1949, the situation was similar in that animals and plants were not considered to be 'manners of new manufacture' which was the requirement for patentability. However, it has been held under the PA 1949 that a micro-biological process, which resulted in an end-product that was capable of being sold, was capable of being patented, eg using micro-organisms to produce antibiotics (*American Cyanamid Co (Dann's) Patent* (1971)).

However, protection is available for the inventor of new varieties of plants under the Plant Varieties and Seeds Act 1964 as amended by the Agriculture (Miscellaneous Provisions) Act 1968, the European Communities Act 1972 and the Plant Varieties Act 1983. Furthermore there is EC Council Regulation 2100/94 on Community plant variety rights which will be in operation from 27 April 1995 (Article 117).

18.11   Other grounds

The other grounds upon which a patent may be revoked are:

• grant to a person not entitled;

• insufficiency;

• the matter disclosed if the specification extends beyond that disclosed in the preliminary application; and

• the protection conferred by the patient has been extended by an amendment which should not have been made.

These grounds raise issues that are more suitably dealt with in a more advanced book on patents and so they will not be discussed further.

Patents: Validity

An examination system maintains the integrity of the register more than does a simple depository system.

Introduction

A patent application is examined for both inventiveness and world-wide novelty.

Examination of a patent application

Several grounds for invalidity under the PA 1949 have been removed; these include inutility, false suggestion, illegality of intended use and secret use. Under the PA 1977 the new grounds for invalidity include unallowable amendment and insufficiency.

Invalidity under the PA 1949 contrasted with that under the PA 1977

There are only five grounds for a patent being held invalid under the PA 1977. These are lack of patentability; grant to a person not entitled; insufficiency, specification extends beyond the application; and, unallowable amendment (s 72(1)).

Grounds for invalidity under the PA 1977

The allegation that a patent is not a patentable invention is the commonest ground for revocation (s 72(1)(a)). A patent must be new, inventive, capable of industrial application and not excluded by ss 1(2) or 1(3).

Patentable invention

An invention is defined negatively, by stating that it is not a discovery, an aesthetic work, a scheme for a mental act, or a method of presenting information. In *STERNHEIMER/ Harmonic Vibrations* (1989) the Technical Board of Appeal of the EPO said that the excluded matters were characterised by not using 'technical methods to produce a concrete technical effect'.

What is an invention?

The practical application of a discovery may be an invention, but not the discovery *per se* (*Genentech Inc's Patent* (1989)), eg a mathematical model cannot be patented.

The correct protection for aesthetic creations is copyright, design right or registered design as may be appropriate in each case.

A scheme for performing a mental act, such as a computer program cannot be patent; nor can the mere presentation of information (*Re the Computer Generation of Chinese Characters* (1993)).

Novelty	The 'state of the art' is defined as anything published or done in public anywhere in the world. It includes the material in other patent applications that have not yet been published at the priority date of the patent application in question.

There is a need for a clear and unambiguous description of the prior material. Alternatively, a pre-dating article that would infringe the patent would suffice. Either of these amounts to an enabling disclosure (*Asahi Kasei Kogyo KK's Application* (1991)). |
| **Documentary disclosure** | Most of the prior material will be contained in documents. These documents must have been 'made available to the public' which means that the information bas been added to the stock of available knowledge (*Gadd & Mason v Manchester* (1892)).

Unpublished patent applications form part of the state of the art for the purpose of novelty. Mosaicing of documents is not allowed (*Martin v Millwood* (1956)). |
| **Prior use disclosure** | The test involves reversing the order of events, ie would the article previously disclosed have infringed the patent? If yes, then it was a prior use disclosed (*Harwood v Great Northern Railway* (1865)). The use of prototype defeats novelty (*Windsurfing International v Tabur Marine* (1985)). |
| **New uses for old ideas** | Generally, new uses for old ideas does not confer novelty (*Molins v Industrial Machinery Co Ltd* (1938)). |
| **Disclosures that are discounted** | If there is a disclosure that breaches a duty of confidentiality within six months of the patent application, then that does not adversely affect novelty (*Saltman Engineering Co v Campbell* (1949)).

The first medical use of an already-known compound will still be patentable (*John Wyeth & Brother & Schering's Application* (1985)). |
| **Inventive step** | PA 1977 ss 3 1(1)(b) and 3 follow EPC Article 56. To attack obviousness, one cannot use the information contained in unpublished patent applications, unlike when refuting novelty.

The person skilled in the art may be a highly skilled research scientist (*Genentech Inc's Patent* (1989)).

Mosaicing of information is permitted to show invention obvious. However, if the mosaic itself was not obvious, then |

there is an inventive step (*Mills & Rockley v Technograph Printed Circuits* (1972)).

A four part test for inventive step was developed in *Windsurfing International Inc v Tabur Marine (Great Britain) Ltd* (1985).

Commercial success is indicative of inventiveness (*Unilever v Gillette* (1989)).

An invention must be capable of industrial application. For this reason, a purported perpetual motion machine was not allowed (*NEWMAN/Perpetual motion* (1988)).

Capable of industrial application

Industrial application means that there is a vendible product (*R v Wheeler* (1819)), eg a machine to make rain from fog (*Elton and Leda Chemicals* (1957)).

Industrial application

A patent for a contraceptive pill was not allowed as being against social morals (*Riddlesbarger's Application* (1936)), but later was permitted (*Schering AG's Application* (1971)).

Subject matter excluded from patent protection

Chapter 19

Patents: Infringement

The value of a patent to a patentee is that he may use it to stop another person from using the subject matter of the invention. Thus, a patent gives control over the commercial exploitation of the invention, which may be duly exploited for a financial reward for a limited period. Furthermore, the mere existence of a patent may be used as a negotiating tool in order to support other rights held by the patentee, for example confidential information relating to the patented product or process, otherwise known as 'know-how'.

The contribution that the inventor makes to the stock of human knowledge by revealing the details of the invention is compensated for by society by the grant of an absolute monopoly that is limited in time. In order to protect his monopoly, the patentee may commence an action for infringement of his patent. Such an action will succeed if the acts of alleged infringement fall within the scope of the claims as properly construed. Once the patent has expired, the patentee cannot stop anyone else from working the patent. The invention now becomes free for all to use, ie it has entered into the public domain of knowledge.

19.1 Introduction

No action for the infringement of a patent can be brought until the patent is granted. The patentee may then sue for acts of infringement that occurred between publication of the application and the grant of the patent (ss 69(1) and (2)(a)), so long as any alleged act of infringement would have infringed not only the patent as finally published, but also the claims of the application as published (s 69(2)(b)). This section is new and applies to all acts of infringement after 1 June 1978. If the patent has been amended after the grant of the patent, then these amendments act retrospectively to the date of the grant of the patent (s 75(3)).

19.2 Timing of infringement proceedings

Section 60 defines infringement in a manner that is similar, but not identical, to that contained within the CPC Articles 29-31.

The question of infringement falls to be considered in two parts. The first of which is whether the act complained of falls within s 60, which delineates the scope of the monopoly granted by the patent. This rarely raises a problem. However, the second limb is contentious. The exclusive right to do those things detailed in s 60 is only granted by the patent to the

19.3 Infringement

invention that is the subject matter of the patent under consideration. It is very rare that the alleged infringing product or process is exactly the same as the patented invention. Thus, it falls to be considered whether the alleged infringing product or process falls within the scope of the claims of the patent as properly construed.

19.3.1   Infringing acts under PA 1977 s 60

Section 60 is concerned with the meaning of infringement. It reads as follows:

'(1)   Subject to the provisions of this section, a person infringes a patent for an invention if, but only if, while the patent is in force, he does any of the following things in the United Kingdom in relation to the invention without the consent of the proprietor of the patent, that is to say -

(a)   where the invention is a product, he makes, disposes of, offers to dispose or, uses or imports the product or keeps it whether for disposal or otherwise;

(b)   where the invention is a process, he uses the process or he offers it for use in the United Kingdom when he knows, or it is obvious to a reasonable person in the circumstances, that its use there without the consent of the proprietor would be an infringement of the patent;

(c)   where the invention is a process, he disposes of, offers to dispose of, uses or imports any product obtained directly by means of that process or keeps any such product whether for disposal or otherwise.

(2)   Subject to the following provisions of this section, a person (other than the proprietor of the patent) also infringes a patent for an invention if, while the patent is in force and without the consent of the proprietor, he supplies or offers to supply in the United Kingdom a person other than a licensee or other person entitled to work the invention with any of the means, relating to an essential element of the invention, for putting the invention into effect when he knows, or it is obvious to a reasonable person in the circumstances, that those means are suitable for putting, and are intended to put, the invention into effect in the United Kingdom.'

19.3.2   Supply of staple commodities

Subsection 60(3) states that:

'Subsection (2) above shall not apply to the supply or offer of a staple commercial product unless the supply or the offer is made for the purpose of inducing the person supplied or, as the case may be, the person to whom the offer is made to do an act which constitutes an infringement of the patent by virtue of subsection (1) above.'

Thus, the supply of basic commodities which are then used to produce an infringing article is not inofitself an infringing act (*Benno Jaffé und Darmstaedter Lanolin Fabrik v John Richardson & Co (Leicester) Ltd* (1894)). This is will not even amount to procuring the infringement, unless there is some common design between the supplier and the primary infringer, or there is an inducement by the supplier that the infringer should infringe (*Belegging-en Exploitatiemaalschappij BV Lavender v Witten Industrial Diamonds Ltd* (1979)). There is a tendency, however, for the courts to consider that s 60 provides a complete list of acts that may amount to patent infringement, and thus procuring the infringement, or inciting another to infringe, are not actionable unless the procurer or incitor is a joint tortfeasor (*Amstrad Consumer Electronics plc v British Phonographic Industry Ltd* (1986)).

Balcombe LJ in *Daily v Etablissements Fernand Berchet* (1992) stated:

| **19.4** | **Construction of the claims** |

'The task of construction of claims of a patent specification is one which does not require any specialised skill, but only the application of the same canons of construction that are applied to every written instrument to be construed by a court.'

This statement must be read in the light of case law on construction, which permits a technical word to have a technical meaning, even if the general public is unaware of that meaning. For example, the Highways Act 1835 empowered the borough surveyor to prune and lop trees. The plaintiff sued the borough surveyor who had removed the top part of the trees from the plaintiff's property. The court held that the words 'prune' and 'lop' had a technical meaning when used in this context, namely removing excess growth to improve growth and removing side branches respectively. The borough surveyor had 'topped' the trees, ie removed the crown of the tree which he was not empowered to do (*Unwin v Hanson* (1891)).

When a claims falls to be considered for the question of validity it is assumed that the draftsman would take into account an obvious attack on novelty or inventive step. In contrast, when the question of the interpretation of a claim falls to be considered in the light of an allegedly infringing article, the true meaning of the claims should not be tempered by reference to the allegedly infringing article (*Nobel's Explosive Co Ltd v Anderson* (1894)). This difference in approach is logically because, when drafting a claim, 'obviousness' and 'novelty' problems would be uppermost in the mind of the patent agent. However, there is no reason for the patent agent to have in mind all the possible combinations that may be produced in the future.

19.4.1   Textual construction

Originally, there was no requirement to include any claims in a patent. Then, slowly, claims of a very general nature were included. For example, 'The general arrangement and construction of the improved lamp hereinbefore described and represented in figures 1 to 4 of the accompanying drawings' (*Wenham Co Ltd v Champion Gas Lamp Co Ltd* (1891)). When claims were as broad as this the court was required by necessity to look at the 'pith and marrow' of the invention (*Clark v Adie* (1877)).

Gradually, the claims became more precise, and this correspondingly lead to the construction of the claims based far more on the textual interpretation of the exact words that were employed to define the monopoly sought. Thus, for example, Lord Porter said in *Electric & Musical Industries Ltd v Lissen Ltd* (1939), that:

'if the claims have a plain meaning in themselves, then advantage cannot be taken of the language used in the body of the specification to make them mean something different.'

However, the House of Lords reached no clear consensus on this matter and Lord Russell in the same case said:

'The function of the claims is to define clearly and with precision the monopoly claimed, so that others may know the exact boundaries of the area within which they will be trespassers. Their primary object is to limit and not extend the monopoly. What is not claimed is disclaimed.'

19.4.2   'Pith and marrow' construction

However, there continued to be the idea that there was a special doctrine that applied to the construction of patent claims, that was somewhat wider than the literal textual construction of the words used, so that an alleged infringement that was not exactly within the scope of the claim, yet utilised the essence of the invention would still be held to be an infringement. This doctrine is often referred to as the 'pith and marrow' approach, the name being an echo of the earlier approach of the court when claims were less precisely drafted. However, this approach will not allow for a nonsense to be made of the wording of the claim. Thus, in *C Van Der Lely*

NV v Bamfords Ltd (1963), the defendant's hay-turning machine was the mechanical equivalent of the plaintiff's, differing only in the fact that the removable wheels of the defendant's machine were on the front, while the plaintiff had claimed a device in which they were on the back. It was held that the word 'hindmost' in the claim could not be read as 'foremost' so as to include within its scope the defendant's machine. Viscount Radcliffe stated that:

'After all, it is [the patentee] who has committed himself to the unequivocal description of what he claims to have invented, and he must submit in the first place to be judged by his own action and words.'

Lord Reid gave a dissenting judgment in *C Van Der Lely NV v Bamfords Ltd* (1963), in which His Lordship proposed that it was necessary in order to prevent sharp practice on the part of a potential infringer to allow a principle of construction in which there could be the substitution of a mechanical equivalent for an integer. This line of dissent was further advanced in a later dissenting judgment by Lord Pearce in *Rodi & Wienenberger AG v Henry Showell Ltd* (1969) in which it was proposed that so long as the essential part of the integer is taken, even if inessential parts have been omitted, then infringement should still be found to occur. The problem with allowing a functional equivalent is that it introduces a large area of uncertainty into the scope of the patent. This uncertainty potentially hinders a rival from entering the market. Within the UK, the *dictum* of functional equivalents has traditionally not found favour.

The case of *Catnic Components Ltd v Hill & Smith Ltd* (1982) concerned the exact construction of a box lintel. One part of this lintel was to be 'substantially horizontal' while another part was to be 'vertical'. The defendant argued that, because the patentee had not qualified the word 'vertical' with the word 'substantially' as he had done when referring to the horizontal part, then the vertical part must be exactly vertical, and not a few degrees off the vertical, even if the slight angle of deviation did not detract from its performance of the required function. All three members of the Court of Appeal found that there was no *textual* infringement, and only one found that there was infringement using the 'pith and marrow' doctrine. The House of Lords, however, unanimously overturned this decision.

19.4.3   Catnic v Hill & Smith

There was only one judgment, which was given by Lord Diplock, in which His Lordship said that the:

'... patent specification is a unilateral statement by the patentee, in words of his own choosing, addressed to those likely to have a practical interest in the subject matter of his invention (ie 'skilled in the art'), by which he informs them of what he claims to be the essential features of the new product or process for which the letters patent grant him a monopoly. It is those novel features only that he claims to be essential that constitute the so-called pith and marrow of the claim. A patent specification should be given a purposive construction rather than a purely literal one derived from applying to it a kind of meticulous verbal analysis in which lawyers are too often tempted by their training to indulge. The question in each case is whether persons with practical knowledge and experience of the kind of work in which the invention was intended to be used, would understand that strict compliance with a particular descriptive word or phrase appearing in a claim was intended by the patentee to be an essential requirement of the invention so that any variant would fall outside the monopoly claimed, even though it could have no material effect upon the way the invention worked.'

Thus with this speech Lord Diplock replaced the doctrine of 'pith and marrow' with the 'purposive approach' for patents granted under the PA 1949.

In *PLG Research Ltd v Ardon International Ltd* (1995), the Court of Appeal held that the purposive approach promulgated by Lord Diplock in *Catnic v Hill and Smith* (1982) was no longer the correct approach. Instead, the Protocol on the Interpretation of Article 69 of the EPC, which is concerned with infringement, should be followed for patents granted under the PA 1977. Furthermore, the UK approach should be consistent with the decisions of the German courts; in particular, the doctrine of functional equivalents should be implemented. However, in *Assidoman Multipack Ltd v The Mead Corporation* (1995), Aldous J held that the Court of Appeal's comments in *PLG Research Ltd v Ardon International Ltd* (1995) were *obiter*, and thus not binding upon him. Moreover, after extensively reviewing the case law, Aldous J concluded that Lord Diplock's approach was in accordance with the Protocol, namely that the claims should be interpreted in a manner that 'combines a fair protection for the patentee with a reasonable degree of certainty for third parties'. Accordingly, the purposive approach as promulgated by Lord Diplock in *Catnic v Hill and Smith* (1982) was still good law for patents granted under either the PA 1949 or the PA 1977. Thus, once again, the doctrine of functional equivalents has failed to impress a UK court.

19.4.4   Development of the purposive approach

Hoffman J in *Improver Corp v Remington Consumer Products Ltd* (1990), re-stated the *Catnic* test in a more accessible form. This case concerned the construction of the phrase 'helical spring' which was used in the invention of a depilating device. The alleged infringing device used a rubber rod that had slits in it, and these slits opened up in order to trap the hairs. The slitted rod performed exactly the same mechanical operation as did the helical spring. His Lordship said:

> 'If the issue was whether a feature embodied in the alleged infringement which fell outside the primary, literal or contextual meaning of a descriptive word or phrase in the claim ('a variant') was nevertheless within its language as properly interpreted, the court should ask itself the following questions ('Lord Diplock's three questions'):
>
> (i) Does the variant have a material effect upon the way the invention works? If yes, the variant is outside the claim. If no: (ii) Would this (ie that the variant has no material effect) have been obvious at the date of publication of the patent to a reader skilled in the art? If no, the variant is outside the claim. If yes: (iii) Would the reader skilled in the art nevertheless have understood from the language of the claim that the patentee intended that strict compliance with the primary meaning was an essential requirement of the invention. If yes, the variant is outside the claim.'

It was held in this case that there was no infringement, because the wording of the claims for a helical spring did not cover a slitted rubber rod. In Germany, the courts held that the patent was valid and infringed (mentioned in *Improver Corp v Raymond Industrial Ltd* (1991)). The difference in the results reflects the different approaches of the UK courts to those on the continent, and until a pan European appeal court is established such dichotomous results will continue.

The variants that are considered must be obviously immaterial, rather than whether or not the variants are obvious. Furthermore, the variants considered would usually have little or no effect upon the efficiency of the invention.

19.5   Defences

Unlike copyright, there are a number of statutory defences that are available to a defendant in a patent infringement. There are, of course, also common law defences.

19.5.1   Licence

An act that falls within the ambit of the claims is not an infringement if it is done with the permission of the proprietor. The licence may be either explicit or implicit, ie having arisen purely from the necessary implication of the circumstances. A licence cannot be granted by only one of several co-owners of a patent. Rather for such a licence to be valid, it must be granted with the consent of all the co-owners (s 36(3)).

19.5.2	Statutory defences	Subsection 60(5) gives a number of specific examples of acts that are not infringements. It reads as follows:

'An act which, apart from this subsection, would constitute an infringement of a patent for an invention shall not do so if -

(a) it is done privately and for purposes which are not commercial;

(b) it is done for experimental purposes relating to the subject-matter of the invention;

(c) it consists of the extemporaneous preparation in a pharmacy of a medicine for an individual in accordance with a prescription given by a registered medical or dental practitioner or consists of dealing with a medicine so prepared ...'

19.5.3	Private and experimental use	'Privately' has been held to mean 'for a person's own use' (*Smith Kline & French Laboratories Ltd v Evans Medical Ltd* (1989)). This exemption does not cover the situation where the use serves a dual function of private and commercial purpose, but only excludes those cases concerned solely with private use, that are also non-commercial in nature.

It is permissible to use the subject-matter of the invention for experimental purposes, so long as the experiment itself is concerned with that subject-matter. Thus, it is not permissible to perform an experiment which merely uses the subject-matter of the invention in order to facilitate the study of some other issue. The exemption is drawn narrowly, thus the purpose of the experiment must be to discover things not already known, and it is not sufficient that the use is merely in order to gather data in order to satisfy a regulatory condition before approval may be granted (*Monsanto Co v Stauffer Chemical Co* (1985)).

19.5.4	Prior users of the invention	It has always been a principle of patent law that the grant of a patent cannot stop any person from continuing what he has always done prior to the grant of the patent. In most cases, this is of no consequence, because by the very nature of a patent it should be inventive and novel, and thus there should be no prior users. However, in order to protect the position of any prior user special provisions are present within the PA 1977 to permit the continued use. These provisions are contained within s 64, as amended by the CDPA 1988 Schedule 5 para 17, and are effective from the 7 January 1991.

This protection only covers those activities of the same nature that were done before the priority date of the patent, and so there may be no further development of those activities without risking the new acts becoming infringing acts.

Section 44(3) provides that 'in proceedings against any person for infringement of a patent it shall be a defence to prove that at the time of the infringement there was in force a contract relating to the patent made by or with the consent of the plaintiff ... containing ... a condition or term void by virtue of this section'. The section enumerates a number of such terms that, broadly, all relate to restrictive practices. This defence is rarely invoked, but when it does occur it provides a complete defence (*Chiron Corporation v Organon Teknicka Ltd (No 3)* (1994).

19.5.5   PA 1977 s 44

It is a general principle of continental intellectual property law that once a product has been put on the market by, or with the consent of, the owner of the intellectual property rights in the goods, which in this case are the patent rights, then the proprietor of those rights cannot limit what the purchaser does with the goods thereafter, ie the proprietor's rights are exhausted once the goods have passed to the purchaser.

19.5.6   Exhaustion of rights

The existence and exercise of patent rights have the potential to distort trade between Member States of the EU. Accordingly, there are a number of Regulations that exist to regulate these issues. The principal regulations are the know-how Block Exemption 556/89 and the Patent Block Exemption 2349/90. The latter was due to expire on 31 December 1994, but it has been extended to 30 June 1995, by which time the Commission intends to replace both block exemptions with a single Technology Transfer Block Exemption. However, this has not yet been finalised. In addition to these Regulations, the provision against restriction on free trade and anti-competitive practices apply to patent rights.

Lastly, the principle of non-derogation from grant, which was adopted by the House of Lords for copyright matters in *British Leyland Motor Corporation Ltd v Armstrong Patents Co Ltd* (1986), was based upon a line of authority that originated in the field of patents. This has already been discussed in detail in Chapter 8.

19.5.7   Non-derogation from grant

Patents: Infringement

A patent gives the proprietor the exclusive rights to certain activities concerning the subject matter of the patent. This exclusive right is given in return for disclosing fully the patented invention.

Introduction

An action for infringement may only be commenced after the grant of the patent. However, the patentee may seek damages from the publication of application if it is in the same form as the final patent (ss 69(1) and (2)).

Amendments act retrospectively (s 75(3)).

Timing of infringement proceedings

Under the PA 1977, infringement is determined exclusively by s 60, (cf CPC Articles 29-31).

Infringement

Broadly, there is an infringement of a patent for a product if it is made, disposed of or kept.

Similarly, a process is infringed occurs if it is used, offered for use or a product obtained directly from the process is disposed of or used. Furthermore, there is an infringement if an essential element of the invention for putting the invention into effect is supplied.

Infringing Acts under PA 1977 s 60

The supply of staple commercial commodities is only an infringement if it has been done for the purpose of inducing infringement. Thus, the supply of staple commodities *per se* is not an infringement (*Benno Jaffe v Richardson* (1894)). There needs to be a common design to infringe (*Lavender v Witten* (1979)).

Supply of staple commodities

Balcombe LJ in *Daily v Etablissement Fernand Berchet* (1992) said that the normal canons of construction should be used in patent cases. However, technical words may have a technical meaning (*Unwin v Hanson* (1891)).

Construction of the claims

The early broad claims lead to a 'pith and marrow' approach (*Clark v Addie* (1877)). With increased precision, came a stricter, more literal, interpretation of the invention claimed.

Textual construction

'Pith and marrow' construction	One cannot go against the plain meaning of the words used in a claim (*Van Der Lely v Bamfords* (1963)).

Lord Reid, dissenting, proposed a more purposive construction. |
| ***Catnic v Hill & Smith*** | In *Catnic v Hill & Smith* (1982), Lord Diplock promulgated a 'purposive construction rather than a purely literal one'. This approach is valid for patents granted under the PA 1949 and the PA 1977 (*Assidoman Multipack Ltd v The Mead Corporation* (1995)). |
| **Development of the purposive approach** | If a variant is obviously immaterial, then it will be held to infringe (*Improver v Remington* (1990)). |
| **Defences** | There is infringement only if the infringing acts were done without the licence of the proprietor of the patent.

Various statutory defences exist. For example, if done privately and for purposes which are not commercial (s 60(5)(a)); experimental purposes relating to the subject-matter of the invention (s 60(5)(b)); and, extemporaneous preparation in a pharmacy of a medicine (s 60(5)(c)).

Private use has been held to mean 'for a person's own use' (*Smith Kline & French v Evans* (1989)). To gain the protection of s 60(5((b), the purpose of the experiment must be to discover new information (*Monsanto v Stauffer* (1985)).

Prior users of the invention are not liable for infringement (PA 1977 s 64 (as amended by the CDPA 1988 Schedule 5 para 17).

If there is a contract that contains a void condition by reason of s 44, then that will also provide a defence (*Chiron Corporation v Organon Teknicka Ltd (No 3)* (1994).

The principle of exhaustion of right applies to patent matters. Furthermore, they are regulated by various block exemptions. The existing block exemptions are soon to be replaced by a single Technology Transfer Block Exemption Regulation. Save for this Regulation, the normal principles relating to anti-competitive practices apply. Lastly, the principle of non-derogation from grant was originally developed in the patent field and still applies today in this field as well as in the field of copyright. |

Chapter 20

Trade Marks: Historical Introduction

During the great expansion of industrialised and international trade that occurred during the second half of the 19th century, there was an increasing demand from trading organisations and companies for some system whereby their trading identities could be protected from imitation by competitors. Before 1875 there was no system of registration in the UK for trade or service marks, and thus a competitor could imitate another's mark so long as the use was not fraudulent or deceitful.

As far as the traders were concerned this allowed too much latitude to their competitors. This was a particular concern when the goods were destined for sale overseas, because the local population might not be able to read English and thus acquaint themselves with the written statements by which the competitor distinguished his goods from those of the original trader. The indigenous purchaser would instead rely on the overall similarity of any pictorial mark, and hence could be misled by a similarity that fell short of actual fraud or deceit.

For example, in Singapore, a certain brand of cough sweets were sold under the name 'Hacks'. However, native customers, being unable to read Roman script, referred to them as 'red paper cough sweets', an allusion to the red cellophane wrappers that contained the sweets themselves. It was held that cough sweets, wrapped in a similarly coloured cellophane wrapper, sold by a rival under the name 'Pecto', were not sufficiently distinguished to prevent there being a misrepresentation that could found an action for passing-off, but no possible cause of action lay for trade mark infringement (*White Hudson & Co Ltd v Asian Organisation Ltd* (1965)).

This principle, that the mark must not mislead a prospective purchaser into believing that the goods originate from a source different from the one which the mark seems to indicate, continues to underpin trade mark legislation to the present day. In this respect, the law governing trade marks has remained remarkably constant over the last 100 odd years.

In 1875 the first UK statute concerned with trade marks was passed. This was the Trade Marks Registration Act 1875, and it allowed the owner of a trade mark to institute proceedings for the infringement of a trade mark so long as the mark had been

20.1 Introduction

20.2 Early legislation

registered in accordance with the Act. The very first trade mark to be registered incorporated the red triangle for Bass & Co Pale Ale, as brewed by Bass, Ratcliff & Gretton Ltd. This trade mark is still registered and is jealously protected by its proprietors. For example, youth hostels used to be depicted on ordnance survey maps by a small red triangle; however, they are now depicted with a green triangle.

This original Act was amended the next year by the Trade Marks Registration Amendment Act 1876. The change allowed a trader to sue for infringement of an unregistered trade mark only after its registration had been refused by the Registrar.

Over the next 50 odd years, the laws relating to trade marks was changed on many occasions. The continuing alterations were due to the legislature changing its position on how trade marks should be protected so that the interests of the business community were balanced with those of the general public.

Prior to the Trade Marks Act 1919, there was no distinction made between trade marks, ie, the proprietors of all trade marks were granted the same rights. However, the 1919 Act divided the register into Part A and Part B marks. The latter type of marks were easier to register, because the requirements for such marks were less stringent; correspondingly, however, a Part B mark afforded less protection for its proprietor. It was possible for a Part B mark to be upgraded to Part A if, through use, it was shown to meet the higher standards required.

It may be seen by the large number of Acts passed in a short period of time (11 in 62 years), that not only was Parliament very active in trying to protect the interests of the legitimate traders, but also that the area was a difficult one to regulate.

20.3   Trade Marks Act 1938 and its amendments

By 1937 the Acts that were still in force had been heavily amended, and the time had come to rationalise the situation. Thus, in 1938, the Trade Marks Act 1938 was passed to consolidate all that had gone before. The 1938 Act was a complicated piece of legislation that reflected the complicated background it was designed to replace. Unfortunately, it was not a model of clarity: in fact, it has been the butt of much judicial comment over the years on how not to draft legislation.

The 1938 Act remained the principal Act governing trade mark law until the coming into force of the Trade Mark Act 1994 on 31 October 1994. Thus, it is important to understand the developments that occurred under the 1938 Act in order to understand the UK foundation for the 1994 Act.

In 1974 the Mathys Committee recommended a number of changes to the law concerning trade marks. However, the only recommendation that was eventually adopted was the extension of the trade mark laws to include marks used to distinguish services. This change was incorporated by the Trade Marks (Amendment) Act 1984 which introduced a registration system for service marks, ie marks designed to distinguish services rather than goods. The second amendment to the original TMA 1938 was by the Patents, Designs and Marks Act 1986 which allowed marks to be kept otherwise than in documentary form, ie, the Register of trade marks could now be kept on computer. Both of these Acts came into force on the same day, namely 1 October 1986.

The principal Act of 1938, as amended, created two closely related systems, one for trade marks and one for service marks. However, the overall result is that the law on trade and service marks was scattered between the three principal Acts of 1938, 1984 and 1986.

In addition to the principal Acts already mentioned, there were special provisions made for the duration of the Second World War (the Patents, Designs, Copyrights and Trade Marks (Emergency) Act 1939 and the Patents and Designs Act 1946). It is usual practice for a country at war with another country to confiscate any intellectual property as well as sequestering its assets. For example, during the First World War, the US confiscated the trade mark 'Aspirin', which belonged to Bayer, the German pharmaceutical company. This trade mark had been used for the analgesic, acetylsalicylic acid. The US government sold the trade mark to Sterling; but, in September 1994, the US subsidiary of Bayer bought back the rights to the name, along with the trade marks 'Phillips' Milk of Magnesia' and 'Alka-Seltzer'. So, once more, the trade mark 'Aspirin' belongs to its German originators.

Even though there was no system of registration for trade marks until the Trade Marks Act 1875, before that time there were many statutes that were concerned with the marks found on silver and gold articles. These marks dealt with the certification of such goods, ie whether or not the goods had been approved officially.

Other official marks that indicated that an item was of a sufficient standard included the gun proofing marks. There are still two extant Acts that are concerned with gun barrels, namely the Gun Barrel Proof Act 1868 and the Gun Barrel Proof Act 1950.

The marks that certify plate silver are regulated by a variety of Acts that include the Plate Assay (Sheffield and

20.4   Certification marks and other ancillary matters

Birmingham) Act 1772 and the Hallmarking Act 1973. The latter act was designed to make fresh provisions for the composition, assaying, marking and description of articles of precious metals. It repealed a vast number of old Acts that covered such diverse matters as the 'Act for encouraging the bringing in wrought plate to be coined' 1696, the Gold and Silver Thread Act (Ireland) Act 1761, and the Wedding Rings Act 1855.

The Chartered Associations (Protection of Names and Uniforms) Act 1926 is designed to protect the names, uniforms and badges of associations incorporated by Royal Charter.

| 20.5 | **Trade Marks Act 1994** | After the creation of the European Economic Community in 1958, it rapidly became apparent that there needed to be one trade mark system that covered all the Member States of the community. This would be necessary in order to facilitate the free movement of trade between the Member States in accordance with Articles 30-36 of the Treaty of Rome. |

After extensive discussions, preliminary proposals were published in 1980 that included a draft regulation and a draft directive. After further consideration by the European Parliament an amended draft Regulation and a draft Directive were published (31 December 1984, and 31 December 1985 respectively). The aim of the Regulation was to establish a Community trade mark, that would have effect throughout all of the Member States.

Before agreement had been reached on the Regulation it was thought that immediate steps were needed in order to ensure that the differences in the trade mark laws of the various Member States did not impede the free movement of goods and the freedom to provide services and so distort competition within the common market. As a result, the development of the Directive was pursued, which was intended to harmonise the individual laws of Member States, and this resulted in the First Council Directive 89/104/EEC. It was felt by the Commission that the harmonisation of domestic rights was easier to achieve than the introduction of a new pan-Community right that would operate throughout the whole Community.

| 20.5.1 | Directive 89/104/EEC | The Directive was adopted on 21 December 1988, and by 28 December 1991 the Member States were to have brought into effect the necessary laws and administrative procedures needed to comply with the Directive (Article 16(1)). The Council, acting upon a proposal from the Commission, deferred this date to 31 December 1992 (Article 16(2)). |

However, no further deferments were allowed under the Directive. The UK has been in breach of this obligation since the end of 1992 until 31 October 1994 when the Trade Marks Act 1994 came into force.

In addition to Directive 89/104/EEC, the UK is signatory to a number of international agreements that impose certain obligations which need to be fulfilled. The two main international agreements are the Paris Convention for the Protection of Industrial Property 1883 as revised and amended and the Protocol to the Madrid Agreement concerning the International Registration of Marks 1989. These international agreements are concerned with the priority that should be accorded to applications made in different countries and also with how internationally recognised marks should be treated.

Directive 89/104/EEC only has relevance to the members of the European Union, while the Madrid Protocol has a wider application as may be gathered from Article 16(1) which states that apart from copies in English, French and Spanish, official texts should be established in Arabic, Chinese, German, Italian, Japanese, Portuguese and Russian. The Paris Convention is a truly international convention with 114 signatory States as of 15 October 1993.

In response to these obligations the Government produced a white paper entitled the 'Reform of Trade Marks Law 1990' which recommended that the current domestic law needed to be amended in a number of significant areas. The overall aim was to re-state the law of trade marks to meet the needs of the present trading community, and at the same time to clarify and simplify the text of the law.

The Trade Marks Act 1994 is intended to implement Directive 89/104/EEC to approximate the law of the Member States relating to trade marks; to give effect to the Madrid Protocol so that the UK may ratify that Agreement; and, also to meet the UK's other international obligations under the Paris Convention 1883. Furthermore, the new Act makes provisions for the introduction of the Community Trade Mark, which will be introduced by Regulation 40/94. It is also the aim of the Government to restate the law in clearer terms so as to meet the needs of modern commercial practice.

This Act radically affects the substantive law on trade marks within the UK. The Trade Marks Act 1938 (as amended) will continue to be applied to all acts of infringement committed before the commencement date of the new Act (TMA 1994 Schedule 3 para 4(1)). Thus, given the six year period of limitation for tortious wrongs and the delay in

20.5.2   Response by the UK

20.5.3   UK domestic legislation

bringing an action to trial, it is not unreasonable to suppose that the law under the TMA 1938 as amended will continue to be relevant for intellectual property law practitioners until the end of the century. Furthermore, some of the principles that have been developed under the 1938 Act will continue to apply after the new regime has come into effect. As a consequence, it is still necessary to consider the TMA 1938 in some detail.

20.5.4   Community Trade
          Mark Regulation 40/94

The Community Trade Mark Regulation was adopted on 20 December 1993. It created a unitary trade mark that will be effective throughout the whole European Union. This new property right will be administered by the Community Trade Marks Office (the 'CTMO'), which is to be situated in Alicante, Spain. The formal title for the CTMO is the Office for Harmonisation of the International Market (Trade Marks and Designs). The Office will also administer the new Community Design Right when it is introduced. The location of the headquarters was one of the last hurdles to be overcome before the final agreement of the Regulation. Another hurdle was the working language of the Office. It has now been decided that there will be five languages: English, French, German, Italian and Spanish (Art 115(2)). It is expected that applications for registration for the Community trade mark may begin to be submitted in 1996.

The Regulation came into force on 14 March 1994, which was the sixtieth day after it had been published in the Official Journal of the European Communities (Article 143(1)). Member States have three years from then (Article 143(2)) to set up the Community Trade Marks Courts as required under Article 91, and to provide the regulatory mechanism for converting a Community trade mark application into a national trade mark application as required under Article 110.

It will be recalled that a Regulation has direct effect, and thus does not require any further implementation before it may be relied upon. This is in contrast to a Directive. Thus, any provisions which may be made by the Secretary of State under the TMA 1994 s 52, are limited to facilitating the implementation of the Regulation, rather than effecting the implementation *per se*.

It is envisaged that the new Community trade mark will operate alongside the domestic trade mark system, in a similar manner to the European Community and domestic patent systems. Eventually, the unitary trade mark may replace the individual trade marks that exist currently in the different Member States.

Sections 53 and 54 of the TMA 1994 are concerned with the Madrid Protocol. The Secretary of State may, by order, make such provisions as he thinks fit for giving effect in the UK to the provisions contained within the Protocol (s 54(1)). An order shall be made by statutory instrument (s 54(4)).

The Protocol will provide a system whereby applications made by a single filing will be acceptable for national registration in the countries which have ratified the Protocol. The Protocol is in essence a watered-down version of the Madrid Agreement. It was designed to allow more countries, like the UK, to reach some agreement on the international treatment of trade marks, when, for whatever reason, those countries did not wish to comply with the full Agreement. The UK ratified the Protocol on 6 April 1995.

Sections 55–60 of the TMA 1994 concern the Paris Convention. It was arguable that, even though the UK is a signatory to the Paris Convention, the UK had not fulfilled all of its obligations under the Convention. The TMA 1994 rectifies these failings.

A Convention country is defined as a country, other than the UK, which is a party to the Paris Convention (s 55(1)(b)). Section 4(3) of the TMA 1994 covers the absolute grounds for refusing an application for registration of a mark which are specified in ss 57 or 58. These marks are concerned with national emblems of Convention countries and the emblems of certain international organisations. These provisions between them now fulfil the obligations of the UK under Article 6*ter* of the Paris Convention.

Section 56 of the TMA 1994 is concerned with the protection of well-known trade marks that are protected under the Paris Convention by Article 6*bis*. Such a mark would not be registered in the UK, because, if it was, there would be no need for this provision as it would be protected under the normal infringement provisions for domestic trade marks. The proprietor of such a mark may seek an injunction to restrain any use that causes confusion (s 56(2)).

Section 60 fulfils the obligations under Article 6*septies* and clarifies the position where an application for registration of a trade mark is made by an agent or representative of the proprietor of the mark in a Convention country.

Provision is made to amend the TMA 1994 if the Paris Convention is itself amended or revised (s 55(2)). However, no alteration to this part of the Act may be made unless the Paris Convention is first altered. Thus, the Government obviously considers that it has now fully complied with all of its obligations under that Convention.

20.5.5   Madrid Protocol

20.5.6   Paris Convention

20.6   Passing-off and other related rights

It is possible to have a trade mark that is not registered, and yet it still may have some protection in law. In such cases, obviously, protection cannot be sought from the legislation that deals with registered trade marks. Instead, reliance must be placed primarily upon the common law tort of passing-off.

The protection provided for registered trade marks by the registration system and for unregistered trade marks by the tort of passing-off are designed to complement each other, and so provide protection to the owner of any mark that is used in the course of trade.

There are other forms of protection available to the trader; for example, the tort of malicious falsehood, which is otherwise know as trade libel or injurious falsehood. This provides protection against a competitor making false statements about the goods of another trader with a view to causing damage to that trader thereby.

In a rather different vein, the Trade Descriptions Act 1968 is designed to protect the consumer from being deceived by unscrupulous traders who are dealing in goods that bear a mark that gives a false impression as to its origin. One of the objectives of this Act is to provide protection against counterfeit goods. The concern of Parliament to protect the consumer against the counterfeiter is also shared by the trader whose goods are being imitated, because he believes that he is thereby losing sales. However, it is not always the case that the sale of a counterfeit item equates with the loss of a sale of the genuine article. For example, a man who purchases an imitation Rolex watch from a market stall for £20 would probably not buy a genuine Oyster Rolex Perpetual, which costs at least £1,000. The torts of passing-off and malicious falsehood are designed to protect the integrity of a business's goodwill and reputation, while the TDA 1968 is designed to protect the general consuming public from various nefarious activities of the less than scrupulous trader. Between them, they help to ensure the probity of the market place.

20.7   Rationale for a registration system

Prior to the introduction of registration of trade marks by the Trade Marks Registration Act 1875, a prospective plaintiff had to prove not only that he was the owner of the mark in question, but also that the mark was distinctive of his goods. This latter point involved not only showing that the mark distinguished his goods from those of other traders, but also that consumers associated the mark with him as the trade source. The requirement to prove these matters placed a great burden on a prospective plaintiff. The purpose of the registration system was to simplify the procedure for protecting the rights of the owner of a trade mark. Registration is *prima facie* proof that the person who makes the application is indeed the owner of the mark, and also that the mark is distinctive of his goods. A mark is registered in respect of particular goods or services, and the protection thereby conferred is limited to those goods or services. The protection is of a monopolistic nature, ie regardless of whether another person has independently created the same mark, that other person will still be held to have infringed the registered mark if that latter person uses the mark in the course of trade on goods for which the mark is registered. There is, however, an exception whereby someone who was using the mark honestly before the applicant's use commenced, may still continue to use that mark.

To ensure that the old system of law did not continue in parallel with the new registration system, a prospective plaintiff could not sue for trade mark infringement unless the mark was validly registered. This is still the case. Thus, no person shall be entitled to institute any proceeding to prevent, or to recover damages for, the infringement of an unregistered trade mark, but nothing shall be deemed to affect rights of action against any person for passing off or the remedies in respect thereof (TMA 1938 s 2 as amended by TM(A)A 1984 s 1(5)(a), and TMA 1994 s 2(2)). In practice, if a registered trade mark is involved, it is usual to sue for both trade mark infringement as well as for passing-off. This protects against the situation where the goods in question are held not to be covered by the registration or the registration is invalid for some reason, and thus trade mark proceedings *simpliciter* would fail. If the trade mark is unregistered, then only passing-off proceedings may be commenced.

Trade Marks: Historical Introduction

Before 1875 infringement was only actionable if it was fraudulent or deceitful. This required the twin issues of 'use in course of trade' and 'distinguishing source of goods' to be established by the proprietor.

Introduction

The Trade Marks Registration Act 1875 introduced a registration system for trade marks. In 1919, the Trade Marks Act 1919 divided the register into Parts A and B. Part B marks are easier to obtain, because they have to meet less stringent criteria; but, accordingly, they offer less protection to the proprietor.

Early legislation

The Trade Marks Act 1938 was the principal Act governing trade marks. The Trade Marks (Amendment) Act 1984 permitted registration of service marks. The Patents, Designs and Marks Act 1986 allowed for computerisation of the trade mark register. Both of the latter two Acts came into force on 1 October 1986.

Trade Marks Act 1938 and its amendments

Certification marks are used to prove that an article meets the official standard for that product. For example, the Gun Barrel Proof Act 1868 and the Gun Barrel Proof Act 1950 are designed to ensure that gun barrels are safe for use. The Hallmarking Act 1973 regulates gold and silver goods.

Certification marks and other ancillary matters

Directive 89/104 EEC aims to approximate the laws on trade marks within the Community, while Regulation 40/94 introduces a unitary Community trade mark.

Directive 89/104/EEC and Community Trade Mark Regulation 40/94

Paris Convention for the Protection of Industrial Property 1883, as revised and amended, is concerned with the protection imposed upon well-known marks.

International Conventions

The Protocol to the Madrid Agreement concerning the International Registration of Marks 1989 provides a single filing system so that an application may be registered in all the member countries.

The White Paper entitled 'Reform of Trade Marks Law 1990' recommended changes to the UK domestic legislation so as to fulfil its international obligations.

Trade Marks Act 1994

The Trade Marks Act 1994, which received Royal Assent on 21 July 1994, came into force on 31 October 1994. Trade mark infringement which occurred before 31 October 1994 is still governed by the TMA 1938 (TMA 1994 Schedule 3 para 4(1)). The TMA 1994 brings the UK domestic law on trade marks into line with modern commercial practice, as well as fulfilling its international obligations under the Paris Convention and the Madrid Protocol.

Passing-off and other related rights

Passing-off protects unregistered trade marks. Malicious falsehood prevents untrue statements being made by competitors. Both these torts protect the integrity of the goodwill and reputation attached to a business.

The Trade Descriptions Act 1968 protects the public, eg from counterfeiters.

Rationale for a registration system

Originally had to prove title, distinctiveness and reputation. The system of registration simplified the procedure, by providing prima facie evidence of these points. Registration confers a monopolistic protection for the registered trade mark. However, one may no longer sue for trade mark infringement of an unregistered trade mark. The tort of passing-off, which protects unregistered trade marks, is preserved under the TMA 1938 s 2 as amended and the TMA 1994 s 2(2).

Chapter 21

Trade Marks: The 1938 Act: Basic Principles

The essence of a trade mark is to distinguish the goods of one trader from those of another, so that a prospective customer, who has on previous occasions contentedly purchased a particular trader's goods, may on a subsequent occasion identify that first trader's goods and purchase them safe in the belief that they will fulfil his expectations.

The statutory definition of a trade mark attempts to encapsulate the function. Thus a 'trade mark' was defined by s 68(1) of the TMA 1938 to mean:

'... except in relation to a certification trade mark, a mark used or proposed to be used in relation to goods for the purpose of indicating, or so to indicate, a connection in the course of trade between the goods and some person having the right either as proprietor or as registered user to use the mark, whether with or without any indication of the identity of that person.'

A 'mark' is further defined so as to include a 'device, brand, heading, label, ticket, name, signature, word, letter, numeral or any combination thereof' (TMA 1938 s 68(1)).

Even though the definition of 'mark' in the context of a trade mark is very wide, it is not wide enough to include the container of the goods for which the mark is to be registered. Thus, the distinctive glass bottle in which Coca-Cola was commonly sold was refused registration (*COCA-COLA Trade Marks* (1986)). In order to prevent the shape of a container being imitated, recourse must be had in the law of passing-off. In *Reckitt & Colman Products Ltd v Borden Inc* (1990) an injunction was obtained to restrain the defendant from selling lemon juice in yellow, lemon-shaped containers that resembled the plaintiff's 'Jif Lemon' containers.

Originally, a trade mark owner had to establish a reputation in the mark before it could be registered. This required the mark to be actually used in practice so that the goods became associated with him. Then the situation became that a mark may be registered not only if it was actually used, but also if its use was proposed (s 68(1)).

In *Imperial Group Ltd v Philip Morris & Co Ltd* (1982) the mark 'NERIT' was registered for a brand of cigarettes. Imperial Group Ltd had no long-term intention of using this

21.1 Statutory definition of trade mark

21.2 Use of the mark or proposed use

mark. The Court of Appeal held that the mark was incapable of registration, because the clause 'proposed to be used' required a definite and present intention to use, and, furthermore, that the use must be primarily intended to engender goodwill in the mark.

It is common commercial practice to launch a product such as a children's toy in one country to test the market reaction. If that reaction is favourable then the product will be released in other countries and in addition, other related products will be produced. An unrelated person could attempt to register the trade marks related to such a new product in the UK, when the product is originally launched elsewhere, with a view to selling the rights to such marks if the product becomes a success. In such a case the person who registers the multiplicity of marks would be held to be dealing in the marks themselves and not in the underlying goods and so the registrations would be rejected since this amounts to trafficking in trade marks (*HOLLY HOBBIE Trade Mark* (1984)).

21.3   Connection in the course of trade

Not only must there be use of the trade mark, but that use must indicate a 'connection in the course of trade'. In *Imperial Group Ltd v Philip Morris & Co Ltd* (1982) it was held that the phrase 'in the course of trade' implied that there was an intention on behalf of the trade mark user to make a profit and to establish trading goodwill. Thus, as a consequence of this ruling the title of a free magazine may not be registered (*UPDATE Trade Mark* (1979)), unless there is an intention to make a profit from advertising revenue (*GOLDEN PAGES Trade Mark* (1985)).

The goods or services must be in existence, or, at least, they must be available in order for there to be a potential trade in those goods or services in connection with which the mark may be used. Accordingly, if the mark does not become apparent until after the purchase of the goods with which it is associated, then that mark cannot be connected with the goods 'in the course of trade', but only in the course of their use. For example, the coloured stripes in toothpaste that are formed when it is extruded from the tube cannot be registered (*Unilever's (Striped Toothpaste) Application* (1980)).

The use of a trade mark on invoices and delivery notes has been held to constitute use in relation to the goods invoiced and delivered (*CHEETAH Trade Mark* (1993)).

21.4   Register of trade marks

The trade mark register was established by the TMRA 1875 ss 1-7. This register is still in existence (TMA 1938 s 1, as amended by the PDMA 1986 s 1 and Schedule 1 para 1, and

TMA 1994 s 63). It is overseen by the Comptroller-General of Patents, Designs and Trade Marks. Incidentally, 'Comptroller-General' is pronounced 'controller-general'. When he is dealing with trade marks he is referred to as the Registrar (s 1(1)).

Originally, the trade marks register comprised only one part. However, the TMA 1919 s 1 divided the register into two parts: Part A and Part B. Part A included all those trade marks which were on the register at the commencement of the 1919 Act, ie 1 April 1920 (TMA 1919 ss 1(2)) and 13(2)), together with all those trade marks that were registrable under (what became) s 9 of the TMA 1938. Part B comprised those marks that were registrable under (what became) s 10 of the TMA 1938. The division into two parts of the register was maintained until 30 October 1994 (TMA 1938 s 1(2)), and applied equally to service marks as well as to trade marks (PDMA 1986 Schedule 2 para 1(1)). However, after the coming into force of the TMA 1994 on 31 October 1994, the register once again became unified.

21.5   Division of the register

Generally, the person who was using the mark was the appropriate person to make the application for registration (s 17(1)). The owner of the mark was called the proprietor and it was to him that the exclusive right to use the trade mark was given in conjunction with any person who was a registered user of the mark (s 28).

The Registrar had an absolute discretion to accept or reject the application for registration of a mark, or impose such limitations or conditions as he thought fit (s 17(2)). If an application for a mark to be registered in Part A failed, it could then have been treated as an application for that mark to be registered in Part B, so long as the applicant agreed (s 17(3)).

21.6   Application for registration

When an application for registration had been accepted, the mark is then advertised in the Official Journal of the Patents Office, which is published weekly (s 18(1)). This enables *any* person to give notice that he objects to the mark as advertised (s 18(2)). After the application had been accepted and objections, if any, had been successfully overcome, then the mark could be registered in Part A or Part B as was appropriate (s 19(1) as amended by PDMA 1986 s 2(3), Schedule 2 para 3 and s 3(2) Schedule 3 Part II). Thus, there was a two-stage process whereby an application for registration was first vetted by the Registrar before it was advertised and then after any objection had been raised, ie objections by third parties apart from the Registrar and the applicant, the mark could proceed to registration.

21.7   Registration

21.8	Classification of goods and services

Section 3 of the TMA 1938 provided that a trade mark must be registered in respect of particular goods or classes of goods, and any question which arose as to the class within which any goods fell should be determined by the Registrar, whose decision was final. This section applied to services marks by virtue of the general section (TM(A)A 1984 s 1(1), as amended by the PDMA 1986 s 2(1) Schedule 1 para 1).

The classification of goods and services into different classes was contained in the Trade Marks and Service Marks Rules 1986 rr 5-8 and Schedules 3 and 4. A separate application was needed for each class, and thus the procedure for registering a mark that was to be used for a number of different types of goods may prove to be expensive (TMSMR 1986 r 21).

Schedule 3 contained the 50 categories that were used to classify marks registered prior to 27 July 1938. Schedule 4 Part I contained 34 classes for goods, while Part II contained eight classes for services. Examples of classes of goods under Schedule 4 include: chemicals used in industry, science and photography (class 1); firearms, ammunition and projectiles, explosives and fireworks (class 13); musical instruments (class 15); games and playthings (class 28); and, alcoholic beverages (except beer) (class 33). Examples of classes of services under Schedule 4 include: advertising (class 35); telecommunications (class 38); and, education (class 41).

A mark could be registered for a complete class of goods, or just a selection of those goods. The importance of the scope of the registration was that it determined the limits of the protection that a registered mark could command and thus the range of goods upon which a mark, when used, could be held to infringe a registered trade mark.

21.9	Introduction to Parts A and B

Trade marks could be registered in either Part A or Part B of the register. The requirements that had to be satisfied before a mark could be registered in Part A were more stringent than those required for registration in Part B. Correspondingly, the protection granted, once registration had been effected in Part A, was greater than that conferred on a Part B mark. Section 9 of the TMA 1938 made provisions for Part A marks, while Part B marks were dealt with by s 10.

Generally, a mark will not be accepted for registration if it interferes with the freedom of honest and legitimate traders to use words or devices common in the English language. Thus 'Next' was refused registration (*NEXT Trade Mark* (1992)).

Trade marks may be contrasted with advertising slogans. The former are usually short in nature, while the latter are usually longer and contain an exhortation to buy the product. In between there may be a short phrase that serves both functions, and, so long as it would be taken as identifying the origin of the goods, the phrase could act as a trade mark. Thus, it was held that the phrase 'I CAN'T BELIEVE IT'S YOGURT' was accepted for registration in Part B of the register (*I CAN'T BELIEVE IT'S YOGURT Trade Mark* (1992)). However, the phrase 'HAVE A BREAK' used in the slogan 'Have a break have a Kit Kat', which is used to advertise the well known chocolate bar 'Kit Kat', was not registrable in either Part A or Part B. The words of the phrase were individually and collectively non-distinctive in respect of snack foods and further the use of the phrase was not in a trade mark sense (*HAVE A BREAK Trade Mark* (1993)).

Broadly, the difference between a Part A mark and a Part B mark is the level of distinctiveness of the mark in question. Thus, very distinctive marks may be registered in Part A, while less distinctive ones may be registered in B.

21.10   TMA 1938 s 9

Exactly how distinctive a mark must be before it is eligible for registration in Part A rather than Part B, or even whether it is worthy of registration at all, has taxed both the legislature and the judiciary.

For a mark to have been registered in Part A, it had to satisfy at least *one* of the five requirements given in s 9(1)(a)-(e). The five requirements were separate and distinct, but were not mutually exclusive and so a mark could have fallen into more than one category. Only in s 9(1)(e) was the word 'distinctive' actually used, but distinctiveness was a requirement for all the categories (*SWALLOW Trade Mark* (1947)). However, just because a mark satisfied at least one requirement it did not mean that the mark would automatically be registered (*CHIN CHIN Trade Mark* (1965)). A mark could satisfy a requirement of s 9 but then could be excluded by the operation of, for example, ss 11 or 12, or denied registration at the discretion of the Registrar.

21.10.1   Necessary but not sufficient condition for registration

Section 9 proceeded to define 'distinctive' to mean:

'... adapted ... to distinguish goods with which the proprietor of the trade mark is or may be connected in the course of trade from goods in the case of which no such connection subsists ...' (s 9(2)).

21.10.2   Statutory definition of distinctiveness

When determining whether or not a trade mark was adapted to distinguish, the tribunal could consider the extent to which:

'(i)   the trade mark is inherently adapted to distinguish; and

(ii)   by reason of the use of the trade mark or of any other circumstances, the trade mark is in fact adapted to distinguish' (s 9(3)).'

Both of these issues have been held to be questions of law (*YORK Trade Mark* (1982)). Inherent adaptability referred to some intrinsic quality of the proposed mark that made it unique when used for the particular goods or services in question.

The approach which the Registrar should have adopted when considering this matter, was to balance the inherent distinctiveness of the mark against the *de facto* distinctiveness that the mark had acquired by reason of its actual use in the market place. Thus, a mark which was inherently very distinctive required less evidence of acquired distinctiveness. In contrast, a mark which inherently had no distinctiveness could not be registered, regardless of how much evidence was adduced of the distinctiveness it had acquired by actual use (*Yorkshire Copper Works Ltd v Registrar of Trade Marks* (1954) and *YORK Trade Mark* (1984)). For example, the mark 'York' used in connection with containers and trailers for freight could not be registered. The House of Lords held that the geographical significance of the mark rendered it 'incapable in law' of distinguishing the applicant's goods, regardless of the fact that evidence had been adduced that the mark was, in actual use, 100 per cent distinctive of these goods (*YORK Trade Mark* (1984)). In contrast, a mark that comprised a unique pattern designed *ab initio* would be likely to possess the inherent quality of distinctiveness to qualify for registration in Part A.

In *Registrar of Trade Marks v W & G Du Cros Ltd* (1913), Lord Parker gave the classic definition of 'inherent adaptability to distinguish', where his Lordship stated that:

'... the right to registration should largely depend on whether other traders are likely, in the ordinary course of their business without any improper motive, to desire to use the same mark, or some mark nearly resembling it, upon or in connection with their own goods.'

21.10.3   Examples

To qualify as a trade mark under s 9(1)(a), the name of the company, individual or firm had to be 'represented in a special or particular manner'. For example, the mark 'Robin Hood' in which the 'R' incorporated an archer, while the 'D' was a target, was acceptable (*Standard Cameras Ltd's Application* (1952)).

Under s 9(1)(b), trade marks may comprise a signature, and thereby qualify the registration in Part A. In *Fanfold Ltd's Application* (1928), Tomlin J said:

'I think it may be rightly said that a signature is distinctive of the individual who signs'.

Section 9(1)(c) concerns words that have been invented in order to act as a trade mark. An early example of an invented word mark is 'Persil', which was coined in 1903. This word is a combination of the names of the principal chemical ingredients of this washing powder, namely perborate and silicate.

An invented word does not necessarily have to be meaningless; for example, 'persil' also means 'parsley' in French. In fact, the value of an invented trade mark is enhanced if it does have some meaning to the purchaser. The case of (*Eastman Photographic Materials Co Ltd's Application*) (1898)) concerned the application to register the mark 'Solio' for photographic paper. Lord Macnaghten stated that:

'If it is an invented word – if it is "new" and freshly coined (to adapt an old and familiar quotation) – it seems that it is no objection that it may be traced to a foreign source, or that it may contain a covert and skillful allusion to the character or quality of the goods. I do not think that it is necessary that it should be wholly meaningless.'

A mark could be registered under s 9(1)(d) as a trade mark, even if it did not qualify under paragraph (a) to (c) of s 9(1), so long as the mark did not refer to the character or quality of the goods or services, and so long as the mark did not signify a geographical name or surname when understood in ordinary usage.

Indirectness could be introduced by requiring that the word in question required translation from a foreign language, thus 'Kiku' was allowed for perfumes, the word being Japanese for 'chrysanthemum' (*KIKU Trade Mark* (1978)). However, the use of a foreign word such as 'belle', being the French for beautiful, would most likely not be allowed, because its laudatory nature is readily apparent to the average Englishman. The word 'Earthmaster' was refused registration, because it was held to be descriptive of the character of the machine that the trade mark user wished to promote (*Chaseside Engineering Co Ltd's Application*) (1956)).

It was still possible to register a mark even if it did not fall within ss 9(1)(a)–(d). However, it would only be registered if evidence of its distinctiveness was adduced. Thus, it was possible to register words of geographical significance or surnames if it could be shown to be distinctive. The smaller, more remote a place name, the greater the likelihood that the registration would be allowed, because there was a smaller chance that any other trader would legitimately wish to use that word, or would wish to trade in the same type of goods from that area, and would thus be inconvenienced if the place name was registered by someone else. Thus, 'Apollinaris' was allowed for mineral water (*Apollinaris Brunnen vormals Georg Kreuzberg AG's Application* (1907)).

Not only could a trade mark consist of words, but it could also consist partly, or entirely, of a device, that is to say some logo or other graphic mark. Yet a *very* simple device may be refused registration, eg the red tab sewn into, and protruding from, the back-pocket seam of a pair of Levi jeans was refused registration (*Levi Strauss & Co's Label Trade Mark* (1991)). However, simplicity of the individual components is not a bar *per se* to registration. Thus, a mark that comprised a large letter 'T' bisected by the word 'diamond', all contained within a lozenge-shaped doubled-lined border was held to be capable of registration (*Diamond T Motor Car Co's Application* (1921)).

The 1938 Act permitted the registration of letters and numerals so long as they were distinctive and the registration would not embarrass the legitimate use by other traders, eg '4711' (*RJ Reuter & Co Ltd v Mulhens* (1953)).

It was permissible for colour to contribute to the distinctiveness of the mark (s 16). The issue for colour marks reduces to one of distinctiveness; thus the black and copper-coloured battery of Duracell has been registered, because it was held to be distinctive in practice (*Duracell International Inc v Ever Ready Ltd* (1989)).

21.11   TMA 1938 s 10

As described above, Part A marks are concerned with inherent distinctiveness or distinctiveness as actually proven in practice. However, if a mark did not quite reach one of those standards of distinctiveness, then it could still be possible for the mark to be registered in Part B of the Register. Registration in Part B afforded less protection for the proprietor of the mark, than would registration within Part A.

21.11.1   Statutory provisions

Section 10 of the TMA 1938 governed the position for the registration of a mark in Part B. It stated that:

'(1)   In order for a mark to be registrable in Part B of the register it must be capable, in relation to the goods in respect of which it is registered or proposed to be registered, of distinguishing goods with which the proprietor of the trade mark is or may be connected in the course of trade from goods in the case of which no such connection subsists, either generally or, where the trade mark is registered or proposed to be registered subject to limitations, in relation to use within the extent of the registration.'

The dividing line between a mark capable of registration in Part B, and yet not meriting registration in Part A, has been the source of much judicial and academic comment over the years. Even though a formulation may be devised, its implementation in practice may be more difficult.

There are two principal differences between the requirements for registration in Part A compared with registration in Part B. The first is that Part A marks must be *'adapted* to distinguish', while Part B marks are *'capable* of distinguishing'. Broadly, 'adaptation' refers to the inherent qualities of a mark to distinguish itself from another; while 'capability' alludes to the fact that in practice a mark has been shown to be distinctive.

21.11.2   Registration in Part A and Part B compared

The second difference concerns names, signatures and invented words. In Part A, if these did not fall into one of the subsections 9(1)(a) to (d), then in order to be registered in Part A, evidence of distinctiveness was required so that they could be brought within s 9(1)(e). In contrast, such marks may be registered in Part B, without adducing evidence that the mark was distinctive, so long as the applicant was able to convince the Registrar that the mark was capable of distinguishing.

The requirement for a mark under the TMA 1994 is similar to the test that existed for a Part B mark under the TMA 1938 (TMA 1994 s 1(1)).

In *WELDMESH Trade Mark* (1965) the trade mark 'Weldmesh' was registered in Part B for steel mesh fences. It had acquired over time 100% distinctiveness and so the proprietor applied for the mark to be re-registered in Part A, because of the additional benefits that would confer. Lloyd-Jacob J said:

21.11.3   Capable of distinguishing under the TMA 1938

'It is, therefore, not unreasonable to regard the two expressions "adapted to distinguish" and "capable of distinguishing" as being deliberately chosen so as to direct the particular enquiry aright, the former emphasising that it is because of the presence of a sufficient distinguishing characteristic in the mark itself that distinctiveness is to be expected to result whatever the type and scale of the user and thus secure an estimation of a positive quality in the mark; and the second that, in spite of the absence of a sufficient distinguishing characteristic in the mark itself, distinctiveness can be acquired by an appropriate user, thereby overcoming a negative quality in the mark.'

The judge then went on to hold that:

'... the conjunction of the two words "weld" and "mesh" is so clearly and directly descriptive of welded mesh goods that the mark applied for is not inherently 'adapted to distinguish' the goods of the applicants', and thus he refused the application for the mark to be re-registered in Part A.

Thus clearly after the introduction of the TMA 1938, it was possible for a mark to be properly registered in Part B because it was not suitable for Part A registration, and yet it did satisfy the requirements of being 'capable of distinguishing' the goods of the proprietor from those of his competitors, and accordingly merited some protection as a registered trade mark.

21.12   Defensive registration

If a trade mark that consisted of an invented word or words had become so well-known in respect of any goods for which it was registered, that the use of that mark for other unrelated goods would have been likely to have been taken as indicating a connection in the course of trade between those unrelated goods and the proprietor of the mark for the original goods, then the mark could be registered for those unrelated goods, regardless of whether or not the proprietor intended to trade in those other goods. Such a registration would not be invalid for want of such proposed use, in contrast to the usual requirements (s 27(1)). This was called defensive registration. This procedure protected the proprietor of a well-known mark from other traders taking advantage of his reputation in the mark for the original goods. There was no provision for the defensive registration of a service mark.

21.13   Restriction on registration

Broadly, the onus on whether or not a mark should be registered was placed upon the applicant. It was up to him to prove that the proposed mark satisfied the requirements in s 9 or s 10, and that it did not fall foul of the prohibitions contained in ss 11, 12 or 15. Even when all these hurdles were crossed, the Registrar could still refuse to register a mark as an exercise of his discretion under s 17(2). For example, in *Arthur Fairest Ltd's Application* (1951) there was an application to register a mark that had been used on lottery tickets, the sale of which was illegal then. The court refused the registration as an exercise of its discretion, because the wrongful use of the word 'registered' might have led some to believe that judicial approval had been given to the tickets, and so, by implication, to the lottery.

There was no presumption in favour of the proposed mark if it already satisfied the other conditions. Thus, registration was all uphill under the TMA 1938. This is now turned on its head under the TMA 1994, for there is a presumption in favour of registration, which may be rebutted only by positive, and limited, reasons for refusal.

Section 11 stated that it would not be lawful to register as a trade mark or part of a trade mark any matter the use of which would, by reason of its being likely to deceive or cause confusion or otherwise, be disentitled to protection in a court of justice, or would be contrary to law or morality, or any scandalous design.

21.13.1   TMA 1938 s 11

Subsections 12(1) and (2) (as amended by the TM(A)A 1984 s 1(4), Schedule 2 para 2) stated that no trade mark should be registered in respect of any goods or description of goods that was identical with, or nearly resembled a mark belonging to a different proprietor and already on the register in respect of the same goods or the same description of goods, save that if there was honest concurrent use.

21.13.2   TMA 1938 s 12

The interplay between these two sections was summarised in *Smith Hayden & Co Ltd's Application* (1946), which concerned the objection by the proprietors of the marks 'Hovis' and 'Ovi', registered for cake mixtures, to the application to register the mark 'Ovax' for improvers and moistening agents to be used in the manufacturer of cakes. Evershed J held that:

21.13.3   Interplay between ss 11 and 12

> 'In the circumstances, the questions for my decision under the two sections of the Act have been formulated, and I think correctly formulated as follows: (a) (under section 11) "Having regard to the reputation acquired by the name 'Hovis', is the Court satisfied that the mark applied for, if used in a normal and fair manner in connection with any goods covered by the registration proposed, will not be reasonably likely to cause deception and confusion amongst a substantial number of person?"; (b) (under section 12) "Assuming user by Hovis Limited of their marks 'Hovis' and 'Ovi' in a normal and fair manner for any of the goods covered by the registrations of these marks (and including particularly goods also covered by the proposed registration of the mark 'Ovax') is the Court satisfied that there will be no reasonable likelihood of deception or confusion among a substantial number of persons if Hayden & Co Ltd also use their mark 'Ovax' normally and fairly in respect of any goods covered by their proposed registration?" '

'Ovi' was registered as an associated mark to 'Hovis' but was never used separately, and thus it was not mentioned in the test under s 11. The application for registration in this case was allowed to proceed, because the court answered both questions in the affirmative, ie there was no reasonable likelihood of confusion under either test. From a careful analysis, the following differences between ss 11 and 12 may be delineated.

Section 11 could apply to a case where the opponent's mark was unregistered all together, or was unregistered for some of the goods that would be covered by the proposed registration, or even to the situation in which the prior mark had only been used on goods of an entirely different description. In contrast, s 12 was concerned only with use upon similar goods.

Section 12, however, was wider than s 11, because it covered the notional use of any of the goods covered by the proposed registration, while s 11 depended upon actual confusion.

21.14   Prohibition on registration under s 11

The mark 'China-Therm', which was to be used on plastic insulated cups, was refused, because such use would have been deceptive (*CHINA-THERM Trade Mark* (1980)). The mark 'Orlwoola' was refused registration on two grounds. If it was used for cloth made of wool, it was merely a homonym of a purely descriptive nature, ie 'all wool', and as such was not permissible; while if used on articles that were not wool, then that use would be deceptive, and hence objectionable (*HN Brock & Co Ltd's Application* (1909)).

A mark would be refused registration if it was contrary to morality. The mark itself had to be inherently objectionable, and so the mark 'hallelujah' for women's clothing was refused because the word had an overwhelmingly religious significance and its use on women's clothing would offend generally accepted mores of the time, and further that its use would offend the religious susceptibilities of a not insubstantial number of persons (*HALLELUJAH Trade Mark* (1976)).

An example of a mark being refused for 'any other reason' would be when there was a great risk to public safety if the two marks were confused, even if such confusion was highly unlikely. Thus, the application for the mark 'Univer' for cardio-vascular preparations for human use was refused, because it so nearly resembled the mark 'Univet' which was registered for veterinary preparations. In this case, the court held that the goods for which the two marks were proposed to be registered were of the same description, and that there was a need to protect the public from the consequences of confusion between these different pharmaceutical products (*UNIVER Trade Mark* (1993)).

21.15   Prohibition on registration under s 12

Section 12 provided the basis for the objection to an application based upon a conflict with a prior registered mark. This section also provided that the Registrar had to consider any honest concurrent use of the marks in question.

Unlike s 11, in which the goods in question may be dissimilar, under s 12 the goods to which the application related must be the same, or of the same description, as the goods to which the registered mark related (s 12(1)(a) and (b)).

In *Ladislas Jellinek's Application* (1946) Romer J held that shoes and shoe polish were not of the same description. He proposed a triple test, namely the nature and composition of the goods; the respective uses of the articles; and the trade channels through which the commodities respectively are bought and sold.

The application for the mark 'Inadine' for wound dressings was refused because of the existing registration for 'Anadin' as an analgesics. The court held that both types of goods were often purchased when the consumer had no symptoms, and furthermore if the purchaser had been asked to obtain a branded product it was not necessarily the case that he would know the type of product required, and so confusion could result (*INADINE Trade Mark* (1992)).

Section 12(2) allowed the Registrar or the court to take into account any honest concurrent use, or other special circumstances when it fell to be considered whether the application for the registration for the new mark should be allowed or not.

The essential matters which had to be considered when dealing with an application under this subsection were outlined by Lord Tomlin in *Alex Pirie and Sons Ltd's Application* (1933). The matters included:

- the extent of use in time and quantity and the area of trade;

- the degree of confusion likely to ensue from the resemblance of the marks as this was an indication of the inconvenience to which the public would be put;

- the honesty of the concurrent use; and

- whether or not any instances of confusion had in fact been proven.

However, the presence of confusion by itself did not then automatically mean that the mark would not be accepted for registration (*BULER Trade Mark* (1975)). Such concurrent use had to be honest, and thus a genuine belief that no confusion would arise was acceptable.

If the application was for the same mark, for the same goods and to operate in the same geographical area, then the Registrar was loathe to allow the application (*Edward Bainbridge and N Green & Co's Application* (1940)). However,

21.15.1   Associated or identical goods or services

21.15.2   Honest concurrent use

there was no statutory bar to registration if this so-called 'triple identity' existed, it was merely the established practice of the Registry (*BUD Trade Mark* (1988)).

21.16   Mark used as the name or description of an article or substance

The 1938 Act made special provisions for the registration of a trade mark that was used as the name or description of an article or substance (s 15). Broadly, a registration of such a mark that had acquired such a usage after the date of its registration should not by itself render the mark invalid (s 15(1)).

The common law position was stated by Fry J in *Siegert v Findlater* (1878):

> 'The person who produces a new article and is the sole maker of it, has the greatest difficulty (if it is not an impossibility) in claiming the name of that article as his own, because until somebody else produces the same article there is nothing to distinguish it from.'

Even though this rule had an obvious applicability to patented products, it extended further to include those cases where the proposed trade name, at the date of the application for registration, was the name of the article itself, in contradistinction to the word being the name of goods of a particular type emanating from a particular trade source. So, for this reason, the word 'pizza', as well as the homonym 'pitza', was refused registration for pizza pies (*PIZZA Trade Mark* (1975)).

Trade Mark: The 1938 Act: Basic Principles

The fundamental purpose of a trade mark is to indicate a connection in the course of trade between the goods and the proprietor (s 68(1)). A mark includes any device, ticket, name, signature, word, letter or numeral (s 68(1)). It was not possible to register the shape of a container for goods (*COCA-COLA Trade Marks* (1986)).

Statutory definition of trade mark

The mark must be used or proposed to be used (s 68(1)).Thus the use of a ghost mark is not enough (*Imperial Group Ltd v Philip Morris & Co Ltd* (1982)). Trafficking in marks is not permitted (*HOLLY HOBBIE Trade Mark* (1984)).

Use of the mark or proposed use

There must be an intention to make a profit (*Imperial Group Ltd v Philip Morris & Co Ltd* (1982)). The mark must be in existence when the goods are traded (*Unilever's (Striped Toothpaste) Application* (1980)).

The use of the mark on invoices is sufficient to constitute use for the purpose of the TMA 1938 (*CHEETAH Trade Mark* (1993)).

Connection in the course of trade

The Register is still in operation (TMA 1938 s 1 and TMA 1994 s 63).

Register of trade marks

The TMA 1919 s 1 divided the register into Parts A & B, as from 1 April 1920. From 31 October 1994 the register once again become unified by virtue of the TMA 1994.

Division of the register

The procedure was the same for an application to register a mark in either Part A or Part B. The Registrar had absolute discretion whether or not to register a mark (s 17(2)).

Application for registration

Once accepted by the Registrar, the mark had to be advertised in the Official Journal (s 18(1)). This gave the opportunity for any person to object (s 18(2)).

Opposition to registration

Once advertised, and after objections, if any, have been overcome, then the mark would become registered (s 19(1)).

Registration

Goods and services must be registered with respect to the prescribed classes (s 3). The classes were set out in the TMSMR

Classification of goods and services

1986 rr 5-8 and TMA 1938 Schedules 3 and 4. Schedule 3 contained the 50 classes used before 27 July 1938, while Schedule 4 contained the 40 goods classes and 8 service classes currently in use.

Introduction to Parts A and B

Part A marks were governed by s 9, while Part B marks were governed by s 10.

The word 'next' was refused registration, because such a registration would fetter the legitimate use by honest traders of part of the English language (*NEXT Trade Mark* (1992)).

So long as a phrase was used in a trade mark sense it could be registered as such (*I CAN'T BELIEVE IT'S YOGURT Trade Mark* (1992)).

TMA 1938 s 9

A Part A mark must have been 'adapted to distinguish'. Distinctiveness was required by all categories of Part A marks in s 9(1)(a)-(e). (*SWALLOW Trade Mark* (1947)). Hence distinctiveness was a necessary but not sufficient condition for registration. A mark could have been excluded by the operation of ss 11 or 12, or at the Registrar's discretion (s 17(2)).

Definition of distinctiveness

'Adapted to distinguish' (s 9(2)) means inherently adapted or in fact distinguishes, which is a question of law (*YORK Trade Mark* (1982)). Consequently, inherently non-distinctive marks could not be registered (*Yorkshire Copper v Registrar* (1954)).

Examples

Usually a special representation of name would suffice (s 9(1)(a)) (*Standard Cameras Ltd's Application* (1952)). All signature marks were prima facie distinctive (*Fanfold Ltd's Application* (1928)).

An invented word could not imply the character of the goods, but it could mean something (*Eastman Photographic Materials Co Ltd's Application* (1898)). Words that were descriptive of the character of goods were not allowed (*Chaseside Engineering Co Ltd's Application* (1956)).

It was possible to register a name that had a geographical significance but distinctiveness was required. The smaller, more remote, the place, the greater the likelihood of success (*Apollinaris Brunnen vormals Georg Kreuzberg AG's Application* (1907)).

Very simple marks would generally not be allowed (*Levi Strauss's Label Trade Mark* (1991)); however, simplicity *per se* is no bar (*Diamond T Motor Car Co's Application* (1921)).

Colour could contribute to distinctiveness (*Duracell International Inc v Ever Ready Ltd* (1989)).

Lower standard of distinctiveness was required for registration in Part B. Concomitantly, there was less protection conferred. In contrast to a Part A mark, a Part B mark only had to be capable of distinguishing (s 10).

TMA 1938 s 10

A Part A mark had to be adapted to distinguish, while a Part B mark had to be merely capable of distinguishing.

Part A falling within s 9(1)(e) marks required evidence of distinctiveness, of which there was no need for Part B marks.

In *WELDMESH Trade Mark* (1965) the court held that not all Part B marks were fit for promotion to Part A.

Registration in Part A and Part B compared

Only invented words could be registered for defensive registration (s 27(1)).There was no provision for the defensive registration of a service mark.

Defensive registration

A mark may be excluded from registration by the operation of ss 11, 12 or 15, or operation of the Registrar's discretion (s 17(2)) (*Arthur Fairest Ltd's Application* (1951)).

Restrictions on registration

Registration prevented for deceptive, confusing or other marks contrary to law (s 11).

A mark may also be refused registration if there is a conflict with a similar mark that is already registered (s 12(1)).

However, if there has been honest concurrent use of the similar mark, then the Registrar may take this into account when considering the application (s 12(2)).

TMA 1938 ss 11 and 12

Section 11 could apply to unregistered marks and dissimilar goods. It also required actual confusion; while s 12 invoked the concept of notional use on similar goods, and in that sense was wider because there was no need for actual confusion to have occurred (*Smith Hayden & Co Ltd's Application* (1946)).

Interplay between ss 11 and 12

A plastic insulating cup was held to be deceptive (*CHINA-THERM Trade Mark* (1980)).

The mark 'Orlwoola' was refused as being either deceptive or descriptive (*HN Brock & Co Ltd's Application* (1910)).

For a mark to be scandalous, it had to offend the generally accepted mores of the time (*HALLELUJAH Trade Mark* (1976)).

There was a triple test of the nature, use and trade channels through which the goods would be sold in order to determine if the goods were associated or not (*Ladislas Jellinek's Application* (1946)).

Prohibition on registration under s 11

Prohibition on registration under s 12

If there has been honest concurrent one, then the Registrar would consider that when considering the application of the new mark; both the quality and quantity of the use must be taken into account (*Alex Pirie and Sons Ltd's Application* (1933)).

If a mark became used as a name or description of an article or substance after registration, then the mark could still be valid (s 15(1)). However, if it acquired such usage prior to application, then it would be refused (*PIZZA Trade Mark* (1975)).

Chapter 22

Trade Marks: The 1938 Act: Infringement and Defences

<table>
<tr><td>

The introduction of a system for registering of trade marks in 1875 made infringement proceedings easier, and thus increased the usefulness of a trade mark. As the protection conferred by registration is monopolistic in nature, the proprietor has the exclusive right to use that mark as a trade or service mark, so long as the mark was valid. However, the protection conferred is only for use with the particular class, or classes, of goods for which the mark has been registered, and so the use of an identical mark for dissimilar goods or services would not constitute an infringement. Under the TMA 1994, it is possible to infringe a mark when it has been applied to dissimilar goods so long as the mark in question has a reputation in the UK.

For an infringement of a trade or service mark to have been committed, one or more of the essential features of the mark must have been appropriated (*Saville Perfumery Ltd v June Perfume Ltd* (1941)). An essential feature included the overall idea or impression that the mark left with a prospective purchaser, and consideration may be given to the sound of the mark when it was spoken aloud, as well as the visual effect it had upon the eye. However, a mark could only be infringed by a graphic representation, and not by the audible reproduction of the mark. This stemmed from the historical nature of marks being a visual identification placed on goods.

It is the overall impression that the mark made on a prospective purchaser that was important. If this impression resulted from an imperfect recollection of what actually constituted the mark, then the allegedly infringing mark would be judged against that imperfect recollection. Section 4(1), supplemented by s 6, governed the actions that were to constitute infringement. There were special provisions for Part B marks in s 5. However, infringement was limited by the operation of ss 4(2), 4(3), 4(4), 7 and 8.

</td><td>

22.1   Introduction

</td></tr>
<tr><td>

Section 4(1) detailed the limit of trade mark infringement. A valid registration of a mark gave the proprietor of that mark the exclusive right to the use of the trade mark in relation to those goods for which it had been registered. That right was deemed to be infringed by any person who, not being the proprietor or registered user, used in the course of trade a mark identical with or nearly resembling it in relation to any

</td><td>

22.2   Infringement of a trade mark under TMA 1938 s 4(1)

</td></tr>
</table>

goods in respect of which it was registered, and in such manner as to render the use of the mark likely to be taken either (a) as being use as a trade mark, or (b) in a case in which the use is use upon the goods or in physical relation thereto or in an advertising circular or other advertisement issued to the public, as importing as reference to some person having the right either as proprietor or as a registered user to use the trade mark or to goods with which such a person as aforesaid is connected in the course of trade (TMA 1938 s 4(1) as amended by the TM(A)A 1984 s 1 (4), Schedule 2 para 1). This section had been described as being of 'fuliginous obscurity' (*Bismag Ltd v Amblins (Chemists) Ltd* (1940)).

The reference in subsection 4(1)(b) to 'importing a reference' to a trade mark in advertising material was introduced explicitly to overrule the House of Lords decision in *Irving's Yeast-Vite Ltd v FA Horsenail (t/a The Herbal Dispensary)* (1934), where it had been held that the advertisement 'Yeast tablets ... A substitute for Yeast-Vite' had not been an infringement of the trade mark 'Yeast-Vite'. This was the way in which Parliament prohibited comparative advertising and it became the bane of all advertising consultants over the years.

22.3   Infringement of a service mark under TMA 1938 s 4(1)

The infringement of service marks was governed by s 4(1) (as amended by the TM(A)A 1984 s 1(2), Schedule 1 para 2(1) and (2)). The modified section was very similar to the trade mark version.

In *Aristoc Ltd v Rysta Ltd* (1945) there was an application to register the mark 'Rysta' for a repair service of stockings. Objection was raised by the proprietor of the mark 'Aristoc' which was registered for the manufacture of stockings. The House of Lords held that a user in connection with a repair service was not a trade mark user, because the repair service did not denote a connection 'in the course of trade' and that it was not appropriate to use a trade mark to denote a such temporary connection with the goods as a repair service. Hence the application for registration was refused, because in essence the application was for a service, namely the repair of stockings, and at that time trade marks could only be registered for goods, which in this case would have been the manufacture of stockings.

22.4   Use as a trade mark

Section 4(1) gave the proprietor the exclusive right to *use* the mark. It did not confer the right to use the mark in the first place. Thus, for example, the mere fact that a mark was registered would not provide a defence for the proprietor of that registered mark against an action for passing-off.

In *Carless, Capel & Leonard v F Pilmore-Bedford & Sons* (1928) it was held that petrol pumps in the shape of a lighthouse did not infringe the lighthouse trade mark of the plaintiffs which was registered for petrol, because the petrol pumps did not indicate the trade source of the petrol, merely the physical location at which petrol could be obtained.

The primary purpose of a trade mark is for the identification of the trade source and not as an advertisement. As a consequence, the mark may be so small that it is not easily seen by the naked eye, yet it still acted as a trade mark, because it indicated the trade source of the goods (*Unic SA v Lyndeau Products Ltd* (1964)). In contrast, the use of the words 'Treat Size' was held to be descriptive of the product, which was a confectionery. Hence, it was held that the words were not an infringement of the registered trade mark 'Treets' (*Mars GB Ltd v Cadbury Ltd* (1987)).

A mark used on goods to advertise others may or may not be used as a trade mark in relation to either or both goods: it was a matter of fact and degree. The use of the mark 'Kodak' in the phrase 'Do it! Use Kodak films and plates' printed on T-shirts, was held not to be a use of the mark in respect of clothes, because its manner of use did not indicate the source of the T-shirts but rather its use was merely ancillary to Kodak's photographic trade and was primarily intended to advertise the same (*KODIAK Trade Mark* (1990)).

The trade mark need not be visible at the time of sale, but may be observed at a later time. For example, it was held that it was an infringement of a registered trade mark to play a pirate video tape upon which the mark had been recorded magnetically (*Esquire Electronics Ltd v Roopanand Bros* (1991)).

The allegedly infringing mark must have been used on goods that corresponded to the class of goods for which the trade mark was registered in order for there to be an infringement. However, a common sense, rather than a strict legalistic, approach is adopted by the courts when determining whether or not the goods are similar. Thus, a mark registered in class 39 (which includes stationery) was infringed by metallic staples bearing the same mark, even though, according to the classification index used for registered marks, metallic staples belonged in class 13 (*Ofrex Ltd v Rapesco Ltd* (1963)).	**22.5 Goods of a similar nature**
Under s 4(1)(b) importing a reference to another trade mark would have amounted to infringement of that other mark. If a trade mark consisted of a trader's name, it would appear not to have been an infringement of that mark, if the reference was to it as a name and not as a trade mark. Hence the statement 'not connected with Parker Knoll plc' was held	**22.6 Importing a reference**

not to infringe the Parker-Knoll trade mark (*Parker-Knoll plc v Knoll Overseas Ltd* (1985)). This was a fine distinction that was hard to draw in many cases. For example, the words 'Frazer's Chemicals have manufactured hair lacquer for Pompadour Laboratories Limited for many years', was held not to import a reference to the trade mark '*Pompadour*' (*Pompadour Laboratories Ltd v Stanley Frazer* (1966)); but an advertisement that included the clause 'Dell was rated ahead of Compaq' was held to import a reference and was thus an infringement (*Compaq Computer Corporation v Dell Computer Corporation Ltd* (1992)).

Furthermore, the comparative advertisement need not be issued to the general public; it is sufficient if it is released to a specialist class of the public, eg retailers (*Chanel Ltd v Triton Packaging Ltd* (1993)).

22.7	**Nature of the person who is deceived**	An allegedly infringing mark would constitute an infringement if it was likely that the purchasers of the goods upon which the offending mark was placed would be deceived or would be liable to confuse the goods so marked with the goods of the legitimate trade mark owner. Evidence of confusion would be adduced by the plaintiff; however, the court decides who is the appropriate person who must be shown to be confused in order to establish the course of action. Usually, the purchaser was taken to be the domestic consumer, and not the retailer (*William Edge & Sons Ltd v William Niccolls & Sons Ltd* (1911)); however, if the consumer could not obtain the goods until after they had been selected by a retailer, as was the case for prescription drugs, which could only be released by a pharmacist, then the appropriate person was the retailer (*Glaxo Laboratories Ltd v Pharmax Ltd* (1976)). If the goods were to be exported then the appropriate purchaser would be a citizen of the country in which the goods were actually sold, and not a member of the public of the UK (*George Ballantine & Son Ltd v Ballantyne Stewart & Co Ltd* (1959)).
22.8	**Comparison of marks**	Rarely will the situation arise in which the allegedly infringing mark appears on goods that are displayed adjacent to goods that bear the offended registered mark. The usual scenario is for the different goods to be sold at different times or places. Thus, a potential purchaser is not given the opportunity to compare directly the contested marks side by side. Instead, the allegedly infringing mark will be compared by the potential purchaser with an imperfectly remembered image of the registered mark. On many occasions, a double take is necessary in order to distinguish the mark in question. The issue of infringement will arise when greater attention than the

goods merit is required in order to differentiate the marks. Often, the first impression given by the two marks upon the court will be determinative of the question of infringement.

A mark will create a certain impression, which will be retained by the prospective purchaser far longer than the exact details will be remembered. This lasting impression is called the idea of the mark and is used when comparing two marks. Taking as an example the first registered trade mark, namely the red triangle used for beer made by Bass Brewery, the idea retained by the viewer is simply an equilateral triangle of solid red. On old ordnance survey maps, Youth Hostels were depicted by a small red triangle to which Bass took objection. Apart from the fact that the triangles were congruent, another issue was the possible confusion between a hostel and a hostelry. The matter was resolved, out of court, by altering the symbol for Youth Hostels to green triangles. The idea of a green triangle is clearly distinct from that of a red triangle, and so removed any lingering possibility of comparison by a thirsty rambler reading an ordnance survey map.

In the case of the red triangle, the mark was so simple that all of its features could be recalled. For a more complicated mark, the recollection may be imperfect, yet the general idea of the mark will still be recalled. This is a *sine qua non* of a successful trade mark, for if the mark leaves no impression upon the viewer then it has failed in its objective of enabling the purchaser to identify the goods of a particular trade, so that on future occasions he will buy those goods in preference to another trader's goods.

An example of imperfect recollection for a word mark is given by 'watermatic', which was held to be an infringement of 'aquamatic' when used on toy water pistols (*Harry Reynolds v Laffeaty's Ltd* (1957)). Even though the words are quite different, the idea conjured up by each mark is similar, namely a high-powered water pistol, and so the marks were held to be confusingly similar. Similarly, a device for car headlights that consisted of the lamps being depicted as the eyes of a cat was held to infringe a registered trade mark in which a line drawing of the front of a car was distorted so as to resemble a cat (*Taw Manufacturing Co Ltd v Notek Engineering Co Ltd* (1951)). In contrast, it was held that '99' did not infringe '999', because the idea of the former was duplication of the number, while the idea of the latter was triplication (*Ardath Tobacco Co Ltd v W Sandorides Ltd* (1925)). Therefore, as the idea behind the two marks was different, there was no likelihood of comparison between them.

22.8.1   Idea of the mark

For word marks, the first syllable is often considered to be the characteristic part that forms the memorable feature. In *London Lubricants (1920) Ltd's Application* (1925), Sargant LJ said:

> '... the tendency of persons using the English language to slur the termination of words also has the effect necessarily that the beginning of words is accentuated in comparison, and, in my judgement, the first syllable of a word is, as a rule, far the most important for the purpose of distinction.'

22.8.2   Whole mark to be considered

When comparing one mark against another, the impression which the whole mark gives must be considered. For example, a case of infringement involved the depiction of the head of a bull on the label for mustard and a drawing of a charging buffalo. Taken in isolation the drawings of the animals were quite different, one being merely of the animal's head, while the other was of the whole animal. However, coupled with the remainder of the label, the overall impression was similar, and hence there was a likelihood of comparison (*Farrow's Application* (1890)). In this case, emphasis was placed upon the visual impression of the marks, while the literary content was relegated in importance. Stirling J said in conclusion:

> 'Now, judging simply by eyesight ... that a person buying – not a wholesale or retail dealer who was dealing in mustard – but an ordinary person who had been accustomed to buy mustard in tin boxes like this with the bull's head upon it, if he were left to himself might very readily mistake the buffalo in Farrow's for the bull's head in Coleman's; and this conclusion is supported by the evidence. It is said that that would be so in some places, and particularly in Wales, where Mr Coleman's article has a large sale, and where the English language is not familiar to many of the inhabitants.'

Where, however, there is a common element, or elements, between the marks under comparison, then regard must be had to whether that element is common in the trade before the court could consider the question of infringement. So 'Pepsi-Cola' was held not to be an infringement of 'Coca-Cola' because 'cola' was common in the trade which comprised non-alcoholic drinks (*Coca Cola Co of Canada Ltd v Pepsi Cola Co of Canada Ltd* (1942)).

22.8.3   Comparison of marks as actually encountered

The comparison that should be made when considering infringement is between the alleged infringing mark, and the registered trade mark as actually used in practice, rather than how it appears on the register. In the case of *Christiansen's Trade Mark* (1886), Lindley LJ said:

'It appears to me, therefore, that ... the trade mark is to be looked at not simply as it appears on the Register, but with reference to the evidence which shows how it is going to be used in the trade.'

In this context, evidence which has been obtained under laboratory conditions that indicates a likelihood of confusion will not be accorded much weight by the court. This is particularly true when the court feels that the laboratory conditions bear no resemblance to what would occur in the market place (*Laura Ashley Ltd v Coloroll Ltd* (1987)).

The question of infringement of word marks was summarised by Romer J in *Lever Brothers, Port Sunlight, Ltd v Sunniwite Products Ltd* (1949) (approving Parker J in *Pianotist Co Ltd's Application* (1906)), when the judge said:

'You must consider the two words. You must judge them both by their look and their sound. You must consider the goods to which they are to be applied. You must consider the nature and kind of customer who would be likely to buy the goods. In fact you must consider all the surrounding circumstances, and you must further consider what is likely to happen if each of these trade marks is used in a normal way as a trade mark for the goods of the respective owners of the marks.'

A trade mark owner could impose contracted restrictions on the future use of his marked goods, which, if breached, would amount to an infringement of the trade mark (s 6(1)). In this way, the integrity of the trade mark could be preserved and hence its commercial value maintained for the proprietor.	**22.9 Infringement by breach of restrictions under s 6**
The infringement of those marks that were registered in Part B of the Register was governed by the TMA 1938 s 5. Broadly, the rights given to the proprietor of a mark that was registered in Part B was the same as the rights given to the proprietor of a mark that was registered in Part A. There was, however, an extra provision for Part B marks that was contained in s 5(2), which stated that in any action for infringement of a Part B mark, no injunction or other relief would be granted to the plaintiff if the defendant established to the satisfaction of the court that the use of which the plaintiff complained was not likely to deceive or cause confusion, or to be taken as indicating a connection in the course of trade between the offending goods and some other person having the right either as proprietor or as registered user to use the trade mark.	**22.10 Infringement of Part B marks**

Section 5(2) does not provide a true defence, it is merely a bar to the granting of remedies to an aggrieved plaintiff. This distinction is important, because under the transitional provisions to the TMA 1994 it will not be an infringement of an existing registered mark to continue, after the commencement of the TMA 1994, any use which did not amount to an infringement under the TMA 1938 (TMA 1994 Schedule 3 para 4(2)). If s 5(2) provided a true defence, it would mean that no infringement had occurred and thus the transitional provisions could be invoked. However, if an act that fall within s 5(2), and on a true construction this merely alleviated the grant of any relief, even though infringement had been established, it would mean that such an act would then attract liability after the commencement of the TMA 1994. There is no equivalent of s 5(2) in the new Act, and because of the transitional provisions its effect will not carry on after commencement.

22.11 Defences to an action for infringement of a trade or service mark

The commonest manner in which the scope of acts which could amount to an infringement was restricted was by the imposition of a disclaimer on the exclusive use of part of the registered mark (ss 4(2) and 14). This had the effect that the proprietor could not stop other traders from using those parts of his registered mark which had been disclaimed. For example, the registered trade mark in Part A of a stylised cooking pot with the words 'The Mongolian Barbeque' had the words disclaimed. Thus it would not be an act of *trade mark* infringement for another restaurant to use those words. However, such use may amount to passing-off if there is a misrepresentation.

Another example concerned the device 'Diamond T' which consisted of the letter 'T' in a lozenge border, the word 'diamond', the letter 'T' and a lozenge border were all disclaimed for exclusive use individually (*Diamond T Motor Car Co's Application* (1921)).

22.11.1 Infringement limited by being genuine goods or services

The second major restriction on the scope of acts that amounted to trade mark infringement was the use of the trade mark upon genuine goods, that is upon goods with originated from the proprietor of the trade mark (s 4(3)(a)).

If the article was genuine, but not of the appropriate standard for the particular mark that was being used, then there could still be a case of trade mark infringement. For example, the defendant was prohibited from altering the two-door 'Silver Shadow' Rolls-Royce to appear like the four-door 'Corniche' model, while it still bore the Rolls-Royce trade marks (*Rolls-Royce Motors Ltd v Zanelli* (1979)).

In *Accurist Watches Ltd v King* (1992), the UK registered user of the trade mark became insolvent, and so the supplier of the watches invoked a 'reservation of title' clause to reclaim the genuine watches that it had supplied. It was held that as the mark had been applied with the consent of the proprietor and that the watches were genuine, then the supplier could re-sell these watches, even though it was not the registered user in the UK and even though it intended to sell the watches at a discount.

The doctrine of exhaustion of rights provides that once goods marked with a trade mark have been placed on the market with the consent of the proprietor, then the proprietor cannot exercise any control on the subsequent movement of those goods, ie his rights have been exhausted after the first transaction (*Centrafarm BV v Sterling Drug Inc* (1974)). This obviously has a bearing on trade mark infringement proceedings based on the use of a registered trade mark placed upon genuine goods. This area of law, however, has been greatly influenced by European legislation. As a consequence, it makes a significant difference on the legality of certain actions on whether or not the proprietor is resident within the EU.

22.11.2   Exhaustion of rights

If a parent company which is outside the EU, expressly forbids a subsidiary from marketing a product within the UK, and only allows it to sell the trade marked product in another country, then the subsidiary may be stopped from making parallel imports into the UK (*Colgate-Palmolive Ltd v Markwell Finance Ltd* (1989)). The situation is the opposite if the parent company did not expressly prohibit the parallel import (*Revlon Inc v Cripps & Lee Ltd* (1980)).

The situation is different again if the parent company is resident within the European Community. Under the Treaty of Rome 1957, Articles 30-36 establish the principle of the free movement of goods within the Community. Article 30 prohibits any quantitative restrictions on imports (*Rewe-Zentral AG v Bundesmonopolverwaltung für Branntwein* (1979)). If a measure falls within the scope of Article 30, it may only be saved if it is one of the 'mandatory requirements' or by the operation of Article 36, which is concerned with industrial or commercial property. Thus, the *existence* of intellectual property rights is recognised; however, the derogation from the general principle of free movement of goods by the *exercise* of those rights is only permitted to the extent that the 'specific subject matter' of those rights needs to be safeguarded (*Deutsche Grammophon GmbH v Metro-SB-Großmärkte GmbH & Co KG* (1971)). In *SA CNL-Sucal NV v HAG GF AG* (1991) (known as *HAG II*), the court stated that:

'The specific subject matter of a trade mark right is to grant the owner the right to use the mark for the first marketing of a product and, in this way, to protect him against competitors who would like to abuse the position and reputation of the mark by selling products to which the mark has been improperly affixed. To determine the exact effect of this exclusive right which is granted to the owner of the mark, it is necessary to take account of the essential function of the mark, which is to give the consumer or final user a guarantee of the identity of the origin of the marked product by enabling him to distinguish, without any possible confusion, that product from others of a different provenance.'

Thus, the first marketing of the marked product is protected by the action of Article 36, because that is all that is needed to protect the specific subject matter of this right. There is no need for the trade mark owner to limit the resale of the marked goods, for the rights of the trade mark owner are exhausted after the first sale.

It is essential, however, that this first marketing is done with the *consent* of the trade mark proprietor. This is known as the doctrine of consent. The decisive factor in considering the issue of consent is whether or not there was a *possibility* of quality control of the goods so marked, rather than the actual exercise of such control.

Thus, the specific object of a trade mark is exhausted once the owner has consented to its first marketing. If, for whatever reason, the trade mark was assigned to a third party having no economic links with the assignor, then the assignor was not to have implied consent to the future application of that mark. In *IHT Internationale Heiztechnik GmbH v Ideal Standard GmbH* (1995), the trade mark 'Ideal Standard' for heating equipment was held by the French and German subsidiaries of the parent company American Standard. In 1984, the French subsidiary sold its rights to the trade mark to a third party, which in turn assigned the trade mark to a fourth party who had no link with the parent company. This fourth party made heating equipment in France under the mark 'Ideal Standard' which, in turn, was sold by IHT Internationale, a German company, in Germany. The German Ideal Standard subsidiary attempted to stop the use of the mark in Germany by IHT Internationale. The ECJ held that IHT Internationale could be prevented from using the mark, and the assignment to an unrelated company did not imply consent to the use of the mark. The court went on to hold that 'for a trade mark to be able to fulfil its role, it must offer a guarantee that all goods bearing it have been produced under the control of a single undertaking which is accountable for their quality. In this way, the ECJ has reasserted the principle that trade marks are territorial in nature.

Section 4(3)(b) provided that it was not an infringement of the right of a registered trade mark to use a mark in relation to goods adapted to form a part of other goods.

    Thus, it was permissible to indicate on spare parts or other additions made by third parties, that they were compatible with the genuine article. For example, the phrase 'clothes fit for BARBIE doll' was held by the High Court of Hong Kong to fall within this section, and thus avoid liability for infringement (*Mattel Inc v Tonka Corporation* (1992)).

If two marks were registered that were identical or nearly resembling each other, then neither infringed the other (s 4(4)).

By virtue of s 7, unregistered common law rights that had been acquired over the years could be preserved, even though a trade mark had subsequently been registered. The commonest manner in which this comes to light is where a mark has been registered and then used exclusively in one location. Subsequently, when the business expands, it moves into another location only to find someone using a similar mark. This section ensures that the local user is protected from the expansion of the other mark. Such a scenario often occurs with mobile food ones such as ice-cream vans or fish and chips vans and the like.

Section 8 provided that no registration of a trade mark should interfere with any *bona fide* use by a person of his own name.

    In *Baume and Co Ltd v AH Moore Ltd* (1957) *bona fide* use had been held to mean:

    '... the honest use by the person of his own name without any intention to deceive anybody or without any intention to make use of the goodwill which has been acquired by another trader.'

The deliberate use by the defendant of his name as a brand name, whilst aware of the plaintiff's trade mark in a manner which was likely to led to confusion, has been held not to be *bona fide* (*George Ballantine & Son Ltd v Ballantyne Stewart & Co Ltd* (1959)). It was quite hard, if not impossible, to establish *bona fides* if a company changed its name to be similar to a competitor's.

22.11.3	Infringement limited by being a component part
22.11.4	Concurrent rights in trade or service marks
22.12	**Vested rights in trade or service marks**
22.13	*Bone fide* use of own name

Trade Marks: The 1938 Act: Infringement and Defences

Registration allows that the ownership and reputation of mark to be assumed by the plaintiff. Monopolistic protection was conferred, that could be renewed for as long as the mark was used. Infringement only covered the goods for which the mark was registered. Infringement required that one or more of the essential features had been appropriated. Infringement could only occur by a graphical representation, and not orally.

Infringement was governed by ss 4(1), 5 and 6, but was limited by ss 4(2)-(4), 7 and 8.

Introduction

A validly registered mark gave the proprietor the exclusive right to use the mark.

The use of the alleged infringing mark must be as a trade mark, ie as indicating the trade source of goods (s 4(1)(a)).

Alternatively, infringement could occur by importing a reference, ie comparative advertising (s 4(1)(b)). This subsection was introduced by Parliament explicitly to overrule *Irving's Yeast-Vite Ltd v FA Horsenail* (1934): in order to infringe, the offending mark must be either identical or nearly resembling the registered mark.

The difference between a trade in the goods themselves and a repair service in those goods is sufficient (*Aristoc Ltd v Rysta Ltd* (1945)).

Infringement mark under TMA 1938 s 4(1)

The offending mark must be used as a trade mark, thus petrol pumps in the shape of lighthouses did not infringe a mark which portrayed a lighthouse (*Carless, Capel & Leonard v F Pilmore-Bedford* (1928)).

The mark may be very small, because it may still fulfil its function to indicate trade origin (*Unic SA v Lyndeau Products Ltd* (1964)).

The use of a confusingly similar mark as an advertising gimmick was not an infringement of the registered mark (*Mars GB Ltd v Cadbury Ltd* (1987)).

Use as a trade mark

Goods of a similar nature	The courts adopts a common sense approach, whether or not the goods are similar (*Ofrex Ltd v Rapesco Ltd* (1963)).
Importing a reference	Comparative advertising was not allowed (s 4(1)(b)) (*Bismag Ltd v Amblins (Chemists) Ltd* (1940)). However, one could refer to the company name of a competitor in the advertisement (*Pompadour Laboratories Ltd v Stanley Frazer* (1966)).
Nature of the person who is deceived	The prospective purchaser was usually assumed to be a domestic consumer, rather than a retailer (*Edge v Niccolls* (1911)). Such a purchaser would take ordinary care in selection (*George Angus & Co Ltd's Application* (1943)).
Comparison of marks	Direct side-by-side comparisons rarely occur in the market place. The first impression upon the judge will often decide a case in practice.
Idea of the mark	The 'idea' of the mark is the *sine non qua* of a trade mark. For example, 'watermatic' infringed 'aquamatic' (*Harry Reynolds v Laffeaty's Ltd* (1957)). In contrast, '99' did not infringe '999' (*Ardath Tobacco Co Ltd v W Sandorides Ltd* (1925)). In a word mark, the first syllable is often the most important, because it is a tendency for people to slur the ends of their words (*London Lubricants (1920) Ltd's Application* (1925)).
Whole mark to be considered	However, not just the idea of the mark, but also the whole of the mark must be considered (*Farrow's Application* (1890)). If there are elements that are common in the trade, then they should be ignored (*Coca Cola v Pepsi Cola* (1942)).
Comparison of marks as actually encountered	The comparison of the marks should be as they are to be found in practice (*Christiansen's Trade Mark* (1886)). Word marks should be judged by both the ear and the eye (*Lever Bros v Sunniwite Products* (1949)).

A trade mark owner could impose restrictions, which if breached, amount to an infringement.

Infringement of Part B marks was governed by ss 5 and 6, which broadly followed that for Part A marks. No remedy would be granted to an aggrieved plaintiff, even when infringement had been proved, if there was no confusion or no indication of a connection in the course of trade.

There would be no infringement of a registered trade mark if the part copied had been disclaimed under s 14.

The use of a registered trade mark on a genuine article was permissible. However, the appropriate mark had to be used for the appropriate quality of goods (*Rolls-Royce Motors v Zanelli* (1979)).

The principle of the exhaustion of rights meant that once the goods had been put on the market with the consent of the trade mark owner, then he could not control any further transactions using that mark. Thus, parallel imports could not be stopped by the exercise of trade mark rights (*Rewe-Zentral AG v Bundesmonopolverwaltung für Branntwein* (1979)).

The first marketing must be with the consent of the trade mark owner (*SA CNL-Sucal v HAG GF AG* (1991)). Thus, if the trade mark in one country has been assigned to a third party which is totally independent of the assignor, consent cannot be implied (*IHT Internationale v Ideal Standard GmbH* (1995)).

There is no infringement of a trade mark if it used on spare parts so as to indicate compatibility with the genuine article (s 4(3)(b))). Thus, clothes marked for BARBIE dolls were allowed (*Mattel Inc v Tonka Corporation* (1992)).

Section 7 provided protection for unregistered rights in actual use since before the registration of the trade mark against infringement proceedings issued by the owner of the registered trade mark.

Section 8 provided protection for the *bona fide* use of one's own name. Usually difficult to establish in practice.

Chapter 23

Trade Marks: The 1994 Act: Basic Principles

Trade mark law was introduced into UK legislation by the Trade Marks Registration Act 1875. There were then eight intervening Acts affecting trade marks before the Trade Marks Act 1938, which in turn was amended by six other Acts. The result was that Trade Mark law had a long and complicated history. What was worse was that a lot of it was still relevant. Aldous J in *Loudoun Manufacturing Co Ltd v Courtaulds plc (t/a John Lean and Sons)* (1994) said 'In order to resolve the issue [before me today] and to decide what was the proprietary right in question, it was necessary to go back to the position before the Trade Marks Registration Act 1875.' The Trade Marks Act 1994 swept away all the previous UK legislation, and starts with a clean slate.

The Trade Marks Bill was introduced into the House of Lords and received its first reading on 24 November 1993, and received Royal Assent on 21 July 1994. The Trade Marks Act 1994 came into force on 31 October 1994 (TMA 1994, s 109(1) and Trade Marks Act 1994 (Commencement) Order 1994). The Preamble to the Act sets out the aims that it is designed to fulfil. These include the making of new provisions for registered trade marks, the implementation of Council Directive 89/104/EEC, the making of provisions in connection with Council Regulation EC/40/94, to give effect to the Madrid Protocol 1989 and to give effect to certain provisions of the Paris Convention 1883.

This Act will fundamentally alter trade mark law within the UK. It will remove most of the historical basis from which the present law is derived, and replace it with the purposive approach that is adopted on the Continent. In this manner, its overall aim is similar to the Patents Act 1977.

23.1 Introduction

The Memorandum of the European Communities on the creation of an EEC trade mark states that 'Both economically and legally the function of the trade mark as an indication of origin is paramount.'. It then continues to state that:

> 'By virtue of their role as an indicator of origin and quality and as a means of advertising, trade marks are indeed an indispensable means of promoting trade and in doing so assist the further interpenetration of national markets. They help manufacturers to acquire new markets and thus help to promote the expansion of economic activity beyond national borders.'

23.2 Trade Marks Act 1994 and Directive 89/104/EEC

From these sentiments, it is clear that the European Commission believes that the trade mark legislation has a large effect on the pan-European market, and so the harmonisation of such laws in order to prevent distortion of the internal market is of central importance to the European Commission.

However, in contrast to this official view, it is open to argument that trade marks are actually local in nature. Unlike a patent that embodies a novel idea that can be accepted and appreciated as such in all the separate countries that form the EU, a trade mark often depends for its success on subtle nuances of meaning. An example concerns the word 'NOVA', which Vauxhall wished to register as the name of its new car. In Spanish, 'nova' is a homonym for 'it doesn't go'. Not exactly the idea a car manufacturer wishes to create for a new model! The EU comprises a wealth of very different cultures and attitudes that may prove too diverse to be amenable to a single trade mark for any given product. The future of the Community Trade Mark will depend on how the consumers in the various member countries react to an undifferentiated approach.

The Trade Mark Act 1994 purports to implement Directive 89/104/EEC, and thus comply with the obligations that are concomitant with the UK's membership of the European Union. During the passage of the Bill through both Houses, the Government refused to accept many amendments that would have varied the wording of a clause away from that contained within the Directive. The Trade Mark Act 1994 is similar to the Patents Act 1977, because that also purported to implement a Directive, namely the CPC. However, in the case of the PA 1977, the wording of the Act was different from that of the Directive in various places. These differences have lead to the ECJ to hold that those parts of the Patents Act 1977 are in contravention of the CPC. Accordingly, the Government wished to avoid similar rulings on the TMA 1994, and so faithfully followed the wording of Directive 89/104/EEC. This means that UK practitioners are left with the often vague wording of a European Directive rather than the more formal wording they have been used to hitherto.

Directive 89/104/EEC may be adjudicated upon by the ECJ, and any rulings within that forum on legislation that is identical to the domestic legislation will bind the courts in the UK. Furthermore, rulings within other European Courts will have to be considered as presumably persuasive and not binding authority, so as to ensure that the new regime is developed and applied in a similar manner across the European Union. In addition to the rulings of these courts, there is an 'Annex' to the Directive. This contains 'Statements' in which the Council and Commission indicate what they believe is the meaning of a particular Article of the Directive. There is little doubt that the ECJ and other Continental courts will take these statements into consideration. It is possible that the courts within the UK will adopt a similar approach to these statements as they do to references to *Hansard*, ie they will only consider them when the text is unclear (*Pepper (Inspector of Taxes) v Hart* (1993), and Practice Direction (*Hansard Extracts*) (1994)).

The definition of what constitutes a mark that may be registered has been widened. Service marks are no longer treated separately from trade marks, but are included in the definition of trade marks. Thus, the parallel systems for service marks and trade marks that existed under the TMA 1938 is swept away, and replaced by a single, unitary, system. Furthermore, the Register is no longer divided into Part A and Part B: there is only a single category. This restores the position to that which was in existence before the Trade Marks Act 1919. The level of distinctiveness required by a mark before it may be eligible for registration is phrased in the same way as was applicable to Part B marks, ie 'capable of distinguishing'. Even though the wording is the same as for the old Part B marks, it does not necessarily follow that the old case law will be applicable. This is because that case law was decided in the framework of deciding between Part A and Part B marks and marks that could not be registered all. Now, the test is between registrable and unregistrable marks as determined by a *European* understanding of distinctiveness.

The new law creates a presumption that a mark should be registered, so long as it does not fall within the specified grounds for refusal (TMA 1994, ss 3-5). This reverses the position under the TMA 1938, whereby the applicant had to show that the mark ought to be registered. Thus the burden of proof has altered, and so it should be easier to register new marks. As a corollary to this change, the Registrar no longer has an absolute discretion to refuse an application for registration, instead the only grounds for refusal are contained within the Act (TMA 1944, ss 3-5).

Infringement is no longer restricted to purely visual representation, but may now also be, for example, by an audible reproduction of the mark.

Most of the restrictions that control the assignment and licensing of trade marks have been removed. Thus, the Registrar no longer monitors and protects the interests of the general public which was a guiding principle behind the old

23.3   Principal changes

legislation. The responsibility for ensuring that marks are bought and sold in a manner that will not lead to the confusion or deception of the general public now rests with the proprietors of those marks. However, it is still the position that the assignment of the goodwill of a business includes the related unregistered trade marks, because usually the goodwill in a business is based upon the use of an unregistered trade mark (TMA 1938 s 24(6)).

The old restrictions on licensing have been removed, and so has the prohibition against trafficking in trade marks. This increased freedom is likely to promote the area of character merchandising.

The Act makes explicit provision that no proceedings will lie for the infringement of an unregistered trade mark *per se*, but it also states that it does not affect the law relating to passing-off (s 2(2)), thus maintaining the position under the 1938 Act. Furthermore, the optional Article 4(4)(b) of the Directive has been implemented, which prohibits the registration of a mark if, or to the extent that, its use in the UK is liable to be prevented by virtue of any rule of law (in particular, the law of passing-off) protecting an unregistered trade mark or other sign used in the course of trade (s 5(4)(a)). Under the TMA 1938, there was no explicit provision to this effect. Instead s 11 of the TMA 1938 was used to prevent the registration of marks whose use would cause confusion with an earlier unregistered mark.

There is no longer a requirement that a trade mark should indicate a connection *in the course of trade*. The consequence of this is that, for example, charities or local authorities may register their distinctive logos.

However, for infringement the use must still be in the course of trade certification marks will continue to be registrable for goods, but, in addition, will now be possible for services. Under the TMA 1994, the Registrar will assume control for all aspects of the registration, and maintenance of certification, whereas under the TMA 1938, some functions were performed by the Department of Trade and Industry. Section 50(1) defines a certification mark as 'a mark indicating that the goods or services in connection with which it is used are certified by the proprietor of the mark in respect of origin, material, mode of manufacture of goods or performance of services, quality, accuracy or other characteristics'.

Collective marks are introduced for the first time within the UK. They differ from certification marks in that they are protected in the name of an association, the members of which carry on business supplying the goods or services concerned.

Thus, the association, consisting of a number of individual members, is the proprietor of the mark, in contrast to other marks where the proprietor is an individual person or company.

A mark was defined by the TMA 1938 s 68 as including, 'a device, brand, heading, label, ticket, name, signature, work, letter, numeral or any combination thereof', and continued by saying that a trade mark indicated a connection in the course of trade between the goods and the trader. The House of Lords held that the Coca Cola glass bottle was not capable of registration *per se* (*COCA COLA Trade Marks* (1986)). The bottle was only refused registration on account of it being three-dimensional and so not within the definition of a mark. It had already been held by the House of Lords that so long as a three-dimensional article could be represented in two dimensions, then it could be registered if it met the criterion of distinctiveness (*Smith, Kline & French Laboratories Ltd v Sterling-Winthrop Group Ltd* (1976)).

23.4   Definition of a trade mark

The TMA 1994 s 1(1) provides a completely different definition for a trade mark. It states:

'1(1) In this Act a 'trade mark' means any sign capable of being represented graphically, which is capable of distinguishing goods or services of one undertaking from those of other undertakings, particularly words.

A trade mark may, in particular, consist of words (including personal names), designs, letters, numerals, or the shape of goods or of their packing.'

This follows the wording of Article 2 of the Directive.

This broad definition is designed to define the basic function of a trade mark, namely to indicate the origin of goods or services and to distinguish them from those of other undertakings.

Furthermore, in order to overcome the textual difficulties that resulted from splitting the TMA 1938 into two, one for trade marks and the other for service marks, the new Act follows the European methodology of using the phrase 'trade mark' to refer to marks used in relation to goods as well as marks used in relation to services. So there will not exist the confusing situation of two versions of the law relating to marks used for goods and services.

Section 2(1) provides that a registered trade mark is a property right that is obtained by the registration of the mark under the Act, and that it is the proprietor of the mark who has the rights and remedies provided by the Act. In particular, a registered trade mark is personal property (s 22), which is the same as for a patent (PA 1977, s 30(1)), while copyright is merely stated as being a 'property right' without further elaboration (CDPA 1988 s1(1)).

23.4.1   Any sign

The definition expressly provides that three dimensional objects may now be registered as trade marks. This, in effect, overturns the decision in *COCA-COLA Trade Marks* (1986), in which the classic glass bottle was denied registration. The concern of the Mathys Committee, which reported in 1974, was that such a development would confer a monopoly in the shapes of basic containers. However, in practice, no-one could use a bottle that was same shape as the Coca-Cola bottle without committing the tort of passing-off, A similar situation has already arisen in the UK. The makers of the 'JIF' lemon successfully prevented the introduction by a rival manufacturer of a product that contained lemon juice in a yellow plastic lemon-shaped container, on the grounds that it would amount to passing-off as a 'JIF' lemon (*Reckitt & Colman Products Ltd v Borden Inc* (1990)). However, any residual concern is met in the new Act which provides certain absolute grounds for refusal to register a mark that comprises the shape of an article (s 3(2)).

The list of examples contained in s 1(1) is not intended to be exhaustive, and so it will be for the courts to determine whether or not solid colours or shades of colours, or signs denoting sound, smell or taste may constitute a trade mark. Part of the rationale for the new Act is to bring the substantive law into line with what is currently occurring in the market place, and if a mark functions as a trade mark then it ought to be registrable.

23.4.2   Capable of graphical representation

The limiting requirement that the mark must be represented graphically serves the dual pragmatic purpose of ease of keeping the register by the Trade Mark Office, and ease of searching the register by interested parties. If, for example, real exhibits of smells or sounds could be deposited, then they would be both difficult to store physically and difficult to examine from a remote location.

Clearly, old marks may be represented graphically. Solid objects may be equally represented by perspective drawings. Musical marks could be represented by conventional notation. It is less clear how some of the more exotic suggestions for novel marks may be represented, eg would the chemical composition of a smell be satisfactory? More likely, the print-out from an analytical device such as a gas chromatogram would be used to characterise a complicated smell such as a perfume.

The requirement that a mark be capable of distinguishing the goods or services of one undertaking from those of other undertakings is a question of fact. Thus, if there is sufficient evidence of distinctiveness in practice, this will allow registration. Hence the new law will confer rights on all marks that prove themselves in the market place, and thus overcome the anomaly of the 1938 Act whereby some marks that were *de facto* distinctive could still not obtain registration.

23.4.3   Capable of distinguishing

The new definition is wide enough to include sounds and smells. The question of distinctiveness is particularly important in such a case. For example, is the hearer to have perfect pitch? It would seem unlikely that an audible mark which depended upon such refinement would be distinctive to the majority of the potential consumers. Even though the example of taste is not given, it is akin to smell. Thus, would Pepsi endeavour to register the taste of its soft drink, adducing evidence that it was distinctive as shown by the results of blind tasting in the 'The Taste Challenge' which it mounts between its product and unnamed competitors? However, even if a taste could be proved to be distinctive, it may still not qualify for registration, because it is appreciated after the article in question has been sold and is in the process of being consumed (*Unilever Ltd's (Striped Toothpaste) Application* (1980)).

The purpose of Directive 89/104/EEC is not to harmonise the procedure of the Member States, but merely to approximate the substantive law on trade marks so as to facilitate the free flow of marked goods within the Community. Full harmonisation of the substantive law and procedure will await the implementation of Regulation 40/94, and even then that will only be for the Community trade mark, for the various different national trade mark laws will still operate in parallel in each country. However, Parliament has taken this opportunity to make some preliminary provisions for the anticipated introduction of the Community trade mark. Also, the opportunity has been taken to simplify the overall procedure for the application for registration of a national trade mark, and to bring it more closely into line with the expected form that will be used for the Community trade mark. This will be to the advantage of commerce, and trade mark agents, as only one procedural system will need to be mastered.

23.5   **Procedural changes**

23.5.1   Principal provisions

Under the old law, an application for registration had to be restricted to a single class of goods or services, and thus, if registration was sought in more than one class, a corresponding number of separate applications had to be made. This cumbersome application procedure has been removed, and multi-class applications are now permitted (s 32(2)(c)).

Previously, it was possible to amend the proposed trade mark, even to the extent that the final mark as approved by the Registrar might be quite different from the original one. It is not possible for a mark to be amended in the application procedure under either the Madrid Protocol or the proposed Community trade mark system. Accordingly, Parliament has taken this opportunity to prohibit amendments to the mark during the application procedure (ss 39(2) and 44(1)). Thus, if a mark is not approved for registration, a fresh application will need to be filed, with, correspondingly, a fresh set of fees being levied. It will, however, still be permissible to amend the class of goods for which a mark is to be registered (s 41).

Under the proposed Community trade mark system, objection to a proposed mark may only be taken by a proprietor of a mark already on the register. The Registrar would only take a passive role by searching the register for potentially conflicting interests, and then advising the parties concerned. It is then for those parties to mount a successful opposition. However, for the present, the old system will still operate (ss 37 and 38).

Under the TMA 1938, a trade mark was initially registered for seven years, and could then be renewed every 14 years thereafter indefinitely. This has changed, so that both the initial period of registration, and the renewal periods, will now be for 10 years (ss 42 and 43).

Trade Marks: the 1994 Act: Basic Principles

Royal Assent of the TMA 1994 was granted on 21 July 1994, and it came into force on 31 October 1994. This Act adopts a continental approach to trade mark legislation.

Introduction

The TMA 1994 usually follows exactly the wording of the Directive. The Directive is judiciable by the ECJ, and so the UK Courts will have to consider these judgments. There are statements by the Council and Commission on meaning of the Directive which are annexed to the Directive. The status of these statements in UK courts has yet to be determined.

Trade Marks Act 1994 and Directive 89/104/EEC

The definition of a trade mark has been widened to include, for example, 3D marks, ie the shapes of containers.

Marks for goods and services are now treated in the same manner. There is a single register, ie it is no longer divided into Parts A and B. A mark must be capable of distinguishing, ie similar to the old standard of distinctiveness required for a Part B mark. There is a presumption that a mark should be registered, so long as it meets the requirements of s 1(1).

Infringement is no longer restricted to visual representation, but may, for example, be aural.

Most restrictions on assignments and licensing have been removed.

Collective marks have been introduced.

Principal changes

Any sign capable of being represented graphically and that is distinguishable may be registered as a trade mark (s 1(1)).

Containers will now be allowed, thus overruling *COCA COLA Trade Marks* (1986).

Definition of a trade mark

Section 1(1) is not exhaustive, thus sounds and smells may be included.

Any sign

There is an absolute requirement that the sign must be capable of being represented graphically.

Capable of graphical representation

Capable of distinguishing

The essential purpose of a trade mark is to distinguish the trade source of goods. The test is phrased in the same manner as for old Part B marks.

If a mark distinguishes in fact, then it is capable of distinguishing in law.

Procedural changes

There is a simplification of the registration procedure.

Full harmonisation will, however, await the implementation of the Community Trade Mark Regulation.

Principal provisions

There is only a single register, because there is only one test for distinctiveness.

Multi-class applications are now permitted. There are very tight restrictions on permissible amendments of an application.

Registration will be for 10 years, as will renewal for each successive period.

Chapter 24

Trade Marks: The 1994 Act: Registration

The definition of a trade mark under Article 2 of the Directive and s 1(1) is very wide. In order to ensure that marks are only registered when they actually serve the function of a trade mark, there are number of grounds upon which a mark may be refused registration. The Directive contains mandatory provisions in Article 3(1), as well as optional provisions in Article 3(2). It is forbidden for the national law to provide for any grounds which are in addition to those mentioned in the Directive. The TMA 1994 has incorporated the mandatory and optional requirements of Article 3 into ss 3 and 4.

The term 'absolute' means that the grounds for refusal of registration are based upon the inherent properties of the proposed mark itself, rather than based upon any conflict of the proposed mark with other earlier marks, in which case the grounds are labelled 'relative'.

24.1 Absolute grounds for refusal of registration

The four principal grounds for refusing registration are contained in subsection 3(1). The first is that the mark does not satisfy the requirements of s 1(1) (s 3(1)(a)); the second being that the mark is devoid of any distinctive character (s 3(1)(b)); the third relates to marks that consist exclusively of signs or indications of kind, quality, quantity, intended purpose, value, geographical origin, the time of production of goods or of rendering services, or other characteristics of goods or services (s 3(1)(c)); and the fourth concerns marks that have become customary in the current language or in the *bona fide* and established practices of the trade (s 3(1)(d)), save that if such a mark has acquired distinctiveness in use before the date of the application for registration, then it shall not be denied registration by virtue of para (b), (c) or (d). It should be noted that distinctiveness acquired by reason of use is not sufficient to overcome a defect under para (a), ie the mark does not satisfy the conditions required by s 1(1) in order to constitute being a 'mark' for the purpose of the Act.

24.1.1 TMA 1994 s 3(1)

Section 3 implements Articles 3(1)(a) to (d) and the mandatory part of Article 3(3). There was an optional proviso that would have allowed the distinctive character to be acquired after the date of application or even after the date of registration. This latter proviso has not been included in the new Act. The reason for this is that the new Act already widens what is eligible for registration to those marks that have proved their distinctiveness in the market place. Parliament felt that this was wide enough, there being no need to include marks that have not yet proved themselves as functional trade marks.

Paragraph (b) prohibits the registration of those marks that lack distinctive character, which would, for example, include purely laudatory terms and the shape of bottles that have become generic. An example of a shape that has become generic is the container that held the anti-dandruff shampoo sold under the name 'Head and Shoulders'. The supermarkets who produce their own brand of anti-dandruff shampoo also sell this product in a bottle of similar shape to the original. Thus, now, a white bottle with a long neck, and a flatter bulbous bottom has become associated with this type of medicated shampoo.

Paragraph (c) prohibits the registration of marks that comprise *exclusively* of descriptive material. Thus, a mark that contains some, but not all, descriptive material may be registrable so long as it is distinctive. An alternative ground for refusing the registration of certain anti-dandruff bottles could be found under para (d), because the bottle has become customary in the *bona fide* and established practices of the trade. However, in this case, the *bona fides* of the competitor may be called into question. Another consideration is that the customary use must be by the trade. Thus, if the mark has fallen into common parlance in domestic circles, this may not prevent registration. An example would be the term 'hoover' for a vacuum cleaner: *manufacturers* only use the latter and not the former term, *customers* often confuse the two.

24.1.2   TMA 1994 ss 3(2)-3(6)

The remaining subsections of s 3 contain other grounds for the refusal of an application for registration. Further conditions concerning the registrability of shapes of goods are contained in s 3(2), which provides that such a mark may be refused registration on the grounds that it consists exclusively of the shape which results from the nature of the goods themselves (s 3(2)(a)); or the shape of goods which is necessary to obtain a technical result (s 3(2)(b)); or the shape which gives substantial value to the goods (s 3(2)(c)). This follows Article 3(1)(e). The statements to the Directive indicate that the shape of the goods includes the shape of the packaging. The reference to a shape that gives substantial value can only mean a shape that somehow enhances the product in some functional manner, and cannot be a reference to a shape that, because it has become associated with quality, a higher price may be commanded. For example, the Jif plastic lemon container adds value by allowing the public to identify it easily, but the shape itself has no functional value and thus would not be excluded from registration on this point. In contrast, the carrying handles built into certain cardboard containers for cans have a functional purpose for which the purchaser would be willing to pay. Thus, the shape of the handles could not be registered as a trade mark, because it gives substantial value to the goods and so is excluded by the operation of s 3(2)(c). There is no proviso to this subsection to the effect that any problems to registration may be overcome by demonstrating that distinctiveness has been shown in use.

The discretion which the Registrar could exercise over whether or not a mark should be registered is abrogated: if a mark satisfies the conditions for registration the Registrar shall register it (s 37(5)). There will, however, remain a residual power to refuse registration, not as an exercise of discretion, but as a matter of substantive law that the proposed mark is contrary to public policy or to accepted principles of morality (s 3(3)(a)); or of such a nature as to deceive the public (for instance as to the nature, quality or geographical origin of the goods or services (s 3(3)(b)). This follows Articles 3(1)(f) and 3(1)(g). Section 3(3)(b) is similar in effect to s 11 of the TMA 1938.

By section 3(4) a mark shall not be registered if, or to the extent that, its use is prohibited in the UK by any enactment or rule of law or by any provision of Community law. Thus, for example, the registration of 'Anzac' will still be prohibited as this is still protected by the 'Anzac' (Restriction on Trade Use of Word) Act 1916. Furthermore, a trade mark shall not be registered if or to the extent that the application is made in bad faith (s 3(6)). This would include, for example, an application to register a 'ghost mark' as illustrated by the mark 'NERIT'. These sections follow Articles 3(2)(a) and 3(2)(d).

In addition to the grounds contained within s 3, a trade mark shall not be registered in the situations specified in s 4, which is concerned with specially protected emblems (s 3(5)).

24.2   Specially protected emblems

Apart from the provisions in s 3 for the refusal to register a mark, there are special provisions in s 4 which cover marks of particular importance. Thus, unless consent has been given by Her Majesty the Queen, or the appropriate member of the Royal Family, a mark shall not be registered which consists of, or contains, the Royal arms (s 4(1)(a)), or any of the Royal flags (s 4(1)(b)), or a representation of any member of the Royal Family (s 4(1)(c)), or any words which indicate Royal patronage (s 4(1)(d)). This follows Article 3(1)(h).

Further provisions prevent the registration of the national flag of the UK, or the respective flags of the component parts (s 4(2)(a) and (b)), if the use of any of them as a trade mark would be misleading or grossly offensive. As part of the Government's general policy of making the law relating to trade marks more readily comprehensible to the public at large, the national flag of the UK is identified parenthetically as being commonly known as the 'Union Jack'. It may be commonly be known as such, but this usage is not correct. The term 'Union Jack' is a colloquial expression that in proper usage refers only to the situation when the Union Flag is flown on the jackstay of one of Her Majesty's ships.

Section 4(3) provides protection against the registration of a mark that falls within s 57, which concerns national emblems of Convention countries, and s 58, which concerns the emblems of certain international organisations. This fulfils the UK's obligations under the Paris Convention Article 6*ter*.

There seems to be no explicit section which implements Article 3(2)(b). This states that no mark shall be registered if it covers a sign of high symbolic value, in particular a religious symbol. Obvious examples include the Jewish Star of David, the Christian Cross, and the Islamic Crescent. Presumably, the prohibition under s 3(3)(a) against the registration of a mark that is contrary to the accepted principles of morality would cover such an attempt. However, the Directive felt the need to make an explicit provision, and so it is surprising that explicit mention was not made in the TMA 1994, especially as the Government (generally) strenuously resisted attempts to deviate from the wording of the Directive.

| 24.3 | **Relative grounds for refusal for registration** | Article 4 is concerned with the relative grounds for refusal of registration. These concern the situation when there is a conflict with an earlier trade mark or earlier right. Opposition to the registration of a mark under these relative grounds may be made by the Registrar of his own motion, as well as by any interested party, whether they are aggrieved or not. However, under s 8(1) the Secretary of State may, by Order, provide that a trade mark shall not be refused registration on these relative grounds unless objection on these grounds is taken in opposition proceedings by the proprietor of the earlier mark. Such an Order may not be introduced until at least 10 years after the introduction of the Community Trade Mark (s 8(5)), which occurred on 14 March 1994. |

Even before the Secretary of State makes such an Order, the powers of the Registrar have been restricted considerably from what they were under the TMA 1938. Thus, for example, if the proprietor of the earlier trade mark or other earlier right agrees to the registration, then the Registrar cannot prevent such a registration (s 5(5)). There are provisions for the Registrar to carry out a search of the register 'to such extent as he considers necessary of earlier trade marks' (s 37(2)).

Earlier trade marks are defined in s 6, to include a registered trade mark, an international trade mark and a community trade mark, all of which must have an application date earlier than that of the trade mark where application is under consideration.

The fettering of the powers of the Registrar to oppose an application for registration, coupled with the removal of the restriction on the assignment of marks that were associated together under the TMA 1938 is potentially capable of leading to confusion in the market place. Previously, the Registrar monitored the system to ensure that every possible step was taken to protect the general public from being confused by the existence of similar marks in the market place, but unrelated in terms of their proprietors. Now it is up to those proprietors themselves to ensure that the value of their marks is maintained by being vigilant in their monitoring of the applications and prudent in the division of hitherto associated marks.

Thus, under s 5(1) a trade mark shall not be registered if it is identical with an earlier trade mark and used for identical goods or services as the earlier protected trade mark. This is further elaborated in s 5(2) which prohibits the registration of a trade mark that, because of its identity with a protected earlier mark and the similarity of the goods or services for which the mark is used, or because of the similarity with a protected earlier mark, and the identity or similarity of the goods and services, there is likelihood of confusion on the part of the public. This follows Article 4(1)(a) and (b). The use of the word 'protected' covers the situation where the trade mark is not registered.

24.3.1   TMA 1994 ss 5, 6 and 7

Further, a trade mark shall not be registered that is identical with, or similar to, an earlier trade mark and is to be registered for dissimilar goods, if the earlier mark has a reputation, and the use of the latter mark would, without due cause, take unfair advantage of, or be detrimental to, the distinctive character or the repute of the earlier trade mark (s 5(3)). The meaning of 'reputation' is not defined in either the Act or the Directive. On the continent, a mark is held to be 'of repute' when it is well known among the general public. Evidence of such knowledge is achieved by conducting surveys that measure the unprompted awareness of the mark to the person being listed. Generally, more than 50% of those questioned have to recognise the mark before it is held to be 'of repute'. The UK courts are notoriously sceptical of survey evidence; however, on this matter, they may have no choice but to accept it.

These three provisions mirror those for infringement of a trade mark contained in s 10(1)-(3).

A trade mark shall not be registered if, or to the extent that, its use in the UK is liable to be prevented by virtue of any rule of law (in particular, the law of passing-off) protecting an unregistered trade mark or other sign used in the course of trade (s 5(4)(a)), or by virtue of an earlier right, in particular by virtue of the law of copyright, design right or registered design (s 5(4)(b)). A person thus entitled to prevent the use of a trade mark is referred to as the proprietor of an 'earlier right'. The protection conferred by s 5(4)(a) is narrower than that conferred by the TMA 1938 s 11.

The term 'earlier trade mark' is defined in s 6 to mean a registered trade mark, international trade mark (UK) or a Community trade mark which has a date of application for registration earlier than that of the trade mark in question, taking account (where appropriate) of the priorities claimed in respect of the trade marks.

Provision has been made to protect the position of an honest concurrent user (s 7). This section was only introduced in the last stages of the passage of the Bill. It provides that a trade mark application may be refused registration if an objection based on the grounds in s 5 is raised by the proprietor of the earlier trade mark or earlier right, but that the Registrar cannot refuse the registration of his own motion (s 7(2)).

24.4 Defensive registration

Under the TMA 1938 it was permissible to register a mark even when there was no intention to use that mark as a trade mark for the goods for which it was registered. This was called defensive registration and was permissible by virtue of TMA 1938 s 27. This could only be done for marks which consist of an invented word or invented words. This is in order to protect both the general public and the trader from another competitor who took advantage of the reputation of a well known mark to promote goods that were unrelated to the goods for which the mark is registered. There was, however, no equivalent for service marks.

Defensive registration is not permitted by Articles 10 and 12 of the Directive. Defensive marks already registered will be permitted to stay on the register for five years before they are revoked (Article 10(4)(b)).

However, the provision of s 5(3), which follows the optional Article 4(4)(a), acknowledges the present trading practice of producing a range of unrelated goods, but which all emanate from the same trade source. The general public would be likely to assume that a new product that bore the same or similar mark to that born by the other goods, came from the same trade source, and thus would be deceived if the situation was otherwise. Thus, s 5(3) provides that a mark shall not be registered, even if the application is for dissimilar goods to those for which a similar mark, which has a reputation in the UK, is already registered. This in effect renders the need for defensive registration unnecessary. Thus if, for example, the trade mark Coca Cola was only registered for soft drinks, then no other trader could register it for T-shirts or stationery, because the public would be likely to regard Coca Cola as the source and not the applicant. Thus, the 'Coca-Cola' mark will be protected from having its reputation damaged or diluted by its appearance on other goods that have not emanated from a source controlled by the proprietor of the mark.

Trade Marks: The 1994 Act: Registration

Absolute grounds for refusal of registration

There are mandatory provisions contained within Article 3(1), and optional ones within Article 3(2). No other grounds may be implemented by national law to found a ground of objection to registration. The absolute grounds refer to the inherent properties of the mark being considered, while the relative grounds refer to the conflict of the mark in question with earlier marks and rights. The absolute grounds are contained in ss 3 and 4 of the TMA 1994, while the relative grounds are in s 5.

TMA 1994 s 3(1)

The absolute grounds include: the mark does not satisfy s 1(1) (s 3(1)(a)); the mark is devoid of distinctive character (s 3(1)(b)); the mark consists exclusively of descriptive elements (s 3(1)(c)); or the mark has become customary within the established *bona fide* practice of the trade (s 3(1)((d)).

TMA 1994 ss 3(2)-3(6)

There are limitations on the shape of containers that may be registered (s 3(2)). Furthermore, registration may be refused if the mark is contrary to public policy or likely to deceive (s 3(3)); or will not be registered if the use of the mark is prohibited by any rule of law (s 3(4)). Marks that conflict with specially protected emblems will not be registered (s 3(5)). Registration may be refused for being in bad faith (s 3(6)).

Specially protected emblems

The Royal arms, flags and representations of the Royal family are all protected (s 4(1)). Registration will be refused to marks that comprise the Union Flag or the flags of the separate countries that form the UK, if their use would be misleading or grossly offensive (s 4(2)). The emblems of Convention country and certain international organisations are also protected (s 4(3)).

Relative grounds for refusal for registration

Registration will be refused if there is a conflict with an earlier registered trade mark or an earlier right. Opposition may be made by the Registrar of his own motion. However, the Secretary of State may make provisions that only a proprietor of earlier mark/right may object (s 8(1)). The power of the Registrar is curtailed in that he cannot object to registration if the proprietor of the earlier mark/right agrees to registration (s 5(5)).

TMA 1994 ss 5, 6 and 7	Thus, registration will be refused if there is a conflict with an earlier identical earlier mark (s 5(1)); or if the conflict is with a similar mark for similar goods, coupled with the likelihood of confusion (s 5(2)); and, lastly, if the conflict is with a mark that has a reputation, if registration would be unfair or detrimental to that earlier mark (s 5(3)).

Conflict with an unregistered mark (s 5(4)(a)) or other right (s 5(4)(b)), will also prevent registration.

Honest concurrent use is protected under s 7. |
| **Defensive registration** | Not allowed by Articles 10 and 12 of the Directive. Existing defence marks will be allowed to remain on the register for five years (Article 10(4)(b)). However, the operation of s 5(3) will protect most important marks by preventing other similar marks being registered for dissimilar goods. |

Chapter 25

Trade Marks: The 1994 Act: Infringement

The issue of infringement is central to any system of property rights. This is dealt with by Article 5, and broadly the definition of infringement has been widened from what existed under the TMA 1938. In essence infringement under the TMA 1938 necessitated that the offending mark be used in the course of trade in relation to the goods in question (TMA 1938 ss 4 and 5). The verbosity and obscurity of the language of ss 4 and 5 has been well chronicled over the years in the law reports. One of the stated aims of the new Act is to implement the Government's policy of simplifying the language used in statutes.

The rights conferred by registration are delineated by s 9, while s 10 details the acts that constitute an infringement. Section 11 indicates those acts that will not constitute infringement of a registered trade mark, while s 12 deals with the principle of exhaustion of rights, and s 13 deals with the limitations of rights as imposed by the registration being subject to a disclaimer. Sections 14-21 deal with infringement proceedings.

25.1 Introduction

Section 9(1) confers exclusive rights upon the proprietor of the trade mark which is infringed by the use of the trade mark in the United Kingdom without his consent. The acts amounting to an infringement are specified in s 10. The rights of the proprietor have effect from the date of registration (which in accordance with s 40(3) is the date of filing of the application for registration), provided that no infringement proceedings may be begun before the date on which the trade mark is in fact registered (s 9(3)(a)); and no offence under s 92 (unauthorised use of the trade mark) is committed by anything done before the date of publication of the registration (s 9(3)(b)).

Consent may be oral. Written consent is only needed for a formal licence. Infringement is limited to those acts detailed in s 10, and thus an application under s 16 for delivery up is not an action for infringement. This is a small, but important difference, because, for example, it would mean that in the county court, an application for delivery up should proceed by way of originating application, rather than by way of summons.

25.2 Rights conferred by registration

25.3	**Infringement**	The acts that amount to infringement are contained in s 10. Subsection (1) and (2) follow Articles 5(1)(a) and (b); subsection (3) follows Article 5(2); and subsection (6) follows Articles 6(1) and 5(5) of the Directive. The provisions generally mirror those for the relative grounds for refusal of a trade mark, with the exception that the infringement provisions only refer to registered trade marks, while the registration provisions refer to earlier trade marks and rights that are protected.

These infringement provisions may be summarised as follows:

(1)   identical mark with identical goods;

(2)(a) identical mark with similar goods, or

(2)(b) similar mark with identical or similar goods,

> so long as there is a likelihood of confusion;

(3)   identical or similar marks with dissimilar goods, if the mark has a reputation and the use would damage that reputation;

(4)   outlines the meaning of 'use';

(5)   fixes liability on the actual manufacturer of the offending mark if he has guilty knowledge;

(6)   permits comparative advertising if done fairly.

25.3.1	Application of the provisions	The definition of use has been widened to extend beyond the definition that was in existence under the TMA 1938. Thus, the infringing use is no longer limited to a printed or visual representation (TMA 1938 s 68(2)). Now, infringing use of a trade mark will include, in addition, use by means other than graphic representation (TMA 1994 s 103(2)). Presumably, if the mark is a sound, then the use of that mark will include the audible reproduction of it. The provision may extend even further, and it may be an infringement of a written mark to reproduce it orally, for example, on a radio advertisement. There is no equivalent provision in the Directive.

No evidence of confusion is needed if an identical mark is used on identical goods. However, evidence of confusion is needed if either the marks are only similar rather than identical, or if the goods are only similar rather than identical, or both marks and goods are only similar. Furthermore, the likelihood of confusion, includes the likelihood of association with the trade mark (proviso to s 10(1)). The concept of association has been developed in the Benelux countries, and is much wider than is normally envisaged. For example, a cigarette product was held to be associated with a woman's hygiene product. The issue is whether or not the public would think that it was possible for the two products to be produced by the same corporation.

It will also be an infringement of a registered trade mark if an identical or similar sign is used on goods that are different from those for which the mark is registered if the trade mark has a reputation in the UK, and the use of the sign takes unfair advantage of, or is detrimental to, the distinctive character of the repute of the trade mark (s 10(3)). This provision mirrors that which prevents the registration of such a mark if the earlier mark has a reputation.

This is a fundamental departure for the UK law of trade marks, because, in essence, an action for trade mark infringement is now possible for goods for which the mark is not registered, ie a *de facto* unregistered trade mark. Previously, the *quid pro quo* of registration and the corresponding simplification of an action for infringement was that no action could be taken for infringement unless there was a prior registration of the trade mark for goods in the right class. The lack of such a registration meant that the proprietor had to rely on the law of passing-off, and that in turn necessitated the need to prove reputation and ownership, the two issues which registration presumed. It remains to be seen whether or not the operation of s 10(3) displaces the need for an action based on the test of passing-off. It is likely that a suitable case could be pleaded in the alternative so as to cover all possible eventualities. The need to prove reputation to the satisfaction of the court could pose problems to a plaintiff, for it is unlikely that a defendant would concede the point, except in the most extreme of cases, eg *Coca-Cola* or *IBM*, say.

Under the 1938 TMA, the use of the mark had to be in relation to the goods or services in question. This phraseology was slightly vague, and so it was left to the courts to delineate the boundaries of infringement. In endeavouring to make the new law more readily understood by the commercial world, a number of examples of what would constitute use have been given in the new Act. These are detailed in subsection 10(4). This is not an exclusive list, but only indicative of the type of actions that would be considered to count as the use of a sign that would lead to an infringement. Other uses could equally be held to be an infringement by the courts as the case law develops.

Secondary infringement by a person who helps make articles bearing the offending trade mark is prohibited, but there is a requirement of knowledge (s 10(5)). However, this subsection only applies if the registered trade mark is applied, and does not extend to similar marks, unless, presumably, the difference is *de minimis*.

The last subsection permits comparative advertising, whereby one trader identifies the goods of another trade by means of that other trader's registered trade mark so long as the use is in accordance with honest practices in industrial or commercial matters. This practice is very common between large multi-nationals, even though under the TMA 1938 s 4(1)(b) importing a reference to another trader's mark was prohibited. The new provisions are in line with the draft Directive on Comparative Advertising 1991. This Directive was supposed to be implemented by 31 December 1992; however, it has proved more controversial than first expected, and so its adoption has been delayed. There is now a further 1994 (amended) draft proposal. There is no fixed date for the adoption of this version as yet.

An action for infringement may be brought by the proprietor of the trade mark (s 14(1)), and by an exclusive licensee (s 31(1)). The full range of remedies is available (s 14(2)), including an order for delivery up (s 16(1)).

25.4	**Limitations on infringement**

A trade mark is not infringed by the use of another registered trade mark in relation to goods or services for which the latter is registered (s 11(1)). This is similar to the provisions of the TMA 1938 s 4(4).

A trade mark is not infringed by the use of a person of his own name or address (s 11(2)(a)); or the use of indications concerning the kind, quality, quantity, intended purpose, value, geographical origin, the time of production of goods or of rendering of services, or other characteristics of goods or services (s 11(2)(b)); or the use of the trade mark where it is necessary to indicate the intended purpose of a product (in particular, as accessories or spare parts) (s 11(2)(c)), provided that the use is in accordance with honest practices in industrial and commercial matters. These provisions follow Articles 6(1)(a) to (c). The Statements to the Directive indicate that the term 'person' refers to a natural person; however, in the UK, the term 'person' also includes a body of persons whether corporate or incorporate (Interpretation Act 1978 s 5 and Schedule 1). This could be an area of possible conflict between the domestic and the European Courts. However, in accordance with Continental usage, the courts have never been keen to allow companies the benefit of s 8(a) of the TMA 1938 which allowed a 'person' freely to use his own name without interference from any trade mark registration.

Furthermore, a registered trade mark is not infringed by the use in the course of trade in a particular locality of an earlier right which applies only in that locality. An earlier right means an unregistered trade mark or other sign which has been used continuously in relation to goods or services by a person or a predecessor in title, from a date preceding the earlier of either the registration or use of the registered mark, so long as the earlier right had such goodwill as could be protected by an action for passing-off (s 11(3)). This implements the aim of Article 5(4), but uses terminology that is directed at the existing law of passing-off in the UK.

A registered trade mark is not infringed by the use of the trade mark in relation to goods which have been put on the market in the European Economic Area under that trade mark by the proprietor or with his consent (s 12(1)), so long as there is no legitimate reason for the proprietor to oppose further dealings (in particular, where the condition of the goods has been changed or impaired after they have been put on the market) (s 12(2)). These provisions follow Articles 7(1) and (2).	**25.5 Exhaustion of rights**

These provisions replace those which were contained in the TMA 1938 s 6 which extended the scope of infringement to include certain acts that were contained within a written contract. Only certain acts that related to the subsequent alteration of the goods were covered by s 6, and apart from the restrictions contained there, the proprietor of the trade mark had little control over the goods on which that mark appeared once the goods had been sold by him, ie his rights with respect to the use of the trade mark extended only to the first sale, and thereafter they were exhausted.

An applicant for registration of a trade mark, or the proprietor of a registered trade mark, may disclaim any right to the exclusive use of any specified element of a trade mark (s 13(1)(a)), or, agree that the rights conferred by the registration shall be subject to a specified territorial or other limitations (s 13(1)(b)), and where the registration of a trade mark is subject to a disclaimer or limitation, the rights conferred by s 9 are restricted accordingly. The Registrar no longer has the power to insist upon a disclaimer. It is likely that an applicant will only disclaim material as a result of an opposition that, unless compromised, would result in the application failing.	**25.6 Disclaimers**

All the transitional provisions are contained in Schedule 3. Paragraph 4(1) states that ss 9-12 of the TMA 1994 apply in relation to an existing trade mark as from the commencement of this Act, and s 14 (an action for infringement) applies in relation to an infringement of an existing trade mark committed after the commencement of this Act, subject to sub-para 4(2). The old law continues to apply in relation to infringements committed before commencement.	**25.7 Transitional provisions for infringement actions**

Paragraph 4(2) states that it is not an infringement of (a) an existing trade mark, or (b) a registered trade mark of which the distinctive elements are the same or substantially the same as those of an existing registered trade mark and which is registered for the same goods or services, to continue after the commencement any use which did not amount to infringement of the existing trade mark under the old law. Part (b) of this sub-para is to prevent a proprietor from trying to re-register his trade mark in an attempt to circumvent the provisions of para 4(2).

Interestingly, the defence under the TMA 1938 s 5(2) is so worded that no relief is available to the aggrieved plaintiff, rather than providing that if the defendant's activities fall within the requirements of that subsection, then no infringement has occurred. Thus, such activities would now constitute an infringement, and would not be saved by Schedule 3, para 4(2).

| 25.8 | **Anti-counterfeiting provisions** |

A proprietor of a registered trade mark may, on giving written notice, request the Commissioners of Customs and Excise to treat as prohibited goods a specified consignment of goods that is to be imported into the UK (s 89(1)). Any such goods will be liable to forfeiture, unless the goods have been imported for private and domestic use (s 89(2)). Section 90 empowers the Commissioner of Customs and Excise to make such regulations as are necessary to implement s 89.

The Government expressed concern in the White Paper on the Reform of Trade Mark Law 1990 over the rise in counterfeit goods that are appearing on the market. As an interim step, the CDPA 1988 s 300 inserted ss 58A-D into the TMA 1938, which created the new offence of fraudulent application or use of a trade mark. These sections have now been repealed by the TMA 1994, and different, stronger, provisions have been enacted within the principal Act, namely ss 92-98.

There was particular concern that a trader should not be able to avoid liability under the Trade Descriptions Act 1968 by displaying above the counterfeit goods a sign to the effect that the goods were not genuine, which thereby allowed the trader to argue that nobody was deceived by the false application of the trade mark to the goods (*Kent County Council v Ralph Robert Price* (1993)).

The early draft clauses within the Trade Mark Bill were so widely drawn that almost all infringements would also have amounted to a criminal offence. The final version in s 92 is more tightly drawn. The mark applied must be identical to, or be likely to be mistaken for, the registered trade mark (s 92(1)).

The goods to which the mark is applied must be identical to those for which the mark is registered, or else if the goods are different, then the trade mark must have a reputation in the UK and the use of the sign takes or would take unfair advantage of, or is or would be detrimental to, the distinctive character or the repute of the trade mark (s 92(4)).

In all cases the use must be done with a view to gain for himself or another, or with intent to cause loss to another, and without the consent of the proprietor. A defence is provided to a person who can show that he believed, on reasonable grounds, that the use of the sign in the manner in which it was used, or was to be used, was not an infringement of the registered trade mark (s 92(5)).

Provision is made for the order of the forfeiture and destruction of counterfeit goods (s 97).

These anti-counterfeiting provisions all relate to goods; there are no similar provisions that relate to counterfeited services.

Trade Marks: The 1994 Act: Infringement

This Act attempts to replace the obscure language of TMA 1938 ss 4 and 5 with clearer wording.

Introduction

The infringement provisions follow those contained within Article 5 of the Directive.

The exclusive rights are conferred upon the proprietor (s 9(1)). An action may be commenced after registration (s 9(3)), which is defined to be the date of filing of the application (s 40(3)).

Rights conferred by registration

Consent may be oral, or by conduct, and provides a complete defence.

Primary acts of infringement amount to using the mark as a trade mark (s 10(1)). Secondary acts of infringement require knowledge (s 10(5)). These latter acts are intended to capture the printers and manufacturers who actually produce the marks in question.

Infringement

Comparative advertising is permissible so long as it is fair (s 10(6)).

Infringement may be otherwise than by graphical representation as well as by graphical representation (s 103(2)).

Application of the provisions

No evidence of confusion is needed if the use is by identical marks (s 10(1)).

Otherwise evidence of confusion is required (s 10(2)).

Secondary infringement requires the use of identical marks (s 10(5)).

An infringement action may be brought by proprietor (s 14(1)) or by the exclusive licensee (s 31(1)).

There is no infringement if the use is by another registered mark (s 11(1)).

Limitations on infringement

A person may use his own name and address (s 11(2)(a)). Furthermore, it is permissible to use a mark to indicate the purpose of product, ie spare parts compatibility (s 11(2)(c)).

Exhaustion of rights

The principle of the exhaustion of rights operates when marks are put into circulation within the EU with the consent of the trade mark owner (s 12(1)).

This may be overridden if there is a good reason to control the further circulation, eg quality control of repackaged pharmaceuticals (s 12(2)).

Disclaimers

Disclaimers limit the rights conferred by s 9 (s 13). The Registrar no longer has the power to insist on disclaimers.

Transitional provisions for infringement actions

New acts of infringement are covered by the new Act (Schedule 3 para 4(1)). There is no infringement for acts that were permitted before commencement (Schedule 3 para 4(2)).

Anti-counterfeiting provisions

Commissioners of Customs and Excise may seize goods after written notification (s 89(1)). There has been introduced a new offence which comprises fraudulent application of a trade mark (s 92). An order for forfeiture and destruction is possible under s 97.

Chapter 26

Passing-Off

The tort of passing-off is a common law offence, yet it has received statutory recognition in the Trade Mark Act where it is stated that the creation of the Trade Mark Registry and the corresponding action for trade or service mark infringement does not abrogate any action that may lie at common law for passing-off (TMA 1994 s 2(2)).

26.1   Relationship to trade mark law

The Trade Mark Act is concerned with the protection of registered trade marks, while the law of passing-off is concerned with the protection of marks that identify the goods as emanating from a particular trade source and yet have not necessarily been registered as trade marks. Thus, this area is often referred to as providing protection for unregistered trade marks.

There are certain provisions in the new Trade Marks Act that do provide some protection for a mark being used on articles for which the mark has not been registered (s 10(3)).

In such a situation the proprietor of the registered trade mark is gaining protection for, in essence, an unregistered trade mark for those goods. This is equivalent to being able to sue for the infringement of an unregistered trade mark, which is generally not permissible (TMA 1994 s 2(2)), save that a prospective plaintiff must prove reputation. Previously, such a use by a competitor could only be prevented by an action for passing-off, which requires not only proof of reputation, but also of a misrepresentation. An action for trade mark infringement under s 10(3) is unlikely to displace the tort of passing-off all together for the simple reason that the are still many unregistered trade marks in use, and these cannot avail themselves of the advantages conferred by s 10(3) of the TMA 1994.

Passing-off protects a property right which is not easily defined. In *AG Spalding & Bros v AW Gamage Ltd* (1915), Lord Parker said 'the right is a right of property ... property in the business or goodwill likely to be injured by the misrepresentation'.

An action for passing-off is dependant upon the business having goodwill attached to it. Goodwill is usually achieved by actually trading, even though advertising before the launch of a new product may establish goodwill in that product once it is launched (*British Broadcasting Corporation v Talbot Motor Co*

Ltd (1981)). Generally there is a need for an extended period of time to have elapsed before an action may be commenced. This is to allow the unregistered mark to achieve sufficient goodwill that the courts will seek to protect it. This delay is in contrast to commencing an action for trade mark infringement, which may occur as soon as the application has been accepted. The fact that a trade mark may be actively protected once it has been registered is one of the advantages of registered trade marks over unregistered trade marks.

Before 1986, when it became possible to register service marks for the first time, the tort of passing-off provided the only means of protection for the business get-up of services. This was indicative of the wider scope of passing-off over trade mark protection. The TMA 1994 extends to marks for services, as well as goods, but registration is still a prerequisite before an action for trade mark infringement is commenced.

| 26.2 | Relation with competition law | Under Article 10*bis* of the International Convention for the Protection of Industrial Property 1883 (as subsequently revised and amended), Convention countries, of which the UK is one, must make provisions in the domestic legislation for the protection of traders from unfair competition. The phrase 'unfair competition' is given a broad meaning which tallies with the manner in which it is used on the continent. In the UK, there is no single statute by which unfair competition is defined and prohibited. Instead there are number of other possible causes of action which include the common law actions of passing-off and malicious falsehood and the causes of actions created by the Competition Act 1980 and the Unfair Trade Agreement Act 1976. All these causes of action are designed to protect one trader from the unfair trading habits of another. In contrast the Trade Descriptions Act 1968 and the other criminal provisions of the Trade Marks Act 1994 and the CDPA 1988, as well as the tort of deceit, provide protection for members of the general public from the less desirable trading practices of fraudulent traders. |

If the action complained of affects trade not only in the UK, but also in another Member State of the European Union, then the anti-competition provisions of the Treaty of Rome may be invoked, namely Articles 30-36, 85 and 86. These may be used within the domestic courts, because the Treaty of Rome has direct affect within the UK, and thus the individuals resident within it may rely on the rights that it confers.

| 26.3 | Definition of passing-off | Passing-off consists of four fundamental elements, which stated briefly comprise (a) the misrepresentation by (b) a trader that will (c) damage the (d) goodwill of another. Thus, |

in essence, as Lord Halsbury said in *Frank Reddaway & Co Ltd v George Banham & Co Ltd* (1896), 'nobody has any right to represent his goods as the goods of somebody else'.

There is no *mens rea* requirement that the defendant is acting fraudulently, maliciously or even negligently. Since there is no requirement for a *mens rea* element on behalf of the defendant, the tort may be completed even if the defendant is completely innocent in the sense that he has no knowledge or belief that he is committing an act that satisfies the elements of the tort. As a consequence, both injunctive relief and damages may be awarded if appropriate (*Gillette UK Ltd v Edenwest Ltd* (1994)). The present definition of passing-off is contained in the judgment given by Lord Diplock in *Erven Warnink BV v J Townend & Sons (Hull) Ltd* (1980) (the '*Advocaat*' case) in which his Lordship said that:

> '*Spalding v Gamage* and the later cases make it possible to identify five characteristics which must be present in order to create a valid cause of action for passing-off: (1) a misrepresentation (2) made by a trader in the course of trade (3) to prospective customers of his or ultimate consumers of goods or services supplied by him (4) which is calculated to injure the business or goodwill of another trader (in the sense that this is a reasonably foreseeable consequence) and (5) which causes actual damage to a business or goodwill of the trader by whom the action is brought or (in a *quia timet* action) will probably do so.'

In this definition, parts (2) and (3) constitute the trading element of the tort.

In *Reckitt & Coleman Products Ltd v Borden Inc* (1990), which concerned the Jif lemon containers, Lord Oliver reduced this definition to just three elements, namely the existence of the goodwill, a misrepresentation and damage. It is under these three headings that the elements of the tort of passing-off will be treated below.

The term 'goodwill' is central to the tort of passing-off. Without it, an action will not get off the ground. However, the precise meaning of the term is not always clear from the case law. In particular, it has been known for courts to confuse the issue of 'goodwill' and 'reputation' (*Taittinger SA v Allbev Ltd* (1993)). The courts will now have to distinguish more carefully between these two terms because of the use of the latter term in the TMA 1994, s 10(3).	**26.4 Goodwill**
Not only must goodwill exist, but it must be owned by the plaintiff and be attached to his business interests. Goodwill is not to be confused with the reputation that may also be	26.4.1 Goodwill and reputation

associated with a business. Goodwill has been defined as 'the attractive force which brings in custom' (*Commissioners of the Inland Revenue v Muller & Co's Margarine Ltd* (1901)), ie it is directly concerned with the future trade that a business may expect to achieve. The expectation of future sales is obviously an asset to the business, and thus enhances the value of the business.

Reputation is more akin to how well the business or product is known to the purchasing public, and whether or not what the public knows is favourable. A manufacturer with a large favourable reputation is more likely also to have goodwill, and that will lead customers to purchase its produce; however, this is not invariably the case. For example, the American beer 'Budweiser' was sold originally in the UK only on US Air Force bases. The beer had a large reputation, especially amongst those members of the British public that had travelled within the US. Yet it did not have any goodwill within this country, and so an action for passing-off failed against the Czechoslovakian brewers (*Anheuser-Busch Inc v Budejovicky Budvar NP (t/a Budweiser Budvar Brewery)* (1984)).

26.4.2   In the course of trade

Goodwill attaches only to businesses and not to individuals acting in their domestic capacity. Thus, one neighbour cannot complain of another using the same name for his house (*Day v Browrigg* (1878)).

Charities do not trade in goods or services in the normal sense. Yet the law of passing-off has been used to prevent an organisation from using similar names to those of well established charities, eg *British Legion v British Legion Club (Street) Ltd* (1931), and *Dr Barnardo's Homes: National Incorporated Association v Barnardo Amalgamated Industries Ltd* (1949)) What is being protected in these cases is the good name of charity, so that it may continue to be used to raise funds for services which benefit society.

There is no need for the goodwill to be attached exclusively to only one trader. It is possible for the goodwill to be shared amongst a group of traders. Collective reputations are common in the drinks industry, where, for example, all the Champagne Houses could claim that they have a joint and several reputation that needs to be protected (*HP Bulmer Ltd v J Bollinger SA* (1978)). However, passing-off protects the goodwill within the UK, and thus the prospective plaintiffs must have a *locus standi* within the jurisdiction. Thus, a consortium of producers of Parma ham could not prevent the defendant from selling pre-sliced and packaged ham taken from genuine Parma hams (*Consorzio del Prosciutto di Parma v Marks & Spenser plc* (1991)).

The goodwill normally has to be associated with the goods in question. Thus, if the defendant starts to sell goods of the same type as the plaintiff, ie there is a common field of activity, then, so long as the goodwill can be shown to reside with the plaintiff, a case for passing-off could be made out.

However, if the defendant deals in goods that are different from those of the plaintiff, then the plaintiff must show that his goodwill extends beyond the limited ambit of the goods that he actually produces, and that the public would assume that those different goods did in fact originate from him. Thus, for example, in *Rolls Razor Ltd v Rolls (Lighters) Ltd* (1949) the plaintiff dealt in razors, while the defendant dealt in lighters. It was held that the goodwill of the plaintiff did not extend from razors to lighters, and so the case for passing-off failed. The field of activity may be defined quite narrowly. Thus, for example, there may be a sufficient difference between the trade of a retailer and that of a wholesaler, to define two different areas of activity (*Fortnum and Mason plc v Fortum Ltd* (1994)).

It is, however, possible for the goodwill of the business to extend beyond the products that it supplies. For example, in *Lego Systems Aktieselskab v Lego M Lemelstrich Ltd* (1983), the makers of the children's building blocks were able to prevent the makers of plastic garden equipment from using the name 'Lego'.

There must be some particular feature by which the general public may identify the goods or services of the trader, and that the defendant has misappropriated in some manner that has lead to the damage to the plaintiff. There is no limitation upon the form that this distinguishing feature may take, so long as it serves to identify the goods. Commonly, a name or logo will perform such a function. This protection even extends to *noms de plume*, for example the name 'Kem' which was the mark of a famous cartoonist (*Marengo v Daily Sketch and Sunday Graphic Ltd* (1948)).

The whole get-up of the goods, which consists of the packaging and the presentation of the goods at the point of sale, may be the distinctive feature. It is possible for the shape of the product to be the characteristic feature that distinguishes the article, for example, a sachet of laundry blue (which is the colloquial term for the cleaning and bleaching agent) mounted upon a short stick (*William Edge & Sons Ltd v William Niccolls & Sons Ltd* (1911)).

The attractive force, which constitutes goodwill, may result from advertising as well as from the particular appearance or get-up of the product: the critical test is whether or not the

26.4.3   Common field of activity

26.4.4   Distinguishing feature

'product has derived from the advertising a distinctive character which the market recognises' (*Cadbury-Schweppes Pty Ltd v The Pub Squash Co Ltd* (1981)).

The whole get-up of the product must be taken into account when considering the issue of passing-off. For example, in the Canadian case of *Mr Submarine Ltd v Voultsos* (1977) it was held that the decor of the sandwich bars was distinctive and capable of founding a cause of action in passing-off.

26.4.5   Secondary meaning

If the mark which the plaintiff wishes to protect has some obvious meaning which does not *prima facie* identify the product as coming from a particular trade source, then he must establish that in practice the mark has become indicative of his product only. In such a case the mark is said to have acquired a secondary meaning that is distinct from its obvious primary meaning (*William Wotherspoon v John Currie* (1872)). An example would be where the mark is descriptive of the class of products to which the plaintiff's product belongs. In *Frank Reddaway & Co Ltd v George Banham & Co Ltd* (1896), the mark was 'Camel Hair Belting' which *prima facie* is merely descriptive of a product made from camel hair. In this case, the plaintiff managed to show that the term had acquired, through 13 years of use, the secondary meaning which linked it with its particular product, and so succeeded in the action for passing-off.

In contrast to a mark acquiring a secondary meaning, it is possible for a mark that was initially distinctive to become so well known that it now becomes a generic term. An example concerns the floor covering, linoleum. In this case the term had became sufficiently non-distinctive at a very early stage that it could no longer be protected (*Linoleum Manufacturing Co v Nairn* (1878)).

26.4.6   Concurrent reputations

If two traders commence trading at approximately the same time with similar trade names or logos, then the general public will not have had long enough to distinguish between them and so an action by one of the traders against the other will fail. In *Compatibility Research Ltd v Computer Psyche Co Ltd* (1967), two computer dating agencies commenced business only one month apart, and both used the scientific symbols that represent the male and the female of the species. It was held that a trader who set a new business had no monopoly in that trade, and so could not prevent a rival trader copying his ideas. The distinction to be drawn is between competition, which could not be prevented, and passing-off by the use of a name or sign that has become distinctive of another's trade, which could be prevented. However, every case depends on its facts. In *Stannard v Reay* (1967) three weeks was held to be long enough for a new business, which consisted of the first mobile fish and chip van on the Isle of Wight trading under the name of 'Mr Chippy', to prevent a similar concern from trading under the same name.

Just because there are two or more trading entities that enjoy a reputation in an identical or similar mark, does not mean that they may prevent the use of that mark by any third party unrestricted by geographical considerations. The protection conferred by passing-off only extends as far as the goodwill associated with the business. For example, if two companies operate in different parts of the country, and each has a goodwill associated with it that covers the area of operation, then each may exclude the other from their home region (*Cavendish House (Cheltenham) Ltd v Cavendish-Woodhouse Ltd* (1970)). Furthermore, in any intermediate zone, neither may have sufficient goodwill in order to confer protection, either from each other or from another, third, trade rival (*City Link Travel Holdings Ltd v Lakin* (1979)).

A fundamental of the tort of passing-off is to protect the business interests of a trader within the jurisdiction, ie England and Wales. The trade that generates the goodwill must be done in the UK (*Anheuser-Busch Inc v Budejovicky Budvar NP (t/a Budweiser Budvar Brewery)* (1984)).

There need only be a small amount of trade in the UK. An extreme example occurred in *Maxim's Ltd v Dye* (1977), in which the defendant was stopped from using the name 'Maxim's' for his restaurant in London, because, even though the plaintiff's restaurant served food exclusively at the restaurant on the Champs Elysée in Paris, it was felt by the court that customers from London would travel to Paris for a meal, and thus the goodwill was so strong that the attractive power extended over the Channel.

26.4.7 Geographical limitations

The commonest type of misrepresentation is where the defendant attempts to pass-off his goods for those of the plaintiff by a simple substitution of one product for another.

There may still be a misrepresentation, even if the defendant has attempted to distinguish his goods from those of the plaintiff. For example, in *J Bollinger v Costa Brava Wine Co Ltd* (1961), the defendant was restrained from calling their sparkling wine 'Spanish Champagne', because it did not originate from the Champagne region of France, but rather was made in Spain by a similar method. It was held that since champagne was only drunk by the majority of the public on very rare occasions, that the level of knowledge and

26.5 Misrepresentation

discernment that could be attributed to them was small, and so there was a likelihood of confusion. The Spanish version is now sold under the name of 'Cava'.

In direct contrast to the Champagne case is the British Sherry case of *Vine Products Ltd v Mackenzie & Co Ltd* (1969). In this case, the Spanish producers of sherry failed to stop the British producers from labelling their product 'British Sherry' or 'Cyprus Sherry' as the case may be. The Spanish attempted to persuade the court that the word 'sherry' should be reserved for the produce that came from the Jerez region of Spain. In this case, it was held that the public had had over 100 years in which to be educated as to the differences, and thus no confusion would arise in the market place.

If the mark that is used is of a descriptive nature, then even small differences in the name of a competitor will be sufficient to avoid liability. So, 'Office Cleaning Association' was held not to encroach on the rights and reputation established by 'Office Cleaning Services' (*Office Cleaning Service Ltd v Westminster Window and General Cleaners Ltd* (1946)).

The misrepresentation must be significant, in that it would mislead a significant proportion of the general public. Thus, the proprietors of the *Morning Star* were refused an injunction to restrain the publication of the *Daily Star*, as only 'a moron in a hurry' would be likely to be mislead (*Morning Star Co-Operative Society Ltd v Express Newspapers Ltd* (1979)).

The misrepresentation must be relied upon by the purchaser. Thus, there was no passing-off in selling the blue-coloured adhesive putty 'Sellotak', which resembled 'Blu-Tack', because at the point of sale the blue colour of the putty could not be seen by the purchaser as it was contained within the packaging and so could not amount to a misrepresentation. Any subsequent confusion that may arise, because of the similar colour, would have only a very small influence on future sales and so could be dismissed (*Bostick Ltd v Sellotape GB Ltd* (1994)).

Usually, the defendant claims that his goods or services are the same as those of the plaintiffs. However, the reverse situation is also possible, ie where the defendant claims that the goods of the plaintiff were actually made by the defendant. For example, in *Bristol Conservatories Ltd v Conservatories Custom Built Ltd* (1989) the defendants showed prospective customers photographs of the plaintiff's conservatories, and passed them off as having been made by the defendants. This situation is sometimes called inverse, or reverse, passing-off, but the Judge did not make such a distinction.

It is very common for survey evidence to be adduced to show that confusion has, or is likely, to occur. The courts usually take a very dim view of such evidence (*United Biscuits (UK) Ltd v Burtons Biscuits Ltd* (1992) and *Dalgety Spillers Foods Ltd v Food Brokers Ltd* (1994)). Alternatively, evidence from trap orders may be used, and such evidence is permissible (*Marie Claire Album SA v Hartstone Hosiery Ltd* (1993)).

Another way in which there may be a misrepresentation is where the defendant supplies goods of a different quality from those which the customer ordered, even if the goods supplied are genuine to the plaintiff. Thus, in the case of *AG Spalding & Bros v AW Gamage Ltd* (1915), the defendant supplied the plaintiff's 'Orb' football when the 'New Improved Orb' football had been requested.	26.5.1 **Misrepresentation as to quality**
Generally, a person is allowed to trade under his own name, even if a small amount of confusion arises because of that. Thus, the proprietor of the Royal Albert Hall was unable to enjoin Albert Edward Hall from organising the Albert Hall Orchestra (*Corporation of the Hall of Arts and Sciences (Commonly known as The Albert Hall) v Albert Edward Hall* (1934)). However, the trader must be acting honestly, and not trying to deliberately take advantage of the reputation of a name established by some other trader.	26.5.2 **Mere confusion insufficient**
As passing-off is a tort there is a need to prove that damage *has flown* from the actions complained of, or that it is likely that damage *will flow* from those actions. The damage usually takes the form of substituted sales, ie the defendant has secured a sale, which save for the misrepresentation, would have gone to the plaintiff. Alternatively, the damage suffered by the plaintiff is to his reputation. This latter form of damage is the only type that may occur when the plaintiff and the defendant are trading in different products.	26.6 **Damage**

In *Erven Warnink Besloten Vennootschap v J Townend & Sons (Hull) Ltd* (1979), the plaintiffs were a group of Dutch manufacturers of 'Advocaat'. The defendants started selling in 1974 a drink called 'Keeling's Old English Advocaat' which consisted of powered eggs and fortified Cyprus sherry, and had traditionally been called 'Egg Flip' in the UK. The defendants' drink was sold at a lower price than the plaintiff's. Lord Diplock then said, with respect to the issue of damage:

'... that Keeling's deception of the public has caused and, unless prevented, will continue to cause, damage to Warnick in the trade and the goodwill of their business both directly in the loss of sales and indirectly in the debasement of the reputation attaching to the name

'Advocaat' if it is permitted to be used of alcoholic egg drinks generally and not confined to those that are spirit based.'

In cases in which there is a great dissimilarity in the products between the plaintiff and the defendant, then the possibility for any real confusion, and so probability of damage, is decreased. However, the more disreputable the activities of the defendant in the eyes of the plaintiff, the more concerned the plaintiff will be that if there is an association in the minds of the public, then great damage would flow. Thus, a night club for the rich and famous has enjoined an escort agency, and an upmarket department store has enjoined a moneylender (*Annabel's (Berkeley Square) Ltd v G Shock (t/a Annabel's Escort Agency)* (1972) and *Harrods Ltd v R Harrod Ltd* (1924) respectively).

Passing-Off

Passing-off provides a common law remedy for the protection of unregistered trade marks. Trade mark infringement is limited to the goods for which the mark has been registered, unless the mark has a reputation that would be damaged (TMA 1994 s 10(3)).

Relationship to trade mark law

Goodwill is the property right that is protected by passing-off (*Spalding v AW Gamage* (1915)). One cannot sue for passing-off until goodwill has been established, and this requires time. In contrast, an action for trade mark infringement may be launched as soon as the mark has been registered.

The tort of passing-off has a similar scope to some continental systems of unfair regulation. For that reason, the UK Government has no intention of introducing any further unfair competition legislation.

Relation with competition law

The essential elements are goodwill, misrepresentation and damage. The classic definition was given by Lord Diplock in *Erven Warnink BV v J Townend & Sons (Hull)* (1979).

Definition of passing-off

Innocence is no defence, as there is no *mens rea* element involved in the tort (*Gillette UK Ltd v Edenwest Ltd* (1994)).

Goodwill must not be confused with reputation (*Taittinger SA v Allber Ltd* (1993)).

Goodwill

Goodwill is the attractive force which brings in custom (*IRC v Muller's Margarine Ltd* (1901)). Reputation is akin to how well known, and how well regarded is the name of the business by the public.

A large reputation may exist in the US, but that does not constitute goodwill in the UK (*Anheuser-Busch v Budejovicky Budvar* (1984)).

The use of the mark has to be in the course of trade, and so domestic use is permissible (*Day v Browrigg* (1878)). Even though charities do not trade in goods or services as such, the courts have protected them (*Dr Barnardo's v Barnardo Amalgamated* (1949)).

In the course of trade

Consortiums are protected (*HP Bulmer Ltd v J Bollinger SA* (1978)).

Common field of activity

Typically, there is a need for a common field of activity, hence the goodwill only extends to similar goods. Thus, razors and lighters have been held to be different areas of trade, and so the goodwill did not extend to both areas. (*Rolls Razor Ltd v Rolls (Lighters) Ltd* (1949)). Similarly, retailers and wholesalers are different trades (*Fortum and Mason plc v Fortum Ltd* (1994)).

The larger the goodwill, then the larger the sphere of influence of the goodwill. Thus, Lego could prevent the use of the name on garden furniture (*Lego Systems A/S v Lego M Lemelstrich* (1983)).

Distinguishing feature

A *nom de plume* may serve as a distinguishing feature (*Marengo v Daily Sketch* (1948)). The whole get-up and decor of a shop may constitute the distinguishing feature, and so be protectable (*Mr Submarine Ltd v Voultsos* (1977)).

Secondary meaning

If the mark is descriptive, it must acquire a secondary meaning that distinguishes the plaintiff, eg the term 'camel hair belting' became distinctive of the plaintiff and so could be protected (*Frank Reddaway & Co Ltd v George Banham & Co Ltd* (1896)). What was once distinctive may lose that distinctiveness by becoming generic (*Linoleum Co v Nairn* (1878)).

Concurrent reputations

It is possible for two organisations to develop a concurrent reputation, in which case neither can stop the other (*Compatibility Research v Computer Psyche* (1967)). However, goodwill may be acquired quickly if there is a large trading volume (*Stannard v Reay* (1967)).

Geographical limitations

The goodwill may be restricted to a particular area (*Cavendish House (Cheltenham) v Cavendish-Woodhouse* (1970)). As a consequence, the boundary zone may be unprotectable by either party against each other or against a third trader (*City Link Travel Holdings Ltd v Lakin* (1979)).

It is not impossible for a foreign business to acquire goodwill in the UK (*Maxim's Ltd v Dye* (1977)).

Misrepresentation

The commonest misrepresentation is for the defendant's goods to be substituted for plaintiff's.

Small differences may be sufficient to distinguish rival services (*Office Cleaning v Westminster Cleaners* (1946)).

Survey evidence is of dubious value (*United Biscuits (UK) Ltd v Burtons Biscuits Ltd* (1992) and *Dalgety Spillers Foods Ltd v Food Brokers Ltd* (1994)).

Evidence from trap orders is permissible (*Marie Claire Album SA v Hartstone Hosiery Ltd* (1993)). However, the misrepresentation must be significant enough to have influenced the normal consumer, and not just a 'moron in a hurry' (*Morning Star Co-Operative Society v Express Newspapers* (1979)).

Misrepresentation as to quality

Inverse passing-off is where instead of pretending that the defendant's products are the plaintiff's, the defendant misrepresents that the plaintiff's products are its own (*Bristol Conservatories Ltd v Conservatories Custom Built Ltd* (1989)).

Selling inferior goods as better goods is actionable (*Spalding & Bros v AW Gamage Ltd* (1915)).

Mere confusion is not actionable (*The Albert Hall v Albert Edward Hall* (1934)).

Mere confusion insufficient

Lost sales is the commonest form of damage.

Damage

Chapter 27

Duty of Confidentiality

Most branches of intellectual property are now protected by statutory provisions, eg the Trade Marks Act 1994 for trade marks. The common law provides protection for an unregistered trade mark by an action for passing-off, and it also provides protection against some forms of unfair competition by an action for malicious falsehood. Equity also provides a valuable cause of action for the protection of intellectual property, namely the protection of confidential information by an action for the breach of the duty of confidentiality.

In addition to the equitable duty of confidentiality, which regulates the preservation of confidential information between private individuals, State secrets are regulated by the Official Secrets Act 1989.

However, the equitable duty of confidentiality is not to be confused with a right to privacy, for no such thing exists in English law. The issue of the privacy of the individual and the intrusion by the press was the subject of the Report of the Committee on Privacy and Related Matters 1990 (the Calcutt Report). However, the Government has not indicated any intention at present of introducing legislation in this area.

Most inventions result in a product which, once it is on the market, may be dismantled and so the internal workings may be deduced and reproduced. Thus, the only effective protection for such an invention is a patent that will confer a true monopoly on the inventor. If, however, the importance of the idea lies not in the end product, which may be analysed, but in its preparation, then that method of production may be kept effectively confidential by imposing a duty of confidentiality on any person who is connected with the production process. In this manner, a good idea may often be exploited for far longer than the 20 years of protection granted by a patent. The protection will last until that process is discovered independently, and then the originator will lose his monopoly.

In industry it is common for the underlying product to be protected by a patent, and then for the details of how to make that product in the most efficient manner to be protected by collateral agreements that cover the confidential production

27.1 Introduction

27.2 Interplay between confidentiality and patents

information. Such collateral agreements are often called 'know-how' agreements.

| 27.3 | **Recipe of Coca-Cola** |

Both the potential power and inherent weakness of relying upon confidential information alone is shown by the recipe for the popular soft drink 'Coca-Cola'. This drink was concocted in 1887 by an Atlanta pharmacist Dr John Pemberton, and even though there have been many imitators, it is still a great success. The drink was named after the two principal ingredients that it was purported to contain, namely cocaine from the coca plant, and caffeine from the cola nut. The original version never contained any cocaine, and the other ingredients have altered over the years, eg phosphoric acid has replaced citric acid because it is cheaper. The secret of its success was always stated to lie in the unique blend of ingredients. The recipe of the components and their amounts was a closely guarded secret, code named '7X'.

With the advance of modern analytical tools, it would now be possible to determine the exact composition of such a mixture. However, the recipe has become known through other channels, and it may now be stated openly that Coca-Cola is composed of 120 parts of oil of lemon, 80 parts of oil of orange, 40 parts of oil of nutmeg, 40 parts of oil of cinnamon, 40 parts of oil of neroli, and 20 parts of oil of coriander.

This aspect of the secret for the drink is now no longer capable of protection by imposing a duty of confidentiality. There remains, though, the exact manner in which these ingredients are mixed. This aspect of the secret formula is still subject to confidentiality agreements, and thus cannot be revealed without breaking that duty.

| 27.4 | **Relationship with copyright protection** |

Section 171(1)(e) of the CDPA 1988 states that nothing in that Act is to affect the operation of any rule of equity relating to breaches of trust or confidence. Many of the old copyright cases concern the publication of previously unpublished material. Often the judgments did not make it clear upon what grounds relief was granted. For example, in *Prince Albert v Strange* (1849), which concerned the improper copying of some unpublished etchings made by Queen Victoria and the Prince Consort for private distribution, the court found for the plaintiff on the grounds of breach of trust, breach of confidence, and breach of contract.

Copyright in a work only comes into existence once the work has been recorded in some manner or other. The duty of confidentiality may arise regardless of whether the information that is to be kept confidential is recorded in any manner (*Printers and Finishers Ltd v Holloway* (1965)). Thus, copyright cannot be used to protect an idea that has been merely told to another person, while a duty of confidentiality could.

The exact legal basis upon which a duty of confidentiality is based is open to debate. There have been attempts to base the cause of action upon a new equitable property right that vested in the confidential information. Later there have been attempts to base the cause of action in contract, whether express or implied, between the giver and the receiver of the confidential information. Even though this last approach has a certain appeal, it restricts the people who are bound to respect the duty of confidentiality to those who were either party to the contract, or those who have induced a breach of that contract (*British Industrial Plastics Ltd v Ferguson* (1940)). This contractual approach has proved in practice to be too restrictive, and has lead to artificiality in many situations.

Currently the position is that the duty of confidentiality is based upon an equitable obligation of 'good faith' (*Fraser v Evans* (1969)) that is not dependant upon a contractual relationship between the parties. By adopting this position the courts have returned to the earliest formulation which was based upon a 'breach of faith', that was independent of any contractual relationship (*Morison v Moat* (1851)). If, however, there is a contractual relationship between the parties, then in addition to the restrictions imposed by the contract, equity may add further restrictions if it is just to do so.

The importance of delineating the precise nature of the cause of action comes when cases are considered that fall near the limit of what may found a cause of action. Such situations involve the liability of indirect recipients and the liability of those people who, in some way, have acted innocently.

27.5   Nature of the duty of confidentiality

The nature of the duty of confidentiality is that it is unconscionable for a person who has received information on a confidential basis to reveal that information (*Stephens v Avery* (1988)). This broad and developing equitable doctrine states that he who has received information in confidence shall not take unfair advantage or profit from the wrongful use or publication of it (*Attorney-General v Jonathan Cape Ltd* (1976)). Nor may he make any use of it to the prejudice of him who gave it, without obtaining his consent or, at any rate, without paying him for it (*Seager v Copydex Ltd* (1967)).

As this cause of action has an equitable basis, it is capable of protecting not just matters of commercial sensitivity, but

27.6   Equitable nature of the duty of confidentiality

also matters of a purely domestic nature, like for example the private confidences between husband and wife (*Duchess of Argyll v Duke of Argyll* (1967)).

27.7 Working definition of the duty of confidentiality

In *Coco v AN Clark (Engineers) Ltd* (1969), Megarry J listed the requirements that were necessary for the duty of confidentially to arise. First, the information itself must 'have the necessary quality of confidence about it' (*Saltman Engineering Co Ltd v Campbell Engineering Co Ltd* (1948)); secondly, that information must have been imparted in circumstances importing an obligation of confidence; thirdly, there must be an unauthorised use of that information. The judge questioned whether the plaintiff must show that the unauthorised use was to his detriment.

27.8 Necessary quality of confidence

The type of information that may be protected by a duty of confidentiality is very wide. In *Saltman Engineering Co Ltd v Campbell Engineering Co Ltd* (1948) Lord Greene MR said:

'The information, to be confidential, must, I apprehend, apart from contract, have the necessary quality of confidence about it, namely it must not be something which is public property and public knowledge.'

In *Coco v AN Clark (Engineers) Ltd* (1969) Megarry J said:

'Something that has been constructed solely from materials in the public domain may possess the necessary quality of confidentiality: for something new and confidential may have been brought into being by the application of the skill and ingenuity of the human brain. Novelty depends on the thing itself, and not upon the quality of its constituent parts. Indeed, often the more striking the novelty, the more commonplace its components.'

In *Thomas Marshall (Exports) Ltd v Guinle* (1979), Megarry VC said:

'If one turns from the authorities and looks at the matter as a question of principle, I think (and I say this very tentatively, because the principle has not been argued out) that four elements may be discerned which may be of some assistance in identifying confidential information or trade secrets which the court will protect. I speak of such information or secrets only in an industrial or trade setting. First, I think that the information must be information the release of which the owner believes would be injurious to him or of advantage to his rivals or others. Secondly, I think the owner must believe that the information is confidential or secret, ie that it is not already in the public domain. It may be that some or all of his rivals already have the information: but as long as the owner believes it to be confidential I think he is entitled to try and protect it. Thirdly, I think that the owner's belief under the two previous heads must be reasonable. Fourthly, I think that the information must be judged in the light of the usage and practices of the particular industry or trade concerned. It may be that information which does not satisfy all these requirements may be entitled to protection as confidential information or trade secrets: but I think that any which does satisfy them must be of the type which is entitled to protection.'

The following types of information, *inter alia*, have been protected: the technical subject matter of a patent (*Cranleigh Precision Engineering Ltd v Bryant* (1966)); commercial records such as customer lists (*Anton Piller KG v Manufacturing Processes Ltd* (1976)); marketing procedures (*Stephenson Jordan & Harrison Ltd v MacDonald & Evans* (1952)); information of a political significance (*Fraser v Evans* (1969)); a professional questionnaire (*Interfirm Comparison (Australia) Pty Ltd v Law Society of New South Wales* (1977)); and even marital confidences (*Duchess of Argyll v Duke of Argyll* (1967)).

27.8.1 Examples of protected information

The duty of confidentiality may be used to protect a mere idea, regardless of whether or not it has been recorded in any manner. So long as 'the content of the idea was clearly identifiable, original, of potential commercial attractiveness and capable of being realised in actuality', the idea may be protected (*Fraser v Thames Television Ltd* (1984)). The requirement of originality is required to protect ideas for television shows, for otherwise protection may be claimed for an idea that has already been put into practice.

27.8.2 Protection of a mere idea

Information in the public domain cannot be the subject matter of a duty of confidentiality. There are a number of ways in which information that was originally confidential may become public knowledge. For example, if the defendant can show that he already knew the information that is purportedly being imparted to him in confidence, then he will not be bound by any duty of confidentiality that the plaintiff may try to impose (*Johnson v Heat and Air Systems Ltd* (1941)). Alternatively, the information may have become common knowledge since the imposition of the duty of confidentiality through no fault of the confidant, in which case the courts will not impose any liability on the confidant. For example, information that relates to a share price in a company may be confidential until it is published by the company. On publication of that information, the duty of confidentiality

27.8.3 Information in the public domain

disappears, because there is no longer any confidential subject matter.

Apart from information becoming public because it has been released by the person who could impose a duty of confidentiality, the information may have been made available by the original recipient to whom the information was conveyed in confidence. In such a situation, as far as the original recipient of that information is concerned, he should still treat the information as confidential and he is not allowed to use that information freely, because to do so would be a breach of the duty of confidentiality that he owes to the supplier of that information (*Speed Seal Products Ltd v Paddington* (1986)). However, it is submitted, that subsequent recipients would be free to use this information, so long as they acquired it without notice because, as far as any subsequent recipient knows, the information is not confidential but instead is in the public domain.

If the information has only been revealed to a small number of people then the courts may prevent further revelations occurring. For example, when aboriginal religious secrets had been disclosed in confidence by the elders of the Pitjantjara tribe to an anthropologist who then included this information in a book about to be published, the members of the Pitjantjara Council obtained an injunction to stop the publication of the work in order to prevent the secret information reaching the uninitiated (*Foster v Mountford* (1978)).

27.8.4 Excluded matter	Regardless of the exact nature of the information, as a matter of policy, not all types of information will be protected by the courts. Thus, 'trivial tittle-tattle' will not be protected (*Coco v AN Clark (Engineers) Ltd* (1969)). However, if the trivial material is worth money to someone, then the courts may consider it capable of protection (*Church of Scientology of California v Kaufman* (1973)). If the information is scandalous or immoral, then the court will not protect it (*Stephens v Avery* (1988)). This reflects the equitable origins of the duty of confidentiality, for there is no confidence in an iniquity (*Gartside v Outram* (1857)).
27.9 **Obligation of confidence**	In most commercial or industrial relationships that involve the communication of confidential information, the duty of confidentiality is imposed between the parties by contractual means. Thus, the confidential information is exchanged in return for consideration, and the duty of confidentiality is one of the obligations upon the recipient of the information, alongside the concomitant rights, that arise out of the contract.

However, a duty of confidentiality may arise by other means than contract. It may arise in a purely personal situation in which one person tells another some information in confidence. In this case there is no consideration, and thus no contract under English law. If the recipient of the information agrees to accept the information in confidence, then equity will assert that a duty has arisen. If, however, the recipient does not accept that the information is given in confidence, or claims that the giver of the information made no explicit allusion as to the confidential nature of the information, then the question arises whether or not the recipient is under a duty of confidentiality.

Situations that are not clearly defined, such as the domestic scenario indicated above, highlight the differences between the various legal bases upon which the duty of confidentiality may arise. If a duty of confidentiality is considered to arise solely from contractual relationships, then no duty could occur in a purely domestic situation, unless some consideration could be found. However, if it is held possible for property to reside in confidential information, then the transfer of that information to another party would establish a duty of confidentiality, because the duty goes hand-in-hand with the confidential property. In this case, the duty would arise regardless of whether or not the recipient of that information had accepted the duty. Moreover, if confidentiality is considered to be a property right, then the duty would arise even when the recipient is unaware of the duty.

The courts have steered a mid-path between the contractual approach and the property approach. Accordingly, a court will hold that a duty of confidentiality will arise when:

> '... the circumstances are such that any reasonable man standing in the shoes of the recipient of the information would have realised that upon reasonable grounds the information was being given to him in confidence, then this should suffice to impose upon him the equitable obligation of confidence.' (*Coco v AN Clark (Engineers) Ltd* (1969)).

This objective test has certain limitations. For example, the situation in which a third party deliberately listens in on a confidential conversation, either by eavesdropping or by the use of sophisticated surveillance equipment. In *Malone v Commissioner of Police of the Metropolis (No 2)* (1979), it was held by Megarry VC that a third party overhearing a confidential conversation was not bound by a duty of confidentiality, and as a consequence no duty of confidentiality could be imposed so as to restrict the dissemination of the information obtained from an official telephone wire-tapping.

27.9.1   Duty imposed by contract

In the commercial world it is very common for the duty of confidentiality to be imposed and regulated by contractual terms. This has the benefit of certainty and precision as to what may and may not be done by the recipient of the confidential information. For example, a news agency could prevent its subscribers from disseminating the daily Stock Exchange and horse racing results which it supplied to them, simply because the contract did not allow this to be done (*Exchange Telegraph Co Ltd v Gregory & Co* (1896)).

27.9.2   Duty imposed by a relationship of fidelity

The formal relationship that exists between an employer and employee is delineated by a contract of employment. This contract rarely mentions explicitly the duty of fidelity: rather, this is deemed to be an implied term of the contract (*Jarman & Platt Ltd v I Barget Ltd* (1977)). Subsumed within the duty of fidelity is a duty of confidentiality. During the period of employment, not only must the employee not act in a manner that is detrimental to the business of the employer, but he must preserve the confidential information of his employer.

It is not a breach of the duty of fidelity for an employee, whilst he is still employed, simply to make plans or preparation for his future post-termination activities, so long as those plans do not include trade secrets or other confidential information the use of which may be restricted by the imposition of a valid restraint of trade covenant (*Ixora Trading Inc v Jones* (1990)).

Goulding J in *Faccenda Chicken Ltd v Fowler* (1985), held that information acquired by an employee during the course of his employment could be divided into three categories. First, there is information which, because of its trivial character or its easy accessibility from public sources, cannot be regarded by reasonable persons or by the law as confidential at all. Such information may be imparted during the employment or afterwards to anyone. Secondly, there is information which the employee must treat as confidential (either because he is expressly told it is confidential, or because from its character it is obviously so) but which once learned necessarily remains in the employee's head and becomes part of his own skill and knowledge. So long as the employment continues, he cannot otherwise use or disclose such information without infidelity and therefore breach of contract. But when he is no longer in the same employment, the law allows him to use his full skill and knowledge for his own benefit, even if that is in competition with his former employer. If an employer wants to protect information of this nature, he can do so by an express stipulation restraining the employee from competing with him (within reasonable limits of time and space) after the termination of his employment. Thirdly, there are specific trade secrets so confidential that, even though they may necessarily have been learned by heart, and even though the employee may have left the original employment, they cannot lawfully be used for anyone's benefit except the original employer's.

While there may be a stringent duty of fidelity placed upon an employee during his employment, this duty is relaxed extensively when the employee leaves. Therefore, a worker may be free to change his job and to seek new employment without the hindrance of obligations to his previous employer. There are only two restraints that an employer may impose on an ex-employee. The first restraint protects trade secrets, while the second protects the goodwill of the business. Originally, these restrictions were developed by using express covenants within the contract of employment. Such covenants are often called 'restraint of trade' covenants, or, more briefly, 'restrictive' covenants, because they hinder the free movement of an employee after he has left the employment of his old employer to find a new job that may be in competition with his old employer.

27.9.3   Restraints of trade covenants

Restraint of trade covenants may prohibit the ex-employee from setting up in competition on his own account, or from joining a competitor, or from soliciting the customers of his ex-employer, because any such action would damage the business goodwill of his former employer (*Wessex Dairies Ltd v Smith* (1935)). However, such restrictions will only be enforceable if they are reasonably necessary to protect the legitimate commercial interests of the old employer. In order for a restraint of trade covenant to be held reasonable and so enforceable, it must usually be limited in time, space and scope. If a covenant is unnecessarily wide then the courts will not re-write the covenant so as to impose a reasonable restriction, instead the covenant will be held to be an undue restraint of trade and so it is void *ab initio* as it is contrary to public policy.

As explained earlier, in the case of an ex-employee, there is always an equitable duty of confidentiality which restricts the person from disseminating trade secrets, ie the third category of information outlined by Goulding J in *Faccenda Chicken Ltd v Fowler* (1985). However, in addition, there may be explicit restrictive covenants to prevent a person from divulging information that does not constitute a true trade secret, but that does fall within the second category of information potentially capable of protection. However, the prohibition that is imposed by the restrictive covenant cannot be so wide as to prevent a person from reasonably earning a living. This means, in practice, that it cannot prevent him from using information that forms part of his general knowledge and skill of the particular trade in which he is engaged.

| 27.9.4 | Duty imposed by a fiduciary relationship |

It is not necessary for the duty to be imposed by contract, even though when that is the case, the extent of the duty is usually clearly delineated. The duty of confidentiality may arise because a fiduciary relationship exists between the parties, and part of that duty may include a duty of confidentiality covering certain information. There are many situations in which a fiduciary relationship may arise, for example, between a trustee and a beneficiary, between a principal and his agent, between a director and his company, and between a solicitor and his client.

It is not a breach of the fiduciary duty owed by a company director to the company currently employing him, if he intends to set up a business in competition with his current company, after his directorship has ceased. Nor is it a breach of that duty to take any preliminary steps to investigate or forward that intention, so long as there is no actual competitive activity while he remains a director of the first company (*Balston Ltd v Headline Filters Ltd* (1990)).

| 27.9.5 | Purely equitable obligation |

A purely equitable obligation which would impose a duty of confidentiality may occur in a relationship of a domestic nature, such as between husband and wife (*Duchess of Argyll v Duke of Argyll* (1967)). A duty of confidentiality may be imposed upon subsequent recipients of the information, and so form a chain of confidence (*Fraser v Thames TV Ltd* (1969)). In each case the duty that is owed by each subsequent recipient is to the person who imposed that duty upon him, and also to the original source of the confidential information.

In *Fraser v Evans* (1984) Lord Denning MR said that:

'Even if [a person] comes by [the confidential information] innocently, nevertheless once he gets to know that it was originally given in confidence, he can be restrained from breaking that confidence.'

In *Stephenson Jordan & Harrison Ltd v MacDonald & Evans* (1951) the court imposed liability on an innocent recipient of the confidential information from the time that he had become aware of the true nature of the information that he had acquired.

27.10 Breach of the duty of confidentiality

There is a distinction to be drawn between breaching the duty of confidentiality by revealing the confidential information, and breaching the duty by using that information. Thus, even if a defendant has breached his duty of confidentiality, and revealed the information so that it is now in the public domain, he may still be prohibited from using that information himself. The justification for this is that even though the information may now be available to the general public, the defendant has been in possession of it for a sufficiently long time to have learnt how to implement it to its best effect. Accordingly, he could profit more quickly from that information than a recipient to whom the information has just been imparted. Furthermore, it would be inequitable for the original recipient to profit from his own breach of duty. This is called the 'springboard doctrine' and was first developed to protect the confidential information that was used for the construction of a technical piece of equipment (*Terrapin Ltd v Builders' Supply Co (Hayes) Ltd* (1967)).

It is a vexed question whether or not the plaintiff needs to show that he has been damaged by the breach of a duty of confidentiality. In *Jarman & Platt Ltd v I Barget Ltd* (1977), it was assumed that damage to the plaintiff was a necessary condition before damages could be claimed. However, in *Coco v AN Clark (Engineers) Ltd* (1969), Megarry J doubted whether it was necessary to show that damage had been incurred by the plaintiff before he could claim damages, cf the tort of trespass to land. In practice the courts take a pragmatic approach, and will, if necessary, infer that damage has been occasioned to the plaintiff in some form. For example, when the breach of confidentiality has involved the publication of private matters, then the damage may consist of mental and emotional stress (*Duchess of Argyll v Duke of Argyll* (1967)).

27.11 Damage

Equity will not protect confidential information that relates to a criminal activity. This would run contrary to the spirit of the Court of Equity. Equally, the court will justify such decisions by reference to public policy, because it is reasoned that it is in the public interest for the iniquity to be revealed and that justice to society as a whole, rather than a particular segment of it, prevails. However, there are many situations that do not concern criminal activity *per se*, but still involve a tortious or other legal wrong. The interests of the public are usually raised as a defence when confidential information has been released and the defendant is attempting to avoid liability. So, for example, the duty of confidentiality could not be used to prevent the exposure of an agreement that should have been registered under the Restrictive Trade Practices Act 1976 (*Initial Services Ltd v Putterill* (1968)).

27.12 Public interest

The court may even order a defendant to breach a duty of confidentiality, so that the plaintiff may pursue third parties who are violating the plaintiff's rights. So, for example, the Commissioners of Customs and Excise were forced to reveal the names of the importers of a drug that was protected by a patent, so that the patentee could initiate proceedings directly against the persons who were infringing the patent (*Norwich Pharmacal Co v Commissioners of Customs and Excise* (1974)).

27.12.1   Use as a defence

The courts have sanctioned the breach of a duty of confidentiality on the grounds that the breach is in the public interest. For example, a new breathalyser that was about to be introduced by the police force was found to give inaccurate readings. However, the results of the laboratory that made this discovery were contained in a confidential report. An employee of the laboratory leaked the report to a national newspaper in order to expose this shortcoming. The court felt that, in the circumstances, if the report had been handed only to the police force or the Home Office, there was a small chance that it might have been suppressed. This in turn could have lead to the imprisonment of innocent people, which was unacceptable to the court (*Lion Laboratories Ltd v Evans* (1985)). Thus, in this case, it was accepted by the court that there was a defence to the breach of duty, because it was in the interests of the public to know about the potentially inaccurate readings of the new machine.

Duty of Confidentiality

Official Secrets Act 1989 regulates State secrets, while the equitable duty of confidentiality regulates confidences between private individuals.

Introduction

Patents offer an absolute monopoly for 20 years against imitators. In contrast the duty of confidentiality lasts until there is an independent discovery.

Interplay between confidentiality and patents

The component parts and their proportions are now in the public domain. However, the exact production process is still confidential.

Recipe of Coca-Cola

Copyright and confidentiality are often invoked to ensure privacy for unpublished works. However, in contrast to copyright, there is no need to record information before it may be protected by a duty of confidentiality (*Printers & Finishers v Holloway* (1965)).

Relationship with copyright protection

The nature of the duty of confidentiality is one of good faith, ie an equitable duty (*Fraser v Evans* (1969)). In addition, the duty may also be founded in contract, in which case there is a need for consideration.

Nature of the duty of confidentiality

The duty may arise in a purely domestic arrangement (*Duchess of Argyll v Duke of Argyll* (1967)). As a corollary to the equitable nature, there should be no profit allowed to be kept from wrongful use of the confidential information (*AG v Jonathan Cape Ltd* (1976)).

Equitable nature of the duty of confidentiality

Megarry J in *Coco v AN Clark (Engineers) Ltd* (1969) stated that there are three requirements before a duty of confidentiality may arise. First, the information must have the necessary quality of confidence. Secondly, a duty of confidentiality must have been imposed. Thirdly, there must have been a breach of that duty which has led to an unauthorised use or revelation of that information.

Working definition of the duty of confidentiality

Lord Greene MR said that the necessary quality of confidence attaches to information that is neither public property nor public knowledge (*Saltman Engineering v Campbell Engineering* (1948)).

Necessary quality of confidence

Megarry J said that the necessary quality of confidence resulted from the application of the skill and ingenuity of the human brain (*Coco v AN Clark (Engineers) Ltd* (1969)).

Examples of protection information

Examples include technical secrets (*Cranleigh Precision Engineering Ltd v Bryant* (1966)); customer lists; (*Anton Piller KG v Manufacturing Processes Ltd* (1976)); and marketing procedures (*Stephenson Jordan & Harrison v MacDonald & Evans* (1951)).

Protection of a mere idea

A mere idea may be protected if it may be clearly identified, and it is original, of potential commercial attractiveness, and capable of being realised in actuality (*Fraser v Thames TV* (1984)).

Information in the public domain

The recipient of purported confidential information is not bound by the purported duty of confidentiality if he already knew the information (*Johnson v Heat and Air Systems Ltd* (1941)).

However, the defendant is still bound if the confidential information has become public knowledge through his fault (*Speed Seal v Paddington* (1986)).

Even if there has been restricted dissemination, the information may still be treated as confidential by the courts (*Foster v Mountford* (1978)).

Excluded matter

'Trivial tittle-tattle' will not be protected by the courts (*Coco v AN Clark (Engineers) Ltd* (1969)).

There is no protection for an inequity (*Gartside v Outram* (1856)).

Obligation of confidence

Whether or not a duty of confidentiality has arisen is an objective test (*Coco v AN Clark (Engineers) Ltd* (1969)).

However, third parties are not bound, eg official telephone wire-tappers (*Malone v Commissioner of Police* (1979)).

Duty imposed by contract

Contract may prohibit the secondary use of the information (*Exchange Telegraph v Gregory & Co* (1896)).

Similarly, the contract will determine the identity of the parties who are bound by the duty of confidentiality (*Fraser v Evans* (1969)).

A duty of fidelity is implied in a contract of employment (*Jarman & Platt Ltd v I Barget Ltd* (1977)).

Duty imposed by a relationship of fidelity

This duty, however, is not breached by making post-termination plans (*Ixora Trading Inc v Jones* (1990)).

Goulding J, in *Faccenda Chicken Ltd v Fowler* (1985), detailed three types of information that could be gained in employment. The first was of a general non-protectable nature. The second was confidential information that could be protected by a restrictive covenant. The third comprised trade secrets, and is protectable in all circumstances.

Restrictive covenants must be reasonable or else they are unenforceable. It is a reasonable requirement for the ex-employee not to undermine the business of his old employers (*Wessex Dairies Ltd v Smith* (1935)).

Restraint of trade covenants

The duty owed by a company director would be broken if he competes with the company currently employing him (*Balston Ltd v Headline Filters Ltd* (1990)).

Duty imposed by a fiduciary relationship

In a domestic management, eg between a husband and wife, a purely equitable duty may arise (*Duchess of Argyll v Duke of Argyll* (1967)).

Purely equitable obligation

The springboard doctrine states that the person who leaked the confidential information should not be allowed to benefit from his own breach (*Terrapin Ltd v Builder's Supply Co (Hayes) Ltd* (1967)).

Breach of the duty of confidentiality

In *Jarman & Platt Ltd v I Barget Ltd* (1977), it was implied that damage was a prerequisite before damages could be awarded.

Damage

In *Coco v AN Clark (Engineers) Ltd* (1969), Megarry J was doubtful if this was the case, ie a breach of the duty would be actionable without proof of damage, cf trespass to land.

The exposure of improper trading practices could not be restrained even though it was in breach of a duty of confidentiality (*Initial Services Ltd v Putterill* (1968)).

Public interest

The court may order a defendant to breach the duty of confidentiality in order that a plaintiff may pursue other wrong-doers (*Norwich Pharmacal v Customs and Excise* (1974)).

Use as a defence

It was held to be in the public interest for the flaws in a new breathalyser to be exposed to the general public (*Lion Laboratories Ltd v Evans* (1985)).

Chapter 28

Threats and Malicious Falsehood

It is a legitimate expectation of an honest trader that his competitors will not make groundless threats against him, nor that they will make derogatory remarks about his business. In both cases the damage that could be inflicted on an honest trader's business could be immense. In order to help ensure that no unfair advantage is gained by a perpetrator of such nefarious activities, the legislature and the common law have provided some protection. In the case of groundless threats to instigate legal proceedings for the infringement of intellectual property rights, the provisions are contained within the different statutes that regulate the different rights. The protection provided against untrue statements is founded upon the common law action for malicious falsehood. The purpose of both is to protect the honest trader, and to allow him to continue his business activities in peace.

28.1 Introduction

It may readily be appreciated that the threat to initiate court proceedings for the infringement of a patent, or other intellectual property right, may have an adverse effect on another trader's business. The potential damage to the trader's business is even greater if the threats are made against the other trader's customers. If the owner of the intellectual property right then commences litigation against the alleged infringer, it falls to the court to decide whether or not there was an infringement. If the case is not made out, then the defendant is cleared. However, if the threatener does not issue proceedings, but instead just continues to claim that an infringement is occurring, the alleged infringer needs a mechanism whereby he can clear his name.

28.2 Threats

To help an honest trader in this situation the legislature has proscribed the issuing of groundless threats based on some, but not all, of the possible causes of action that relate to intellectual property. Provisions have been made for threats relating to the infringement of a patent (PA 1977 s 70), a registered design (RDA 1949 s 26, as amended by the CDPA 1988 Schedule 3 para 15), an unregistered design, ie design right (CDPA 1988 s 253), and for trade marks (TMA 1994 s 21). The protection is broadly the same in all four situations, and it provides that an aggrieved person may seek an injunction to prevent the continuance of the threats, and may recover damages for any loss that has flowed from the threats. Further, it provides a spring-board for the aggrieved person from which to start an action for revocation of the registered right if that is appropriate. It is to be noted that there are no provisions in the UK to prevent groundless threats relating to works in which copyright may subsist. Moreover, prior to the TMA 1994, there were no provisions under the TMA 1938 that related to groundless threats in trade mark matters.

28.2.1   Early history

The origin of this remedy lies in provisions that originally provided for threats in patent actions. Each branch, which currently appertains to a particular right, has developed subsequently from this common root in a similar manner.

Prior to 1883 there was no statutory remedy for the protection of persons who were threatened with infringement proceedings in patent actions. A person so aggrieved only had recourse to the common law. So a proprietor of a patent might threaten another for infringement proceedings, and so long as the threats were issued *bona fide*, no action could be taken against him. The injured person would only be successful in seeking an injunction to restrain the continuance of the threats if the statements were made *mala fides* and were injurious and untrue (*Halsey v Brotherhood* (1880)), and that the threatener intended to continue to repeat them (*Sugg v Bray* (1885)).

Under the Patents, Designs, and Trade Marks Act 1883 s 32, provisions for a remedy in the case of groundless threats of legal proceedings in patent actions were introduced for the first time.

By the Patents and Designs Act 1907 s 36 and 61 these provisions were extended to apply *mutatis mutandis* to threats in registered design actions.

28.2.2   Present legislative framework

With the introduction of the Registered Design Act 1949, the remedies for groundless threats of infringement proceedings in registered design actions were enacted in their own right (s 26), rather than by reference to the then relevant prevailing patent law (PA 1949, s 65).

Patent cases are now covered by the PA 1977 s 70 which, even though different in detail is to the same effect. The addition of sub-section 26(2A) to the RDA 1949 was to bring the law on registered designs into line with the corresponding law for patents.

Other minor changes in the RDA 1949 s 26 were needed because of the introduction of the design right by the CDPA 1988. The latter right was given protection against threats by the CDPA 1988 s 253 in similar terms to the amended protection given to registered designs.

The provisions contained in the TMA 1994 s 21 broadly follow the protection that is conferred on patents, registered designs and unregistered designs.

The wording of the section is very wide in that 'any person aggrieved' may bring an action, and so become the potential plaintiff. This, for example, would include the manufacturer of the article alleged to infringe (*Bristol-Myers Co v Manon Frères* (1973)). However, when the aggrieved person is complaining about a threat that relates to an article that he no longer produces, then he is not a person aggrieved for the purposes of this section (*Reymes-Cole v Elite Hosiery Co Ltd* (1961)).

28.2.3 Potential parties to the action

The defendant may be any person who has issued a threat, irrespective of whether or not that person has an entitlement to, or an interest in, a relevant intellectual property right or an application for a such a right. Hence a person, even one who acts as an agent for another, would be liable *personally* for any threats that he may issue. This is of particular consequence for a solicitor (*Benmax v Austin Motor Co Ltd* (1953)), or other agent, who may write a letter on behalf of his clients. In *Earles Utilities Ltd v Harrison* (1935), Farwell J said:

> 'I am not aware that there is anything in section 36 [of the then relevant Act] which specifically protects a solicitor who chooses to disregard the provisions of the section.'

Usually the threats are made directly to the person who is being threatened with infringement proceedings; this may be either the manufacturer or the customers. The protection is, however, wide enough to cover indirect threats; for example, when the statements are made to a person that his agent or another third party is to be sued (*Olin Mathieson Chemical Corp v Biorex Laboratories Ltd* (1970)). In such a case, the person aggrieved is the person threatened with the proceedings, and not the actual person to whom the threats were issued.

28.2.4 Person threatened

So statements to a customer, or a potential customer, that proceedings will be brought against the manufacturer would give rise to a cause of action with the manufacturer as the plaintiff (*Surridge's Patents Ltd v Trico-Folberth Ltd* (1936)), as would threats made to a company carrying an advertisement of the manufacturer (*Jaybeam Ltd v Abru Aluminium Ltd* (1975)). The threats do not have to be communicated to the aggrieved person, but may instead merely constitute the expression of a threat in relation to any person (*John Summers & Sons Ltd v The Cold Metal Process Co* (1948)). In such a case, the aggrieved person is the person to whom the threats related.

The threat must have been uttered within the jurisdiction (*Egg Fillers and Containers (Aust) Proprietary Ltd v Holed-Tite*

Packing Corporation (1934)), but the threatened action may be abroad, as may be the threatener.

28.2.5   Nature of the threats

The threats may be made by 'circulars, advertisements or otherwise'. The words 'or otherwise' are not to be construed *ejusdem generis* (*Speedcranes Ltd v Thomson* (1978)). Hence, oral threats are within this section (*Farr v Weatherhead and Harding* (1932)). Furthermore, *bona fides* is no defence to a threats action (*Skinner & Co v Perry* (1893)).

28.2.6   Difference between a mere notification and a threat

The Registered Design Act 1949 s 26(3) states that for the avoidance of doubt it is hereby declared that a mere notification that a design is registered does not constitute a threat of proceedings within the meaning of this section. Similar provisions are found in the sections relating to patents, unregistered designs and trade marks (PA 1977 s 70(5), CDPA 1988 s 253(4) and TMA s 21(4) respectively).

The notification that the owner has a right does not constitute a threat (*Johnson v Edge* (1892)). It is even permissible to issue a general warning that anyone infringing the intellectual property right in question must expect proceedings to ensue (*Speedcranes Ltd v Thomson* (1978)), so long as the warning does not indicate that everyone in the trade is at risk of being sued (*Martin and Miles Martin Pen Co Ltd v The Selsdon Fountain Pen Co Ltd* (1949)). In *Challender v Royle* (1887), Bowen LJ said that:

'Everybody, it seems to me, has still a right to issue a general warning to pirates not to pirate, and to infringers not to infringe, and to warn the public that the patent to which the patentee is entitled, and under which he claims, is one which he intends to enforce.'

In *Finkelstein v Billig* (1930), where the main part of the letter from a Patent Agent concerned an allegation that a certain article would infringe the client's patent when granted, the letter continued 'Incidentally, our client also has a registered design covering this article'. It was held here that this did not amount to a threat in respect of the registered design.

If the notification is to the general public is so phrased that no particular person may be identified as being threatened then there is no threat within the meaning of this section (*Boneham and Hart (t/a F Boneham & Co) v Hirst Bros & Co Ltd* (1917)). This is so even if the plaintiff thinks that he is being threatened (*HW Howson Ltd v Algraphy Ltd* (1965)). It is, however, very easy to cross the border from what is permissible to what is not.

The threat complained of in *Johnson v Edge* (1892) was:

'Notice to grocers and others. Information of extensive violation of Mr William Edge's patent rights has been received. All parties are warned not to infringe these rights.'

Lindley LJ said:

'Now this is addressed to the trade; what would they understand by it? If they have turned their attention to it after Mr Johnson sent out these things, they would say: "Oh, that is addressed to Harrison and Johnson – we know those two; they are making more or less things like Mr Edge; it must be those things." It must be, therefore, an intimation – it would be construed to be an intimation by Mr Edge – that he considered these things an infringement of his patent.'

It was held that this was not mere general warning. There was no need for any person to be identified explicitly: it was sufficient that the alleged threat referred to a specific person by necessary implication. In *Boneham and Hart (t/a F Boneham & Co) v Hirst Bros & Co Ltd* (1917) the alleged threat stated that a certain registered design had 'evoked some rubbishy imitations' and that legal proceedings would be taken against any infringer. It was held that the threat was clearly directed against somebody.

The cumulative effect of all the correspondence must be taken as a whole, and if that is threatening then that is sufficient even though no single incident contains a threat (*Willis & Bates Ltd v Tilley Lamp Co* (1944)). Further, the whole background in which the alleged threat occurred should be taken into consideration in deciding whether or not it was a threat (*Surridge's Patents Ltd v Trico-Folberth Ltd* (1936)).

It will be recalled, however, that there is no statutory bar to making threats that proceedings will be commenced based upon an infringement of copyright. However, in *Jaybeam Ltd v Abru Aluminium Ltd* (1975) where the letter in question threatened proceedings for copyright infringement, but it also included at the end a mere notification of the existence of a registered design, it was held by Whitford J that any businessman would think that he was being threatened in respect of not just the copyright proceedings, but also in respect of the registered design. Thus, it is not safe to make threats of copyright proceedings, unless the threat contains no reference to other IPRs that do attract such protection.

There is no need for any specific mention of legal proceedings, if an ordinary person would infer that such proceedings were threatened, then a cause of action exists (*Willis & Bates Ltd v*

28.2.7   Threat of legal proceedings

Tilley Lamps Co (1944)). In *Rosedale Associated Manufacturers Ltd v Airfix Products Ltd* (1957) a letter was sent to the plaintiffs which stated that the clients of the writers of the letter were the proprietors of a registered design in castellated toy buckets, and that the writers of the letter were given to understand that the plaintiffs were supplying castellated toy buckets. The letter continued:

> '... in these circumstances our clients have thought it right to instruct us to advise you of the position. You must understand that our clients are prepared to protect their interests with the utmost vigour.'

Lloyd-Jacob J held that the first part of the letter fell clearly within the proviso which related to mere notification (RDA 1949 s 26(3)). However, with respect to the second sentence, he continued:

> 'In my judgment, it is impossible to suppose that that paragraph in the letter was concerned merely with giving an intimation that a registered design was the property of Airfix. Coupled with the statement in the first paragraph that Airfix had reason to suppose that there was an offer for a supply of castellated toy buckets by Rosedale at the time the letter was written, the letter is to my mind a threat of proceedings.'

In *Paul Trading Co Ltd v J Marksmith & Co Ltd* (1952) a letter stated that the offending article was a 'copy', and then asked for the name of the manufacturer or supplier so that the writer could contact him. It was held by Lloyd-Jacob J that this was not a threat of proceedings. Furthermore, the context in which the threat was delivered was relevant in deciding whether or not the offending statement was a threat. If it was clear to the recipient that there was no likelihood of proceedings being issued against him, then there is no threat (*O and M Kleeman Ltd v Rosedale Associated Manufacturers Ltd* (1954)).

The person threatened must be threatened with legal proceedings and not just legal liability. This is an important distinction that turns on the exact phrasing of the alleged threat. In *Earles Utilities Ltd v Harrison* (1935) the letter, which had been written by the solicitor, read: 'Dear Sirs, I understand you are acting as distributors of a certain kettle which is an infringement of Patent No 165,299, vested in a client of mine. Unless I receive forthwith your assurance that you will at once cease the distribution of such kettles, I shall have no alternative but to advise my client to apply for an injunction. Please, therefore, give this matter your immediate attention.'

In dismissing the action Farwell J said:

'... it has been known for a client to refuse his solicitor's advice. In my judgment, that cannot be said to be a threat.'

The threats must be groundless, which may mean that there is no underlying intellectual property right, or that it is invalid, or that the alleged infringement is in fact not an infringement. If the defendant can justify the threats, then the action will fail against him.

28.2.8   Groundless threats

In contrast to the usual procedure in defamation actions, if the defendant intends to justify the threats then this will not prevent an interlocutory injunction being granted (*Johnson Electric Industrial Manufactory Ltd v Mabuchi-Motor KK* (1986) in contrast to *Bestobell Paints Ltd v Bigg* (1975)).

The CDPA 1988 Schedule 3 para 15(3) inserted a new subsection into the RDA 1949, namely s 26(2A), whereby any threat 'to bring proceedings for an infringement alleged to consist of the making or importing of anything' was excluded from the ambit of the threats section. Thus, there is no statutory bar to bringing groundless threats that concern certain acts of primary infringement within the UK (*Therm-a-Stor Ltd v Weatherseal Windows Ltd* (1981)). This sub-section was introduced to bring the law on registered design into line with patents. The relevant sub-section for unregistered designs and trade marks is to the same effect.

28.2.9   Exclusion provisions

Thus, the threats provisions only cover the core acts of infringement, namely selling or otherwise dealing with the offending article. The threat provisions do not extend to the making or importation of anything covered by the IPR in question (PA 1977 s 70(4), RDA 1949 s 26(2A), CDPA 1988 s 253(3), and, in the case of trade marks, the use of this exclusion is extended to include the application of the mark to goods or their packaging and the supply of services under the mark (TMA 1994 s 21(1)).

If an aggrieved person cannot seek reddress under these statutory provisions, then he may seek a declaration that the acts complained of do not constitute an infringement. This was the course of action followed by the plaintiff in *Leco Instruments (UK) Ltd v Land Pyrometers Ltd* (1982), because the threat alleged copyright infringement for which there is no statutory protection. Alternatively, the facts of a particular case may be sufficient to start proceedings for malicious falsehood.

This common law remedy is of particular use if the statements complained of do not amount to a threat of legal proceedings, or otherwise do not fall within the relevant sections of the PA 1977 s 70, RDA 1949 s 26, TMA 1994 s 21 and the CDPA 1988 s

28.3   **Malicious falsehood**

253 (*Mentmore Manufacturing Co Ltd v Fomento (Sterling Area) Ltd* (1955)). This tort may also be used when it is not possible to prove the necessary elements of the tort of passing-off.

When a competitor is engaged in a comparative advertising campaign with the plaintiff, then malicious falsehood would often be pleaded along with trade mark infringement, which arose by virtue of TMA 1938 s 4(1)(b) (*Compaq Computer Corporation v Dell Computer Corporation Ltd* (1992)). Under the new Trade Marks Act 1994 comparative advertising will be permitted so long as it is in accordance with honest practices in industrial or commercial matters (TMA 1994 s 10(6)). Malicious falsehood has also been pleaded in tandem with the alleged infringement of an unregistered trade mark, ie passing-off (*Ciba-Geigy plc v Parke Davis & Co Ltd* (1994)).

Potentially, the courts could have extended the ambit of the tort of malicious falsehood, as they have done with passing-off, so as to provide some measure of protection against unfair competition in the broad sense. The courts have, however, not done this, and so this tort is usually used only in the most blatant cases.

To make out this cause of action, the statements must be both untrue and made maliciously. As long as the requirements of the Defamation Act 1952 s 3(1) are fulfilled, then there is no need to allege or prove special damage (*RJ Reuter v Muhlens* (1953)). If, however, the requirements of the DA 1952 s 3 are not made out, then the plaintiff must allege, and prove, that he has sustained actual financial loss and that such loss must have been caused by the malicious falsehood (*Brady v Express Newspapers plc* (1994)). So long as the statements are confined to the plaintiff's property and commercial interests, and are not directed at his personal reputation and good name, then the case is one of malicious falsehood and not libel (*CHC Software Care Ltd v Hopkins & Wood* (1993)). Where the facts support a cause of action for both libel and malicious falsehood, it is not an abuse to prosecute the malicious falsehood in preference to the libel (*Joyce v Sengupta* (1993)).

When threats of a copyright infringement action are made, it may be possible to prevent their continuance by basing proceedings on malicious falsehood or unlawful interference with the plaintiff's business (*Jaybeam Ltd v Abru Aluminium Ltd* (1975)).

An interlocutory injunction will not normally be granted to prevent the continuance of the malicious falsehood if the defendant intends to justify his remarks (*Polydor Ltd v*

Harlequin Records Shops Ltd (1980) and *Mainmet Holdings plc v Austin* (1991)), which is in contrast to the situation where a threats action is brought, but similar to the situation in defamation actions. However, if the court is satisfied on the evidence that the statements are untrue and made maliciously, then an interlocutory injunction may be granted (*Kaye v Robertson* (1991)).

Malicious falsehood is also called injurious falsehood or trade libel, or slander of goods. These terms seem to be used interchangeably by the judiciary.

Malice is now taken to mean that the statements were made *mala fide*, ie with a dishonest motive (*Greers Ltd v Pearman & Corder Ltd* (1922)). Proof that the defendant knew that the statements he was making were untrue is potent evidence of malice, and in such a case it is irrelevant whether or not the defendant intended to profit himself from the action. If the defendant believed the statement to be true, yet made it for the purpose of injuring the plaintiff, then such an act will also be malicious (*Wilts United Dairy v Thomas Robinson & Sons Co Ltd* (1957)).

28.3.1   Malice

If a person alleged infringement and the act did fall within the scope of his monopoly, and yet the threatener knew that his monopoly was invalid, it would appear that such a threat was malicious. However, was it untrue? In *Challender v Royle* (1887), Cotton LJ said:

28.3.2   Falsehood

'I cannot see how, if a patent is invalid, there can be any act done in infringement of a legal right when the legal right depends only on the validity of that patent.'

On the other hand, it may be said that infringement and validity are separate questions, and that at any rate a registered design or trade mark, once granted, is valid until taken off the register.

A true statement, no matter how harmful to the plaintiff, is not actionable under this tortious head. Furthermore, the onus of proof that the statement is untrue is on the plaintiff.

If a competitor engages in comparative advertising and in so doing merely indulges in hyperbolic puffing about the virtues of his own product, then the courts will not interfere to restrain that activity (*McDonald's Hamburgers Ltd v Burgerking (UK) Ltd* (1986)). Thus, such statements as 'A's flour is as good as B's' are mere puffs and not actionable. However, if the product under comparison was not flour, or some such similar pedestrian article, but, say, pharmaceutical products, such a statement would be examined more closely by the courts to ensure that it was scrupulously correct (*Ciba-Geigy plc v Parke*

Davis & Co Ltd (1994)).

The defendant must make some false statement concerning the goods of the plaintiff (*Timothy White v Gustav Mellin* (1895)), but even then the falsehood must not be minor, but be of such substance that a reasonable man would take it as a serious claim (*De Beers Abrasive Products Ltd v International General Electric Company of New York Ltd* (1975)).

28.3.3   Damage

Originally, the plaintiff had to prove that special damage had been incurred. This tended to restrict the application of this tort to matters that directly concerned either property or the business of the plaintiff (*Haddan v Lott* (1845)).

There is now no requirement to prove special damage if the statement in question was

- calculated to cause pecuniary damage to the plaintiff and was published in a writing or other permanent form; or

- was calculated to cause pecuniary damage to the plaintiff in respect of any office, profession, calling, trade or business, held or carried on by him at the time of the publication (Defamation Act 1952 s 3).

'Calculated to cause' does not add to the *mens rea* element of the offence, but may be established by the objective test of 'being likely to cause' (*Customglass Boats Ltd v Salthouse Brothers Ltd* (1976)).

If, however, the requirements of the DA 1952 s 3 are not made out, then the plaintiff must allege, and prove, that he has sustained actual financial loss and that such loss must have been caused by the malicious falsehood (*Brady v Express Newspapers plc* (1994)).

Threats and Malicious Falsehood

The threats provisions and the test of malicious falsehood present some protection for the honest trader against groundless threats and derogatory remarks.	**Introduction**
Protection is provided by statute for the various IPRs, eg patents (PA 1977 s 70); registered designs (RDA 1949 s 26 as amended by the CDPA 1988 Schedule 3 para 15); unregistered designs, (CDPA 1988 s 253); and, trade marks (TMA 1994 s 21).	**Threats**
Prior to 1883, there was no remedy available against *bona fide* threats. The Patents, Designs, and Trade Marks Act 1883 s 32 introduced a remedy in patent matters for groundless threats. The Patents and Designs Act 1907 s 61 extended this protection to registered designs.	**Early history**
Protection for registered designs was enacted in its own right by the RDA 1949 s 26. Minor changes were made to the RDA 1949 by the CDPA 1988 to accommodate the introduction of design right. Protection in trade mark matters was introduced for the first time with TMA 1994 s 21. There is still no protection for threats in copyright proceedings.	**Present legislative framework**
'Any person aggrieved' may bring an action. The defendant may be any threatener including a solicitor (*Benmax v Austin Motor Co Ltd* (1953)).	**Potential parties to the action**
The threat may be direct or indirect, ie to a manufacturer or to his customers. Even threats to a publisher carrying advertisements is sufficient (*Jaybeam Ltd v Abru Aluminium Ltd* (1975)).	**Person threatened**
The threats may be oral as well as written (*Farr v Weatherhead and Harding* (1932)).	**Nature of the threats**
The mere indication the existence of a right is not a threat (*Johnson v Edge* (1892)). Furthermore, a general warning is permissible (*Speedcranes Ltd v Thomson* (1978)). However, the cumulative effect of any action may amount to a threat (*Willis & Bates Ltd v Tilley Lamp Co* (1944)).	**Difference between a mere notification and a threat**

Threat of legal proceedings	The threat of proceedings may be deduced, if it is not explicit (*Rosedale Associated Manufacturer v Airfix* (1956)). Yet, if it is clear that no action would be taken, then there is no threat (*O and M Kleeman v Rosedale Associated Manufacturers* (1954)). There is no threat if only the legal liability is pointed out (*Earles Utilities Ltd v Harrison* (1935)).
Groundless threats	The threats must be groundless, ie no valid IPR underlying the threat. Justification of the threat will not prevent interlocutory relief being granted (*Johnson Electric v Mabuchi-Motor KK* (1986)).
Exclusion provisions	Threats relating to the making or importing of anything are excluded (RDA 1949 s 26(2A), PA 1977 s 70(4), PDPA 1988 s 253(3) and TMA 1994 s 21(1)). The threats provisions basically cover only selling or otherwise distributing.
Malicious falsehood	This is a common law remedy. It is often pleaded in comparative advertising cases (*Compaq Computer v Dell Computer* (1992)). There must be a false statement that has been made maliciously that results in damage (but DA 1952 s 3 may obviate the need for this). Malicious falsehood is concerned with business, as opposed to personal, reputation (*CHC Software v Hopkins & Wood* (1993)). If the facts fit both libel and malicious falsehood, then may plead either (*Joyce v Sengupta* (1993)). Justification will prevent interlocutory relief being granted (*Mainmet Holdings plc v Austin* (1991)). Malicious falsehood is also called injurious falsehood or trade libel.
Malice	Statements made *mala fides* (*Greers Ltd v Pearman & Corder Ltd* (1922)); or with an intention to injure the plaintiff (*Wilts United Dairy v Thomas Robinson & Sons Co Ltd* (1957)).
Falsehood	Mere advertising hyperbolic puffing does not amount to a falsehood (*McDonald's Hamburgers Ltd v Burgerking (UK) Ltd* (1986)). The falsehood must be significant and taken seriously (*De Beers Abrasive v International General Electric* (1975)).

There is no need to prove damage, if the statement is calculated to cause pecuniary damage (DA 1959 s 3). **Damage**

'Calculated' means 'likely to', and thus does not introduce a *mens rea* element (*Customglass Boats v Salthouse* (1976)). Otherwise must prove special damage (*Brady v Express Newspapers plc* (1994)).

Index